CREATING
COMPETENT
COMMUNICATION

C R E A T I N G
C O M P E T E N T
COMMUNICATION

DONALD YODER
University of Dayton

•

LAWRENCE HUGENBERG
Youngstown State University

•

SAMUEL WALLACE
University of Dayton

WCB Brown &
Benchmark
PUBLISHERS

Madison, Wisconsin•Dubuque, Iowa•Indianapolis, Indiana
Melbourne, Australia•Oxford, England

Book Team

Editor *Stan Stoga*
Developmental Editor *Mary E. Rossa*
Production Editor *Scott Sullivan*
Designer *Eric Engelby*
Art Editor *Rachel Imsland*
Photo Editor *Robin Storm*
Visuals/Design Developmental Consultant *Marilyn A. Phelps*
Visuals/Design Freelance Specialist *Mary L. Christianson*
Publishing Services Specialist *Sherry Padden*
Marketing Manager *Carla J. Aspelmeier*
Advertising Manager *Jodi Rymer*

Brown & Benchmark

A Division of Wm. C. Brown Communications, Inc.

Vice President and General Manager *Thomas E. Doran*
Editor in Chief *Edgar J. Laube*
Executive Editor *Ed Bartell*
Executive Editor *Stan Stoga*
National Sales Manager *Eric Ziegler*
Director of CourseResource *Kathy Law Laube*
Director of CourseSystems *Chris Rogers*

Director of Marketing *Sue Simon*
Director of Production *Vickie Putman Caughron*
Imaging Group Manager *Chuck Carpenter*
Manager of Visuals and Design *Faye M. Schilling*
Design Manager *Jac Tilton*
Art Manager *Janice Roerig*
Permissions/Records Manager *Connie Allendorf*

Wm. C. Brown Communications, Inc.

President and Chief Executive Officer *G. Franklin Lewis*
Corporate Vice President, President of WCB Manufacturing *Roger Meyer*
Vice President and Chief Financial Officer *Robert Chesterman*

The credits section for this book begins on page 471 and is considered an extension of the copyright page.

Cover Image: Painting by Leonardo Nierman. Courtesy of Bryant Galleries

Copyedited by Clare Wulker

To Elbee, my companion, my inspiration, but more importantly, my lifelong

friend.   *L. H.*

To my mother and family who have always given me unconditional support

and to RAD who continually inspires me.   *D. Y.*

To my father.   *S. W.*

CONTENTS

CHAPTER 7

Skills for Nonverbal Communication 149

CHAPTER 8

Skills for Listening 175

UNIT III

Strategies for Interpersonal and Group Contexts 197

CHAPTER 9

Strategies for Interpersonal Communication 199

CHAPTER 17   *Strategies for Giving Information 401*

CHAPTER 18   *Strategies for Persuading Others 425*

This text is written for beginning students who want to learn the skills and strategies for creating competent communication. The text is designed to be used in a hybrid or blend basic communication course that combines theoretical understanding of communication with pragmatic applications of communication skills. Both novice and experienced teachers can use this text which is accompanied by a complete instructor's manual.

Creating Competent Communication develops three fundamental themes: First, communication is a transactional process in which people mutually and simultaneously cooperate to create shared meanings. Second, communication situations are more alike than different. Third, communication skills differ from communication strategies.

Most texts approach communication from the perspective of the sender (action approach) or the receiver (reaction approach). These perspectives focus on the individual's behaviors as they attempt to encode and decode messages. Individuals who understand communication processes and skillfully send or receive messages are considered to be competent communicators.

The transactional approach adopted by this text, however, maintains that communication is simultaneously created by all participants. Since both people cooperate to create shared meanings, competence cannot be judged by one individual's actions. Therefore, this text discusses communication competence as occurring through the collective actions of both people. From this perspective, a person cannot be competent alone; that is, there is no such thing as a competent communicator. Rather, communication can be more or less competent depending on the communicators' collective behaviors. The focus changes, therefore, from what one person does to create a message, to what both persons do to help each other create shared meanings.

A second theme is that communication situations are more alike than different. Public speaking, group discussions, interviews, and interpersonal relationships are often approached with the assumption that these contexts are different in the kinds of communication skills required and the nature of the communication processes involved. To assume that contexts are inherently different also presupposes that skills learned in one context are not transferrable to others. From this perspective, for example, people would have to learn different skills for interpersonal communication than they would use for public speaking. Similarly, skills used for presenting information in a group discussion are to be forgotten or ignored when communicating interpersonally. Such an assumption is not true.

We assume that all face-to-face communication contexts are composed of the same characteristics, require similar skills, and involve the same principles and processes of communication, whether the context is stereotyped as public speaking, group discussion, interview, or interpersonal. Indeed, it is often difficult even to label a specific context as public speaking or group communication or any other context. The point is that each communication context includes the same variables that differ only in the degree to which they influence the communication. All contexts require organized messages, though the degree to which a message is organized may be different. All contexts require a number of people, though the specific number of people may vary. Analysis of others is necessary for all contexts, though the amount and type of preparation may differ. All communication requires skills for encoding and decoding messages, though the specific manner in which people speak and listen may change. Each context, therefore, is defined by a unique combination of characteristics present at specific levels. The focus is on determining the influence of the characteristics present and adapting communication strategies accordingly.

Third, we maintain that communication skills differ from communication strategies. Communication skills are the specific behavioral responses of an individual in a communication situation. Communication strategies are the planned adaptation of skills to achieve a specific communication purpose. For example, a football player may learn various skills for blocking an opponent, but planning whom to block and how to block to achieve a specific goal becomes a strategy. Similarly, a communicator can learn skills for different ways to organize a message, or various listening skills, or several techniques for creating a verbal message. The specific organizational pattern the communicator chooses, the specific listening skills the communicator uses, or the specific verbal message the communicator creates is a strategic decision.

In summary, the transactional approach to communication focuses on how people cooperate to achieve competent communication. Because communication contexts are more alike than different, communication skills transcend the specific context. To adapt to the specific characteristics of a particular communication context, communicators must use their skills to create communication strategies that help them help each other to mutually create shared meanings.

Plan of the Text

In light of our three fundamental assumptions, unit I focuses on communication processes and principles that are characteristic of all face-to-face communication. Unit II teaches specific communication skills that apply to all contexts. Units III and IV adapt these skills to specific strategies for a variety of face-to-face communication situations.

Unit I discusses the three assumptions we make about communication. Specifically, the chapters explain the processes and principles of communication, the nature of communication competence, the processes of perception, the influence of self on communication, and the characteristics of communication situations.

Unit II examines specific skills required for all communication situations. It presents skills for analyzing the communication situation, organizing verbal messages, creating and interpreting verbal and nonverbal messages, and listening. Unit II shows how these skills apply to a variety of settings.

Unit III discusses the nature and processes of communication in interpersonal relationships, interpersonal conflicts, group discussions, group decision making, interviews, and intercultural communication situations. These chapters demonstrate how to use communication skills learned in unit II to create specific strategies. Through these, communicators help each other create shared meanings and cooperatively achieve communication goals.

Unit IV examines the strategies for presenting information and persuading others in one-to-many, public speaking situations. These chapters apply the skills learned in unit II to create strategies to help others comprehend and remember information as well as to change attitudes and behavior. Appendix A gives specific advice on outlining techniques. Appendix B presents several sample speeches that highlight important public speaking strategies.

Each chapter also contains several pedagogical aids to help students learn the material. Chapter outlines, glossaries, and exercises highlight important material and help students apply communication concepts and skills to their own experiences. A unique pedagogical feature—"Before You Go On" Questions—help students summarize and comprehend material as they read each chapter. The answers to these questions provide a chapter summary.

Acknowledgments

The authors sincerely express their gratitude to their students, colleagues, and professors who helped them formulate many of the ideas and assumptions in this text.

We appreciate the many helpful comments and insights we received while writing *Creating Competent Communication.* We would especially like to thank our reviewers: Carol Armbrecht, North Central College; Robert Bohlken, Northwest Missouri State University; Mary Ann Cunningham and Janene Frahm, College of Marin; Bobbie Klopp, Kirkwood Community College; Monte Koffler, North Dakota State University; Kathie Leeper, Northwest Missouri State University; Donna Lund, Robert Morris College; Robert Mild Jr., Fairmont State College; Rebecca Parker, Western Illinois University; Janet Sprague-Williams, Waubonsee Community College; and Doris Werkman, Portland State University.

I UNIT

Introduction to Communication

A course in communication can be the most important course you take. Your ability to communicate is essential to success in school, in your career, and in your personal and professional relationships. Communication is more than just common sense. Even though you have been communicating constantly throughout your life, you can improve your communication through study and practice. Knowing how communication works can increase your chances of creating competent communication.

Studying unit I should convince you that the concepts discussed go beyond a common sense perspective. An understanding of this unit not only gives you a grasp of the process of communication but it also helps you to comprehend the following chapters.

This textbook is based on the concept of **communication competence** and treats communication as a transaction involving two or more people. Chapter 1 defines the transactional approach to communication by presenting a model and principles. Chapter 2 discusses the functions of perception, the effects of self-identity and self-esteem on your communication, and the characteristics of communication situations. Chapter 3 defines the concept of communication competence and begins to outline steps to create and improve competence in communication.

When you complete unit I, you should understand that communication is a process that involves two or more people sending and receiving messages simultaneously. You should also understand that, just as it takes two people to communicate, it takes two people to create competent communication. You cannot be competent alone; you must cooperate with others to create competent communication.

1 CHAPTER

Understanding Communication

• *A communication course? Why do I need a communication course?*

• *I've been communicating since I was a baby and I've been doing pretty well all these years.*

• *No one ever told me that I need to communicate better.*

• *Communication courses are okay, but they're not as important as my business and engineering courses.*

A s you review your communication experiences, you may believe you have all the communication skills you need. But, are you sure you have the necessary communication skills to face an important interpersonal conversation with a supervisor at work? Or, how about listening to a good friend who needs your help? Or, what if you have to address a gathering of neighbors to close an environmentally unsafe landfill in your community? All of these examples of communication events demand that you possess and use good communication skills. Are you ready and able to handle each of these situations?

The Importance of Communication

Each day, you are involved in situations that demand good communication skills. The skills discussed in this text can help you in your personal and professional lives. Soon you will graduate from college and begin interviewing for jobs in your chosen career. Researchers have discovered that good written and oral communication skills are among the most important skills a person brings to a job and a career.[1] After completing a survey of major companies, the Wyatt Company reported that "Many employers feel they are not doing a very good job of communicating business direction or the long-term plans of their organization. For this reason, they feel more emphasis is needed on this type of communication."[2] They concluded their report by stating, "The role of communication as a motivational tool will continue to grow."[3] The concepts, skills, and strategies for preparing and communicating ideas that we discuss in this book will help you both personally and professionally.

As mentioned in the beginning of the chapter, many people take for granted that they communicate well. All of us spend most of our lives talking and listening to others. You try to understand others and make them understand you. Some of you may have taken courses in public speaking or listening or interviewing or group discussion to help you learn to communicate. Others may not have had formal courses in communication, but learned important skills through practice and trial and error. For most people, however, an introductory course in communication is their only instruction in the skills necessary for competent communication.

Yet almost every day of our lives most of us have experienced difficulties communicating with others. If asked to make a list of situations where someone else's communication was not as clear as it could have been, you could easily come up with many specific instances. Your list might include one-to-one communication situations with friends and members of your family. It might also include a group situation such as a study group for school, a work group on the job, or a social group or club. Finally, you might also recall some communication situations of a more public nature where the communication could have been better. Often, people recognize that many communication situations are not successful but do not know how to improve them. Instead, they continue to communicate in nonproductive ways and to encounter communication difficulties. By learning and using appropriate communication skills and strategies, they could minimize these difficulties.

Importance to Career Success

The average person spends thirty-five to forty years in a career. Typical measures of career success are how much money he makes, the location of her office in relation to other employees, the type of car he drives, the number of promotions she receives, and many other tangible artifacts of a person's advancement in a career. No matter how you plan to measure your career success, good communication skills are necessary for you to succeed.

How much time will you spend talking and listening during the next thirty-five to forty years in your career? Typically, you will spend approximately 75 to 80 percent of your career talking with or listening to others.[4] Throughout this book, we explore communication skills and teach you strategies that can improve that 75 to 80 percent of your career.

The ability to communicate enhances your chances of advancement in any career. Surveys of people in engineering, public relations, manufacturing, retail sales, personnel, and almost any other career consistently find that communication is the most important skill in getting the job, doing the job well, and advancing in the career.[5] Surveys of college alumni indicate that they often perceive communication courses as more valuable to job success than technical courses in engineering, accounting, management, finance, or other specialized career fields.[6] A vice president for a large, Fortune 500 steel-producing company reported that communication skills are important for a prospective employee to bring to the job. She contended that although her company can teach a new employee how to do a job, it does not have the necessary personnel to teach an employee how to communicate well.

Importance in Interpersonal Relationships

Your interpersonal relationships with friends and family are quite important to you. You develop and maintain lifelong friendships and companions because of your abilities to communicate well with them. Think about one or two of your current close relationships. One of the bonds that keeps a relationship close is the ability of both of you to communicate competently.

We all need friends and intimate relationships. Our abilities to communicate with others competently influences these relationships. The skills and strategies discussed in this textbook can help you through a difficult situation with a spouse, a girlfriend or boyfriend, brothers, sisters, or parents.

There is always room to improve communication skills. Before learning specific communication skills in chapters 4 through 8, however, you must understand the nature of communication. This chapter discusses different perspectives of communication, defines communication, and shows how the communication process works.

People need friends and intimate relationships.

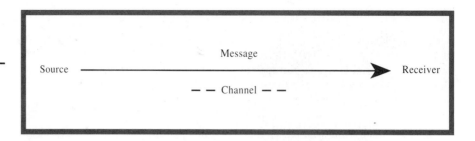

Approaches to Understanding Communication

One way to illustrate the communication process is to provide a model showing the necessary elements and the relationships between them. Any model of communication focuses on one instant of the process, just as a photograph captures a sprinter halfway through a race. Models help us describe the complex process of communication and give us a way to analyze it.

Each model has a different use, yields a different insight into how communication functions, and provides a perspective to understand and improve communication. There are many ways to describe communication. Action models approach the communication process from the message sender's point of view. Reaction models approach the communication process from the receiver's perspective. The transaction model we describe in this text approaches the communication process from the shared perspective of the sender and the receiver.

The Action Approach

An obvious part of communication is the process of sending messages. Initial models of communication developed by speech communication educators and professionals pictured communication as a one-way or linear process.[7] Figure 1.1 shows the **action approach;** a sender sending a message to a receiver through a channel.

A source or **sender** originates the message and tries to determine what to communicate and how best to communicate it. The **message** is the content being sent, verbally or nonverbally, to the receiver. The **channel** is the medium that carries the message to the receiver. For example, when we talk with someone, the airwaves carry the message. Similarly, when we are observing someone's gestures and movements, the light waves carry the information to us. Finally, the **receiver** is the person for whom the message is intended.

The action perspective defines communication as the intentional sending of verbal and nonverbal messages to a receiver to attain a goal. A person who thinks about how to communicate an idea to someone, and then does it, is reflecting the source-oriented approach to communication.

One example of this source-oriented approach involves the concerns of native Americans about the use of *Indians, Braves, Redskins,* and other Native American names as nicknames for sports teams. When talking with Native Americans, some people fail to take into account their heritage and their desire

*Many people assume a
public speech is one-way
communication.*

to protect that heritage. Such persons assume Native Americans understand why
teams use these names. They perceive nothing wrong with the message; it is clear
and unoffensive to them. In this typical problem, both sides are primarily concerned with their own views of the situation. This reduces the likelihood of
competent communication.

Public speaking illustrates the source-oriented approach. For centuries,
communication educators demonstrated how communication works in public
speaking situations. In their efforts to train students to be better public speakers,
they emphasized creating effective messages and delivering those messages in a
correct form. These teachers taught speakers to use correct reasoning; appropriate evidence; clear organization; and vivid, clear language. Some teachers even
taught students specific gestures that aroused emotions and emphasized major
ideas.

Although they taught speakers to recognize the characteristics of the receiver and to adapt messages to the audience, these teachers focused on training
speakers to perform specific actions. Their assumption was that anyone who constructed an appropriate message and sent it correctly created the desired effect
on the audience. The public speech has been and continues to be interpreted as
being source-oriented.

By focusing on the source of a message, the action model is concerned
with only the sender's actions in creating and sending a message. Such communication is a one-way process. Thus, a sender who constructs and sends clear
messages has met all responsibilities in the communication situation. Senders
might claim, "I don't know what the problem is; I made my point perfectly clear."
Or they may state, "If I had only said something else, we wouldn't have had this
fight." When communication breaks down, this model blames the source of the
message. Conversely, good communication is due to the speaker's ability to send
a clear message.

Understanding Communication

The action approach to communication looks at the skills and performance of the individual; someone who performs well is considered a competent communicator. The source-oriented approach to communication ignores the importance of the receiver of the message. By focusing only on the speaker and message, the action approach to communication ignores the receiver's communication. The sender's perceptions of the listeners and their responses become secondary to constructing and delivering a competent message.

"Before You Go On"

You should be able to answer the following question:

Why are there problems in communication when the emphasis in the communication process is on the sender?

For a long time, students and communication instructors accepted this action, or one-way, approach to communication. Later, as a result of better understanding of communication, the reaction approach to communication included the receiver of the message.

The Reaction Approach

The **reaction approach** views communication as a two-way process in which a sender and receiver exchange messages. Rather than being concerned primarily with the form and delivery of a message, the reaction approach is concerned with how the receiver interprets and responds to the message. This focus on the way a person responds to a message, and how the sender subsequently adapts to the response, suggests communication is sequential. A source has to send a message before the receiver can respond; the receiver has to respond to the message before the sender can adapt and send the next message. People take turns sending and receiving much like people playing tennis. They volley messages back and forth, first in one direction, then the other.

The receiver's response to the sender's message is **feedback.** Feedback tells the sender how accurately the message is being received. Positive feedback tells the sender the message was understood; negative feedback suggests that the sender must change the message to achieve understanding. For example, you ask someone what time it is and he correctly answers, "Eight-thirty." This appropriate, positive feedback to the original message suggests the original message was understood. If in responding to the same message, however, another person inappropriately responds, "It's Wednesday," the negative feedback tells the sender that the message was misinterpreted. As illustrated in figure 1.2, feedback completes the communication loop between sender and receiver.

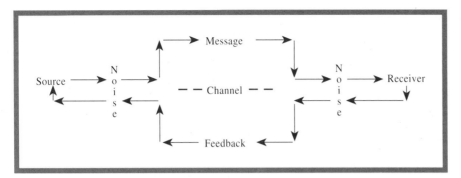

FIGURE 1.2
A reaction model of communication.

Another element of the reaction approach is **noise,** or anything that interferes with the messages being communicated effectively. The two types of noise are external noise and internal noise. *External noise* exists in the environment and interferes with the message. Obvious examples of external noise include police sirens, airplanes overhead, dogs barking, or a loud car driving by. Other examples are a baby crying in church, a radio playing, someone talking loudly at the next table in a restaurant, a door slamming, or a glass breaking in the kitchen at home. *Internal noise* exists in our minds. It consists of daydreaming, thinking of what you did yesterday, anticipating what you will do this weekend, and being tired or emotional. These factors interfere with your attention on the communication or your accurate interpretation of the message. (Chapter 3 discusses internal noise, or distractions, in detail.)

The receiver's point of view defines communication as the meaning and response given to another person's verbal and nonverbal messages. This means any verbal or nonverbal behavior we perceive, interpret, and give meaning to is communication. We may interpret even unintentional actions as meaningful communication. For example, an instructor seeing a student sit with legs crossed at the ankles, leaning back in the chair, arms folded across the chest, and eyes looking at the ceiling, might conclude the student is not paying attention. Regardless of whether the student meant to send this message (or any message), the instructor received and interpreted her behaviors as communication. In another instance, when visiting an instructor's office to seek help for a class assignment, Julie noted her instructor putting papers into a briefcase and putting on a jacket. At the same time, the instructor said there was plenty of time to work with her today. Which message or messages is Julie going to believe? That is, which of these behaviors or statements is she going to interpret as the correct message? Whichever message she emphasizes and interprets determines her feedback, regardless of what the instructor meant.

The reaction approach emphasizes communicators' abilities to listen and respond to each other's messages. Just as the action approach focuses on necessary communication skills for sending a message, the receiver-oriented approach demands good listening skills. Many people, however, have had no formal training to improve listening skills. Focusing solely on receiver skills in communication makes success as difficult to obtain as focusing solely on sender skills. The fact is, you take for granted that your communication skills are good enough for others to understand you and for you to understand others.

"Before You Go On"

You should be able to answer the following question:

How do the sender-oriented approach and the receiver-oriented approach cause differences in the communication process?

The foundation of the reaction model is that the sender of the message acts as a message-initiator and the receiver creates feedback to the original message. This suggests that people take turns when communicating, being first a sender then a receiver. This view of communication does not account for our abilities to listen and talk, observe and talk, and/or think and talk at the same time.

The Transaction Approach

Additional developments in understanding the communication process created the **transaction approach.** The transaction definition of communication emphasizes that senders and receivers share responsibility in the communication process. As a result, the transaction approach defines **communication** as the mutual creation of shared meaning through the simultaneous perception of verbal and nonverbal behaviors within a specific context. As simultaneous receivers and senders of messages, we process our own verbal and nonverbal behaviors at the same time we are interpreting another's messages. Thus, the communication process does not begin when one person speaks or when someone receives a verbal or a nonverbal message from another person. There is no identifiable beginning or end to true communication.[8] The communication process occurs with both people simultaneously. While we are stating our message to others, we are also receiving and interpreting information from the environment and other persons. Likewise, while we are listening to messages from others, we are sending nonverbal messages through eye contact, facial expressions, posture, and movement. This definition of communication highlights the need for shared responsibility for competent communication. Indeed, sending and receiving are processes we engage in simultaneously, not roles that people take turns doing. People do not either send or receive, they send and receive simultaneously.

For example, when you ask someone to do something, you try to read that person's reaction while you are communicating. When you ask someone for a date, you may interpret every movement as a response and a potential reaction

indicating either a yes or a no. You listen to every sound uttered, you watch each facial expression, observe posture and movements, and look into the person's eyes. At the same time, the other person is doing the same thing to you. Both of you are trying to understand the other person's **verbal** and **nonverbal communication** while communicating verbally and nonverbally. Your friend is sending verbal and/ or nonverbal messages to you while receiving verbal and/or nonverbal messages from you at the same time. You are both cooperatively creating a shared meaning, a shared understanding.

As figure 1.3 illustrates, each person is simultaneously perceiving four sources of information. Each person is perceiving the social and physical environment, the self, the other person's behavior, and their own behavior. All of these elements comprise the communication situation. All of these sources of information are interdependent, that is, a change in one affects all of the others. For example, if you are depressed (self), you may behave in a sullen manner (own message), perceive you have no friends (social environment), that it is a gloomy day (physical environment), and interpret another person's comment, "Cheer up!" as derogatory (other's message). If something good happens, such as winning the lottery, your interpretations of the situation change. You may feel happy, friendly to everyone, and interpret the other's message as helpful or humorous. The interaction of the four sources of information constantly changes the communication situation. This requires communicators to constantly adapt to each other to create competent communication.

In the transaction approach, communication occurs within a specific physical and social environment. The specific situation influences communication.[9] As you see in figure 1.3, the participants and all communication elements define the

FIGURE 1.3
*A transaction model of
communication.*

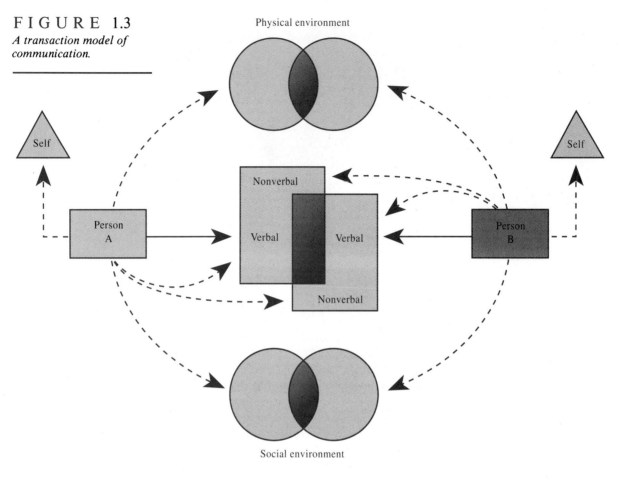

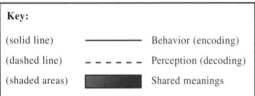

Key:

(solid line)	————	Behavior (encoding)
(dashed line)	- - - - -	Perception (decoding)
(shaded areas)	▓▓▓	Shared meanings

communication situation. The physical surroundings—the location of the communication, the climate, the setting, and the occasion—that communicators simultaneously perceive influence their communication. Similarly, their perceptions of social roles, cultural background, relationship to each other, and social rules and norms affect their communication.

Perceptions of the situation influence how we communicate, what we communicate, and to whom we communicate. You encode and interpret messages differently in church than when sitting in a local fast-food restaurant with friends. Similarly, you communicate differently with instructors in class than you do in their offices. These simple obvious examples demonstrate how perceptions of all the elements of the situation influence communication.

To demonstrate the differences among the action, reaction, and transaction approaches, consider the following example of miscommunication and how each approach explains the communication problem.

PARENT: *I have to go run an errand. Before you can play with your friends, you must finish cutting the grass. When I get home, the grass in the yard had better be cut.*

CHRIS: *No problem, it won't take long.*

The parent goes on an errand leaving Chris to complete the task of cutting the grass. When the parent gets home, only the grass in the front yard is cut, not the grass in the backyard. When Chris returns from playing with friends, the parent expresses displeasure with the fact that Chris did not follow directions.

PARENT: *I told you to cut the grass and you only did the front yard. Did you think I wouldn't notice you hadn't cut the grass in back?*

CHRIS: *You only said the front yard. I remember because I said it wouldn't take long. If I had known I had to cut the backyard, too—it would have taken all day.*

PARENT: *You just didn't listen. When I say cut the yard, you should know I mean both back and front.*

CHRIS: *If you wanted the backyard cut, you should have said so. I didn't do anything wrong—I did just what you said.*

Obviously, both the parent and Chris assumed they understood the message. Each blamed the other for the **miscommunication.**

The parent took an action approach and assumed that the grass would be cut in both yards. The action approach assumed the message was clear and precise. Hence, the parent assumed the child was at fault for not listening carefully.

Chris assumed that the parent's message meant only the front yard. The child took a reaction approach and assumed a correct **interpretation** and appropriate response to the parent's direction. From the reaction point of view, Chris had listened correctly, hence the parent was at fault for not constructing a clear message.

From a transactional perspective, the problem is not solely with the parent's message to Chris, nor with the child's interpretation of the message. The example illustrates a shared responsibility for the miscommunication. The parent shares some of the blame for assuming that the directions were clear enough. The child also shares some of the responsibility for assuming the interpretation was correct. **Communication competence** is a process requiring that all participants work at understanding the message and sharing similar meanings.

You now understand some of the complexities of the process of human communication. Competent communication is not as easy as opening your mouth and stating a message. Competent communication is more complex than assuming that your message is understood or that you understand someone else's message. Competent communication takes hard work by both people. The rest of the book discusses communication skills and strategies to help us create competent communication with others.

"Before You Go On"

You should be able to answer the following question:

What are the differences between the action, reaction, and transaction views of communication?

Principles of Transactional Communication

The transaction approach to communication can be understood by examining five key principles:

1. Communication is a process.
2. Communication is shared responsibility.
3. Communication is more than the sum of its parts.
4. Communication is irreversible.
5. Communication is personal.

Each of these principles flows from the simultaneous nature of sending and receiving messages and the interdependence of the elements of communication depicted in figure 1.3.

Communication is a Process

When we describe a process, we mean something that has no clear beginning or end. The idea of *process* suggests that communication is continuous.[10] It is virtually impossible to determine the exact starting or stopping points in human communication.

Process also suggests that you constantly send and receive verbal and nonverbal messages. Communication cannot be turned on or off at will. Even though they are not always intentional, we constantly send and receive messages.[11] Nonverbal messages (i.e., movement, posture, facial expressions, clothing, and so on) are continuously being received and interpreted. Even someone sitting alone talking on a hospital house phone communicates something to each passerby. At the same time, each passerby communicates something to the person on the phone. You cannot not communicate.

There is no clear distinction when communication begins or ends. When we communicate, meaning is influenced by prior experiences, communication with that person or similar people, and many other past events. Each of these can influence current communication, though the amount and type of influence are sometimes difficult to detect.

The transaction approach assumes communication goes both ways simultaneously.

Communication Is Shared Responsibility

Communication becomes interdependent because your messages and interpretations of the other's messages depend on each other. As you send messages, your interpretations of the other person's behaviors influence your communication. As your messages change, the messages you receive are altered, too. Similarly, the other person's messages to you depend on their perceptions of your messages.

Therefore, communication is shared responsibility between participants. Each person is responsible for competent communication. Participants are not senders or listeners; all participants are co-creators of successful communication. No one participant has more or less responsibility than others in the situation for the successful creation of meaning. The goal of communication is, therefore, to create mutual understanding.

This shared responsibility in transactional communication suggests that competent communication involves a shared or similar meaning for participants' communicative behaviors. Conversely, when communication is not competent, the participants do not have shared or similar meanings. (As we discuss in chapter 3, transactional competence is not simply one individual's skills or behaviors, but is mutually created through people's interaction. Therefore, we do not refer to a competent communica*tor*, but rather to creating competent communica*tion*.)

Competent communication ————————— No communication

Communication competence is not an all-or-nothing proposition. There are degrees of communication competence. You might have competent communication with someone in some situations, or about some topics, or in part but not in every aspect of communication. Similarly, you may share part of the meanings or partially understand each other, but not completely. The closer we are to competent communication, the better.

If you are communicating with one of your friends and miscommunication occurs, you cannot say that "I was competent and the other person was incompetent." Nor can the other person say, "I was competent and you were not." You are both responsible for creating more or less competent communication.

"Before You Go On"

You should be able to answer the following question:

How do we identify communication as competent?

Communication Involves Content and Relationship Messages

The **content** of a message is the idea expressed through people's words and actions. When people think of communicating, they normally think only of the content dimension of the message. However, this is not the total communication.

The **relationship** elements of communication are the emotions people feel about each other, their relative power and status, their attraction for each other, and their involvement with each other's lives. People usually communicate relationship messages through vocal tone, space, touch, eye contact, and other nonverbal communication behaviors. We may think people dislike us when they don't look at us, or have power over us because they yell, or are attracted to us because they touch us.

Every communication has both a content message and a relationship message. Even a simple "Hi" may say both "I am greeting you" (content) and "I like you" (relationship). When a student calls a professor "Dr. Jones," the message expresses both the person's name (content) and the student's lower status (relationship). The content and relationship aspects of communication interact and influence each other. The same content message, "Hi," may be perceived differently if spoken by an enemy, a boss, a lover, or a stranger. When trying to interpret other's messages, we need to understand that the content affects how we perceive the relationship, and that the relationship influences the meaning we give to the content. We must create shared meanings for both the relationship and the content dimensions of communication.

Communication is Irreversible

Messages are interpreted as they are received. Once perceived, messages cannot be taken back. Most of us have said something we wish we could take back—the fact is no one can. Once a message is shared, it becomes part of the receiver's experience and influences subsequent messages during the transaction.

People sometimes forget this principle and try to forget the message was ever sent. They pretend the effects of the message can be erased. When people say, "I'm sorry, forget I ever said that," or "Let me start over," or "Let's pretend that fight never happened," they are forgetting the principle that communication is a whole unit and cannot be reversed. Perhaps the best example of this principle is illustrated by communication during a courtroom trial. During "L.A. Law" or "Perry Mason," the judge sometimes instructs the jury to disregard comments made by an attorney or a witness. The fact is, when applying this principle, the members of the jury cannot disregard what they have just heard. It has already had impact on their perceptions, understandings, and feelings on the case.

Communication is Personal

Each person is different and brings individual experiences to communication situations. No one can separate the self from communication. The self is intertwined in the process and affects the perception and interpretation of the messages during communication. Our interpretation of messages is based on our past experiences with the same word, a similar action or behavior, or a similar set of circumstances. Each of us has a different realm of experience that only applies to us. This is why two people can view the same communication situation at the same time and interpret its meaning and significance differently.

Similarly, your culture and the groups you belong to influence your meanings. You use special language with your friends that no one else understands. Special occupations create jargon that only others in that occupation understand. And, the same word means different things in various areas of the United States. Pick up any dictionary and note how many of the words have multiple definitions. Because words do not have universal meanings, communication with others takes considerable work and cooperation to determine what each person means. We discuss the use of language at length in chapter 6.

Because communication is personal, each person must try to understand the idiosyncracies, emotions, psychological state, and past experiences of the other. Whether the communication is between two or many people, each person gives different meanings to the verbal and nonverbal messages. Awareness of these personal meanings is part of the task involved in competent communication; everyone must work together to create shared meanings.

1.   Why are there problems in communication when the emphasis in the communication process is on the sender?

When the focus is solely on the sender, the emphasis is on the skills needed to put the message together and send it to someone else. Each of us assumes we are good senders, and therefore good communicators of messages. With this belief, it is easy to see why many people emphasize sender-oriented approaches to communication.

In addition, this orientation takes the other participants out of the communication situation. It really does not matter who the receiver is when the focus is on the communication skills required to put together and send messages. The receiver's skills, such as paying attention and listening, are not an important part of communication.

2.   How do the sender-oriented approach and the receiver-oriented approach cause differences in the communication process?

From a sender's point of view, communication is the intentional sending of messages, both verbally and nonverbally, to a receiver with the goal of understanding. The sender plans for and executes the message for these purposes.

From a receiver's point of view, communication is the reception and interpretation of messages. These include both intentional and unintentional messages. Whenever the receiver interprets actions and behaviors as messages, communication occurs.

3.   What are the differences between the action, reaction, and transaction views of communication?

Communication as an action is a one-way communication between sender and receiver. There is no feedback to complete the communication relationship between receiver and sender. Although the receiver is considered, she is not part of the communication process.

Communication as a reaction includes feedback from the receiver to the sender of the message. Feedback related to the original message from the sender assists the sender in seeing to what degree the receiver understands the message. The channel of communication is also included in this communication model. Noise, whether internal or external, interferes with the message being sent clearly through a communication channel.

Communication as a transaction suggests that the messages between sender and receiver occur simultaneously. That is, while we send messages, we also receive messages from others. Thus, the situation is important in communication. The setting, the occasion, the physical characteristics of the situation, and other factors impact on communication.

The transaction view of communication accounts for factors influencing how communication occurs between people. For example, the backgrounds of both people influence the communication. Perceptions, values, beliefs, attitudes, and opinions of both people influence the communication. The transaction view is more complete than the action and reaction views.

4.   What does the statement, "Communication is a process" mean?

It is not clear when human communication begins or when it ends. As a process, communication is influenced by many past events in a person's life: past communication experiences, memories of significant events, educational experience, family upbringing, and so forth. Likewise, today's communication events influence future communication situations.

5.   How do we identify communication as competent?

For communication to be deemed competent, both people must create a similar, shared meaning. It is human nature for us to blame others when miscommunication occurs. We are sure that we said the right words or interpreted messages correctly. After all, we could not cause the miscommunication.

Communication is not something we do by ourselves. It takes two people to communicate, hence, both people are equally involved in making the communication a success or failure. Rather than finding blame for ineffective communication, we need to focus on how we can help each other communicate more effectively. We should not focus on what we did or what the other person did, but on what we did together to create the current communication situation. Both the sender and receiver share equally when communication is a success because both are competent together. They also share equally when miscommunication results.

S T U D E N T   E X E R C I S E S

---

1.   Communication is a continuous process.

Have you ever tried to identify a specific instance when communication began with someone? Perhaps you tried to determine who started a fight, or when a conflict began, or which specific events led to an argument. Perhaps you tried to identify who was at fault in a particular problem or other event in which you participated. Why is identifying the cause of a fight or the person who was at fault in a situation so difficult?

Try to identify when communication in your classroom begins. Does it begin when you walk into the classroom? When your instructor enters the room? Did it begin when you registered for the class? Did it begin when you talked with some of your classmates about the class? When you talked about the instructor? In your experience, which factors affect the communication in the classroom? Have you had similar classes that influenced your communication in this class?

Relate your responses to these questions to the concepts about the nature of human communication presented in this chapter.

2.   A career interview about communication.

Take a few minutes to talk with someone in the profession you would like to enter at the end of college. Ask about the communication skills he has used (or wished he had used) on the job. Ask him to describe the communication skills he sees in his co-workers. Which skills are most important? What are the common communication problems?

Talk for a few minutes about specific communication skills you want to learn to improve your chances of entering your career and then succeeding in that career.

3.   Defining communication.

Ask some members of your family and some of your friends to define or describe communication. Don't give them any hints. After you have gathered seven or eight definitions, examine the similarities and differences among them. Determine whether their definitions fit into the action, reaction, or transaction views of communication discussed in this chapter. What does this say about how people view the process of human communication?

4.   Defining competence.

Ask some of your friends to define communication competence. How do they know when their communication was competent? Spend a few minutes generating your own responses to the same questions. Ask your friends to describe some communication situations when they felt that they were communicating competently. Ask them also to describe some communication situations when they felt they were communicating incompetently.

After you have done this, ask your friends what they have done to increase the likelihood that they are communicating competently. Talk about how they are helping others in the situation communicate competently.

What can you conclude about how others view communication competence? Compare the response to this question to the discussion of communication competence in this chapter.

G L O S S A R Y

action approach The approach to understanding communication that focuses on the one-way process of a source sending a message.

channel The carrier of messages, both verbal and nonverbal, from a sender to a receiver.

communication The use of verbal and nonverbal communication between people trying to create shared meaning.

communication competence The degree to which both sender and receiver have obtained a similar, shared meaning during communication; it implies direct and shared responsibility by both sender and receiver.

feedback The message from a receiver to a sender included in reaction and transaction models of communication.

interpretation The act of making sense of one's perceptions.

message The data or information communicated between sender and receiver and receiver and sender either verbally, nonverbally, or both.

miscommunication When the messages between the sender and receiver are not similar or shared. Both the sender and receiver must assume responsibility when miscommunication occurs.

noise Anything that interferes with the communication channels carrying the messages between people.

nonverbal communication Messages sent between people by using the tone of voice, the rate of speaking, appearance, gestures, eye contact, and facial expressions rather than words.

process The notion that there is no clear beginning or ending to communication. It highlights the fact that communication is ever-changing and dynamic.

reaction approach A view of two-way communication that suggests a sequencing of messages from sender to receiver and then from receiver to sender.

receiver The person the sender's messages are targeted for or a person who perceives a message from someone and gives it meaning.

sender The person who communicates a message to a receiver through initiating the communication. (Also referred to as the source of the message.)

situation All elements comprising the communication interaction including the self, people, the social context, the occasion, and the physical environment.

transaction approach A view of communication in which both people simultaneously send and receive messages. Both people co-create the meanings in communication and thus share responsibility for its successes and failures.

verbal communication The words people use to communicate messages to others. Usually viewed as intentional because persons have to consciously put the messages they have in mind into words.

NOTES

1. For additional development of these ideas, see Samuel L. Becker and Leah R. V. Ekdom, "The Forgotten Basic Skill: Oral Communication," *Iowa Journal of Speech Communication* 12 (1980), 1–18; Allen Blitzstein, "What Employers Are Seeking in Business Graduates," *The College Forum* (Winter 1980–1981), 7; Lawrence W. Hugenberg, Alfred W. Owens II, and David J. Robinson, *Structures for Business and Professional Speech: A Working Resource Manual* (Dubuque, Iowa; Kendall/Hunt Publishing Company, 1982), 1–12; Ben W. Morse, "Theoretician to Pragmatist: What Burger King Hath Done to Me." Paper presented during the Midwest Basic Course Directors' Conference, Cincinnati, Ohio, February 1991; and Ritch L. Sorensen, Grant T. Savage, and Elizabeth Orem, "A Profile of Communication Faculty Needs in Business Schools and Colleges," *Communication Education* 39 (April 1990), 148–60.

2. The Wyatt Company. *The Wyatt Communicator* (Chicago: The Wyatt Company, June 1989), 7.

3. Ibid., 26.

4. This idea is developed in detail in Kenneth R. Mayer, "Building Oral Communication Skills in the Business College Curriculum," *Collegiate News & Views* 35 (1982), 13–17; Rodman L. Drake, "Leadership: It's a Rare Blend of Traits," *Management Review* 74 (August 1985); A. S. Bednar and R. J. Olney, "Communication Needs of Recent Graduates," *Bulletin of the Association for*

Business Communication (December 1987), 22–33; and E. M. Eisenberg and S. R. Phillips, "Miscommunication in Organizations," in *"Miscommunication" and Problematic Talk,* eds. N. Coupland, H. Giles, and J. Wiemann (Newbury Park, Calif.: Sage, 1991), 244–58.

5.   Dan B. Curtis, Jerry L. Winsor, and Ronald D. Stephens, "National Preferences in Business and Communication Education," *Communication Monographs* 28 (1989), 6–14.

6.   Ritch L. Sorensen and Judy C. Pearson, "An Alumni Perspective on Speech Communication Training: Implications for Communication Faculty," *Communication Education* 30 (1981), 299–304.

7.   For excellent explanations of the one-way or linear model of communication, see Claude E. Shannon and Warren Weaver, *The Mathematical Theory of Communication* (Urbana: University of Illinois Press, 1948); Howard H. Martin and Kenneth E. Andersen, eds., *Speech Communication: Analysis and Readings* (Boston: Allyn and Bacon, 1968); and Frank E. X. Dance, "Toward a Theory of Human Communication," in *Human Communication Theory: Original Essays,* ed. Frank E. X. Dance (New York: Holt, Rinehart and Winston, 1967), 288–309.

8.   Dean C. Barnlund, "A Transactional Model of Communication," in *Foundations of Communication Theory,* eds. Kenneth K. Sereno and C. David Mortenson (New York: Harper & Row, 1970), 83–102.

9.   For additional understanding of the importance of the situation on communication, see Lloyd Bitzer, "The Rhetorical Situation," *Philosophy and Rhetoric* 1 (1968), 1–15; and Kenneth Burke, *A Grammar of Motives* (Cleveland, Ohio; Meridian Books/World, 1962).

10.   David Berlo offers a clear explanation of process in *The Process of Communication* (New York: Holt, Rinehart and Winston, 1960), 174–82.

11.   Paul Watzlawick, Janey H. Beavin, and Don D. Jackson, *Pragmatics of Human Communication* (New York: W.W. Norton & Company, 1967).

OUTLINE

Many people think communication only involves the exchange of messages; that is, the verbal and nonverbal behaviors of the people engaging in communication. This is a simplistic view of the communication process. The transaction model of communication introduced in the last chapter includes communicators' perceptions of four interdependent sources of information. We perceive other people's behavior, the environment, our private self, and our own behavior. To understand how communication works, therefore, we need to study the nature and functions of perception, the formation and influence of the self in communication, and the communication situation.

Perception in Communication

Perception is defined as the process by which we give meaning to the world around us. We constantly receive information, or stimuli, about the world through our senses. Most of the stimuli we receive go unnoticed and uninterpreted by our conscious minds. **Reception** refers to this passive receiving of input by our senses. For example, if you are sitting in the library reading, many stimuli are impinging on your senses without your conscious awareness. The noise of the room air conditioner, the shuffling of feet, the buzz of the fluorescent lights, the colors of the walls, the taste of the gum you're chewing, the pressure of the chair against your back, and the weight of the book in your hands are all available to your senses, even though you are usually unaware of them. Only when you focus on the stimuli and attempt to understand them do you engage in the process of perception. Perception is the active process by which we select, organize, and interpret stimuli.

The Functions of Perception

How do we make sense of the thousands of stimuli constantly bombarding our senses? How do we derive meaning from seemingly random and constantly changing stimuli? The process of perception allows us to select, organize, and interpret the world around us.

Selection

We can't possibly give constant attention to each and every stimulus that's available to our senses. From the many sources of information, we select which ones to interpret. To reduce the number of stimuli we interpret, we use the selection function of perception.

Selective Attention One way we limit the number of stimuli on which we focus is through selective attention; that is, we focus on a small number, or set, of stimuli and ignore other stimuli. We can focus our attention at will. We can focus on one sense at a time or on several senses simultaneously, we can focus on a large set or a small set of stimuli, and we can focus for a brief instant or for several seconds. For example, when you see someone coming toward you on the street, you may focus your attention on the entire person, noting height, body shape, and general appearance. On the other hand, you may focus just on hair, or eyes, or shoes. You may just glance at the person or stare. Look at the picture from *Where's Waldo?* What do you notice first? Why is it difficult to find Waldo? Can you see all the pictures at once? What happens as you focus on each character in the picture? Selective attention reduces the number of stimuli we interpret.

Selection of stimuli is not always totally voluntary. A sudden noise, a fragrant odor, an unusual sight, or an unexpected pain can cause us to change the focus of our perception. We crave variety in stimuli and constantly seek new information. If the stimuli is unchanging, we quickly lose interest and seek out different information. Our attention span tends to be about 3 to 5 seconds, so we are constantly shifting our focus to try to make meaning of new stimuli. Whether voluntary or involuntary, selective attention serves to reduce the number of stimuli we perceive.

Selective Retention A second method by which we focus our perceptions is **selective retention.** One source of information, our private self, includes our memories of experiences and events. These memories help us understand current situations as we relate new experiences and ideas to existing memories. Our memories help us give meaning to what we are currently experiencing.

A simple analogy to explain the process of memory is a filing cabinet. If we received a letter from Joe about his camping trip to Utah, we would read it and then file it for later reference. Because we want to find it easily, we put it in a folder labeled "Joe's letter." We might also make copies of the letter and file duplicates in folders labeled "camping," "Utah," and "vacations." Later, someone might ask about Joe. We could find the folder labeled "Joe's letter" and say, "Joe wrote to me about his camping trip." Or we might hear someone talk about Utah and we would look in our Utah folder and say "I have a friend who is in Utah on vacation now." Or we might think about our own vacation and look in the vacation folder and think "I'd like to go camping in Utah on my vacation like Joe is doing." Similar to all filing systems, however, ours is not infallible. We might put Joe's letter in the wrong folder, we might file only part of his letter, we may forget where we filed it, or we may forget to file it at all. If any of these things happen, it is difficult or impossible to retrieve the letter and get complete and accurate information about his trip.

Our memories work somewhat like file cabinets. We associate new information with information already stored in memory. As we selectively attend to stimuli, we file it in our memories. We put it in a mental folder and label the folder so that we can find it again. When we want to retrieve information, we think of the label that stimulates recall of the information.

Because we have so much information to file, and because we don't always develop useful filing systems, our memories tend to be somewhat inaccurate and incomplete.[1] For instance, we forget to label information (we forget a person's name just seconds after we heard it). We misfile the information (we remember an event happening in March rather than April). We file only part of the information (we remember a Halloween party but not everyone's costumes). Or, we forget where we filed the information (we couldn't remember the answer to the test question, even though we had studied it). Therefore, not all memories are totally correct or easily retrieved.

The key to effective memory is to improve our skills in filing the information to make retrieval easier and more efficient. We don't remember just what we want to remember. We remember some things we would rather not, and forget some things important to us. Information used frequently (such as your best friend's phone number) is easier to remember than infrequently used information (such as your dentist's phone number). Information filed with an easily recalled label closely associated with the information is more easily retrieved from memory. Mentally rehearsing the information, developing mnemonic labels for information, and using the information frequently improves selective retention.

The important point about selective retention is that our memories are not perfect. If another person's memory of an event differs from ours, we often argue vehemently that our memory of an event is correct and the other person's memory is wrong. Both people believe their memories of the event are complete and accurate. Because memories are selective, however, both versions of the event are probably somewhat distorted and incomplete.

Selective Exposure We tend to seek information consistent with our view of the world and actively avoid information inconsistent with our perspectives. We selectively search for information to reinforce our attitudes and beliefs and ignore information that challenges them. For example, a person buying a new Dodge Caravan pays attention to advertisements praising the virtues of Dodge Caravans and ignores commercials that promote Ford Aerostars. When we break up with girlfriends or boyfriends, we tend to talk with people who support our decision and avoid those who tell us we made a mistake. **Selective exposure** is the process by which we try to control the types of information available to us so that we can maintain consistency and confidence in our attitudes and our interpretation of the world.

Sometimes we seek information contradicting our decisions and attitudes to strengthen our position. One example is a person who knows she has to defend her decision about the van she purchased to her parents. They wanted her to buy the Aerostar, so she might learn about the Aerostar to refute their arguments. Similarly, you might listen to opinions contradicting your choice of college majors because you know you can easily refute them. In both cases, people are exposing themselves to contradictory information that actually reinforces current interpretations.[2] Selective exposure is one of the processes by which we limit information.

Selective attention, selective retention, and selective exposure are perceptual processes by which we select information from others, from the environment, and from our self. We still have the task of making sense of all the information. One of the ways in which we make sense of the information is through organization.

"Before You Go On"

You should be able to answer the following question:

How does selection limit the information we perceive?

Organization

Organizing information helps us make sense of it. We have difficulty making sense of random, unrelated stimuli. We need to structure the incoming stimuli and to identify relationships among them to handle the quantity of information we perceive. In the process of organizing our perceptions, we give them meaning.

When we organize information, we are essentially saying to ourselves, this is the relationship among all these perceptions; here's what they have in common; here's what they mean. Our organization of perceptions is personal and arbitrary. The stimuli we perceive are not inherently related in any set pattern; they are only grouped together because we decide to organize them in a specific manner. The **organizing function of perception** gives them meaning.

Closure Sometimes we assume information is present when it really isn't there. That is, we add information to existing perceptions to make them more complete and meaningful. We receive part of a message, add information, and assume we know all the message. We perceive part of a picture and assume we know what the rest of the picture is. When we fill in missing information we are engaging in the organizational process of **closure.** When we see someone on campus wearing a sports letter jacket, we may add information and conclude the person is an athlete. We may then assume she likes to talk about sports, that she is less studious than other students, or that she likes to party. Even though the stereotype may or may not be accurate for this person, we behave as if it is. We selectively attended to one piece of information (the jacket) and added information about interests, study habits, and personality. Similarly, we may be assigned a five-page term paper and assume that it must be typed, double-spaced, and include a bibliography, even though the teacher did not specifically say so. We filled in missing information based on our selective retention of similar assignments, experiences with the instructor, or rules for doing term papers.

Closure can be helpful when trying to make sense of perceptions because we don't always have time, resources, or motivation to find out everything. First encounters with new acquaintances require that we make interpretations based on very little actual information to direct our conversation and find mutual interests. Closure helps us make sense of perceptions that are incomplete and otherwise confusing.

Closure can sometimes inhibit accurate perceptions if we don't attempt to validate and subsequently modify our initial interpretations; that is, if we don't try to find the missing information. If we allow closure to freeze our perception and close our minds to further information, we risk making incorrect assumptions and misinterpretations. Inaccurate or incomplete perceptions often cause problems in creating competent communication. (Figure 2.1 shows examples of closure.)

Association Another way we make sense of perceptions is to group stimuli according to the principle of association. **Association** reduces the number of categories we use to classify our perceptions and makes it easier to manage the large amount of information to which we attend.

If we perceive things located close together, we might conclude they belong together because of **space proximity.** For example, if we see two people standing next to each other at a party, we might assume that they are a couple. On hearing a sneeze, we may assume that the person standing where the sound came from sneezed. Spacial proximity of stimuli provides one means of organizing information. (Figure 2.1 shows some examples of association.)

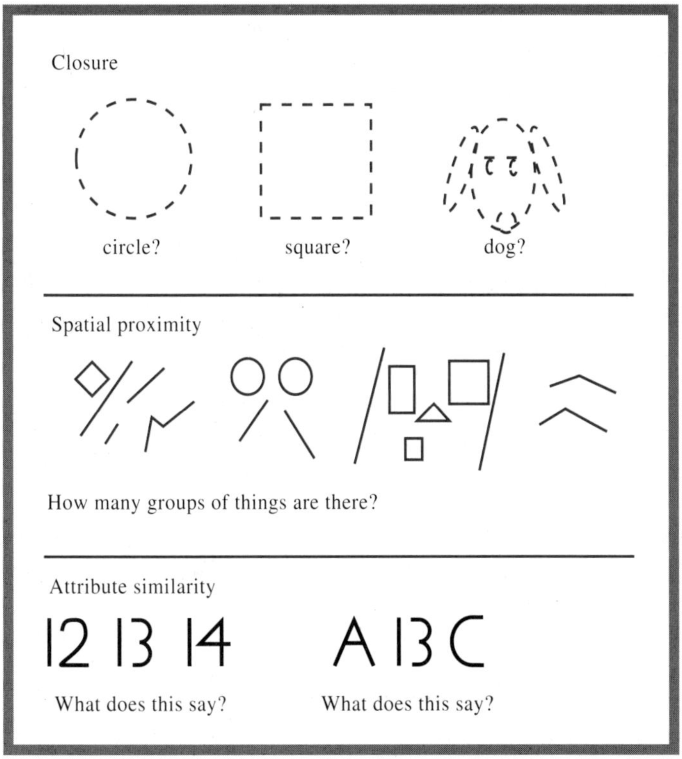

FIGURE 2.1
Examples of perceptual organization.

The figure contains:

Closure

circle?   square?   dog?

Spatial proximity

How many groups of things are there?

Attribute similarity

12 13 14   A 13 C

What does this say?   What does this say?

Sometimes we use **time proximity** to organize perceptions. When two events happen simultaneously or sequentially, we assume that they can be grouped as related events. If someone yawns while we're talking, we might assume they are bored with our conversation, that is, we assume the events are related because they happened at the same time. Similarly, we base cause and effect judgments on the temporal relationship of events—the cause comes before the effect. If we are well-informed during a group discussion and state our ideas clearly, and subsequently we are chosen as leader of the group, we may assume we were selected because we were well-prepared. Whenever we make the conclusion that one event caused another, we are organizing our perceptions according to time proximity.

A third method of association is **attribute similarity.** We organize perceptions or events, people, or things because they have similar characteristics. For example, we might see physical similarities between two people and assume they are related. We might perceive similarities between our love of dancing and a friend's enjoyment of dancing and conclude that we are a lot alike. Whenever we conclude that two or more events are alike, we give them similar meanings based on the attribute similarity principle. (Figure 2.1 shows examples of attribute similarity.)

Once we select stimuli to perceive, we organize our perceptions according to principles of association and closure. The manner in which we organize our perceptions is personal and arbitrary, but it is inherent in the process of human perception. The interpretation function of perception determines the meanings we give to our organized perceptions.

"Before You Go On"

You should be able to answer the following question:

What are three ways you organize perceptions to make sense of them?

Interpretation

Once we have selected and organized information from the environment, the other person's behavior, and our own behavior, we give it meaning. The meaning we give to stimuli is influenced by our physiological biases, our cultural biases, and our psychological biases. Whenever we limit the possible interpretations we can give to stimuli, we have biased our perceptions. **Perceptual bias** slants the meaning we give to perceptions, allows us to perceive stimuli from a limited number of perspectives, or gives a preference for one interpretation rather than others. Our perceptions are inherently biased.

Physiological Biases

Physiological biases are due to limitations of our five senses such as hearing impairments, distortions in eyesight, or insensitivity of touch. Our physical stature also can bias our perceptions. For example, tall people have a different perspective than short people; they see different stimuli and from a different angle than shorter people. For instance a man six feet, four inches tall was on an overly crowded bus with his five-foot, four-inch wife. They had to stand packed in the aisle like sardines. Since he could see over most people's heads, he was perfectly at ease. His wife, however, was distressed because she felt closed in. As a joke, he crouched down to her height to make fun of her and realized that all she could see was the back of the man in front of her. He then realized that her perception of the crowded bus was totally different than his, and he began to understand why she felt claustrophobic. Both these people's perceptions of the bus were limited by their physical height. His physical characteristics had biased his perception in a way different than hers.

Similarly, our physical well-being can bias our perceptions. We perceive events differently when we are tired or sick than when we are alert and well. A cold can interfere with your sense of smell or fatigue can limit your ability to hear important messages. Physiological biases interfere with competent communication by limiting not only each person's understanding of the other's perspective but also the ability to accurately and completely perceive the same stimuli.

Psychological Biases

Psychological biases are our attitudes, values, beliefs, emotions, and needs that influence the way we give meaning to our perceptions. Just as we seek out information consistent with our beliefs and attitudes through selective exposure, we interpret information so that it is consistent with what we already believe to be true. Similarly, our needs and emotions influence how we perceive information. We may laugh at a joke told by a woman, yet be offended if the same joke is told by a man. Similarly, prejudiced people tend to exaggerate the negative qualities of minorities, hungry people estimate the size of food portions as larger than well-fed people, pessimistic people perceive events as more threatening than optimistic people. Our needs, emotions, and attitudes influence how we construct our reality and subsequently, how we behave and adapt to that reality.

Cultural Biases Cultural biases are major influences on our attitudes and beliefs, and subsequently our perceptions. As we discuss in chapter 14, culture is the common frame of reference shared by a large group of people. Culture defines the meanings people give to information and events. The culture in which you live influences how you perceive reality. For example, Andrea was from Colombia, South America, and grew up liking school. In Colombia, going to college was a privilege few people enjoyed. The entrance exams were exceptionally stringent and only the best students were accepted. When she came to college in America, she enjoyed the work and could not understand some of her friends who complained college was too hard, too boring, and too much work. She had the same classes and the same assignments as her friends, but she considered it a challenge, an opportunity to learn important and interesting information, and less work than her classes in Colombia. Because the attitudes and beliefs learned in her culture were different than those of her American friends, she interpreted the same information differently. Her psychological biases influenced the meaning she gave to her perceptions.

Perceptual set is the limitation of our interpretations based on past experiences and/or future expectations. Sometimes we interpret new information as if it were similar to our past experiences. We may perceive our current math classes to be difficult because all of our past math classes have been difficult. Because we perceive it to be difficult, math becomes difficult. Similarly, we tend to interpret new information according to what we expect to perceive. If we expect to have fun at a party, we tend to have fun. Conversely, if we expect a party to be dull, it tends to be dull. Our perceptual biases limit our interpretation of stimuli so that they become what we think they should be.

"Before You Go On"

You should be able to answer the following question:

How are perceptions biased?

Validating Perceptions

With all of the inherent limitations and biases of our perceptions, how can we ever determine if our meanings are correct and accurate? We know we have missed some information through selection. We know we have organized our perceptions according to personal and arbitrary principles. And, we know that we assign biased meanings to our perceptions. The ultimate truth or validity of perceptions is really not possible to ascertain. All we can hope for is some consistency or reliability and some stability in interpreting our perceptions. When our perceptions are consistent, we think they are also true and valid. Next, we examine several ways in which we attempt to validate our perceptions.

Multisensory Validation

One way to determine if our perceptions are valid is to use more than one source of stimuli. We try to find **multisensory validation** or consistency between the perceptions from several of our senses. If you hear a noise, you may look to see if you can find the source of the noise. If you can't you may wonder if you heard the noise at all. If you smell smoke, you may look to see if something is burning. If Bill hears Liz say, "You're such a jerk," he may look at her facial expression to see if she is angry or just joking or even if she is talking to him. In this case, he thought he heard an insult but saw Liz smiling, so Bill reinterprets the message as humor. This makes his perception of what he heard consistent with his perception of what he saw.

When perceptions from different sources are inconsistent, we have difficulty knowing which one is valid, which one to believe. We normally try to choose one of the perceptions as accurate and change interpretations of the other perceptions to be consistent. That's why when Bill was called a jerk, he concluded that the visual message (smiling) was the valid message and reinterpreted Liz's verbal message so that his multisensory perceptions were consistent.

Repetitive Validation

Another way we determine the validity of our perceptions is to repeat the experience to see if we get the same meaning a second time. If we smell something burning, we may sniff the air two or three more times to be sure that we did indeed smell something and that it actually smelled like something burning. If we hear a noise, we may become very quiet and listen for it to happen again. If someone insults us, we may say "what?" to see if we hear the words and intonation the same way the second time. When we make the same interpretation using **repetitive validation,** we believe our perceptions are valid.

Predictive Validation

We also check the validity of our perceptions by making if-then comparisons of events. We formulate a hypothesis and check whether it is true. For example, if Sue perceives that Gary likes her, she might formulate this hypothesis: If he likes me, he will go to the movie with me. Sue then asks him for a date, he says yes, and Sue validated her original perception that Gary likes her. If he says no, Sue may conclude she was originally wrong. We use **predictive validation** when we try to determine a causal relationship among our perceptions. If the causality seems to accurately predict a relationship among perceptions, we assume our initial perceptions were valid.

Consensual Validation

One of the most important sources of validation comes through our interactions with others. We tend to believe our perceptions are accurate if other people have the same perceptions. When we ask, "Do you smell something burning?" we are checking our perception with someone else's interpretation. If they say, "Yeah, I smell smoke," we may conclude there is a fire. If they answer, "I don't smell anything," we may decide we were wrong.

In a sense, the very purpose of communication is to determine **consensual validation.** We try to communicate our perceptions so that others understand and agree with us. We tend to associate with people who perceive things in a manner similar to the way we do because they validate our sense of reality. Through discussion of our perceptions, we co-create a shared reality that we agree is valid.

In the Middle Ages, many people agreed that the world was flat. That didn't make the world flat, but that vision of the world influenced the people's actions because the perception was consensually valid. Consensual validation is not necessarily the way things actually are, but it is the basis on which we act.

"Before You Go On"

You should be able to answer the following question:

What are four ways we validate our perceptions?

We don't always use all of the methods of validation together. If we don't receive consensual validation, we may engage in multisensory or repetitive validation to check our conclusions. If our interpretation is repetitively validated, we may disregard the fact that others don't agree, or we may try to change their minds. The important point about validating our perceptions is that we can interpret events in many ways depending on our selection, organization, and bias. We may consider our perceptions and memories as the most valid and believe that people who disagree with us are mistaken. We need to remember, however, that other people's perceptions are as valid for them as our perceptions are for us. We may even have to realize that our interpretations might be inaccurate, distorted, or wrong. By maintaining open minds, we can consider perceptions different from ours as potentially valid. Creating consensual agreement about the meanings of our perceptions is the goal of competent communication.

One of the difficulties in creating consensual validation is the influence of each person's self on the interpretation of perceptions. The transaction model shows that the self is interdependent with the communication process. As you learned in chapter 1, communication is personal; it is impossible to separate the self from communication. The next section explains the role of self in competent communication.

The Self in Communication

An inherent part of every communication situation is each person's self. The self influences our perceptions of the environment, our own behavior, and the other person's behavior. Our past experiences, moods, physical state of being, emotions, attitudes, values, and beliefs comprise the **self.** Thus, they are interdependent with every aspect of communication. To understand the process of communication, you must understand how each of us perceives the private self.

The Nature of the Self

The self has three interrelated dimensions: self-identity, ideal self, and self-esteem. Each of these dimensions affects our perceptions of our own behavior, others' behavior, and the environment. Conversely, our perceptions of our own behavior, others' behavior, and the environment affect our perception of the self. To understand this interdependence, we must examine the three dimensions of the self.

Self-Identity

Each of us has a perception of who we are that gives us our identity. Have you ever tried to write a list of statements that thoroughly described who you are? If you have, then you probably realize that your self is a complex collection of multiple perceptions. These perceptions of self can be classified into the following five dimensions:

1. The *physical self* includes height, weight, body shape, attractiveness, gender, athletic ability, and similar perceptions.

2. The *social self* includes the roles we assume in our communication with others. When we describe ourselves as students, brothers, daughters, sorority sisters, or math club members, we are describing roles we play. Each role defines social relationships with others. For instance, one can't be a teacher without students. Or, a club member without other people in the club. Thus, a variety of roles define the social self.

3. *The psychological self* includes personality, emotions, needs, beliefs, values, and attitudes. Labels such as friendly, intelligent, shy, anxious, caring, and nervous describe personality and emotions. Conservative, radical, pro-life, and racist describe the beliefs, values, and attitudes that are also part of the psychological self.

4. The *moral self* relates to whether we are honest, trustworthy, ethical, religious, or manipulative. Moral self-identity is part of who we perceive ourselves to be.

5. The *behavioral self* describes our activities, hobbies, or interests. When we describe ourselves as campers, cooks, coin collectors, Yankee fans, pianists, or gardeners, we are defining ourselves by what we do.[3]

Although we categorize our perceptions in these five separate dimensions of **self-identity,** all of our self-perceptions are interrelated. Naturally people emphasize some characteristics more in some contexts than others and they may change over time. We emphasize the physical self when we play sports and the moral self-identity when we perform community service projects. Over time, body shapes and sizes may change, we may stop collecting baseball cards, we may become parents, and we may change our attitudes about education. Self-identity is not a static picture of who we think we are, but a constantly changing collection of interrelated perceptions.

We play many roles in our daily communication with others.

Our activities define our behavioral self.

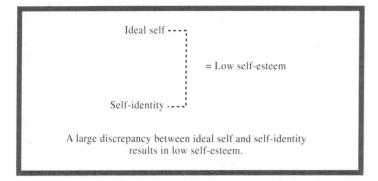

FIGURE 2.2
Relationship of self-identity, ideal self, and self-esteem.

Ideal Self

We not only have a perception of who we are, we also have an idealized version of the self, that is, we have a perception of who we would like to be. The **ideal self** has the same five dimensions as the self-identity. The ideal self can be similar to the self-identity or it may be different. For example, Jim may perceive himself as fat but have a slim or athletic ideal self. When people make statements such as "I need to quit procrastinating," or "I need to listen more carefully to my Mother," or "I want to learn to scuba dive," they are implying that at least part of the ideal self is different than who they currently think they are.

Self-esteem

When we compare our self-identity (who we think we are) with our ideal self (whom we want to be), we make a judgment about the self. This evaluation of the self is **self-esteem.** The difference between the ideal self and self-identity determines self-esteem. If the discrepancy between the ideal self and self-identity is large, persons have a negative evaluation of the self or low self-esteem. If the ideal self and self-identity are similar, persons have a positive evaluation or high self-esteem. (See figure 2.2.)

The magnitude of this discrepancy between the ideal self and self-identity interacts with the degree of importance we place on the specific part of our self-identity. The more important the attribute, the more negatively we evaluate any discrepancy. The less important the attribute, the more tolerant we are of discrepancies between the ideal self and self-identity.[4] For example, Jennifer has an ideal—being a straight A student—but doesn't really care that much about grades. Then she probably is not overly concerned when she receives a C. If being an A student is very important to Jennifer, however, then receiving even an A⁻ might make her feel like a failure. If being thin has high importance as an ideal attribute of David's physical self, then being even two pounds overweight may cause him to hate himself (as with people who suffer from anorexia nervosa). For others who want to be slim but aren't that concerned with their bodies' appearance, being even twenty pounds overweight doesn't negatively influence their self-esteem.

Self-esteem also affects interpretations of other people's behavior. People with low self-esteem interpret other people's behavior more negatively. They perceive a slight disagreement as a message that a person hates them. People with low self-esteem may be more reluctant to communicate with others, more influenced by persuasive messages, and more willing to conform to social pressure than people with high self-esteem.[5]

Self-identity and self-esteem are powerful perceptions that also influence how we interpret another's communication. We perceive communication in such a way that it conforms to our self-concept. The *self-fulfilling prophecy* states that we behave in ways consistent with our self-identity and self-esteem, which in turn validates our perceptions of self. For instance, people who consider themselves to be poor students often study less because they think studying won't do any good. When they do poorly on an exam, they conclude "I told you I was a poor student—what do you expect?"[6] Similarly, people who think they are excellent public speakers speak frequently, without inhibition. As they speak more, they get better and people compliment them, reinforcing a positive self-identity and self-esteem. The self-fulfilling prophecy is the circular influence of self-esteem on behavior and behavior on self-esteem. It illustrates the interdependence of the self and behavior in transactional communication.

"Before You Go On"

You should be able to answer the following question:

How do the ideal self, self-identity, and self-esteem interact to describe the self?

Formation and Development of Self

How do we establish and develop our self-concepts? Where does the ideal self come from? The primary influence on the formation and development of self is our communication with others.[7] We tend to become who others tell us we are; we see ourselves as others perceive us. Remember, we try to develop consistency in our perceptions partly through consensual validations. We check the validity of our perceptions of self by comparing them with how others say they perceive us. When people they trust tell them that they are smart or handsome or empathic or good bowlers, people perceive themselves that way. When no one laughs at their jokes, people who think they are funny may reevaluate their self-perceptions and conclude they can't tell jokes well.

Similarly, we derive self-esteem from our interactions with others in face-to-face communication. We tend to believe people's perceptions and feedback about the self if we have close personal bonds with them. You may not care if a stranger compliments your singing after a concert, but burst with pride when your mother or father says the same thing. People who are important to us, such as parents, siblings, and close friends, have a significant influence on our evaluation of ourselves.

Similarly, the family and friends also influence the ideal self. We may try to be what our parents want us to be. We may try to model close friends' behavior so we can be accepted by our peer groups. Messages such as "Big boys don't cry," or "Cool kids wear Nikes," or "Why aren't you more like your big sister," or "A tall guy like you should be good at basketball," give people pictures of what the ideal self should be.

The media also influence the ideal self. Television shows, commercials, movies, print advertisements, books, music, and magazines portray various ways of perceiving the self. We frequently assume that the media characterize the social norms of acceptable and unacceptable self-images. If the media constantly portrays intelligent and studious people as nerds, a young person may develop an ideal self that finds being intelligent unacceptable. If all the models and movie stars are slim and have blonde hair, we may idealize these features as an indication of what beauty is. If advertisements imply that strong, independent individuals smoke cigarettes, we may assume we have to smoke to be perceived this way. Similarly, we develop notions of ideal selves through education, religious groups and institutions, clubs, and social groups.

We form and develop the self by trying different behaviors and judging how people react to us. By trying the same behavior several times, we determine whether the reaction is repetitively valid. If we obtain consensual validation from different important people whom we trust, and do so a number of times, we may conclude that those behaviors are part of who we are. One way to change the self is to experiment with different behaviors. The only way to know which behaviors to try to change is to become aware of the self-identity. The only way to consensually validate the self-concept is by sharing the self with others through communication.

Communicating about the Self

Others cannot directly perceive your self. They can only infer your self-identity, self-esteem, and ideal self by interpreting your verbal and nonverbal behaviors. Sometimes you project information about your self unintentionally. Others may see you smile, wear bright-colored clothes, and walk with a quick pace. They conclude you are happy and that you feel good about yourself. Such inferences may not always be accurate, but they are inherent in the communication process. Similarly, you make judgments and inferences about another's self.

Another way of communicating your self-perception is through **self-disclosure.** Self-disclosure is intentionally communicating information about the self that others could not easily discover through other means. To tell others that you are tall is not self-disclosure because they can tell that information by looking at you. To tell others that you enjoy being tall, or wish you were, is self-disclosure. The only way others would know how you feel about being tall is if you tell them. Self-disclosure tends to increase the degree of trust people have with each other. If one person self-discloses, others also tend to reveal things about themselves.[8] The sharing of information about ourselves helps others interpret our communication more accurately. It helps them organize our behavior as similar or different than their own and to establish grounds for predictive validation of their perceptions of us. If you tell someone you enjoy folk music, he may organize his perception of you as "similar to my friend, Alice." He may predict you will like Alice and suggest you get together with her and go to a folk music concert. This perception would not be possible if you had not self-disclosed about your interests.

"Before You Go On"

You should be able to answer the following question:

How is the self developed through communication with others?

Perception and the self are two important dimensions of communication. We discuss these concepts throughout the text as they apply to creating competent communication in a variety of contexts. Understanding perception and the self is important when learning to apply appropriate communication skills and strategies.

Characteristics of Communication Contexts

You probably believe that your conversations with friends are fairly competent communication experiences. You frequently talk with people whom you know fairly well, who have similar interests as you, and who seem to understand you. You probably talk together in familiar places such as classes, dorm rooms, the bookstore, and the local hangout. You usually feel comfortable in your ability to send and receive messages accurately in these contexts.

Yet, when you must give a public speech, or participate in a group discussion, or have an interview, with these same friends, or need to communicate with strangers, you may be uncertain about your ability to communicate effectively. For some reason, people often think that these contexts are fundamentally different than their routine, daily conversations. They may think to themselves: "I don't know how to do this. I have never done this before. What will I say? Who wants to listen to me? How should I stand? What should I wear? How long do I have to talk?" These same questions, however, are seldom asked about familiar conversational contexts.

Concerns about communicating in public situations, group discussions, and interviews are sometimes based on the assumption that these contexts require different communication skills and different communication principles. This assumption is not true. Every communication context has the same basic characteristics, requires the same sorts of communication skills, and involves the same principles of communication, whether the context is perceived as public speaking, group discussion, interview, or conversation.

When students in a communication class were asked to describe a communication situation that caused them problems, one person stated:

> I feel totally inadequate when I have to talk to important people. I know what I want to say since I usually plan what I want to say and rehearse the night before. But when I start talking, I feel like what I'm saying is totally disorganized. I also get nervous because people are looking at me and waiting for me to say something profound. It seems like I'm talking for an awfully long time even though I'm often interrupted with questions.

Can you tell from this statement which context is being described? The rehearsed message, the number of listeners, and the organization of ideas may suggest a public speaking context. The questions, however, may suggest an interview or a classroom discussion. Actually, the student was describing a meeting of a community service group that discussed ideas for new fundraising projects.

The point is that each communication context includes the same variables and characteristics; these differ only in the degree to which they are present. Each context requires organized messages, though the degree to which a message is organized may differ. Each context requires a number of people, though the specific number of people varies. Preparation is necessary for each context, though the amount and type of preparation varies. Each context is defined by a unique combination of characteristics that are present at different levels. To create competent communication, you must identify the level to which the characteristics are present and adapt your communication.

As we discuss next, communication occurs within a specific context of physical and social environments. Each context is a unique combination of environmental and social variables to which you must adapt. The communication context gives us clues about which messages to send and how to send them. It also gives us hints concerning how to interpret the other person's messages. Understanding the communication context is an important step in creating communication competence.

"Before You Go On"

You should be able to answer the following question:

How do all communication contexts share the same characteristics?

The Physical Environment

Communication occurs in a **physical environment** that includes the physical surroundings such as the size of the room, arrangement of furniture, climate, color, furnishings and decorations, amount of light, and other stimuli we can physically sense. For example, whether you are communicating in a crowded elevator, an intimate restaurant, at a small party, or a packed football stadium affects the meaning of the communication and the communication strategies you use. People who provide background to the communication, rather than being directly involved in your communication transaction, are considered part of the physical environment.

Supportive Environments

Effective communication occurs when the environment is supportive of the communication efforts. Brightly colored classrooms furnished with comfortable chairs enhance creative thinking and improve students' attention. Furniture arranged so people can easily see each other facilitates group discussions. Partitions that separate areas of a large office into smaller cubicles provide a sense of privacy for employees working one-to-one with clients. Supportive climates minimize distractions and noise that interfere with communication. Supportive climates also affect our attractions to others and enhance the relationships of the communicators.[9]

Counterproductive Environments

When the environment interferes with communication, it is a counterproductive environment. Discussions with a few people in a large auditorium, interviews interrupted by phone calls, technical presentations made with faulty audiovisual equipment, and private conversations in a crowded restaurant are examples of communication in counterproductive environments. Physical environments in which noise and distractions increase the difficulty of communication, or which are inconsistent with the relationships of the communicators, hinder competent communication.

Time

The physical environment also includes time. Classes meeting at 8 A.M. are different than classes held at noon or at night. Meetings on Friday are different than meetings on Monday or Sunday. Conversations occurring on holidays or anniversaries are different than conversations on normal days. The time of day, month, and year influence the meaning of communication and the strategies you use to achieve competent communication.

In addition to the time during which communication occurs, communicators must consider the time available for preparation and the time they have to verbally communicate their ideas. Whenever possible, you should plan your communication. Often people say to themselves after communicating, I wish I had thought of that then—it would have been a great thing to say! or I wish I hadn't said that. It just sort of slipped out. Preparation implies that we should think before we speak.

The context is also defined by the amount of responsibility each person has for the verbal message. Although everyone is continuously sending simultaneous nonverbal messages, people tend to take turns communicating verbally.[10] The length of each turn is influenced by the context. In a conversation, for example, the verbal messages may be relatively short and turns may change rapidly. On the other hand, a public speech lends itself to unequal **verbal responsibility.** The length of time allowed for each person to speak is part of the communication context.

When you monopolize a conversation, when you say nothing during a group discussion, or when you interrupt another's story just to tell yours, you are abusing your verbal responsibility. When you are concise in expressing your ideas in a meeting, when you help others take their appropriate turns in a conversation, or when you speak for the full and allotted time in a public speech, you are correctly analyzing and adapting to the time requirements of the physical context. Effective communication occurs when both people are aware of the amount of time they have to communicate the verbal message and cooperate to fulfill their shared responsibility.

"Before You Go On"

You should be able to answer the following question:

What are the characteristics of the physical environment?

The Social Environment

Communication has both content and relationship dimensions. When you communicate with another, you are creating a relationship as well as communicating ideas. You also are communicating within the cultures of your group memberships. The values and norms of your family, peer groups, clubs, organizations, religious, ethnic, and geographic location influence your communication. People simultaneously belong to a variety of cultures influencing their communication. The social context is comprised of the number of people, the relationships among the communicators and their membership in various social groups, and the purpose of the communication.

Number of People

The context may include any number of people from two, to twenty, to a hundred, or more. The number of people in the context influences the communication strategies selected. Generally, the fewer the people, the more personal the communication. It may be more essential to use a conversational tone, establish direct eye contact, and touch the other person in a one-to-one private conversation than when speaking to a large crowd. It may be easier to adapt a message specifically to one individual in an interview than to ten people in a group meeting. It is even more difficult to adapt to each individual when communicating with a large audience.

The personal relationships among the communicators are more prominent and frequently more important when communicating with a few people. As the number of people in the context increases, the specifics of the individual become diffused into the generalities of the group. However, competent communication requires that all persons in the context feel as if your message is directed specifically to them. Regardless of the number of people, remember that you are communicating with individuals, each of whom has a unique set of perceptions

Group communication is several simultaneous one-to-one transactions.

and expectations. For instance, when speaking with several people, think of it as several simultaneous one-to-one transactions. The number of people is one factor that affects communication competence.

Relationship of the Communicators

Communicators vary in the degree to which they are involved with each other. Familiarity, liking, power, trust, and status are relationship characteristics affecting communication. For example, people tend to be more willing to listen to people who have high status, with whom they are friendly, and whom they perceive as trustworthy and knowledgeable. People also accept ideas more readily when they are involved with the communicator. A supportive relationship among communicators facilitates competent communication. A defensive climate interferes with mutual understanding and the cooperation necessary for competent communication.

Purpose of Communication

The purpose of the communication is a characteristic of the social context. Usually, communication purposes fall into three categories: informative, persuasive, and entertaining. Such distinctions among purposes sometimes help communicators focus efforts on one primary goal. For example, a student may ask, "Do we have to know this material for the test?" An interviewer may say, "I want to convince you to come to work for this company." And, a friend may say, "I have a joke for you." In each case, communicators are indicating their focus on a specific informative, persuasive, or entertainment purpose. In reality, however, every communication context has informative and persuasive and entertainment purposes.

Communication is inherently informative because it allows communicators to share knowledge about each other's perceptions. Informative messages attempt to help people understand and/or remember ideas and facts. As people learn information they change the way they think about the world and other people. Because all messages try to gain understanding and share the communicator's perceptions with others, all messages are to some extent informative.

All messages are also persuasive to the extent that they try to convince others to accept facts, perceptions, and opinions as valid. Persuasive communication calls for people to accept information, attitudes, values, and/or beliefs and tries to convince them to adopt specific actions. To the extent that communication tries to influence people to accept the validity of a specific viewpoint, all communication is inherently persuasive.

Broadly defined, entertainment is the degree to which communication arouses emotions, interest, or involvement. All messages are entertaining in the sense that they require some degree of communication involvement. When entertainment is an important communication purpose, the communicators are vivid, dynamic, and interesting. Vivid, precise, and clear language, dynamic delivery, direct eye contact, and touch can all increase communication involvement, give impact to a message and make it entertaining.

Culture

People belong to various groups and organizations. Each group has its own perspective, values, and social norms. We have different expectations, comply with different rules, emphasize different values, and give different meaning to messages when we communicate in different groups. For example, you probably communicate differently about your social experiences and college classes with your family than with your friends, an employment recruiter, your teacher, or an acquaintance. For instance, at one college, students who went to parties on Friday night referred to the activity as "skipping class." That is, they agreed not to think about school and just relax. When a parent heard her son say he enjoyed skipping class every week she became concerned and called her son's college advisor. She was interpreting the comment from the perspective of a different culture and did not understand the meaning her son gave the same words. Each context emphasizes different cultural norms concerning the language you use, the interpretation you give to events, and the norms for acceptable behavior. We discuss the influence of culture on communication in detail in chapter 14.

Social context is embedded in every communication situation. The relationship of the communicators, their cultural backgrounds, and their communication purposes influence their interpretation of their messages. By analyzing the social context, communicators choose appropriate strategies to help each other communicate competently.

All face-to-face communication contexts involve the same characteristics. The time in which the communication occurs, the amount of verbal message responsibility, the time available for prior preparation, and the physical surroundings all contribute to the definition of physical contexts. The purpose of communication, the relationship of the communicators, and the culture describe the constraints of the social context.

Analyzing the specific requirements and characteristics of the communication context requires specific skills; we discuss these in chapter 4. Communication competence is based on the interaction of the self, perception, and behavior within specific communication contexts. The next chapter explains the nature of communication competence.

Responses to *"Before You Go On"* Questions: A Chapter Summary

1.   How does selection limit the information we perceive?
You cannot possibly pay attention to every stimuli that is continuously impinging on your senses. You must selectively attend to a small part of the information and, at least momentarily, ignore the rest. Similarly, you tend to seek information consistent with what you already know and believe to reduce the confusion that occurs when you have to deal with contradictory information. As you mentally process your perceptions, your memory stores and files the information. However, because you can selectively remember only some of the information you perceive, your memory is frequently incomplete and incorrect.

2.   What are three ways you organize perceptions to make sense of them?
You have difficulty understanding random stimuli. You need a sense of order and structure to help you make sense of your perceptions. When information is incomplete, you use closure to help complete the perception. You group your perceptions according to their similarities and differences to help them fit together in a meaningful way. Through closure and association, the random stimuli that you perceive become organized and meaningful.

3.   How are perceptions biased?

Your perceptions are biased by your physiological capabilities and physical characteristics. The sensitivity of your senses, your emotional state, and your physical health affect your ability to receive and interpret stimuli. Similarly, your interpretation of information is psychologically biased by your attitudes, values, culture, past experiences, and future expectations. Because of perceptual biases, people have different experiences and interpretations of events, people, and things; these make agreement and common understanding difficult.

4.   What are four ways we validate our perceptions?

Your sense of reality and your understanding of the world around you comes through the sense you make of your perceptions. To determine whether your perceptions are accurate, you can repeat the experience or use more than one sense to determine whether your interpretation was valid. You can also use predictive validation and consensual validation to determine if your perceptions make sense. Only consensual validation involves direct communication with others. Indeed, the purpose of communication is to reach consensual validation as people try to achieve a common understanding and interpretation of their perceptions.

5.   How do the ideal self, self-identity, and self-esteem interact to describe the self?

Your ideal self establishes the goals, values, physical image, and personality that you want to have. Your self-identity is your current image of your physical appearance, social roles, personality and emotions, moral values, and interests. Your self-esteem is based on the degree to which your self-identity matches your ideal self on important dimensions of your self. The more similar your self-identity and ideal self, the higher your self-esteem; the more they are different, the lower your self-esteem.

6.   How is the self developed through communication with others?

You develop self-identity through your communication with people important to you. Peers, family, friends, teachers, clergy, and others provide feedback telling you how others perceive you. Your ideal self is similarly established through the values and goals others tell you are important. You also learn the ideals of your culture through television, movies, books, and other media that help form the ideal self.

7.   How do all communication contexts share the same characteristics?

People sometimes erroneously think that various communication contexts have essentially different characteristics, are influenced by different factors, and thus require different communication skills. However, communication contexts are characterized by the same factors of the physical and social environments, and differ only in the degree to which these factors influence the communication. Therefore, all contexts require the same communication skills for analyzing, creating, and listening to verbal and nonverbal messages. They differ only in the strategies with which these skills are employed to create specific messages for specific purposes.

8. What are the characteristics of the physical environment?

The physical setting in which communication occurs affects the manner in which messages are shared and the meanings people give to the messages. The time of day, the degree to which messages are prepared, the way in which people take turns providing verbal messages, and whether the physical surroundings are supportive or counterproductive are characteristics of the physical environment.

9. What are the characteristics of the social environment?

All face-to-face communication occurs within the constraints of a social environment. The social environment influences the meanings people give to each others' messages and the strategies with which they communicate. The number of people involved in the communication, their relationship and involvement in the communication, their purposes in communicating with each other, and their cultural backgrounds influence their communication.

S T U D E N T   E X E R C I S E S

1. Memories are selective.

Talk with a family member about your memories of past Christmases (or Easter, birthdays, Hanukkah, vacations, or other holidays and special occasions). Share your memories of where you were, what gifts you gave and received, who was present, and funny events that happened. Do they remember the same things you do? Do they have the same meaning for the events? Why do your memories differ?

2. Experiencing physical biases.

Try and change your physical perspective. If you are tall, stoop or kneel down; if you are short, stand on a chair or stool. What do you see? Do you selectively attend to different stimuli? Do you feel comfortable talking to people of different heights?

3. Describing your self.

Write down the first twenty words you think of to answer the question, "Who am I?" Check your list and try to place each description into one of the five categories of self-identity. Which categories did you use most often? Which category came to mind first?

Write ten things you would like to change about your private self, things about your self that you are not completely satisfied with. Now write ten things about your self that you are proud of, that you would not want to change. Which list was easier to write? Why? What categories of self-identity most frequently occurred on each list? Were there differences? Why?

4. Media influences the ideal self.

Watch a half-hour of television or read a magazine. What messages do you find that describe an ideal self? What do the advertisements imply you should look like? How should you behave? What should you be interested in or what should you be doing? Do the stories in the magazine or the TV show tell you similar messages about the ideal self? What impact do you think these messages have on your actual ideal self?

5. Supportive and counterproductive environments.

Describe your classroom environment. Is it supportive or counterproductive? Why? How does it affect communication with classmates? With the teacher?

Assume you were going to dinner with a special person. You want the restaurant to be intimate and romantic. Describe your image of the restaurant and how you think that would affect the conversation. Would your communication with this person differ if you had the same conversation at a fast-food restaurant? Why?

G L O S S A R Y

Association A principle by which people organize perceptions based on a perceived relationship among the stimuli.

Attribute similarity A principle by which stimuli are organized according to perceived similarities of characteristics.

Closure A principle of organizing perceptions in which people assume missing information is actually present to make the perception complete and meaningful.

Consensual validation Agreement with others that the perceptions are accurate.

Ideal self The self-identity a person would like to have.

Multisensory validation Assuming that perceptions are correct because they occur through more than one of the five senses.

Organizing function of perception The manner in which otherwise random stimuli are given structure and meaning.

Perception The process by which people give meaning to stimuli.

Perceptual biases Any limitation or distortion of the meanings given to stimuli.

Perceptual set A perceptual bias due to past experiences or future expectations concerning the presence and meaning of stimuli.

Physical environment The physical setting in which communication occurs including furniture, temperature, color, time of day, and noise.

Physiological biases Limitations on perceptions due to physical characteristics, lack of sensitivity, or lack of development of the senses.

Predictive validation Assuming perceptions are accurate because they accurately forecast future events and meanings.

Reception The passive sensing of stimuli without interpretation.

Repetitive validation Assuming perceptions are accurate because they have been experienced more than once with the same sense.

Selective attention The focus on a relatively small set of stimuli so that all other stimuli fade into the background.

Selective exposure Actively seeking information consistent with established perceptions and avoiding contradictory information.

Selective retention The incomplete and/or distorted retrieval of perceptions from memory.

Self People's perceptions of their own self-identity, ideal self, and self-esteem; their memories, emotions, and physical state, attitudes, values, beliefs, and knowledge.

Self-disclosure Communicating information about the self that others could not easily discern or gather from other sources.

Self-esteem The evaluation of a person's self-identity as it compares with the ideal self.

Self-identity The constellation of images comprising the person's physical attributes, personality, morality, social roles, and interests.

Social environment The number of people, their relationships, culture, and communication purpose.

Space proximity A principle by which stimuli are organized according to geographical location.

Time proximity A principle by which stimuli are organized according to the time in which they occur.

Verbal responsibility The degree to which a person is expected to express a verbal message and the manner in which verbal turns are shared among the communicators.

N O T E S

1. See, for example, George Miller, *The Psychology of Communication* (New York: Basic Books, 1965); D. A. Norman, ed., *Models of Human Memory* (New York: Academic Press, 1970); and William L. Benoit and Pamela J. Benoit, "Memory for Conversational Behavior," *Southern Communication Journal* 56 (1990), 24–34.

2. For a discussion of selective exposure, see Irving Janis and Leon Mann, *Decision Making: A Psychological Analysis of Conflict, Choice, and Commitment* (New York: Free Press, 1977).

3. These five categories of self-identity were derived from Kenneth J. Gergen, *The Concept of Self* (New York: Holt, Rinehart and Winston, 1971); W. H. Fitts, *Manual for the Tennessee Self Concept Scale* (Nashville, Tenn.: Counselor Recordings and Tests, 1965); and R. C. Wylie, *The Self Concept* (Lincoln: University of Nebraska Press, 1961).

4. The relationship between self-identity, ideal self, and self-esteem is discussed in George J. McCall and J. L. Simmons, *Identities and Interactions* (New York: Free Press, 1966); C. S. Carver and M. F. Scheier, "Control Theory: A Useful Conceptual Framework for Personality—Social, Clinical, and Health Psychology," *Psychological Bulletin* 35 (1982), 38–48.

5. The influence of self on communication is discussed in James C. McCroskey, John A. Daly, Virginia P. Richmond, and Raymond L. Falcione, "Studies of the Relationship between Communication Apprehension and Self-Esteem," *Human Communication Research* 3 (1977); 269–77; and John E. Horrocks and Dorothy W. Jackson, *Self and Role: A Theory of Self Process and Role Behavior* (Boston: Houghton Mifflin Company, 1972).

6. W. W. Purkey, *Self-Concept and School Achievement* (Englewood Cliffs, N.J.: Prentice Hall, 1970).

7. For classic discussions of the formation of self through interaction with others see George H. Mead, *Mind, Self, and Society* (Chicago: University of Chicago Press, 1934); and Daryl J. Bem, "Self Perception Theory," in *Advances in Experimental Social Psychology,* vol. 6, ed. Leonard Berkowitz (New York: Academic Press, 1973).

8. For discussions of the role of self-disclosure in communication see Sidney Jourard, *The Transparent Self* (New York: Van Nostrand Reinhold, 1971); P. W. Cozby, "Self-Disclosure: A Literature Review," *Psychological Bulletin* 79 (1973); 73–91; Shirley J. Gilbert, "Empirical and Theoretical Extensions of Self Disclosure," in *Explorations in Interpersonal Communciation,* ed. Gerald R. Miller (Beverly Hills: Sage Publications, 1976), 197–216.

9. J. T. Kitchens, T. P. Herron, R. R. Behnke, and M. J. Beatty, "Environmental Esthetics and Interpersonal Attraction," *Western Journal of Speech Communication* 41 (1977); 126–30.

10. For current studies of turn taking see Mark T. Palmer, "Controlling Conversations: Turns, Topics, and Interpersonal Control," *Communication Monographs* 56 (1989), 1–18; William F. Sharkey and Laura Stafford, "Turn-Taking Resources Employed by Congenitally Blind Conversers," *Communication Studies* 41 (1990), 161–82.

3 CHAPTER

Communication Competence

On a superficial level, communication competence is using skills or

abilities to obtain satisfaction or to accomplish goals. According to this view,

competent communicators should be able to speak and listen well, organize

their ideas, and be sensitive and responsive to others. This view is not

complete, however, because communication competence is much more than a

set of skills for sending messages and interpreting feedback. This chapter

discusses communication competence and makes recommendations for

achieving competence in communication.

The Nature of Communication Competence

As you recall from chapter 1, the action approach to communication focuses on the speaker and the message. A reaction perspective to communication focuses on the receivers. Another approach views communication as a transaction in which the communicators cooperate with each other to create or share meaning.

While there are several approaches to communication competence, there is little agreement on a theory or a specific definition.[1] Even so, the following definition seems to be generally accepted: Communication competence is the ability to choose among available communicative behaviors so that interpersonal goals may be successfully accomplished during an encounter while respecting the goals of others who are participating.[2]

This definition suggests that individuals should be able to accomplish communication goals if they are able to adapt to the communication situation and respond with appropriate behavior. This definition fits well into the action and reaction perspectives of communication. The transactional perspective on communication competence, however, requires going beyond acting, adapting, and responding, to cooperating with the other people involved in the situation. Competent communication involves formulating and executing the appropriate communication skills and strategies as well as helping each other create mutual involvement and shared meaning.

Involvement

We can use **interaction involvement** to examine specific areas of communication competence.[3] A basic definition of interaction involvement is the extent to which individuals participate in communication. Involved communicators focus their feelings, thoughts, and conscious attention on the here-and-now of an interaction in which they are participating. On the other hand, noninvolved communicators are not really tuned in. They often appear distracted or otherwise withdrawn from the interaction.

Being involved means possessing some capability in three areas: attentiveness, perceptiveness, and responsiveness. **Attentiveness** is defined as the extent to which you are alert to the elements or cues in the immediate social environment, including others involved in interactions. Your ability to interpret information is diminished if you fail to notice important elements in the environment or the behavior of people around you.

Perceptiveness is a sensitivity to the meanings given to the behavior of others and the meanings given to your own behavior. To be perceptive, you must be attentive; the information must be gathered before it can be interpreted. You should be concerned with not only understanding the behavior of others but also being aware of and understanding how your own behavior might be interpreted by other participants in communication.

Finally, **responsiveness** is concerned with your judgment about which behaviors are appropriate in given social situations. Responsiveness has both cognitive and behavioral elements. Being responsive means not only knowing which behavior is appropriate but also actually being able to perform the behavior when you think the situation requires it.

For example, a professor thought he was highly involved. He listened to students when they talked to him and appeared very good at understanding their feelings. While he was listening to them, however, he usually wore a blank stare and constantly rocked back and forth in his chair. His behavior was unconscious and he paid no attention to it. The students who talked to him never knew how to interpret this behavior. To them, he looked bored and disinterested. Actually, he enjoyed talking to students. The students liked talking to him because he would sit and listen, but they were nervous about it. They couldn't make sense of his behavior. It often appeared that he did not enjoy talking to them. He was not really involved because he paid little attention to his own behavior.

Behavioral Flexibility

People need to adapt to communication situations. Communication strategies that are appropriate for one situation may not work in another. Since communication is a process, people must also adapt to constantly changing situations. Behavioral flexibility refers to the process by which communicators select and adapt communication strategies to fit the situation.

A good deal of human communication behavior is not completely intentional or well thought out. Rather, it is often largely determined by the roles we play, habits that we have, or rituals that we play out in our day-to-day behavior. As a consequence, much of our communication behavior is almost automatic. Very little thought or attention are involved. For example, it is unlikely that you put much conscious effort into greeting rituals. If you see someone you know, you might shake hands and say, "How's it going?" You probably didn't stay up late the night before establishing goals, organizing your thoughts and formulating strategies to greet that person. However, you might do some preparation for the event if the person is someone very important or special to you, or if you are unfamiliar with a situation.

Most people are highly aware of their behavior only under certain circumstances, for example, when they experience new or unique situations. If you find yourself in a novel situation, you probably cannot rely on behaviors that have worked well in the past. You need to carefully observe the situation as it unfolds, come up with a strategy, then carry it out while constantly observing the situation for unanticipated developments.

A key to competent communication is your ability or willingness to monitor the scripted or ritualistic communication that you engage in every day. You must be on the lookout for new situations that do not fit the script. When you encounter such a situation, you should be able to recognize it as new and be willing to deviate from the script. You should also be willing and able to help your partners in communication define the situation and respond accordingly.

It is probably not necessary to treat every communication situation as new. The communication rituals that make up so much of our daily behavior help provide stability through patterns and consistency. However, it would be wise to treat every situation as if it had the potential to be new. That way, you do not have to bring all your awareness and involvement to bear every time somebody asks, "How are you?" You must still maintain some level of awareness, however, that will alert you to unique, nonscripted situations. Competent communication, therefore, requires a motivation to cooperate with others and to focus attention on the communication environment, including your own behavior and the behavior of others.

"Before You Go On"

You should be able to answer the following question:

Why is it essential for you to focus your awareness and attention on communication situations as you participate in them?

Elements of Competent Communication

Achieving competence in communication involves at least five primary elements: (1) goals, (2) communication skills, (3) environmental analysis, (4) the development and implementation of strategies aimed at achieving the goals, and (5) cooperation with other communicators.

The behavior of the communicators in a particular situation is directly and heavily influenced by the goal of communication. Past research has suggested that competent people seem to have a clear sense of their own goals as well as a sense of the goals of others.[4] They are motivated to engage in communication. They also have a good sense of what is happening as the transaction unfolds or progresses. Because they usually see the big picture, they are more likely to influence and direct the conversation rather than merely responding or reacting to parts of it.

Understand that you don't always know the **goals** of your communication. Goals are often very difficult to define. Sometimes you might have too many goals and not know where to focus your attention, or your goals might turn out to be unrealistic. Also, your goals can change over time. Obviously, it is easier to develop a plan for communication if you have a clear goal to accomplish. Often, however, goals are defined to some extent during the communication interaction.

As goals change over time, they fall into three categories: prospective, transactive, and retrospective.[5] A **prospective goal** is one that you conceive before you enter a communication situation. Having made the goal, you attempt to develop strategies to accomplish it. For instance, you could set a goal to get a raise from your boss. After developing a plan, you try to persuade the boss to give you a raise. During the conversation with your boss, however, you decide that you don't need as large a raise as you originally thought, so you change your goal. This **transactive goal** is developed during the course of communication. The change in goal was the result of the transaction. It doesn't mean that you lost or that you were refused a raise, but that you learned something in the communication transaction that made you reconsider your goal. Later on, after the conversation with your boss, you might identify a **retrospective goal,** which is a way of making sense of what happened. You might think, I didn't get a big raise but that's okay. I just wanted the boss to tell me I was doing a good job.

Even though goals are sometimes elusive and hard to define, they are still central to competent communication. Communication strategies are built around goals. Goals are useful even if they aren't defined until after the fact because they help you make sense of what happened. Understanding what happened after the fact can be as important as understanding what should happen before the fact.[6]

"Before You Go On"

You should be able to answer the following question:

How are goals defined?

People have to adapt to changing physical environments to maintain involvement with the communication.

Skills

Unit II focuses on the second element, communication skills. These skills can be learned, practiced, and improved by anyone who works toward achieving more competent communication. These skills do not just make you look good as a communicator; they also help others help you cooperate to create meaning. Communication skills include speaking and listening, organization, and using and interpreting nonverbal behaviors. These skills are necessary for any communication context; mastery of them contributes to your ability to be involved in competent communication.

Situational Analysis

Analyzing the communication environment is the third element. It includes gathering information about the listener or other communicators, the situation, and anything related in some way to accomplishing the goal. Gathering this information requires attention to and awareness of relevant details. Possession of this information requires constant reassessment of the situation, yourself, the other communicators, and the environment. This allows you to make necessary changes in the strategy to compensate for the unanticipated behavior of the others and changes in the social and physical setting.

Strategies

The fourth element, and the focus of units III and IV, is the development of appropriate strategies used in the communicative effort. These strategies are responses to the requirements of a specific communication context. Choosing an appropriate strategy is based on the information gathered in the individual's situational analysis. When competent communication is achieved, the participants respond to circumstances and themselves with appropriate strategies. Regardless of the communication context, those strategies should accomplish the participants' goals and to help them to share meaning. Strategies involve using your communication skills in particular ways.

Cooperation

The last element, cooperation, is the key to the successful implementation of your strategy. If all of the other participants do not cooperate, that is, do not try to help each other understand, then meaning is not shared.

Involvement in communication is a critical requirement for adapting to the environment. Attentiveness, perceptiveness, and responsiveness are skills that can be learned and improved. One observable result of taking this course should be some improvement in your level of involvement.

At times, however, people lose their focus on the communication interaction. The next section discusses some possible reasons for lack of involvement.

"Before You Go On"

You should be able to answer the following question:

What is the difference between skills and strategies?

Barriers to Competent Communication

On a common sense level, it seems reasonable to suggest that people have a natural tendency to be involved in interactions and to cooperate with others. If there is any truth to this suggestion, we need to ask what causes people to be uninvolved? Is there something wrong with them? Do they hate other people? Are they stupid?

It is possible, although uncommon, for the lack of involvement to be associated with some psychological, physiological, or social disorder. However, the most likely answer is that people become uninvolved because of some distraction. The specific sources of **distraction** are probably as unique and varied as the individuals that they affect. Three common forms of distraction are anxiety, preoccupation, and defensiveness.

Anxiety

Anxiety is an emotional state aroused as a response to unknown or uncertain outcomes of events. In an anxious state, thinking often becomes nondirected and decision making ability becomes impaired. The cause of anxiety can be anything that has an uncertain outcome. Sitting in the dentist's waiting room, studying

for an important examination, finding that you have too much to do in too little time, or even calling someone to ask for a date can arouse anxiety and its symptoms. A common cause of anxiety is communication with other people.

Whatever the source, anxiety is a distraction. You can become more concerned with reducing the anxiety than with being involved in communication. Consequently, an anxious state can be a major distraction of your attention from the immediate communication interaction.

This is not to suggest that all anxiety is bad. Some degree of anxiety is usually necessary to motivate you to participate in communication. If there were no anxiety, there would be little reason for you to act or try to accomplish goals. The solution to anxiety is manageability or control. We discuss this topic in detail in chapter 4.

Preoccupation

At least four sources of preoccupation can distract your attention. Preoccupation is defined as involvement in something other than the here and now of the communication interaction itself.[7]

External preoccupation refers to concentrating on something not connected with the conversation. For example, instead of focusing attention on a class lecture, you think about your date last night or what you intend to have for lunch. Daydreaming is a common form of external preoccupation.

Self-preoccupation means that you focus your attention on yourself and not on the interaction. This is common when speaking before a group. For example, you might wonder if your posture is good, if your hair looks funny, or if you have chili stains on your shirt. A first date is also a likely time for self-preoccupation. You want to make sure that your appearance is acceptable and that your behavior is appropriate. The problem with self-preoccupation is that the focus of your attention is on yourself at the expense of your involvement in the communication interaction.

Conversational preoccupation refers to a situation in which you are so concerned with the way the conversation is going that your attention is distracted from the transaction. For example, while conducting an interview in class, you may become concerned with formulating your next question and you neglect to listen to your partner's answer to your last question. The result is a series of questions and answers, but meaning between the two participants has, most likely, not been shared. Because you were not listening to the answer, you withdrew your participation in the conversation.

In *preoccupation with another person,* another participant distracts your attention. For example, if you are speaking to someone who is very attractive, you might become preoccupied with that person's looks and lose your level of involvement in the conversation itself. If you are talking to someone who is famous or has high status, you could be distracted by who he is and pay little attention to the conversation. Consider, for instance, Carol idolized Tony Perez, the baseball player. She collected his pictures and baseball cards and knew everything about Perez's baseball career. Her dream was to meet him, get his autograph, and talk to him. When the opportunity to meet him finally came, Carol was overcome by it. Perez signed his autograph and thanked her for being such a loyal fan. For a few moments she stood silently, looking completely awestruck. Then Carol finally said, "You have nice teeth." She was clearly distracted by the other participant in the conversation.

Defensiveness

The final source of distraction is **defensiveness.**[8] Defensive behavior occurs when you perceive or anticipate a threat. This sort of threat is rarely physical. Rather, it is most often a threat to the self-concept or self-esteem. When you become defensive, you become more interested in how best to handle the threat. That distracts your attention from the interaction at hand.

As you become more and more defensive, it is less likely that you can accurately interpret incoming messages. Because you are becoming defensive, other participants in the conversation become defensive as well. The result is a defensive climate not conducive to cooperation or shared meaning.

The following six behaviors lead to defensiveness.

1. *Evaluation,* or judgmental communication, often promotes a defensive response.
2. *Control* is related to attempts to influence the choices and behavior of others.

3. *Strategy* implies an attempt to manipulate others so that the communicator can use them to advantage. Often the person using the strategy appears neither completely honest nor sincere.
4. *Neutrality* can create defensiveness because it communicates a lack of concern for others' welfare.
5. *Superiority* is communication creating a feeling of inadequacy in others. This is often demonstrated through stubbornness or an unwillingness to work with or listen to the opinions of others.
6. *Certainty* is a know-it-all attitude. Certainty implies that there is only one truth and that anyone who disagrees is wrong. Appearing to strive to win all arguments, sway everyone's opinions, and answer all questions can make others defensive.[9]

All these behaviors can lead to a defensive climate that can distract an individual and even a whole group. This sort of climate makes it difficult, if not impossible to remain involved in the interaction.

The common thread that runs throughout these sources of misinvolvement is distraction from spontaneous involvement in the interaction. When you focus on anything but the here-and-now of the interaction itself, you are not able to analyze the situation, respond with the appropriate behavior, and cooperate with other participants to share meaning. The result, then, is a failure to achieve competence.

Overcoming Barriers to Competent Communication

Now you know the definition of communication competence, its benefits, and some of the elements that can distract you from achieving it. We can now discuss some examples of strategies used by participants in a communication situation to achieve competence.

It's very difficult, if not impossible, to be completely involved in every conversation that you have every day. As you move from situation to situation, your degree of involvement in any particular one depends on how motivated you are to participate. Even when you are not strongly motivated, consider how much easier it would be to maintain your involvement, if other participants in communication situations would help you. They could notice your low level of motivation and take steps to help you increase it. As you become more motivated to participate, you become more involved, and you could help other people become more involved. Such is the nature of the transaction view of communication. It's two or more people in a communication situation who help each other participate to create shared meaning, or communication competence.

We discuss two strategies next: strategies to encourage involvement in the situation and strategies to counteract distraction from the situation. These strategies form the basis of cooperation among participants that is essential to reach the transactional level of communication. Unit III presents these strategies in a variety of communication contexts.

Unsuitable behavior calls attention to itself because it does not fit the interaction.

Encouraging

Strategies for encouraging involvement motivate others to participate in communication. They include recognition, suitability, adaptability, and satisfaction.

Recognition

By acknowledging what others say or do, you encourage their participation.[10] If someone says "I really liked the baseball game last night," you could recognize that by asking, "Oh? What did you like about the game?" This **recognition** of the content of the communication is an indication of your involvement in the conversation. Once others know you are involved and participating, they can be motivated to become involved. Conversely, if you answered, "That's nice," to the comment about the baseball game, you would indicate that you are not involved in the conversation. When you do not recognize the content of another's communication, they are less motivated to be involved in the conversation because it appears that you are not involved.

Suitability

Your behavior should be suitable. **Suitability** is concerned with behaving in a way consistent with the requirements of the communication situation. Suitable behavior does not call attention to itself because it fits in with the ongoing interaction. Because it fits, it can be an indicator of your involvement. For example, if you are asked what today's date is, a suitable response would be "Today is December 10." An unsuitable response would draw unnecessary attention to itself, create a distraction in the conversation, and it might be taken by others as an indication of your lack of involvement. Examples of unsuitable responses to the question about the date are, "Does anybody care what the date is?", or "The world will end soon." Your suitable behavior demonstrates to other participants that you are involved.

Adaptability

Attempt to adapt your behavior to changing situations. As time passes and communication transactions evolve, the goals of the participants as well as the rules for accomplishing them will probably undergo some change. For instance, assume that you were acting as a guide and escorting a new student around your school. Early in that situation you would tell the student where to go for different activities, and you would probably answer lots of questions. As time passes, however, the new student's goals change. Since you have done such a wonderful job of orientation, the student no longer needs a guide, but perhaps now needs a friend. Exercising **adaptability** you would recognize this change in the situation. If appropriate, you should be able to exchange your role of guide for a new role, friend. Recognizing changes in the situation and adapting to them is an indication of your involvement.

Satisfaction

People participate in communication to get some **satisfaction.** If you feel a sense of satisfaction when you talk to someone or a group of people, chances are good that you will be motivated to do it again when and if the opportunity presents itself. For example, you answer a question in class and the teacher says, "You seem to really know the material." You are satisfied with the communication experience and will likely answer other questions in the future. If the teacher had not responded, or had simply said, "Okay," you may be reluctant to answer future questions. You can help others in the communication situation realize some satisfaction from their participation.

Counteracting Distractions

The general strategies discussed so far are those designed to encourage involvement in communication. We turn now to examples of strategies that may counteract distraction and to help the distracted person become involved. Use of these strategies involves recognizing people who are distracted and taking some action to pull them back into the here-and-now of the conversation. We discuss some strategies for the counteraction of both anxiety and a defensive climate next.

Counteracting Anxiety

Consider the situation in which someone is giving a speech in class and is obviously apprehensive. The speaker has shaking hands, a red face, a shrill voice, and seems unable to focus on the note cards. You might feel embarrassed for the speaker and look at the floor, pretending not to notice. You hope that the speaker can gain some composure to complete the speech assignment. When the speaker looks at the audience, all he sees are the tops of heads because everyone is pretending not to notice. What the speaker needs at this point is support. You can provide that support by looking at the speaker, leaning forward, and showing your interest in what is being said. That show of support can help the speaker overcome his anxiety and focus on the content of the message. When a speaker is unable to present a message, the participants have not shared the intended meaning. By providing support for the speaker, you have helped the participants in the situation create competent communication.

You can help others cope with anxiety in all communication contexts. If you notice someone experiencing the symptoms of anxiety, try to show them some support. Support can be verbal encouragement, a look, a wink, or an encouraging touch. On the other hand, if you are experiencing anxiety, look to the other participants for support. Let them help you to help them understand your message or point of view. Remember, at the center of the transactional view of communication is cooperation to create shared meaning. Giving support to someone experiencing anxiety is part of that cooperation.

Counteracting Defensiveness

As stated earlier, people tend to become defensive when they perceive a threat. Defensiveness creates a climate of suspicion. To allow people to cooperate to share meaning, the defensive climate must be counteracted to create a supportive climate.[11]

Description of others' behavior creates a more supportive climate than evaluation. Walking into a room with the person who recently painted it and saying, "Yeech! What a disgusting color!" will probably offend the person and create a defensive climate. The person feels threatened by your evaluation of the color choice. If you were to use a strategy of *description* and say, "Oh! You decided to paint the room yellow," your comment is less likely to be taken as threatening.

The supportive strategy of *empathy* is a productive way of encouraging involvement. When you are empathic, you tell others that you have a genuine concern for them. Whereas neutrality creates a cold, threatening climate, empathy creates a warm, secure climate motivating participants to be involved.

An attempt to control a situation or other participants produces resistance and a defensive climate. A strategy for creating a supportive climate is to take a *problem orientation*. By communicating a wish to cooperate with the other participants, you create a desire for them to cooperate with you to achieve your mutual goals.

When other communicators perceive that you are using a strategy on them, they can become suspicious of your motives and become defensive. The way to avoid this kind of defensiveness is to behave in an honest, candid, and *spontaneous* way.

People do not like to interact with those who make them feel inferior. As soon as they see that another is trying to be superior to them, they become defensive. However, most people do like to interact with others they perceive as equals. Expressing equality is helpful in establishing a supportive climate.

Finally, a person who appears to have all the answers or to know it all can very easily create a defensive climate. The defensiveness created by this climate of certainty can be counteracted by the creation of a supportive climate of *provisionalism*. This climate is created by a mutual effort to search for solutions to problems and to achieve goals.

These are just a few strategies used to promote involvement and, ultimately, competence in your communication. Unit III has more extensive discussions of strategies.

"Before You Go On"

You should be able to answer the following question:

How is communication competence related to involvement in communication situations?

Responses to *"Before You Go On"* Questions: A Chapter Summary

1.   Why is it essential for you to focus your awareness on the communication situations as you participate in them?
Some of your communication is habitual or ritualistic, so it is likely that you put little thought or involvement into it. You often just respond in an automatic manner. Consider, however, that in some communication situations your standard or habitual behavior is inadequate. These situations require your focused attention and involvement. You should maintain a level of awareness when communicating that alerts you to unusual or unique situations.

2.   How are goals defined?
Some goals are thought out well in advance. However, in reality, not all goals are clear before you participate in communication. You create some goals during the encounter while other goals are defined afterward. All goals are useful, however, because they can focus your efforts and can help you make sense of what took place in a communication encounter.

Goals are significant in communication because they provide a focus for your communication activities. When doing situational analysis, you should be concerned with gathering information related to the goals of the communication. Participants use communication skills and strategies to accomplish their goals.

3.   What is the difference between skills and strategies?

Skills refer to the ability to perform communication behaviors. Speaking, listening, and organizing are a few of the skills essential to communication. Strategies are plans that you develop as responses to situations. Strategies call for you to use your skills in a particular way.

To be able to participate in competent communication, concentrate on two primary tasks: to improve your communication skills and to understand the strategies appropriate for a variety of communication contexts. Improving skills and understanding strategies is the focus of the remainder of this book.

4.   How is communication competence related to involvement in communication situations?

Competence is directly related to involvement in communication situations. Being uninvolved or distracted can cause you to lose focus on the here-and-now of the situation and become uninvolved. Sources of distraction include—but are not necessarily limited to—anxiety, preoccupation, and defensiveness. These distractions can be counteracted through strategies that encourage involvement. These include recognizing the communication of others, exhibiting suitable behaviors, adapting to situations as they change, and helping yourself and others find satisfaction in communicating.

S T U D E N T   E X E R C I S E S

1.   Assessing incompetent communication.

List four or five communication situations in which you (or somebody else) behaved inappropriately. Discuss the following questions: What was the cause or motivation for the behavior? What effects did the behavior have on other participants? What could you (or the other) have done to prevent the behavior or to behave more appropriately?

2.   Cooperation for understanding.

Think of some situations in which you have been misunderstood by others. How did you respond? What, if anything, did you do to help the others try to understand you? What could you have done that you didn't do?

3.   Defensive and supportive climates.

Identify which defensive climate each of the following statements could create. Change each statement to create a supportive climate.

    a. Just do what I tell you.
    b. I know what I'm talking about.
    c. You guys came up with a stupid plan!
    d. I'm sorry, but I can't be concerned with your problems right now.
    e. If you had the intelligence to know what I'm talking about, you would certainly agree with me.

GLOSSARY

Adaptability An ability to modify or adjust behavior to fit changing situations.

Anxiety An emotional state aroused as a response to unknown or uncertain outcomes of events.

Attentiveness The extent to which an individual is alert to cues in the social environment.

Defensiveness Behavior that occurs when one perceives or anticipates a threat; it is most often a threat to the self-concept or self-esteem.

Distraction A preoccupation or involvement with something other than participation in the communication transaction.

Goal An outcome desired from a communication situation.

Interaction involvement The extent to which individuals participate in communication.

Perceptiveness A sensitivity to what meanings ought to be given to the behavior of others and what meanings ought to be given to one's own behavior.

Preoccupation Involvement in something other than the here-and-now of the communication interaction.

Prospective goal A goal conceived in advance of the communication encounter.

Recognition Acknowledgement of what others say or do to encourage their participation in communication.

Responsiveness Knowing what behavior is appropriate in a particular situation and having the ability to perform that behavior.

Retrospective goal Goals defined or identified after a communication encounter has taken place.

Ritual A common, everyday communication event that is acted according to a script developed over time; it has become a habit.

Satisfaction A pleasure or fulfillment obtained from a communication situation.

Situational analysis Gathering information about the listeners or anything else that is related to the goal of communication.

Suitability Behaving in a way that is consistent with the requirements or constraints of a situation.

Transactive goal A goal developed or defined during the course of a communication encounter.

NOTES

1. See, for example, B. H. Spitzberg and W. R. Cupach, *Interpersonal Communication Competence* (Beverly Hills, Calif.: Sage, 1984); J. C. McCroskey, "Communication Competence and Performance: A Research and Pedagogical Perspective," *Communication Education* 31 (1982), 1–8; R. B. Rubin, "Assessing Speaking and Listening Competence at the College Level: The Communication Competency Assessment Instrument," *Communication Education* 31 (1982), 19–32; and A. Bochner and C. Kelly, "Interpersonal Competence: Rationale, Philosophy, and Implementation of a Conceptual Framework," *Speech Teacher* 23 (1974), 270–301.

2. J. Weimann, "Explication and Test of a Model of Communicative Competence," *Human Communication Research* 3 (1977), 195–213. See also J. Weimann and P. Backlund, "Current Theory and Research in Communication Competence," *Review of Educational Research* 50 (1980), 185–99; and J. Weimann and C. Kelly, "Pragmatics of Interpersonal Competence," in *Rigor and Imagination: Essays from the Legacy of Gregory Bateson,* eds. C. Wilder-Mott and J. Weakland (New York: Praeger, 1981).

3. D. J. Cegala, "Interaction Involvement: A Cognitive Dimension of Communication Competence," *Communication Education* 30 (1981), 109–21, and D. J. Cegala, "A Study of Affective and Cognitive Manifestations of Interaction Involvement during Unstructured and Competitive Interactions," *Communication Monographs* 51 (1984), 320–38. See also J. Burgoon and D. Newton, "Applying a Social Meaning Model to Relational Message Interpretations of Conversational Involvement: Comparing Observer and Participant Perspectives," *Southern Communication Journal* 56 (1990), 96–113.

4. D. J. Cegala, "A Study of Affective and Cognitive Manifestations."

5. J. L. Hocker and W. Wilmot, *Interpersonal Conflict* (Dubuque, Iowa: Wm. C. Brown, 1985).

6. K. E. Weick, *The Social Psychology of Organizing* (New York: Addison-Wesley, 1979).

7. Erving Goffman, *Interaction Ritual* (Garden City, N.Y.: Anchor, 1967). See also A. Vangelisti, M. Knapp, and J. Daly, "Conversational Narcissism," *Communication Monographs* 57, 251–74.

8. J. R. Gibb, "Defensive Communication," *Journal of Communication* 11 (1961), 141–48.

9. Ibid.

10. D. Smith and K. Williamson, *Interpersonal Communication: Roles, Rules, Strategies, and Games* (Dubuque, Iowa: Wm. C. Brown).

11. J. R. Gibb, "Defensive Communication," 145–48.

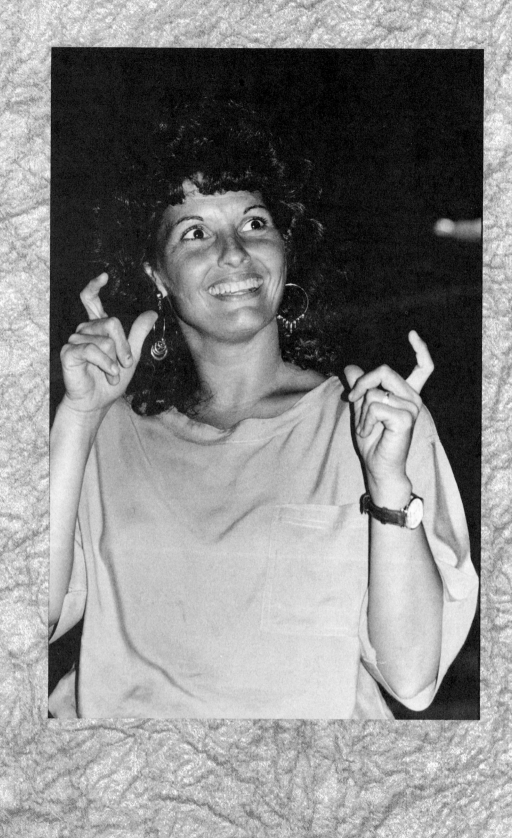

II UNIT

Communication Skills

Many people believe that each communication situation requires unique skills. They think that public speaking situations demand different skills than small group, interviewing, and interpersonal situations. However, one of the central themes of this book is that basic communication skills are used in all communication situations. Because communication situations are more alike than different, they call for similar skills. Although you create different communication strategies for various situations, the communication skills you use remain the same.

For example, when you first learned to play baseball, you were taught a set of basic skills: to throw, to catch, to run, and to hit the ball with the bat. As you grew older and your skills improved, you learned strategy, that is, different ways to use your basic skills to achieve specific goals. The skill of bunting a baseball is different than the strategies for deciding when to bunt, which direction to bunt, and how hard to bunt. Knowing how to throw a curve ball is different than the strategy for deciding when to throw it, how fast to throw it, and where to throw it.

The same concept applies to communication. Communication skills are the basic behaviors you use to recognize and adapt to the constraints of the situation, to express your ideas clearly and with impact, and to understand the other person's ideas. Once you have mastered the necessary skills, you can use them to carry out specific strategies appropriate to your goals in a variety of communication situations. For example, you need to organize all of your messages, though your specific organizational strategy may vary. All of your communication requires listening skills, though how you listen may change in different situations. (Units III and IV discuss communication strategies.)

Unit II examines communication skills basic to any communication situation. Chapter 4 describes the skills of analyzing the elements of communication situations. Chapter 5 looks at different methods for organizing a message and how to begin and end your communication with others. Chapter 6 discusses how to use verbal language to make your ideas clear and vivid. Chapter 7 describes how nonverbal communication skills can help you communicate ideas, emotions, and relationships. Chapter 8 examines listening skills to help you understand and remember other people's messages and to create competent relationships. When you complete unit II, you should understand the skills necessary to create competent communication in many situations.

4 CHAPTER

Skills for Analyzing Communication Contexts

O U T L I N E

- *I don't know what went wrong. I certainly said what I wanted to say, but nobody at the meeting understood my point.*

- *I wish the boss had taken the phone off the hook during our interview so we wouldn't have been constantly interrupted.*

- *I certainly didn't expect that kind of reaction! I didn't know anyone could be so sensitive about ethnic jokes.*

- *I don't know why I get so scared before I go to a job interview.*

- *I wish I had known the audience was going to ask questions; I didn't even get a chance to make my main point.*

These comments indicate that the communicators failed to completely or accurately analyze the communication situation. The process of communication is complex. Too often people consider only what they want to say rather than the needs and listening capabilities of the other person or the constraints and requirements of the particular environment. Analyzing the communication context enables you to be more aware of barriers to communication and to develop specific strategies in preparing for each situation. Being able to recognize and analyze specific communication contexts is essential for competent communication.

As you recall, the transactional model of communication suggests that each person perceives the relationship among four sources of information: (1) the self, (2) personal verbal and nonverbal behavior, (3) the other person's verbal and nonverbal behavior, and (4) the physical and social environment of the communication. All of these elements comprise the communication situation. In making a thorough analysis of the **communication context,** consider how each of these interrelated factors influence your communication.

The initial step in all skills activities is proper preparation. To understand more completely the need for preparation for a skills activity, let's compare communication to playing football. Consider the time and effort a college football team spends preparing for each game. A team spends hours analyzing game films of the other teams to better understand their offensive and defensive game strategies, their skills, their personnel, and their play selection. A team also spends considerable time analyzing its own strengths and weaknesses. The football team then learns a game plan strategy. After this, each team practices the skills necessary to execute their strategies. A team that has analyzed the other team well, developed a successful game plan, and practiced the appropriate skills, has increased the likelihood that it will play well.

Similar to football, communication is a skills activity. Although communication is generally cooperative rather than competitive, it still requires the acquisition of and training in fundamental skills that are prerequisite for success. Like football, effective communication strategies consider the other people in the context, the surrounding environment, and the individual's own abilities and weaknesses. And again, like football, the communication situation does not guarantee a winning outcome for the initial, preplanned strategy. Communicators need to be flexible and continually adapt strategies as the situation develops.

In this chapter, we discuss the skills and procedures necessary to analyze and prepare for communication situations. Analysis includes three general steps: (1) analysis of the private self; (2) analysis of the social environment; and (3) analysis of the physical environment. Detailed analysis enables you to be more effective in achieving competent communication. Remember that careful and thorough preparation takes time and effort. You must be willing to expend this effort to create competent communication.

Analyzing the Self

Your private self is a major influence on your communication. As you learned in Chapter 1, a basic principle of communication is that it is personal. You cannot separate the self from your interpretations of your own behavior, the other's behavior, or the communication environment. Your past experiences, attitudes, knowledge, emotions, and self-concept are continually affecting the meaning you give to messages. Three specific aspects of the self require analysis if communication is to be effective: your communication skills, your emotions, and your attitudes and knowledge.

Analyzing Your Communication Skills

Self-analysis is not as easy as it may sound. How much do you really know about yourself? Have you ever considered, for example, your particular communication strengths and weaknesses? Knowledge of the types of communication in which you excel and the kinds of communication experiences in which you experience difficulty can provide important insights to guide your communication. Knowing how much preparation you need for a particular communication situation, the confidence you have in different communication situations, and the degree to which you need to rehearse for communication are important considerations as you prepare to communicate. You need to know your own limitations so you can compensate for them; you need to know your strengths so you can capitalize on them.

For example, a novice executive had to prepare a formal proposal for the agency's board of directors. She had not made a formal presentation since her beginning communication course in college, and felt somewhat unsure of her ability to do a good job. However, she remembered the processes she had learned in the course and began to prepare for the meeting. Her first step was to determine what she already knew about the proposal, how comfortable she would feel in front of a group of people making a formal presentation, and how much time she would need to prepare effectively. She knew she did not have the skills necessary to present the proposal off the cuff so she spent hours rehearsing her talk. She understood she would be nervous making a formal presentation, so she practiced visualizing only positive outcomes for the message. She gave her talk to her husband and children and friends to get their criticisms and to become comfortable stating her ideas aloud to others. Because of her initial self-analysis, the executive prepared sufficiently to make a successful presentation. She worked to overcome her weaknesses rather than avoiding the situation or simply hoping that she would not make mistakes.

If a thorough analysis of your communication needs reveals weaknesses, then commit yourself to eliminating those weaknesses. In the business world, individuals must learn the skills necessary to communicate effectively in job situations. Your relationships with family and friends depends on your ability to understand and adapt to the needs of the communication situation. Carefully consider your readiness to undertake various communication responsibilities and expend the energies necessary to prepare for situations in which you perceive a likelihood for poor communication. By learning and practicing communication skills, you are better prepared to accept responsibility for your part in creating competent communication.

Ask Others for Feedback

How do you analyze your communication skills? Observing another's reactions to your messages can help you discover strengths and weaknesses. Do others laugh at your jokes, follow your suggestions, and seek your advice on problems? Or do they have to ask you to repeat your statements, act puzzled at your behavior, and argue with your suggestions? The degree to which other people's reactions are what you expect and want is one indicator of your communication strengths and weaknesses.

Another method is to ask others for feedback. Perhaps others have observed that you are a good listener, that you have a picturesque way of phrasing ideas, or that you can clearly state your ideas. If so, you can capitalize on these communication strengths. On the other hand, perhaps others have noted that you ramble in your communication, that your voice is monotonous, or that you constantly say *like,* or *you know.* Maybe, you don't seem to be able to control a group meeting. These are specific communication weaknesses. Competent communicators actively seek feedback from others, listen to what is said, and act accordingly.

Keep a Communication Log

Another method of analyzing your communication skills is keeping a written log of communication situations and analyzing their effectiveness. A written **communication log** describing and evaluating your communication experiences can

quickly indicate trends in your communication effectiveness. You will find that certain communication situations are consistently competent and others consistently offer difficulties.

A sales executive kept a log of his sales calls for the first six months of the year. The log revealed that he was 60 percent successful when his client was a junior executive but only 10 percent successful with senior executives. He realized that he was somewhat intimidated by high-status people and that his closing pitch was, therefore, unassertive and tentative. Working hard to overcome his weakness, he developed new strategies for closing a sale, wore more expensive suits to increase his credibility, and scheduled dinner meetings in a fine restaurant. He found that the new strategies performed in more neutral territory, rather than in the senior executive's office, made him feel less intimidated. By being more assertive, he increased his success rate to 50 percent. This salesman used a communication log to indicate a weakness in his communication. It suggested that he change his verbal message, his nonverbal message, and the environment so that he could be more successful. Only when you, too, have identified your strengths and weaknesses can you begin to improve communication. (Exercise 1 at the end of this chapter gives an example of questions you could answer in your own communication log.)

Use Videotape or Audiotape

A third method of analyzing communication strengths and weaknesses is to be videotaped communicating in specific situations.[1] You might have a friend videotape a speech you give for a class, a meeting of your club, or even a family dinner. Whether you use videotape at home, at your job, or in the classroom during rehearsal or a live situation, you have a chance to see yourself as others see you. Audiotaping can also reveal your tone of voice, how clearly you speak, and the way you construct your verbal message. Be realistic in your self evaluation; self-criticism is generally more severe than another person's evaluation. Your objective in viewing yourself on tape is to see which of your communication skills are effective and which ones need improvement.

"Before You Go On"

You should be able to answer the following question:

Which methods can you use to analyze your communication skills?

Analyzing Emotions

A second factor in self-analysis is to understand your feelings and emotions in various communication contexts. Emotions influence verbal and nonverbal communication because in each transaction you perceive your emotional self as you encode and decode messages. Emotions and behaviors are inseparable.

Your emotions are part of the message you want others to understand. You might be unhappy if someone laughed at you when you told them a secret that had upset you. Similarly, you probably don't want to be taken seriously when you're joking, or offered condolences when you are happy, or ignored when you feel lonely. Communicating your emotions clearly to others begins with understanding exactly how you feel when you communicate.

One of the best methods for analyzing your emotions is to learn to label them precisely. **Labeling** involves finding precise words that separate the specific emotion from all similar emotions. For example, there are many kinds of love— puppy love, infatuation, unendurable longing, brotherly love, sisterly devotion, or I-can't-bear-to-be-without-you love. Anger may vary in intensity from mild dislike to intense hatred. You may be so happy you want to sing, or angry enough to break something, or as proud as a new parent. Using adjectives, adverbs, metaphors, and similes to describe your emotions helps you understand your feelings. This, in turn, can help you understand how emotions are affecting your communication with others. Two specific emotions central to competent communication are enthusiasm and anxiety.

Generate Enthusiasm

A key to competent communication is to use your emotions to help get your message across to others. Just like successful football players use emotions to increase motivation, energy, and drive during a game, successful communicators use emotions to increase their involvement during communication situations. For example, a nurse made a presentation to the hospital's physicians concerning appropriate responsibility levels for the professional nursing staff. During the presentation, he demonstrated a great deal of enthusiasm in delivering his ideas.

The physicians were impressed with the conviction with which the nurse spoke and adopted his suggestions. Similarly, recruiters are impressed with job candidates who show enthusiasm during employment interviews. Conversations are more involving when people express their ideas enthusiastically.

Analyzing the degree to which you are involved in the topic can indicate how convincingly you will communicate about the topic. Your **enthusiasm** shows other people that you want them to understand and believe your messages. Having a strong desire to share your ideas and a conviction that your ideas are important increases your involvement in the interaction. Simultaneously, your emotions help others to become involved.

Manage Anxiety

One of the strongest emotions in communication contexts is communication apprehension.[2] Each of us has experienced extreme nervousness or fear when communicating with others. Communication apprehension is a common experience in a variety of communication situations. Studies indicate, for example, that one out of five people in America has high anxiety when communicating with others.[3]

Anxiety is a response to a perceived threat. People become anxious when they fear some unknown force or unforeseen event will affect them negatively.[4] They anticipate negative results and then become anxious over imagined outcomes. When people are anxious, especially overly anxious, their bodies react in predictable ways. Generally, the heart rate increases, blood rushes to the skin and head, muscles tense in readiness, the mouth becomes extremely dry, and hands sweat.[5] These normal bodily reactions to a perceived threat may actually increase the level of anxiety. For example, people become increasingly anxious when they notice they are blushing, that their knees are shaking due to muscle tension, that their hearts are pounding due to the pumping adrenaline. They think each of these reactions is unnatural. On the contrary, it would be unnatural if the body did not respond in this manner to a perceived threat.

Communication apprehension inhibits effective communication when it is extremely high. Highly anxious people avoid communication situations where they have complete responsibility for the message, they are evaluated, or they feel that everyone's attention is directed toward them. Such anxieties can even prevent people from taking lucrative careers that include high levels of communication responsibility. People who are overly anxious about their communication abilities refuse to share valuable ideas in group meetings and avoid situations in which they must communicate one-to-one. Even when such communication is essential for their careers, they avoid talking to important people in their jobs.[6]

Analyzing your communication apprehension might help you manage its impact on your communication. Tests for communication apprehension, such as the Personal Report of Communication Apprehension (PRCA), can provide insight into the level of apprehension you feel in different situations.[7] Once you have identified the sources and levels of anxiety, you can begin to manage your anxiety so that it supports your communication efforts rather than hinders them. Notice that the focus is on managing anxiety rather than eliminating it.

One way of managing anxiety is **visualization**—visualizing positive results in the communication situation.[8] When you anticipate an upcoming speech, interview, or group meeting, sit down, close your eyes, and visualize success. Do not let a negative thought enter your mind! If you begin to think of negative outcomes, stop immediately, clear your mind and start over. Think of the situation as an opportunity for things to go well, rather than as a threat to your goals and self-esteem. While anticipating upcoming communication events, using this positive mental association and imagery helps you reduce your anxiety to a manageable level.

A second way to reduce anxiety is to use the excess energy caused by the increased heart rate and adrenaline to perform physical activity. Exercises, stretching, isometrics, or other physical activities can burn excess energy created by anxiety. If you find yourself becoming highly anxious as you anticipate a communication situation such as an interview, a meeting, a date, or a speech, try taking a walk, cleaning off your desk, or rearranging your bookcases to burn off the excess energy. Just before (and even during) the communication itself, you can do relaxation exercises such as taking deep breaths, stretching, moving about, or doing simple isometrics. The key is to reduce the physical symptoms of excess anxiety to manageable levels so you can concentrate on the communication situation rather than on yourself.

During the communication situation, strive to keep the communication under control. Perceive anxiety as a positive force. At moderate levels, anxiety increases mental alertness and provides extra energy needed in the communication situation. Effective communicators use the energy and alertness constructively during the communication. Focus your attention and energy on the message and your desire to get the message across to the listeners. As we discussed in the last chapter, if you are preoccupied with yourself, you frequently become overly concerned with appearance and mannerisms. This only increases the levels of anxiety and increases your misinvolvement in the communication. Interestingly, the opposite is also true. When you are involved in the communication and focused on helping the other person understand your message, you use natural and appropriate nonverbal gestures, posture, and facial expressions. The key is to be aware of the self, but focus primarily on your desire to communicate your ideas to the other person.

The last method for reducing and managing communication apprehension is to practice. Experience is often the best teacher. Since anxiety is caused by anticipating future events, the actual outcomes are unknown, and you tend to imagine all kinds of negative consequences. As you acquire more experience, you become more proficient and realize that there is less reason to become overly anxious. For example, if you have had several job interviews, you were probably more comfortable in the last one than the first one. Similarly, your first date was probably more stressful than later dates. You can become accustomed to communication experiences and reduce your anxiety through practice.

Practicing also reduces anxiety because it prepares you for the situation. The better your analysis of the other person's needs, the more carefully you plan the ideas, the more you rehearse how you are going to say the message, the better the communication experience will be. You should feel less anxious if you know

Practicing communication often decreases anxiety.

you are prepared than if you approach the situation with no idea of what you are going to say or do. In addition, careful preparation more likely ensures a positive result for your communication efforts. You will soon realize that you do not have much to fear.

"Before You Go On"

You should be able to answer the following question:

How can analyzing emotions help create competent communication?

Analyzing Attitudes and Knowledge

Self-analysis in preparing to communicate should also include analyzing your knowledge of, interest in, and attitudes toward the topic of your communication. People communicate more effectively about topics in which they are interested and knowledgeable, and toward which they have clearly defined attitudes. As noted earlier, knowing what you are talking about is vital to effective communication and establishing your credibility.

People are often less willing to participate in communication when they don't understand the topic. If you don't prepare for a group meeting, for instance, you may feel reluctant to contribute your ideas. You may avoid conversations with people if you ask yourself what will we talk about? On the other hand, you will probably be eager to talk about subjects in which you are interested and have lots of information. You want to share your ideas about topics on which you have strong attitudes and beliefs. You become highly involved in communication interactions when you perceive you have something important to contribute.

Analysis of your attitudes and knowledge allows you to prepare more effective messages and make the preparation process more efficient. By analyzing your prior knowledge about a topic, you find out which content areas require more research and additional information. Recognizing your **attitudes** can indicate areas of bias that influence your interpretation of messages.

Self-analysis of interests, attitudes, and knowledge takes time. One method is to keep an activities log such as the one in exercise 2 at the end of this chapter. By considering how you spend your time, you get an idea of the activities you find most interesting and which you probably know about. A second method is to consider current events or editorials in the newspaper and television and develop an attitude profile such as the one in exercise 3 at the end of the chapter. After each event, decide how you feel about the issue. Asking yourself what-if questions helps to determine the depth of your attitudes about related topics. Many games, such as Scruples and Girl Talk, provide a way of analyzing yourself through interactions with others. Take time to analyze your attitudes and knowledge, to articulate your thoughts about a variety of issues, and to perform serious and thorough self-reflection.

Analysis of your interests, knowledge, and attitudes can help identify topics and ideas that you are competent and eager to discuss. Increase your capability to create competent communication by increasing your information and knowledge in a variety of topics and by becoming aware of your attitudes about issues. Reading newspapers, magazines, and books can increase your knowledge of current events. Broadening your experiences to include art, theater, sports, hobbies, politics, religion, or community service can create new interests. If you only read the comics, always do and see the same things, and always talk to the same people, your attitudes, interests, and knowledge may become narrow and restricted. Talking about the weather is fine for chitchat, however, having breadth and depth in the topics you can discuss enables you to engage in competent communication with more people, in more situations, and with more ease.

"Before You Go On"

You should be able to answer the following question:

How can you analyze your attitudes and knowledge?

Self-analysis is a constant process by which communicators become aware of their knowledge, emotions, attitudes, anxieties, and communication skills. Once you identify these factors influencing the communication process, capitalize on your strengths and work to overcome weaknesses. As you become aware of the self, you also need to become aware of the other people and the environmental factors that comprise the communication situation.

Analyzing the Social Environment

The social context refers to the culture and society in which the communication occurs. It focuses on the people involved in the communication rather than the physical setting. To analyze the social context, examine: (1) the communication purpose, (2) the other people in the communication, (3) the relationship of the communicators, and (4) the cultural influences on the communication.

Determine the Communication Purpose

In analyzing the social context, consider the purpose of the communication. As we discussed in chapter 2, we communicate to inform, persuade, and entertain. All three of these **general communication purposes** are important in every communication, though a specific message may emphasize one purpose rather than another. People also have **specific communication purposes** concerning particular goals they wish to accomplish. For example, a person may have a general persuasive purpose of convincing another to quit smoking. She may also have specific communication purposes: (1) demonstrating that she cares about her friend, (2) appearing knowledgeable about the dangers of smoking, and (3) convincing her friend to see a hypnotist for treatment. The general and specific purposes guide the construction of your message and the strategies you employ to accomplish your goals.

You will know that you have clearly analyzed your communication purposes when you are able to state them in specific behaviors you want to perform. Similarly, when others can tell you what specific behaviors they want you to do, you will have a clear understanding of their communication purposes. For example, if you want to convince a friend to stop smoking, you may state your communication goals as:

To convince my friend to see a hypnotist next week.

To inform my friend that I care about him.

To have my friend give me a hug after our conversation.

To state three reasons to quit smoking.

Notice that each of these statements identifies a specific behavior that the people perform during the communication or as a result of the communication. They are easy to verify—your friend either goes to the hypnotist or not; you either told your friend you cared about him or not; you either get a hug or not; you either remembered to state all three reasons or not. Clearly stated purposes help us understand the social context, what we want to accomplish, and whether or not the communication purposes were achieved.

Have you ever attended a group meeting that you thought was going to be just a social gathering, only to discover the group was meeting to make an important decision? Communication was probably difficult until all people agreed on a common purpose. Analysis of the **communication purpose** also includes understanding the requirements of the occasion. The occasion influences and limits the choice of communication purposes. For example, a party may not be an appropriate place for shop talk, a speech for a travel club may require you to tell humorous anecdotes about your recent trip to Paris, or a job interview may require you to self-disclose about your reasons for leaving your last job. Adapting to the context and occasion is an important skill in analyzing the communication purpose.

From the action approach, the sender of the message determines the communication purpose. From a reaction approach, the receiver interprets the sender's purpose and responds appropriately. The transaction approach suggests that people jointly negotiate their communication purposes. When analyzing the communication purpose, the speaker considers not only her own reasons for the message, but also how the other person will interpret the message. The receiver not only tries to understand why the speaker is communicating, but also his own reasons for listening and responding. Together they create the purposes for the communication. When they successfully negotiate interdependent purposes, they are communicating competently.

To analyze the purpose of the communication ask yourself:

- What do I want to accomplish in this transaction? Why am I communicating with the other person?
- What do others want to accomplish? Why are they communicating with me?
- What purposes do others want me to fulfill? What do they expect from me?
- What does the occasion demand from me? From them? From us? What communication would be inappropriate for this occasion?

"Before You Go On"

You should be able to answer the following question:

Which factors affect the communication purpose?

Analyzing Others

An important element of any communication situation is the person with whom you are communicating. The philosophy of this text is that people have to co-operate and help each other create shared meanings, that people create competent communication through their joint actions. This perspective requires making a concerted effort to understand how others interpret their perceptions of themselves, of the environment, and of your behavior.

Just as you analyzed your private self, you also need to analyze the other person's knowledge, interests, attitudes, emotions, and communication skills. Determining the degree to which other people are involved in the communication process is a complex task. It is difficult because you must rely on inferences and educated guesses. You must determine the interest level of the other people, their knowledge of the topic, their attitudes toward the topic, their impressions of you, and their expectations and goals for the communication. You can analyze the degree of the other person's involvement through three primary sources of information: (1) demographic characteristics, (2) direct questions, and (3) the number of people in the communication situation.

Analyze Demographic Characteristics

Demographic variables identify characteristics that categorize people in groups, that is, the social and physical characteristics that they share. For example, we can classify people according to physical characteristics of sex, age, race, height, and weight. Other classifications include religion, political preference, socioeconomic background, ethnic heritage, organizational role, occupation, and affiliation with various social organizations.[9]

Demographic characteristics can be helpful in making initial judgments about appropriate strategies for communication. We can make educated guesses about people's interests, knowledge, and attitudes based on perceived similarities between them and other people with whom we have communicated. When we attribute attitudes and personalities to people based on physical appearance and behaviors, we treat them as if they are the same as other people with similar appearances and behaviors. Classification of people in demographic groups is a starting point that helps you relate with the variety of people you encounter.[10]

As we discussed in chapter 2, you cannot treat each and every perception as totally unique and different. When you perceive people, you try to make sense of their behavior by relating it to familiar experiences with similar behavior. Stereotyping is simply a method for organizing your perceptions; your perceptions allow you to predict people's behaviors and attitudes.

For example, you may perceive a person working for a Japanese organization as loyal to the corporation, secure in the workplace, productive, and relatively happy. These deductions may be based on your prior information about the typical Japanese worker. Or, you may meet a someone who is not athletic, wearing horn-rimmed glasses and outdated clothes, and carrying a calculator. You might assume this person is intelligent, studious, shy, and socially inept because of social stereotypes you have seen in the movies and on TV. Other assumptions might include that a woman dressed in a business suit is a feminist, that an elderly person is knowledgeable about social security, or that a homeless person is just lazy. Deductions based on appearance and demographics are made when communicating with all people.

In the absence of more specific information about others, you have no choice but to rely on inferences to determine who you communicate with, what ideas should be expressed, and how you should phrase your ideas. However, take care in making sweeping generalizations about others based solely on demographics. The danger of **stereotypes** is assuming that they are totally accurate and being unwilling to change and refine the stereotypes based on new information. When we freeze an initial stereotype, we cease our analysis and fail to try to understand individual persons. Then, there is little chance for competent communication.

Competent communication occurs when initial impressions are constantly monitored for accuracy and are refined and changed as new information is discovered.[11] Remember, all people in the communication situation are performing

demographic analysis and creating stereotypes. Other persons are stereotyping you even as you stereotype them. Competent communication occurs when people adapt their communication to each other based on actual behavior rather than on frozen, preconceived generalities.

Use Direct Questions

A second area or source of information about the other person is specific data concerning attitudes, values, and knowledge about a topic. These data can be collected by directing questions to people and making conclusions based on their answers. For example, if a corporation's executive accountant wants to propose investing $250 million of company assets in real estate to the board of directors, it would be advantageous to determine the board members' opinions concerning speculative investments. The accountant may talk to each of the members, or write to them, and ask their opinions prior to the board meeting. This knowledge, obtained prior to the communication and used appropriately, would enhance the accountant's chances for success. Knowing the listeners' attitudes and beliefs about the topic could dramatically increase the likelihood of communication success.

This analysis is different from using the demographic variables described earlier. You can directly ascertain others' attitudes, interests, and knowledge about a topic rather than make educated guesses from general characteristics. Generalizations based on specific attitude-value-belief analyses are more specific and, perhaps, more accurate. Asking **direct questions** through interviews, letters, or questionnaires can reveal precise information about a specific topic. The questions to ask relative to your topic fall into three general areas:

1. How much do the other persons know and how do they feel about my topic?
2. How much do the other persons know and how do they feel about me?
3. How do the other persons feel about participating in the communication context?

Answers to these questions are more contextual than answers and generalizations from demographic variables. You can ask these questions prior to a specific communication encounter, or you can ask them during the transaction itself.

Determine the Number of People

Another consideration in analyzing the social environment is determining the number of people involved in the communication situation. You need to know whether you will be communicating with one person, a group of three, or an audience of fifty. Your communication strategies differ depending on the number of people present. Planning seating arrangements, providing copies of materials, deciding on the specificity of your ideas, and planning the length of time you need to talk are just a few of the adaptations you must make based on the number of people.

The more people listening to the message, the more difficult it is to adapt the message to each individual. An interview, for example, allows a person to construct a message designed to arouse the interest of a specific interviewer. However, a speech to fifty employees at an orientation session requires more generalities and fewer personalized remarks.

While the specific strategies you use vary depending on the number of people, the communication skills you use are the same regardless of how many people are present. Clarity of language, organization of ideas, accurate listening, and appropriate nonverbal behaviors are equally important whether you are conversing one on one, participating in a group discussion, or presenting a public speech.

"Before You Go On"

You should be able to answer the following question:

What are two skills for analyzing others' interests, attitudes, and knowledge?

Understand the Relationship among Communicators

As we discussed in chapter 1, all communication has both content and relationship dimensions. The relationship among the communicators influences the way they interpret the content of the message. The degree to which people like each other, the amount of power people have in the relationship, and the trust that exists between them influence the meaning they give to each other's messages. We communicate differently in different relationships. If you have ever said, "I like her because I can kid her without her getting mad," or "I wouldn't talk this way to my boss—she wouldn't believe me," or "I can trust you with my darkest secrets," you are illustrating the influence of relationships on your communication strategies.

As we have discussed in unit I, relationships affect and are affected by the communication among people. Relationships are not just your perceptions and feelings added to the perceptions and feelings the other person has about you. It is more than simply the sum of its parts. Both people create the relationship through the interdependence of their behavior. For example, from a relationship perspective, you can't exert power if the other person is not willing to be influenced by you. You can't lead if no one will follow. Conversely, others can't follow you, if you are unwilling to lead. Relationships are mutually created.

When analyzing relationships, people rely on their own intuition and interpretations of the other people's behavior for clues about the nature of the relationship. By observing how others use eye contact, posture, facial expression, touch, distance, and tone of voice, people make inferences about the current relationship. This interpretation influences how they encode their own messages and, in turn, how they interpret the other's messages.

Seldom do people use metacommunication to discover the nature of the relationship. *Metacommunication* is communicating about communication, that is, people discuss what their relationship means, and how they express their feelings about the relationship. The key questions to ask are

1. How do we feel about each other?
2. Do we trust each other?
3. How do we create and share power together?
4. What kind of climate have we created for this transaction?

Often the best way to discover the answers to these questions is to discuss them openly with the other person. Knowing the answers to these questions helps both parties create competent communication.

Analyze the Culture

Culture is the shared perceptions of reality created among a group of people through their communication. Culture provides a common frame of reference through which people interpret the meaning of their verbal and nonverbal behaviors. It also provides a set of values by which to establish standards and norms for present behavior while providing direction for future actions. You may normally think of culture involving only large societies such as the Japanese, Mexican-

American, Sioux Indian, or Russians. However, other groups also develop a specific culture, for example, religious institutions (such as Catholic or Southern Baptist), ethnic groups (such as Afro-American or Jewish), geographic groups (such as inner city or rural), organizations (such as IBM, the U.S. Marine Corps), or small groups (such as families and clubs). Every person simultaneously belongs to several cultures. For example, a Mexican-American Catholic may live in an inner-city barrio and work for IBM. All of these cultures influence the way the person communicates.

Social norms, that is, rules and standards for acceptable or preferred behavior, evolve from people's cultures. People have expectations of the type, quantity, and quality of communication behavior. They judge whether communication is appropriate based on the social norms they follow. For instance, a teacher at a rural school on a Lakota Sioux reservation in South Dakota found it difficult to teach his students public speaking skills. The students would not look at the audience during their presentations, even when threatened with failing grades for not establishing eye contact. The teacher initially thought that they were just being stubborn or worse, that they were stupid. The parents of one student finally told the teacher that tribal custom dictated that direct eye contact with strangers and with people in authority was considered rude. The students' culture had established standards for appropriate eye contact, and the students would not violate that social norm even when faced with a poor grade in speech class. Because the teacher was from a different culture, he did not know this cultural norm.

Skills for Analyzing Communication Contexts

Knowing which behaviors are acceptable or preferred is essential to creating mutual understanding. We discuss the influence of culture on communication more specifically in chapter 14.

Analyzing cultural influences on people in the communication transaction is not always easy. One problem is that we are **ethnocentric,** that is, we interpret others' culture from our own perspective. Because we assume that our own cultural perspective is valid, we tend to judge different cultures as incorrect or strange. To analyze cultural influences on communication, you must listen to the stories people tell. Find out who they consider to be their heroes and villains. Listen to how they explain past events and what commentary they make about the present situation. In this way, you can ascertain how they interpret their perceptions and how these perceptions may be influenced by their specific backgrounds and social environments. Just as when you stereotype people based on their demographics, be flexible in your analysis of people on the basis of culture. Not all Japanese, or Afro-Americans, or people from small town rural families think and behave in the same way. Similar to stereotypes, membership in a culture is only a general guide to understanding and predicting how specific people might interpret the messages they perceive. Competent communication occurs when people are aware of each other's cultural heritage but adapt to the specifics of the communication transaction.

"Before You Go On"

You should be able to answer the following question:

What skills help analyze the impact of people's relationships and culture on communication?

Analyzing the Physical Context

Communicators should consider and explore the physical characteristics of a communication situation. The size of the room, the arrangement of the seating, the availability of audiovisual equipment, and the comfort afforded the communicators have potential impact on the eventual success or failure of communication. The physical context includes (1) the physical surroundings, (2) the time, and (3) the time requirements for the message.

Physical Surroundings

The physical surroundings influence the quality, efficiency, and fidelity of the messages people communicate. The physical surroundings also affect the motivation and ability of people to become involved in the communication. The color of the room and decorations, type and arrangement of furniture, the size of the space, temperature, and other factors available to the physical senses comprise the physical surroundings. When the communication is to occur in a large auditorium instead of a small conference room around a table, different communication strategies are needed. In a large area, people are more distant from each other and not directly facing each other; this requires more effort to make sure everyone can hear and see the messages. On the other hand, a meeting of a large group in a small, hot room makes it difficult to keep attention on the communication and forces people to sit close to people they may not know. Such discomfort may focus attention on wanting to leave the communication rather than fully participating in it.

The surroundings may be supportive and facilitate communication, or they may be counterproductive and inhibit competent communication. Supportive surroundings make it easy for the communicators to see and hear each other's messages, to use appropriate touch and eye contact, and express themselves in the most productive manner. These surroundings offer few distractions from the communication, and people are able to establish an appropriate relationship.

A counterproductive environment, on the other hand, inhibits competent communication. Noise and visual distractions may interfere with people's attempts to talk with each other. There may be too much or too little space available for the number of people. The room decorations may be inappropriate for the occasion. Whenever the physical surroundings are counterproductive, people either adapt their communication or change the environment.

No environments are inherently supportive or counterproductive—it depends on the nature of the communication. Just as a loud and boisterous party may be counterproductive to a quiet conversation among good friends, a quiet intimate restaurant may be counterproductive for two strangers who have little

Skills for Analyzing Communication Contexts   91

interest in each other. Similarly, a large auditorium may be counterproductive for a lecture to a few people, but supportive for a political rally.

When analyzing the physical surroundings, determine the sort of environment where the communication will occur, and the impact of the environmental factors on the communication. Decide which parts of the surroundings you can control, and to which elements you can adapt. The important consideration in the analysis is identifying potential sources of interference with competent communication and adapting to them.

"Before You Go On"

You should be able to answer the following question:

What are the differences between supportive and counterproductive environments?

Time

Part of the physical environment is the time in which the communication occurs and the duration of the communication. Although time cannot be sensed in the same way as other physical surroundings, nonetheless, it influences the way we express and interpret messages. Analyzing the constraints that time imposes on communication and how it influences the meanings people give to messages is an important skill.

Time of Day

The time of day affects people's communication. For example, people are less alert later in the workday and their minds seem to focus more on going home than on the communication efforts. You may avoid early morning or late afternoon classes because you know you have difficulty paying attention and understanding material at those times. The time of day also is affected by events that have just occurred or are about to occur. For example, you may be more focused on a teacher's lecture if you know there will be a quiz at the end of the class period. On the other hand, you may have difficulty listening to a friend discuss vacation plans if you just found out you couldn't go on the vacation you had planned.

When the communication occurs is important to consider. Analyzing the time context helps you adapt to the needs and concerns of others. Ask yourself

- How will people will feel at that time?

- Will any events that have just occurred affect how people interpret my message?

- What up-coming events will others be thinking about as they listen to me?

Time Requirements for the Message

In addition to the time of day, the physical context includes the time requirements for the message. Some people are late for appointments. Others are not prepared to express themselves clearly. Still others ramble on and on without giving anyone else a chance to state new ideas. None of these people have correctly analyzed the time requirements of the communication context. Communication contexts differ in the amount of time you have and need to prepare your message. Contexts also vary in how much time you have to state your ideas and how punctual you are expected to be.

Time for Prior Preparation

Have you ever said, "Oh, there was something I wanted to ask you but I forgot what it was." Or, "I don't know the answer to that question. I didn't read the assignment for today's class." Or, "I'm sorry to have to call you back, but I forgot to ask you a question." Or, "I just didn't have time to prepare the speech the way I wanted to." If these statements sound familiar, you have experienced a problem with making **time for prior preparation,** an element of every communication situation.

Communication situations differ in the time available for prior preparation. In many cases, the amount of time you have for preparing to communicate determines the depth of analysis you can perform, the amount of practice you can do, and the number of strategies you can plan. If there are two weeks until a meeting, you have considerable time to prepare and should be able to conduct a complete and thorough analysis on the discussion topic. On the other hand, if you are called on to present ideas in an impromptu, or off-the-cuff, manner during a meeting, there is little time to plan an appropriate strategy for conveying your idea. Similarly, when you run into a friend on the street, you need to remember what you wanted to say to him or her on the spot. The key to effective preparation is to anticipate communication situations in which you want to present a message or will be asked to present one. Even the impromptu message can be anticipated and some prior preparation performed.

Anticipating communication situations requires constantly analyzing friends, colleagues, and supervisors. Maintaining a written and/or mental catalog of ideas, observations, comments, biases, and so forth about people with whom you will be communicating helps you be prepared to communicate with them. Then, even if asked at the last moment to speak off-the-cuff, you will have completed some analysis of the information needs of the other person. The initial question in the analysis of a communication situation is: "How much time do I have to prepare the message and analyze the situation?"

Time to Present the Verbal Message

A college senior was asked to be a host for a high school student visiting the campus. The host was to give a tour of campus and take the visitor to lunch at the campus cafeteria. During the tour, the high school student would not say more than two words, no matter what questions the host asked. When the host talked, the visitor seemed disinterested. They ate lunch in virtual silence.

At a recent professional convention, four professors were to present their ideas on innovative teaching methods during an hour-long seminar. The first speaker, however, spoke for almost 45 minutes. The second speaker tried to hurry, but took 10 minutes. The last two speakers were very upset because they did not get a chance to present their ideas at all.

The problem in these two situations was the same: The visiting student and the first professor violated the amount of verbal message responsibility they had in the situation. Have you ever said, "I couldn't get a word in edgewise. He never shut up long enough for me to say anything." Or, "It was not a good interview. I tried to get her to talk, but she just answered my questions with a yes or no and wouldn't elaborate." Or, "I know my speech was only three minutes long instead of ten, but that's all I could think of to say." If you have ever made these statements, you have identified a problem with verbal message responsibility.

Although people continuously communicate nonverbally, they normally take turns presenting ideas verbally. Your **verbal message responsibility** ranges from sole responsibility (as in a training lecture or technical presentation) to shared responsibility when others verbally contribute to the communication situation (as in an interview, a group discussion, or a conversation). The amount of time for which you are responsible for the message influences the number of ideas you discuss, amount of information you include, and the preparation you need. If others are also presenting ideas, your message must be prepared so that it can be quickly adapted to their comments, feedback, and questions. If others have the primary verbal responsibility, you need to prepare to listen and communicate your involvement nonverbally. Therefore, in the analysis of the communication context ask: "How much time do I have for my verbal message?" and "Will I be the only one speaking?"

"Before You Go On"

You should be able to answer the following question:

How does time affect the communication context?

Describing and understanding the communication situation is necessary for competent communication. People react to each other based on their stereotypes of each other, their own attitudes and emotions, and their perceptions of the physical environment. People adapt their communication to the specific communication situation. The next chapters in this unit describe other skills that help you adapt to the context. Unit III and unit IV discuss specific strategies that you can use depending on your analysis of the communication context.

1.   Which methods can you use to analyze your communication skills?
Recognizing your communication strengths and weaknesses is the first step in the analysis of the communication context. Second, you can receive insights about your communication skills from other people's feedback. Videotapes and audiotapes of your communication can vividly demonstrate the way you communicate and let you realize how others receive your messages. A third method requires that you keep a written communication log in which you record and analyze your communication encounters. A communication log helps you find patterns of communication competence.

2.   How can analyzing emotions help create competent communication?
Emotions affect communication on at least two levels. First, emotions affect you internally, that is, your ability to process information, the meaning you give to messages, and the way you encode messages to others. Second, emotions affect the external communication with others, that is, they are part of the message you wish others to understand. You can better understand emotions if you have a precise way of labeling them. Using figures of speech, descriptive modifiers, and precise terminology can help clarify emotions for yourself, and also make them clearer to others. Enthusiasm and anxiety are specific emotions that affect the communication process. Enthusiasm is the desire to share your ideas with others and comes from your involvement in the communication. Anxiety may also enhance communication if effectively managed. Too little or too much anxiety reduces the chances of creating competent communication. Anxiety can be analyzed through written tests and can be managed through positive visualization, physical activity, and relaxation exercises, and practice.

3.   How can you analyze your attitudes and knowledge?
People spend time doing activities that are most meaningful to them and that they know about. An activities inventory can provide insight into your attitudes and knowledge about various issues and topics. Explaining your attitudes toward topics to yourself and others can help you clarify the scope and depth of your attitudes.

4.   Which factors affect the communication purpose?
Communication usually attempts to fulfill three interrelated purposes of informing, persuading, and entertaining. Each person in the communication context has a purpose in expressing his or her own ideas. Each person also expects the other communicators to fulfill specific purposes. In addition, the occasion and setting create expectations for communication. The purposes of communication can be clarified by stating them clearly. Only with clear goals can communicators cooperate to help each other reach them.

5.   What are two skills for analyzing others' interests, attitudes, and knowledge?

The attitudes and knowledge others have about the topic of communication influences how they perceive your message. You can make some general inferences about others' knowledge and attitudes through analysis of demographic information to categorize them. A second method is to ask them direct questions about their attitudes, values, and knowledge through interviews, conversations, or written surveys. Direct questions can provide more specific information than general demographic data, but such information is often difficult to acquire.

6.   Which skills help analyze the impact of people's relationships and culture on communication?

The relationships among communicators affect the meanings of their communication, yet most people do not openly or specifically discuss their relationships. Analysis of relationships is often based on inferences drawn from the way individuals use nonverbal communication. Their facial expressions, tone of voice, use of touch, and eye contact indicate how they perceive the relationship. Culture affects the expression and interpretation of relationship cues. Learning about others' culture through stories, myths, and language can give insight for interpreting their messages and determining how to make our messages meaningful to them.

An important, but frequently neglected communication skill, is metacommunication. People seldom directly talk about how they are communicating, their perceptions of the relationship, and their specific perceptions of each other.

7.   What are the differences between supportive and counterproductive environments?

A supportive climate consists of physical surroundings that facilitate the communication process. The colors, arrangement of furniture, comfort, and amount of noise are consistent with the purposes of the communicators and their needs. A counterproductive physical environment inhibits communication competence. Analyzing the environment requires recognition of the factors that influence supportiveness and controlling the environment to reduce the impact of nonproductive elements.

8.   How does time affect the communication context?

The time during which communication occurs affects the abilities of people to be involved in the communication. Selective attention and retention are affected by the time of day, the length of time the message takes, and the responsibility people take for their role in the exchange of verbal messages. The time available for preparing your communication strategies affects the degree to which your messages are planned and rehearsed. Anticipating upcoming communication events; developing communication skills; and continuously analyzing the self, others, and environments puts preparation time to its best use.

1. Communication log.

Think of your communication experiences with friends, work associates, classmates, family, and teachers during the past week. For each encounter, ask yourself the following questions:

    a. Did the other person understand you the first time you made a statement, or was repetition necessary?

    b. Was the other person satisfied with your response to his or her questions? Did you misunderstand the question because you weren't listening carefully?

    c. Did you enjoy the communication situation or were you bored, uncomfortable, or anxious?

    d. Did the communication occur as you had planned? If not, what was different and what caused the change?

    e. Did you say what you had planned to say or did you forget part of your ideas?

    f. Did you know what your goal was? Did you accomplish your purpose?

    g. If you could do it over, would you do anything differently? Why? Is there any way you could have done it this way the first time?

2. Activities log.

Think of your activities during the past week (or record your activities for the coming week). Go through each day and make a list of everything you did and how much time was spent on each activity. What activities did you do most often? In which activities did you spend the most time? Which activities were most enjoyable? Which activities would you like to do again?

3. Attitude profile.

Watch the television news or read the newspaper. List the topics for each story. Decide if you agree or disagree with the events that occurred and the way people reacted to them. How would you have acted in similar situations? Then read the editorials in the newspaper. Do you agree with them? Are there any circumstances that would make you change your mind? If you wrote a letter to the editor about the topic, what would you say?

4. Communication apprehension.

Consider situations in which you are anxious about communicating and which you wish you could avoid. Also consider situations in which you feel relaxed and eager to communicate. (You may want to ask your teacher to administer an anxiety test such as the PRCA—Personal Report of Communication Apprehension.) In which circumstances are you most anxious? Why? In which circumstances were you most comfortable? Why?

5.   Describe your emotions.

For each of the following general, vague emotions, write several related and more specific emotions. Use descriptive words, metaphors, and other figures of speech to make your emotions vivid and specific.

Love	Hate	Pride	Lonely	Happy
Sad	Worried	Fear	Anger	Insecure

GLOSSARY

anxiety A response to a perceived threat.

attitude A predisposition to respond in a favorable or unfavorable manner to an idea, event, person, or thing.

communication apprehension Anxiety produced during anticipation of, or engagement in, communication activities.

communication context The interdependent interaction of all the elements of communication, including self, others, physical and social environments, and behaviors.

communication log A method of analyzing communication skills by keeping a written record of communication experiences and looking for patterns of strengths and weaknesses.

culture The common frame of reference, or perspective, shared by a group of people reflecting their values, attitudes, and the meanings they give to their perceptions.

demographic characteristics A method for making inferences about listeners by placing them in familiar categories or stereotypes based on observed physical, nonverbal, verbal, or social characteristics.

direct question A method for gathering information about receivers by asking them for information through surveys, questionnaires, interviews, or other direct responses.

enthusiasm The emotional involvement in a message; the desire to communicate a message to others.

ethnocentrism The attitude that one's own culture is more valid, useful, or important than another culture.

general communication purposes All communication has informative, persuasive, and entertainment purposes; specific contexts may emphasize one, two, or all three purposes.

labeling A method for analyzing emotions by finding precise words that separate the specific emotion from all other similar emotions.

specific communication purposes Particular behaviors to be performed during, or as a result of, communication.

stereotype A verbal label for a category of people who are commonly perceived to share similar characteristics, to possess similar knowledge and attitudes, and to behave in similar ways.

time for prior preparation Amount of time a person has to anticipate and prepare for specific communication encounters.

verbal message responsibility The degree to which a person is expected to create and deliver a verbal message; the degree to which people take turns in sharing verbal messages.

visualization A method for managing communication apprehension by visualizing positive results of your communication.

NOTES

1. See, for example, Adeline G. Hirschfield, "Videotape Recordings for Self-Analysis in the Speech Classroom," *Speech Teacher* 17 (1968), 116–18; D. Thomas Porter and G. William King, "The Use of Videotape Equipment in Improving Oral Interpretation Performance," *Speech Teacher* 21 (1972), 99–106; Robert Lake and W. Clifton Adams, "Effects of the Videotape Recorder on Levels of Anxiety, Exhibitionism, and Reticence in High School Speech Students," *Communication Education* 33 (1984), 333–36.

2. For reviews of communication apprehension studies see: James C. McCroskey, "Oral Communication Apprehension: A Summary of Recent Theory and Research," *Human Communication Research* 4 (1977), 78–96; John A. Daly and James C. McCroskey, eds., *Avoiding Communication: Shyness, Reticence, and Communication Apprehension* (Newbury Park, Calif.: Sage, 1984); James C. McCroskey and John A. Daly, *Personality and Interpersonal Communication* (Newbury Park, Calif.: Sage: 1987), especially pages 129–56.

3. Daly and McCroskey, *Avoiding Communication.*

4. Irving Janis and Leon Mann. *Decision Making: A Psychological Analysis of Conflict, Choice, Commitment* (New York: Free Press, 1977).

5. Michael M. Beatty and Ralph R. Behnke, "An Assimilation Theory Perspective of Communication Apprehension," *Human Communication Research* 6 (1980), 319–25.

6. See for example, James C. McCroskey and Virginia P. Richmond, "The Impact of Communication Apprehension on Individuals in Organizations," *Communication Quarterly* 27 (1979), 55–61; Philip M. Ericson and John W. Gardner, "Two Longitudinal Studies of Communication Apprehension and Its Effects on College Students' Success," *Communication Education* 40 (1992), 127–37.

7. James C. McCroskey, "Validity of the PRCA as an Index of Oral Communication Apprehension," *Communication Monographs* 45, 192–203. Other measures of communication apprehension are discussed in: Judee K. Burgoon, "The Unwillingness-to-Communicate Scale: Development and Validation," *Communication Monographs* 43 (1976), 60–9; James C. McCroskey, "Reliability and Validity of the Willingness to Communicate Scale," *Communication Quarterly* 40 (1992), 16–25.

8. Studies on the effectiveness of techniques for reducing anxiety include: Joe Ayres and Tim Hopf, "Visualization: Reducing Speech Anxiety and Enhancing Performance," *Communication Reports* 5 (1992), 1–10; Lynne Kelly, Robert L.

Duran, and John Stewart, "Rhetoritherapy Revisited: A Test of Its Effectiveness as a Treatment for Communication Problems," *Communication Education* 39 (1990), 207–26; Mike Allen, John E. Hunter, and William A. Donahue, "Meta-Analysis of Self-Report Data on the Effectiveness of Public Speaking Anxiety Treatment Techniques," *Communication Education* 38 (1989), 54–76.

9.   Steve Duck, *The Study of Acquaintance* (Westmead, England: Saxon House, 1977).

10.   B. Aubrey Fisher, *Interpersonal Communication: Pragmatics of Human Relationships* (New York: Random House, 1977).

11.   Rod Hart and Don Burks, "Rhetorical Sensitivity and Social Interaction," *Speech Monographs* 39 (1972), 75–91.

A local organizer of a charity fund-raising drive talked with a friend during lunch about last year's fund drive:

Last year we raised over $250,000 for hospital equipment for the young children's wing. I never thought I would see such happy faces as those of the children and their families in that hospital wing. They were recruited from the local university and our high schools did a great job of securing donations. By the way, we need a specific strategy for raising money again this year. Is your lunch okay? I favor using some direct mailers even though almost everyone else prefers using telephone solicitations. We must try to beat last year's total by at least 10 percent. I think we can count on the college and high school students to help us again this year. By the way, did you remember to send them all thank you letters last year? I think the media people will help this year if we can get someone to write some promotional and advertising copy. We have to get busy and find volunteers to help this campaign. I have some good ideas for posters and would like to have you contribute at least five hours per week mailing letters to last year's contributors. If we both pitch in like we have in the past, we can make this another successful campaign.

Notice how this message jumps from one idea to the next with little structure or relationship among the ideas. The organizer's friend probably had some difficulty trying to understand the exact point or points being made. Because the message appears disorganized, it is likely there was some difficulty in identifying exactly what needed to be done. We have all heard messages with similar organizational problems.

The Purposes of Organizing

The **organization** of messages refers to the order in which we communicate ideas and the relationships among them. People have some difficulty understanding information presented in random order. They have to work harder to find relationships among ideas to make sense of them. Listeners use the organizing function of perception to group similar ideas together (association), to emphasize main points (selection), and to fill in information to make the message seem complete (closure). In the previous example, since it is not clear how the message was organized, the organizer's friend is confused about the relationships between the ideas. As a result, the friend organizes the information in the message in a personal manner, and probably differently than the speaker. When speakers leave the organizing process up to the listeners, the messages probably are not understood as intended.

Showing Coherence and Relationships among Ideas

Organize your messages so ideas develop coherently. Listeners expect ideas in messages to be related. Whether giving a public speech, discussing an idea during a group meeting, explaining your job qualifications to a potential employer, or talking with a friend about your plans for spring break, organize your ideas so that others understand the relationships between them.

Let's return to the example at the beginning of the chapter. What are the relationships the organizer intended between the ideas of the smiling faces of the children and their families, the need to raise 10 percent more money, and the request that the organizer's friend work five hours each week on posters for the campaign? Were the children and families recruited from the local universities? Will direct mailers increase last year's total funds by at least 10 percent? Does the fundraiser want media people to volunteer to write advertising copy? In the original message, the fund drive organizer creates relationships that are confusing. Note the difference in the following revision. Do you answer the questions the same way after reading the revised message?

I never thought I would see such happy faces as those of the children and their families in that hospital wing when they heard we raised $250,000 for new equipment. Although last year's campaign was a success, you and I have to develop strategies to raise even more money this year.

Our plan should include the continued use of the high school and college students who worked so hard last year. I will begin securing volunteers and will give you a progress report. In addition, we should think about using direct mailers, even though a lot of people prefer telephone solicitations. We'll have to meet again within a week or so to decide which option we will use this year.

Between now and our next meeting, could you contact the media to see if they will help advertise our campaign? I'll contact our corporate sponsors to be sure they will continue to promote the fund drive with their employees. I would like to send a letter to each company that contributed last year. Why don't we both draft a letter and put a final version together during our next meeting? I think we should meet for lunch again next week to give each other updates on our progress. What do you think?

Skills for Organizing Communication

In the revised message, the speaker organizes the ideas into three main topic areas: last year's success, people's activities that raised the money, and the use of media and corporate sponsors. The message now shows a clear relationship between last year's successful fund drive and the activities that would be needed this year. In this chapter, we discuss ways to organize messages to help others understand your messages.

Showing Coherence in Messages

Remember, listeners expect messages to be organized. If you communicate your ideas in an unorganized manner, you are perceived to be less knowledgeable and, therefore, less believable.[1] Mentally organizing information as it is received is a function of human perception. If the speaker does not provide a clear relationship between information, those who hear the message are forced to provide their own organization to make sense of the message.

Because of their past experiences, people organize information in different ways. That is, you cannot be sure others will organize the information you communicate in the same way you do. In talking with a friend about what you did last weekend, you have to communicate your message in an organized fashion and make that organization clear to your friend. If you just start rambling about all your various activities, making statements as they occur to you with no thought about how they fit with previous statements, your friend would have a hard time following your train of thought. If communication is to be competent, speakers must work to organize their ideas before making statements. Likewise, listeners must work to organize the message during the communication. Together, they co-create a similar organization of ideas and understanding of the message.

In addition to arranging the statements and topics of a message, organization also refers to the way communication between people is structured. In interpersonal or group communication situations, taking turns is one way to organize the communication so participants are not talking at the same time. Turn taking helps others to help you regulate your verbal message responsibility. Communication has an expected flow and direction. For example, when someone asks you a question, you are expected to answer. When someone pauses and looks at you, you may assume it is your turn to speak. When you want to talk in class, you may signal you want a turn by raising your hand. We regulate the flow of verbal communication by conventions establishing whose turn it is to speak. (Chapter 7 examines the use of nonverbal regulators more specifically.) Without an organized flow of communication, talking with someone would be chaotic.

"Before You Go On"

You should be able to answer the following question:

What are two reasons for organizing your messages?

A direct chronological organization pattern helps people understand a sequence of steps.

Skills for Organizing Ideas

You can do many things to organize ideas. In chapter 2 we explained that everyone selects, organizes, and interprets the information they receive. Competent communicators work together to share these perceptions and meanings. You have to help the others understand the way you think; you should not keep it secret and make them guess, you should tell them. You do this by organizing information into patterns and communicating these patterns to others. You have to tell others why you think the way you do and try to get them to think that way or at least understand your way of thinking. In doing this, you co-create interest, relate information to others, try to make your information seem believable, and show them how the information relates to them. The rest of this chapter explains some specific skills to use to better organize your information and ideas.

Types of Organizational Patterns

Organizational patterns specify the order of ideas in a message and indicate their relationships to each other. Although we typically use these organizational patterns when learning public speaking skills, they can and should be used in conversations, interviews, and group situations as well.

The most frequently used ways to organize messages include sequential, spatial, topical, cause-effect, and problem-solution.

Sequential

In sequencing information—also referred to as **chronological organization**—ideas develop according to a time line or a series of events, actions, or procedures. Sequential organization is appropriate when everyone's understanding of the progression or development of ideas, events, patterns, or actions is important. This pattern is usually constructed in a direct **sequential order** from the earliest event or the first step to the most recent event or the final step. When you explain to a friend how to assemble a bicycle, you might begin by telling her to attach the seat to the frame. Next you tell her to attach the brake handles to the handle bars and to put the gear assembly in the proper place on the bicycle. Then she should attach the chain to the gears, and attach the tires to the frame. Finally, you would tell your friend to adjust the brake pads on the wheels and then adjust the seat to the appropriate height. In this situation, the direct sequential pattern of the ideas allows for the development of a clear relationship between ideas. In giving your friend directions, you and your friend see the relationship between steps in the assembly process.

The sequence of events or ideas organized in *reverse sequential order* moves from the most recent to earlier events or ideas. During an employment interview, for instance, a job applicant often begins discussing previous job experiences by describing the most recent job and then reviewing past work experience. A staff sergeant in the Army may teach a group of new recruits how to clean and/or repair a rifle by starting with the assembled rifle and working backward to a completely disassembled rifle. Disassembling the rifle and showing the relationship between the various parts helps recruits understand how the rifle is put together. Both of these examples use the reverse sequential pattern to explain the relationship of ideas and processes.

In selecting one of these two options, consider the following: If it will help others understand your message to see the total picture, select the reverse sequential order. On the other hand, if others will understand your message by seeing the various parts before they are assembled, select the direct sequential order.

"Before You Go On"

You should be able to answer the following question:

What is the major difference between the direct sequential order and the reverse sequential order of organization?

Spatial

Use the spatial pattern to organization when you want to show how ideas relate to each other in geography or location. Often, spatial relationships involve moving from one location to another. The spatial pattern provides a mental map of the *physical relationship* of ideas, objects, events, or processes. For instance, a counselor at your university could explain the different locations of first aid equipment to a group of new students using the spatial pattern. The counselor may explain the equipment available in different buildings or offices on campus, moving from the administration building, through each classroom building, to each residence hall, and ending up at the library. Students receive information based on the location of the first aid equipment in each building in a comprehensive safety program.

Use a **spatial sequence** when communication involves a geographic distribution, the location of specific events, services, products, or objects. Spatial sequences enable listeners to visualize the geographic relationships of the ideas, processes, or events.

Topical

In organizing information into topics, the speaker divides a large category of ideas into specific units or subtopics of information. A message using **topical sequence** provides several smaller categories of information about a larger topic. Before talking with your class about good study habits, for instance, divide the topic into smaller units. You might explain four subtopics of information about good study habits: (1) taking notes, (2) reading textbooks for comprehension, (3) writing papers, and (4) studying for tests. Each of the smaller units helps explain the nature and variety of good study habits.

Sometimes the arrangement of a message organized into topics indicates relationships among the smaller categories (subtopics) of information. One such method is the *climactic topical sequence*. The climactic relationship presents the most important subtopic last. Each idea builds toward the most important point to be made. In the previous example, when talking about study habits, you might decide that your most important point is the way to study for tests. You begin by discussing note taking, reading the textbook for understanding, and writing papers as contributing to good study habits. Nonetheless, you want to focus your receivers' attention on your last, most important idea: studying for exams.

A climactic order can also move from events that occur less frequently to those that occur most often. For example, at a weekly review meeting the manager of a small appliance store would tell the store supervisor about infrequent parts shortages and conclude with frequent turn-around time problems.

Speakers also arrange their information in reverse order, the *anticlimactic pattern,* moving from most important to least important, or from most frequent to least frequent. Use the anticlimactic pattern when you need to make an immediate impact to gain someone's attention.

Another way to show relationships among subtopics is to move from familiar to unfamiliar ideas. This pattern begins with information familiar to others and then develops new ideas. If you are trying to explain word processing to a friend who just bought a home computer, begin by talking about using a typewriter and then introduce the more complex functions of the computer keyboard. Once you have established a common foundation of familiar information (the typewriter), you can proceed to discuss unfamiliar information (the computer keyboard) more clearly.

Whether the information is organized in climactic, anticlimactic, or familiar to unfamiliar order, a topical sequence helps others understand the relationships among subtopics.

Cause-Effect

Organizing messages into a **cause-effect sequence** demonstrates the relationships among conditions and consequences. Use the cause-effect pattern to demonstrate that present conditions have future consequences or that present conditions were caused by a set of past circumstances. As an example, during a meeting on campus, a congressional representative may contend that negative economic indicators, a drop in the ratio of savings to household income, and new federal tax laws may cause the local economy to experience additional unemployment and lower tax revenues next year. The representative suggests that current conditions will cause specific future effects.

Conversely, the dean of your college may explain that there are fewer course offerings, fewer new faculty, and fewer academic advisors as a result of lower student enrollment over the past six years, poor recruitment, poor economic conditions, and less tuition assistance from governmental agencies. The dean emphasizes the relationship between current conditions and previous events. Whether you communicate from cause to effect or effect to cause, clearly create the relationship between current conditions and past or future events.

In using the **problem-solution sequence,** the speaker describes the need for change and offers a solution or plan of action. The problem-solution sequence is also known as the Motivated Sequence.[2] The Motivated Sequence includes these steps:

1.   Attention step
2.   Need step
3.   Solution step
4.   Visualization step
5.   Action step

The speaker gains the listeners' attention, creates a need or reason for change, and then proposes a specific plan to meet the need or problem. The speaker visualizes the advantages and results of the plan and asks the listener to perform a specific action to implement the proposal. In describing the relationship between the need for change and the plan of action, the problem-solution sequence creates reasons to adopt a specific change from present conditions.

When using the problem-solution sequence, ensure that you clearly explain both the need or reason for change and the specific plan of action. When listeners are not convinced that a change is necessary, it does not matter how appealing the solution is. On the other hand, if listeners are convinced that a change should be made, you must present a useful solution others are willing to accept.

Persuasive messages, aimed at trying to change others' behaviors, attitudes, or opinions, usually employ a problem-solution pattern. For example, assume you want a friend to let you borrow her car tonight. You might begin by pointing out that your car is in the garage being repaired and won't be returned to you for several days. You may point out that your date tonight is extremely important to you. You also tell her that you do not have access to any other car. You may tell her that borrowing her car is the only way you can go on this date tonight. You point out that when you drive you are very careful, you have never received a ticket, and you will park the car away from others so it won't get hit. Finally, you promise to let her borrow your car in the future if she needs it. You have presented a need, explained a plan to meet that need, and helped her visualize that the plan is beneficial and workable.

Each organizational sequence describes a specific order of ideas and the relationships among them. You organize messages to show sequential progression, spatial location, topical divisions, causes and effects, and/or solutions to problems. The specific sequence, or combination of sequences, you select helps others understand how you think ideas are related. Choosing an appropriate sequence and communicating that sequence are important skills in competent communication.

"Before You Go On"

You should be able to answer the following question:

Why is the problem-solution sequence usually recommended for a persuasive message?

Skills for Beginning Messages

Sometimes people begin messages by just blurting out the first main idea. They provide no context for the ideas they are discussing to help the listeners understand why they are talking about the topic. Most messages require a beginning to get the listeners' attention and prepare them to focus attention on the message. Regardless of the communication context, the beginning of a message accomplishes four things: It gains interest for your ideas, helps others believe your ideas, gives others a reason to pay attention to your message, and helps others see how you organized your ideas. These opening comments must be related to the goals of the message and focus attention on the rest of the message.

Gaining Interest for Your Ideas

One purpose of introductory comments is to create interest for your ideas.[3] You try to convince others that your message is worth paying attention to and thinking about. Before asking a friend to borrow $500 to buy a car, for example, be sure to create interest in your message. The most common techniques for creating interest include (1) asking questions, (2) using dramatic illustrations, (3) making humorous statements, (4) making a startling statement, and (5) using quotations.

Asking Questions

Questions arouse listeners' curiosity, get them actively thinking about your topic, and directly involve them in the communication. Questions can either be responsive or rhetorical. A **responsive question** asks for a verbal or/and nonverbal response from others. They may raise their hands, stand up, answer yes or no, or give a specific answer. If you are talking with a friend about next term's class schedule, you want her to be thinking of your topic and answer your questions about specific instructors and classes. The responsive question can create interest in your experiences, your opinions, and/or your attitudes.

A **rhetorical question** asks others to respond mentally. This is an effective technique when an overt response may be embarrassing or when a show of hands may be unnecessary to your purpose. For example, a lawyer talking to a group of employees concerning their legal rights in sexual harassment cases may not want to embarrass them by asking for a show of hands by those who have been harassed. However, a rhetorical question asking them to think about their experiences might arouse the employees' interest in the topic and motivate them to listen.

Dramatic Illustrations

Telling about a dramatic incident generates interest in the topic. Such dramatic illustrations may be either fictitious or real. For example, you are trying to convince your friends to wear seat belts in a car. You might use a fictitious dramatic example of someone who died in a car accident through failure to buckle up. You could use a real example if it happened to someone you know. As communicators, we have the option to use real illustrations if they are available, or we can create some to gain dramatic impact. Be ethical when using a fictitious example—tell your listener that it is not true, just that it could be true. **Dramatic illustrations** are useful in arousing your receivers' emotions.

Humorous Statements

Jokes, anecdotes, and humorous statements frequently create interest in an idea. When humor is appropriate for the message, it helps relax others and create feelings of goodwill and friendship. Recognize that humor is a risky way to begin; you risk having others think your message is not funny. To be safe, test your humor prior to the event. For example, if you are going to tell a joke to your date tonight, try it out on your roommate. Usually, you should avoid sexist, ethnic, racist, sexual, and other tasteless humor when introducing an idea. Introductory humor must be directly related to the topic and appropriate for the listener and occasion.[4]

Startling Statements

Startling statements help listeners consider information or facts in unique ways or give them information arousing their curiosity. A secretary trying to convince a boss that there should be a ban on smoking in the office might begin by stating, "We have twenty people in our office who smoke. Combined, they smoke almost 75,000 cigarettes each year in this building. If placed end to end, these 75,000 cigarettes would stretch for nearly four miles!" Statistics are often good sources of startling statements.

Like other interest-generating approaches, the startling statement should be closely related to your communication purpose. Refrain from making startling statements to create interest and then failing to explain or use the information in the rest of the message.

Quotations

Using other people's words can also gain attention. Quotations may state ideas in unique ways that capture listeners' interest. Avoid quotes that are too common; strive to be unique. Look for the unusual statement, the picturesque phrasing of ideas, or the authoritative voice that states an idea. Sources of quotations include newspapers, magazines, literature, and/or your favorite television programs. When using quotes, accurately cite the exact words and give credit to the person you are quoting. When talking informally, this is sometimes impossible and even unnecessary. In more formal situations, however, cite the source of the quotation.

"Before You Go On"

You should be able to answer the following question:

Which five techniques help create interest in your ideas?

Whether using dramatic illustrations, startling statements, quotations, questions, or humorous stories, you should arouse people's interest in your ideas. All messages need an interest-arousing first step regardless of specific communication context. The important consideration is for you to focus others' interest on the message, not yourself. Be careful not to make statements that mislead others or focus their interest on things other than your goals or message.

Helping Others Believe Your Ideas

Another function of a good beginning is to help others believe you. Listeners need to know why they should believe what you are saying. Help others believe you by telling them about your past experience, education or special training, and/or personal involvements with the information. In talking with a friend about the importance of saving money, you can help him believe you by saying:

- I have talked with many other college students about investing in their futures and have had many of them sign up to receive further information.
- I work for a company that handles investment accounts for more than 250,000 college students who are saving for their futures.
- I keep up on the daily activities in the financial marketplace by reading investment reports in the *Wall Street Journal, Barron's,* and *Business Monthly.*

These statements establish your involvement, expertise, knowledge, and interest in investment planning. People are more willing to listen to your sales pitch if they perceive you as believable.[5]

Somethings create your believability before you enter the communication situation. Your status—whether through a position in a company or the local community—your reputation, and any relationship you have with the participants affect your credibility before you even open your mouth. If you have any doubts about how others perceive you, spend some time in your message to establish why they should believe you.

Giving Others Reasons to Listen

People are usually most interested in information that affects them directly. The more immediate the potential effect to the listener, the more interest that person has in the information. A good beginning to a message tells others how they can use the information for personal growth, how to accomplish a specific task, or how to improve their performance. For example, instead of the salesperson simply stating, "Mutual funds are good investments," it might be better to relate the topic of retirement programs specifically to the listeners. The salesperson could state, "When you leave the university in two or three years, how much will you have to spend? If you start tomorrow, and invest just $20 a month in a mutual fund, you will have saved more than $1,000."

Notice how this latter example relates the message directly to the listeners' needs, interests, and actions. The latter statements create a sense of immediate need for the information.

Help Others Organize Your Ideas

Once you have aroused listeners' interest, given them reason to listen to you, and helped them believe your ideas, you still have to tell them what your message is about. Introducing your message requires more than simply announcing the subject, as in the statement, "Today I want to talk with you about saving money in mutual funds." A more effective introduction states the major idea and previews the subtopics to be included in the message. Give your listener an idea about what to expect in your message and how it is organized. In essence, prepare them to understand your ideas.

A proposition statement is a declarative statement about the topic. It lets others know what you plan to say and the approach you are taking. During an interview, for instance, communicate the objectives during the beginning moments rather than letting the participants try to guess and conclude for themselves what the objectives are. Similarly, when talking with friends about your career interests, you can help them relate to you and your message by clearly stating your main idea.

The proposition statement allows others to understand the ultimate goal of the communication. Also remember to preview the ideas you plan to discuss. Stating each idea enables listeners to create expectations and interest in what is to come.[6] This allows others to mentally organize your information which helps them understand your forthcoming message. Take advantage of this first opportunity to tell your listeners exactly what the message is and to emphasize important ideas.

The beginning is an important part of every communication situation. Competent communication is assisted when you prepare others to listen. The length of time available for the message, the amount of prior knowledge others have about you, and the degree to which others are initially interested in the topic influence how you begin your message.

Casual conversations don't always need a preview, nor do you need to spend much time building credibility with your best friend. However, in more formal situations, when your message is important, or when your ideas are complex, consider the skills for preparing people to listen. Skill in developing effective beginnings to messages is one of the most creative, yet difficult, processes in putting a message together. It is also one of the most important.

"Before You Go On"

You should be able to answer the following question:

What are the four elements of effective beginnings of a message and what functions do they serve?

Skills for Relating Ideas through Transitions

Transitions are bridges that connect ideas. Transitions help receivers understand the relationships of ideas in your message. Transitions are necessary when moving from one idea to the next. Transitions accomplish three things:

1. They signal one idea is finished.
2. They provide a relationship to the next idea.
3. They preview the upcoming idea in the message.

Transitions signal that an idea is finished. This can be accomplished through a minisummary of previous information. You might say, "Now that we have discussed the safety needs of new cars"; or, "You should realize by now that we have a serious problem in communicating ideas from department to department in this company." Or, you may say, "We agree that our relationship is important and that our most frequent problem is failing to listen to each other." Each statement provides a quick review or restatement of material.

A second function of transition material is connecting previous information with new information. People like to understand how ideas relate to each other. The following statements are examples of transitions:

- The administration building is not the only building on campus that needs substantial renovation.
- The problem of insufficient parking on campus is not going to go away by itself. We must seriously consider finding a solution.
- We have spent the last hour in this group talking about our reasons for being here. Now we have to move on to discuss how to accomplish our task.

Each statement indicates the relationships between ideas. Transitions indicate to listeners why and how you plan to move on to the next idea.

Finally, transitions announce or preview the next part of a message. They may announce the next idea to be discussed or they may briefly preview the way the next idea will be developed. The following statements illustrate how to accomplish this task:

- The University Theater Department needs to be modernized, let's talk about how this will be accomplished.
- My solution to the parking problem entails both funding from state and federal governments as well as an increase in the student and faculty parking fees to fund the construction of a parking deck.
- We need to begin planning our wedding. Let's talk about where the ceremony will be and how many people we will invite.

Each statement indicates the next topic to be discussed in the overall message. In the first statement, listeners simply learn that renovation will occur, and the specifics of the renovation are presented later. In the second, others know the speaker is introducing not only a solution but also the two main parts of funding the solution. The third statement, made in an interpersonal situation, directs the next few minutes of the conversation toward planning the wedding.

Transitions are necessary between all ideas in a message. Whenever you want to shift attention from one idea to another, transitions help listeners follow your ideas and your thinking. Now, you are ready to learn the skills for ending messages.

Skills for Ending Messages

Effective endings enable you to indicate that your message is coming to an end and help reaffirm understanding. Effective endings offer a final opportunity for you to help others understand the purpose of the message and your major ideas. Weak endings leave receivers wondering if the message is complete or if additional information is to come. The ending performs some of the same functions as beginnings to messages: summarizing major ideas, relating the information to others, and providing closure.

Summarizing the Major Points

Endings include a final summary of the major ideas and information to help listeners remember them. This is your last chance to repeat your major ideas. Though the ideas have been communicated in the beginning of the message and restated during the message, repeating them one more time at the end reinforces their importance. It is not appropriate to introduce new material or to expand on ideas you may have forgotten to develop. Addition of new material at this time tends to be confusing.

Summarize ideas rather than just listing subjects from the message. For instance, "Okay—we agree about the issues of our conflict and decided how we would resolve them," merely labels categories of information and does not reinforce specifics. Rather, a summarizing statement of a conversation where conflict was resolved might be: "I think we've agreed that our conflict has been resolved. We know that we've been mad at each other because I didn't call when I was supposed to, didn't apologize for being late, and showed inattention. We agreed we can work the problem out if I remember to call you when I will be late and show appreciation for the things you do for me." Notice, in the latter summary, we have a better idea of how the conflict was resolved. A good summary focuses on ideas, not topic categories.

Relating the Message to Others

Endings should reinforce the relationship of ideas to the listeners. As with the beginning, the ending ensures that others understand how the information can be used, what actions they may take, or how they should feel. The ending to the preceding message on conflict resolution, might include an additional statement such as, "The next time we have a conflict situation, let's stop a minute and ask ourselves what caused the conflict. What can we do to resolve it quickly so we are both happy? We can't let conflicts over minor issues ruin our relationship."

The ending to a persuasive message may include statements calling for the listener to take some immediate action such as,

- Vote yes tomorrow on the income tax repeal.
- Sign here and you will receive the world's best set of encyclopedias.
- Sign up today for the intramural program and begin a season of fun with a new set of friends.

Each statement suggests specific actions or applications.

Providing Closure

People want to know when the message is over. They need to know when it is appropriate to leave the situation, to applaud (if appropriate), to ask questions, or to express their ideas. By using the same techniques to gain attention at the beginning, closure gives your message impact at the end. Asking a question, using a quotation, or citing a dramatic illustration can provide effective closure. The selection of specific techniques depends on the communication situation, participants in the situation, and the goal of communicating.

Effective closure occurs also when you refer to your opening remarks to give the impression that you have completed your ideas. If you are talking with your instructor about the importance of changing the date of a final, you may use a dramatic illustration about your roommate, John, and how difficult it was on him to take three finals in his major on the same day. In your closure, you might refer to this story by stating, "John took three exams last year on the same day because he was not willing to talk with his instructors. He failed two of them because he did not have enough time to study for each test. I don't want this to happen to myself or to other majors in our program. Moving the test to another day will make a difference. After all, final exams should measure our knowledge, not our stamina." Reference to the story about John reminds the teacher where you began and provides a sense of completeness.

Likewise, you could refer back to a startling statement used during the beginning of your message. If you made the startling statement that people who smoke a pack of cigarettes per day for ten years smoke the equivalent of four miles of cigarettes laid end to end, you might conclude with the statement, "So remember if you smoke the equivalent of four miles of cigarettes, you aren't walking a mile for a Camel, you're smoking it." Closure gives your ideas impact. Your very last statement should be memorable.

"Before You Go On"

You should be able to answer the following question:

What three things should you do when ending a message and what functions do they serve?

Once you learn the skills in this chapter, you can construct a verbal message. Your communication will have a beginning, a middle, and an end that fit together to create a coherent message. You can now construct a verbal message so that others can recognize the purpose of your message, its importance and relevance to them, and the major ideas. You are ready to prepare messages that help others maintain interest in and listen to your ideas.

In the rest of this unit, we discuss specific skills for language usage, nonverbal communication, and listening. In unit IV we discuss how to apply these skills and develop strategies for specific communication contexts.

Responses to *"Before You Go On"* Questions: A Chapter Summary

1.   What are two reasons for organizing your messages?
The primary reasons you organize messages are to help others listen and understand. Without this help, listeners may be confused as they create relationships among ideas. If you do not help them create the relationships among ideas, they may create entirely different relationships than intended. Having a good organizational pattern that is communicated clearly helps others understand relationships among ideas. Organizing your ideas for others also helps you clarify them for yourself.

Another reason to organize your communication is to create a coherent structure to the communication flow between people. Determining and accepting verbal message responsibility is critical to competent communication.

2.   What is the major difference between the direct sequential order and the reverse sequential order of organization?
In the direct sequential order, you take the various parts of a complete process or item and talk about them individually as you put them together. This helps

others see relationships among the various elements before they are put together into the whole.

In the reverse sequential order, you begin with something whole and break it down into its various parts. This helps others see the relationships between the elements as they are taken away from the whole.

3.   Why is the problem-solution sequence usually recommended for a persuasive message?

The problem-solution sequence shapes your ideas into an ordered, psychological pattern that helps others change their minds, attitudes, values, and/or behaviors. The problem-solution pattern begins by creating a problem, or need, for others; after developing a rationale for that problem or need, it shows listeners how that problem or need affects them.

The second part of this pattern is to provide a well-supported solution to the problem or need. The key is to make sure the solution satisfies the problem or meets the need specifically. The speaker spends time developing a clear rationale why this solution satisfies the problem or meets the need with information.

This pattern helps others see relationships between problems or needs and solutions. It helps them decide if the persuasive appeal is strong enough to warrant change.

4.   Which five techniques help create interest in your ideas?

The five techniques include dramatic illustrations, startling statements, quotations, questions, and humorous stories. Regardless of which technique is used in the beginning of the message, it should help listeners generate some interest in the topic.

When using one of these techniques, be sure that whatever beginning you select is relevant to the information you want to include in your message. Do not, for example, tell a joke or create a dramatic illustration that is irrelevant to the rest of your message.

5.   What are the four elements of effective beginnings of a message and what functions do they serve?

The beginning to a message includes the following elements:

1. *Gain interest in your ideas.* Help others listen to what you have to say. The five techniques described in question 4 can help you create interest in your message.
2. *Give others a reason to listen.* Create a reason for others to listen to the message. The best way is to help them see that the information has some immediate effect on them or that it will help them in some way. The more immediate the benefit to them, the more reason they have to listen.
3. *Help others believe what you are going to say.* In each communication event, give others reason to feel that what you are going to say is accurate and the truth. In other words, you have to do something that enhances your credibility and the credibility of your ideas with others.

4. *Help others mentally organize your message.* Remember, the focus of this chapter has been on helping people organize information as they receive it. In the beginning, if you tell others what you are going to tell them, it helps them organize the information that comes later in the communication situation.

6.   What three things should you do when ending a message and what functions do they serve?

When ending your message, you should (1) summarize major ideas, (2) relate the message to the listeners, and (3) provide closure.

In summarizing ideas, help others remember the major things from the message. Tell them again as you are ending your message. In trying to relate the message to others, reinforce the relationship between your listeners and the ideas you presented. Help them see this relationship when ending the message. Finally, let everyone know that you are ending your message. Help others recognize that it is their turn to ask questions, offer comments, or leave the communication situation. Don't leave them guessing.

S T U D E N T   E X E R C I S E S

1.   Developing a beginning for messages.

Using the material from this chapter, construct an effective beginning for a message to be delivered in each of the following situations:

- A meeting you called to discuss whether free literature on safe sex should be provided to college students.
- A formal presentation to the faculty in your major about your ideas for changing degree requirements.
- A chance meeting with one of your co-workers with whom you want to exchange work schedules so you can have the next holiday off.
- A situation where you want your roommate to camp out all night at the ticket window to purchase tickets to a concert by your favorite group.

Construct the beginning to each situation and identify statements that specifically fulfill each function of the beginning of a message: How are you going to create interest in your message? How do you help others to feel that your message is believable? How do you relate the topic to the people you are talking with?

Examine the beginnings you constructed. What did you do differently for each situation? Why did you select different approaches for these beginnings?

Work with a classmate and compare your approaches to each of the situations. Where did they differ? Where were they the same? Ask your classmate to explain why he approached the situation the way he did. Explain to your classmate why you approached the situations the way you did.

2.   Organizing the message.

There are many ways to organize information to help the listener see the relationships between ideas. Let's suppose you have to give a progress report to your instructor on a term paper for a class in your major. The instructor requires a personal progress report with about two weeks to go in the term.

Using each of the organizational patterns discussed in this chapter, organize your message for the instructor. Briefly describe how you would discuss your term paper using these organizational sequences: spatial, sequential (chronological), cause-effect, topical, and problem-solution. Look for the differences in approach each sequence demands in creating the message. Talk about these differences with a classmate. What conclusions can you reach about these various organizational sequences in terms of the information you need to include? In terms of the strategy you want to follow? And, in terms of the communication purpose you have?

3.   Giving humor a try.

Go to the library and take out several anthologies of jokes. Select five or six jokes you think are funny from the books.

Tell these jokes to several of your friends and record their reactions. Tell the same jokes to several members of your family and record their reactions. Look for reactions indicating if others think the jokes were funny or not.

Based on these results, select the joke or jokes you would be willing to tell the class. Make sure your instructor sets aside some class time for this assignment. Compare the reactions to the jokes from your friends and family with the reactions from your classmates. What can you conclude about the use of humor to create interest when beginning your message?

4.   Evaluating the organization of messages.

Take two different communication situations from television and one from a local town meeting and assess the organization patterns followed by the communicators.

   a. Watch a speech from C-SPAN I or C-SPAN II. Make sure you watch the entire speech. It doesn't matter who is giving the speech or what the topic of the speech is. Try to see the organizational pattern the speaker followed. What information did you use to make your determination? Was it from the beginning statements by the speaker? Did the speaker create interest in you for the message? Did the speaker create a reason for you to listen to the message? Did the speaker help you organize the information in the beginning of the speech? Was it from the statements the person made as the speech ended?

   b. Watch one of the news interview programs on Sunday such as "Meet the Press" or "Face the Nation." Examine the structure evidenced by the interviewers. What structure became the predominant one during the program? What information did you use to make this determination? Were multiple patterns evident during the program? Take a look at how the person structured responses to specific questions. Were they organized in an identifiable pattern? What pattern seemed to be most prevalent? How much did the structure of the question dictate the organization of the answer?

c. Go to a local town meeting (i.e., city council meeting, school board meeting, local PTA meeting, or town hall meeting). Get an agenda for the meeting when you arrive. See how the meeting was planned. From the information included in the agenda, determine which organizational pattern was planned. Observe the meeting in its entirety. Compare how the meeting went with how the meeting was planned. Did the organizational pattern from the agenda dictate the overall organization of the meeting? If not, how did it differ? If it differed, how did the leader, or someone else, get the meeting back on track?

Compare your observations with the observations of some of your classmates. Which organizational patterns dominated in particular communication situations? Spend some time discussing why speakers use certain organizational patterns more frequently than others.

G L O S S A R Y

cause-effect sequence The organizational sequence that helps others see relationships between current events and future consequences or past events and current situations.

dramatic illustration A statement that arouses the emotions of others. It may be hypothetical or real. Real illustrations should be used when possible; hypothetical illustrations are acceptable to make a point important to your message.

organization Establishing relationships between ideas in messages to help others understand.

problem-solution sequence The organizational sequence that identifies a problem, or need, readily understandable by others and then suggests a relationship with a reasonable solution to the problem or satisfaction for the need. This pattern is most commonly used in persuasive messages.

responsive question A question that expects a verbal and/or nonverbal response from others. It generates interest in the beginning of a message.

rhetorical question A question that speakers expect others to answer to themselves. It generates interest in the beginning of a message.

sequential or chronological order The organizational sequence that demonstrates relationships between ideas or events in a time sequence, or a chronology. It helps others see the development of ideas or events over time or helps trace events back through time to see which events or ideas led to current events or ideas.

spatial sequence The organizational sequence that creates relationships between ideas in their geographic location or space. It helps others see the geographical or spatial relationships between ideas.

topical sequence The organizational sequence that divides the major point of a message into smaller elements.

NOTES

1. Harry Sharp, Jr., and Thomas McClung. "Effects of Organization on the Speaker's Ethos," *Speech Monographs,* 33 (1966), 182–83.

2. Douglas Ehninger, Bruce W. Gronbeck, and Alan H. Monroe. *Principles of Speech Communication,* 9th Brief Ed. (Glenview, Illinois: Scott, Foresman and Company, 1984).

3. For a lengthy discussion of introductions see: Valerie A. Whitecap, "The Introduction of a Good Speech: Do Good Introductions Predict a Good Speech?" *The Basic Communication Course Annual IV* (Boston: American Press, 1992), 141–53.

4. For additional advice on the use of humor in public speaking, see Judythe A. Isserlis, "Be Relevant, Careful, and Appropriate: Scary Advice on the Use of Humor to the Novice Public Speaker," *Basic Communication Course Annual IV* (Boston: American Press, 1992), 123–40.

5. To read a lengthy discussion of how credibility relates to our ability to persuade others, see Marvin Karlins and Herbert I. Abelson, *Persuasion: How Opinions and Attitudes Are Changed,* 2d ed. (New York: Springer Publishing, 1970); and Franklyn S. Haiman, "An Experimental Study of the Effects of Ethos in Public Speaking," *Speech Monographs* 16 (1949), 190–202.

6. See Steven Booth-Butterfield, "Inhibition and Student Recall of Instructional Messages," *Communication Education* 37 (1988), 312–24.

6 CHAPTER

Skills for Verbal Communication

It used to be that "recession" was a nice way of saying "depression,"

but the hard times seem to be changing, at least when it comes to what you're

supposed to call them. Wall Street analysts think the government is now

testing kinder, gentler substitutes for what has become the dreaded

R-word. . . . Alfred Kahn, the designated inflation fighter under former

President Jimmy Carter, was so intent on avoiding the R-word that he began

referring to "recession" as "banana." (Dayton Daily News, *November 30,*

1990.)

At first, this story may seem strange. What difference does it make what we call the economic situation? How could Alfred Kahn call a recession a "banana"? Why don't people use the correct terms so we can all understand what they are saying? These questions can also be asked of every verbal message you have ever heard, spoken, or written. Why do we use the words we do? What difference does it make? What is the correct word? When you think of communicating, you often think first of how you use language to express ideas.

Language is comprised of three dimensions: First, it is symbolic, that is, language is composed of verbal symbols (words) that give meaning to our perceptions. Second, it is syntactic; language has a structure of meaningful units and agreed-on rules. Third, it is pragmatic because we use language to accomplish a purpose. We are able to communicate with others through words when everyone has similar meanings for the words, when they understand how the words relate to each other, and when they comprehend the purpose of the message. This chapter examines how people create competent communication through the symbolic, syntactic, and pragmatic use of language.

Symbolic Dimensions of Language

Symbols are vocal sounds (or letters) that people have agreed represent something. For example, people have agreed that the letters c a t, or the sounds made when vocalizing the letters, stand for a specific mammal. When you talk about your *cat,* people have a general idea of the animal you have for a pet. It sounds simple. Unfortunately, using the **symbolic dimensions of language** to create meanings is often complex and a major source of misunderstanding. The next section explains why symbols are arbitrary and ambiguous and shows how symbols can have both denotative and connotative meanings. Armed with these basics, you can identify sources of misunderstanding and work to create competent verbal communication.

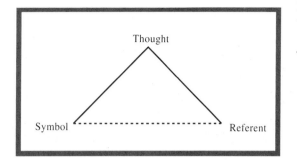

FIGURE 6.1
Triangle of meaning.

Symbols are Arbitrary

The specific symbols we use to refer to things are not connected in any way to the thing itself, that is, the symbol is not the thing. We could call a cat a *gato* (as Spanish-speaking people do), or Fluffy, or frxmus. There is nothing inherent in the animal that requires us to call it *cat*. The reason we have called it a *cat* is because we have agreed to use that symbol for it.

Figure 6.1 illustrates the relationship between the thing we wish to communicate about and the symbol we use to refer to it. The *triangle of meaning* shows that a symbol and the thing it refers to (the referent) are only connected through our thoughts.[1] There is a direct connection between our thoughts and the symbols and between our thoughts and referent. Our thoughts link the symbol to the referent. When we see the animal, we think of the symbol *cat*. When we see or hear the word *cat,* we think about the animal. However, there is no direct connection between the symbol and the animal.

Language is arbitrary because nothing inherent in the referent would cause it to be given a specific symbol. Conversely, nothing inherent in the symbol requires that it refer to a specific thing. We make up the connection between the word and the referent out of our own thoughts.

Because language is arbitrary, we can make up new words to refer to things we need to think about, or we can change the meanings of words to make them refer to something different than they did before. For example, when businesses develop a new product, they have the freedom to call it anything they want to. The developers of a disposable tissue needed a name for it and created *Kleenex*. The word never existed before; the product was called that because the advertisers decided to call it that. They arbitrarily referred to their specific brand of tissue as Kleenex to differentiate it from all other brands.

The meaning of the symbol has changed over the years as people began to use the word *Kleenex* to refer to any tissue, not just the Kleenex brand. The symbol now evokes thoughts of any tissue; when we see any facial tissue we think of the symbol *Kleenex*. Similar changes in meaning have happened for the symbols *Coke, Xerox, Pampers,* and many other everyday words. If symbols were directly tied to the referent, we could not make these changes. Only because language is arbitrary can we create any symbol we wish and change the meaning whenever we choose. As long as people share the same meanings for the symbol, they can use the symbol to share their thoughts with each other.

Because symbols are not the thing, we cannot say that a word means something. Words have no meaning. Meaning is created by people who use the words. Meanings are in people, not words. As Alice discovered in her Wonderland trip through the looking glass, words mean whatever people say they mean—nothing more, nothing less.

Words and Meanings

Humpty Dumpty said, "There's glory for you!"

"I don't know what you mean by 'glory,' " Alice said.

Humpty Dumpty smiled contemptuously, "Of course you don't—till I tell you. I meant, 'there's a nice knock-down argument for you!' "

"But 'glory' doesn't mean a 'nice knock-down argument,' " Alice objected.

"When I use a word," Humpty Dumpty said, in rather a scornful tone, "it means just what I choose it to mean—neither more nor less."

"The question is," said Alice, "whether you can make words mean so many things."

"The question is," said Humpty Dumpty, "which is be master—that's all. . . . Impenetrability! That's what I say!"

"Would you tell me, please," said Alice, "What that word means?"

"Now you talk like a reasonable child," said Humpty Dumpty. "I meant by 'impenetrability' that we've had enough of that subject, and it would be just as well if you'd mention what you mean to do next, as I suppose you don't mean to stop here all the rest of your life."

"That's a great deal to make one word mean," Alice said in a thoughtful tone.

"When I make a word do a lot of work like that," said Humpty Dumpty, "I always pay it extra."

Lewis Carroll, *The Annotated Alice* (New York: Clarkson N. Potter, 1960), 268–69.

Communication is not concerned with discovering the meaning of words, but rather the meanings people give to words. If you argue, "you can't use the word that way. That's not what the word means" you are assuming that words have meanings. It is more correct to say "that's not what I mean when I use the word."

Symbols Are Ambiguous

A word cannot refer to all of the complexities of its referent. When you talk about your car, you are thinking of and referring to a specific vehicle, but the word itself does not describe all of your car's characteristics.[2] Even if you added more words such as, "my red 1992 Dodge Shadow turbo, two-door sedan, with bucket seats and a hatchback," you haven't described all of your car. Words are not all

FIGURE 6.2
Levels of abstraction.

Inside figure:

More abstract

Animal	Vehicle
Pet	Car
Cat	Dodge
Persian cat	Dodge Shadow
Fluffy	My 1992 Dodge Shadow

More concrete

of the thing, that is, words inherently are incomplete. When we use words, we select and focus on certain attributes of the referent and ignore other attributes. The more information and detail we leave out, the more abstract we become.

Symbols refer to categories of things. Abstract words refer to large categories with many possible elements. Specific, concrete words refer to small categories with a few, or even one, member. When you use abstract symbols such as *car,* you refer to a category that potentially includes every car. If you use a symbol to refer to a smaller category, *Dodge,* you include just the cars with that brand name. If you say "my 1992 Dodge Shadow," you mean just that one car which you own, a very small category.

Let's assume you have a pet cat that you arbitrarily named Fluffy. Figure 6.2 lists several symbols you could use to refer to your cat. As we move up this list, we use words that leave out more and more specific details; that is, the symbols refer to larger categories of animals. Each word refers less directly to your specific cat and includes more and more types of animals. As less information is given about the specific animal, the more ambiguous the precise meaning of the word becomes. If you were to talk to an acquaintance about your *pet,* would the other person understand that you meant Fluffy? Or, would he think you were referring to a dog or a goldfish or a parrot?

Language is ambiguous; this becomes even more pronounced when we use words such as *freedom, justice,* or *love.* If you say "I love you," to someone, does that person know which kind of love you mean? Does the person recognize the specific feelings you have, the specific way in which you define the relationship, the specific kinds of behaviors you expect or want? Chances are, the ambiguity of the language will require much discussion before you reach an agreement on the specific meaning of the word *love.*

Symbols Have Two Dimensions of Meaning

Verbal symbols acquire meaning from the people who use them. To create competent communication, people must share similar meanings for the symbols they use. Meanings occur when people connect a symbol with a referent through their thought processes. Just as people's thought processes are never identical, their meanings for words are never identical. As we discussed in chapter 1, communication is personal. We have different experiences, memories, selves, emotions, perceptions of situations, and ways of thinking that influence how we interpret verbal messages.

Personal, **connotative meanings** cannot be truly shared because no one can know precisely what is inside our heads. The words *home* and *father* have different meanings for you than they do for anyone else. You can talk about your perceptions and feelings about your father and your home as much as you want, but no one will be able to have the same connotative or emotional meaning for these words as you.

The symbol father *has special connotative meanings.*

Denotative meanings for symbols allow people to communicate with each other. Denotative meanings are the shared definitions of words, that is, the socially agreed-on referents for symbols. When you use a standard dictionary, you find definitions that society has agreed on as meanings for symbols. In *Black's Law Dictionary,* you discover what members of the legal profession have agreed that words mean. Dictionaries of slang and colloquialisms contain words used by smaller geographic, ethnic, and cultural social groups. Dictionaries are examples of formalized collections of denotative meanings.

Denotative meanings are not only in a dictionary. As few as two people can create an agreed-on referent for a symbol. For instance, in a small private school in Nebraska, six students on the competitive debate team decided to refer to teacher's pets as "hushies" because they were always saying, "Hush, here comes the teacher." The term was not in any dictionary and no one outside this group knew what the term meant, but it had a precise and socially agreed-on denotative meaning for these students. We have also created denotative meanings for several terms in this text. For example, you now have a denotative meaning for the symbol *transactional communication,* even though you cannot find it in a dictionary. As long as we agree on the denotative meaning for the word, we can use the word to communicate.

Sometimes communication focuses on one dimension of meaning more than the other. In some cases, the focus is on the emotional or connotative meaning. When former President Ronald Reagan changed the term for a nuclear weapon from *MX Missile* to *The Peacekeeper,* he was trying to change the way people responded emotionally to the term. Both *MX Missile* and *Peacekeeper* had the same denotative meanings—it was, after all, the same missile—but *Peacekeeper* was intended to arouse more positive emotions. Similarly, government officials referred to the *Vietnam Conflict* while protesters called it the *Vietnam War.* The term *conflict* had different legal denotative meanings and different connotative meanings than *war.* The people detained in Iraq during the 1990 Persian Gulf Crisis—or was it the Iraq War?—were *hostages* according to the American government, but termed *guests* by the Iraqi government. Some people coined a new term and called them *guestages.* Each term referred to the same people, but had different legal denotations and widely different connotative meanings. Once people negotiate and agree on denotative meanings, they can communicate ideas at the denotative level. We can also use denotative meanings to provide some insight into our private connotative meanings. Denotative and connotative meanings occur simultaneously with all verbal communication. Competent communication is created when people use verbal symbols that evoke similar denotative and connotative meanings.

"Before You Go On"

You should be able to answer the following question:

What impact do the symbolic dimensions of language have on communication?

Pragmatic Dimensions of Language

Verbal language is used for specific purposes, that is, it has a pragmatic or practical function in human communication. We use language to express ideas, define relationships, define group identity, and influence the way we think. Language can fulfill several purposes simultaneously, though there may be a primary purpose intended or created. Competent communication occurs when everyone in the transaction clearly understands the **pragmatic dimensions of language.**

Language Expresses Ideas

We use language to inform, persuade, entertain, and express emotions. We use language to inform by sharing our ideas and perceptions so that others understand what we think. Sometimes we want to convince others to think or behave a certain way, so we use language to persuade. Often language creates enjoyment and pleasure, arouses specific emotions in others and ourselves, or creates interest and makes our ideas exciting. Other times, our purpose is to express how we feel about something. For example, we may want to tell others we love them or that we are angry and afraid; sometimes we just want to vent frustration through language. These different functions are often difficult to separate and often occur simultaneously. When we inform others of our ideas, we also try to persuade them they are valid ideas. We use language to make our ideas interesting and entertaining. In most situations language fulfills all of these functions as we strive to express ourselves in ways meaningful to others.

Language Defines Relationships

A second purpose of language is to define relationships. The specific words we choose express not only the content of our ideas but also imply how we perceive our relationships with others. We express liking, respect, power, status, and confidence through the language we use. For example, you probably use different words when communicating with your mother, your friends, your pastor, and your little brother. You might use slang or even profanity with your friends but not with your mother or pastor. You might order your brother to do something for you, but may ask your mother if she would mind doing it. You may use a pastor's title to show respect and status, or a nickname to show friendship and equality with your peers. You might use formal, polite, and proper language when speaking to a teacher, but informal, sarcastic language to joke around with a friend. If you called your mother Mrs. Smith and your professor Little Joey, you may be using language to define relationships inappropriately. Competent communication occurs when people use language consistent with their shared perceptions of the relationships.

Language Defines Group Identity

As we discussed earlier, a social group that uses symbols defines their denotative meanings. Similarly, when people use language that a group has defined a special way, they identify themselves as members of that group.[3] You may have a specific word at your school to refer to campus housing, the food service, or local hangouts. By using these terms, you identify yourself as a student at your specific university since people who do not attend would not know their meanings. If you know what PanHel is, you might be identifying yourself as a member of a fraternity or sorority because some people use that term to refer to their governing body, the PanHellenic Council. People outside of these social groups would probably not know the specific meaning of the terms, that is, they would not be able to identify with the group through language.

A special case of language that defines group identity is jargon. Often a shorthand referent for a longer, more complex phrase, jargon has a more specific meaning than the common word or phrase for which it substitutes. This makes communication easier and more accurate for members of the group. For example, some criticize teachers and textbooks for using jargon rather than more common, everyday words and phrases. Yet, this jargon facilitates more precise discussions of complex ideas and allows the teacher (and students who learn the jargon) to identify with other students, scholars, and professionals in the discipline.

Jargon is often specific to the purposes of a profession, a hobby, an activity, or a specialized set of experiences. Examine the lists of jargon in the following box. Notice how the language carries precise meanings for the people using the

Examples of Jargon

JARGON USED BY DENTISTS

Amalgam = filling

endo = root canal

extractions = pulling a tooth

radiograph = X-ray

crown = cap

gingiva = gums

bugs = bacteria

thirds = wisdom teeth

2 X 2's = gauze pads

occlusion = bite

rouge = polishing agent

dentifrice = toothpaste

JARGON USED BY COMPUTER OPERATORS

load = place data/program in computer memory

run = execute program

get = obtain a file from storage

home = top, left position on the computer screen

byte = a single piece of computer data

disk = media used to store bytes of information

download = move files from one system to another

ASCII = a generic computer language

drive = a device that reads information on a disk

---

symbols as they communicate about the activities and knowledge necessary to accomplish their purposes. At the same time, the jargon identifies the person with a specific group that has similar denotative meanings for the words. When people use jargon with others who do not understand the specialized meanings, it becomes difficult to create competent communication. As in all other uses of verbal communication, competence occurs only when people have shared meanings for the symbols.

Language Influences Thoughts

Can we think without language? Does the language we use shape the way we think about the world? Some researchers think that language influences our ability to perceive the world.[4] The proposition that language influences our ability to perceive and understand the world is called the *Sapir-Whorf Hypothesis*.[5] For example, Eskimos have more than twenty words referring to different types of snow. These words allow them to perceive subtle differences in the characteristics of the snow. If you are a skier, you perhaps know several terms for different types of snow that you have learned to perceive.

Similarly, you may have heard people who speak other languages describe the difficulties of translating from one language to another. They point out that some phrases just can't be translated; the meaning is based in a way of thinking that cannot be expressed in the other language. Although these examples are of language differences among societies and cultures, even in everyday conversations we tend to use language to influence the way people think. Understanding is more than just determining the meanings of words. It also involves understanding how the words shape perceptions and ways of thinking about the world.

One way in which we try to control thinking by controlling symbols is to make decisions concerning socially acceptable language.[6] Some words are taboo in specific groups and societies, that is, we do not use them because they reflect unacceptable ideas. For example, some groups may make taboo certain words for sexual intercourse, normal bodily functions, religious figures, body parts, or death. Interestingly, these same ideas can be referred to with socially acceptable substitute words called **euphemisms.** We can refer to genitals, making love, and gluteus maximus. We can say dog gone, darn, gol darn, gee whiz. Euphemisms allow us to express taboo ideas without using **taboo words.** The specific words and phrases that are taboo (as well as the accepted euphemisms) vary from group to group and also change over time. Social groups use euphemisms to control the way people think by controlling the way they express ideas.

A second way we influence thought by controlling language is through the meaning of symbols. There has been a widespread effort by many groups to de-sex our language. People promoting the use of gender-neutral words argue that using masculine referents for people or occupations in general, causes people to think of men and exclude women.[7] For instance, chair*man* suggests that we think of men in leadership positions rather than women. Similarly, fireman, policeman, and mailman create the thought that people in these roles are necessarily men. By using chairperson, fire fighter, police officer, and mail carrier, our language de-emphasizes the gender role stereotype and we think differently about the occupations and roles.

Similarly, language related to the metric system is difficult for many Americans to adopt as standard usage because it is difficult to think in metric terms. Does an immediate and meaningful picture come to mind if you hear someone described as 173 centimeters tall and weighing 66 kilograms? Are they tall? Heavy? How long would it take you to drive 805 kilometers? Would you have an immediate picture if the same descriptions were given in more usual symbols of five feet, eight inches tall and weighing 145 pounds? Would you know how long it would take you to drive 500 miles? Thinking is influenced by the language we use. One reason that you learn jargon in your classes is that you begin to perceive the world differently when you have a specific vocabulary to guide your perceptions. Competent communication is based on the realization that the words a person uses affect the way in which he or she thinks.

The functions of verbal communication operate at both the conscious and unconscious level. We are sometimes highly aware of the language we use, other times we use whatever words come to mind without thinking about their impact. For example, in the classroom situation, you might call a professor Dr. Jones without much thought because it seems natural to do so. After you graduate, you may consciously decide that your relationship has changed and you should call Dr. Jones by her first name. Sometimes we use slang without thinking that it might be taboo, or that it may inappropriately define the relationship. In a formal situation, such as a job interview, however, we may consciously avoid slang and use proper language. Competent communication depends on the ability of both people to use language that is mutually understood and acceptable.

"Before You Go On"

You should be able to answer the following question:

What are the four pragmatic dimensions of language?

Syntactic Dimensions of Language

The way words relate to each other also governs the meanings people give to language. The syntax of a language involves the rules by which words are structured into meaningful units. When you group words into phrases, sentences, paragraphs, speeches, or other units of writing and speaking, you are trying to tell the other person how you want the words to relate to each other. You are trying to give the other person hints as to the meanings of the symbols by providing a context and structure to your ideas. **Syntactic dimensions of language** are based on socially agreed-on rules related to grammar.

Grammatical rules relate to the manner in which words are strung together to form phrases, sentences, paragraphs, or other meaningful units of thought. When you hear or read a sentence, you don't interpret the meaning of each word individually but, rather, in the context of all the other words in the message. For example, you would not interpret the individual words *I, hit, home, run* individually but rather as the entire sentence "I hit a home run." You might understand the sentence to mean that the person scored during a baseball or softball game. You might get a different meaning, however, if the person did not follow agreed-on rules for describing a baseball game and said "a hit, home I run," even though it means virtually the same thing. We are often unaware of the syntactic rules, unless they are violated.

When you communicate with a person from a different culture, a different social group, or a different background, you may be unaware of the specific syntactic rules that the other person understands. For example, a three-year-old child was confused by a violation of rules. She was watching her father play a game of backgammon with a friend and she asked her father "Is that your game?" He replied, "No, it's my game." After repeating the question several times, and receiving the same reply, she gave up in exasperation. When her father gave a contradictory answer, he had not followed the rules that she expected. Without knowing the rule that contradictory answers can be given for humor, without knowing rules that would allow her to change the question, she was stymied in her quest for a simple and meaningful answer.

Verbal symbols are expressed in oral and written form. When we write, we are consciously aware of syntax. We strive to use correct sentence structure, appropriate phrasing, and correct grammar to aid the reader in determining our meaning. We are often less careful about syntax when we communicate orally. Conversations often violate the rules of correct grammar required in written language, and yet people understand each other. Competent communication does not mean that everyone must always use precise and formally correct syntax. However, people are confused by statements that violate the communication rules they understand and expect to be followed. Competent communication requires that the communicators agree on the rules by which ideas are formulated into meaningful units.

What are syntactic rules of language that communicators use when creating competent communication?

The symbolic, pragmatic, and syntactic dimensions of language occur in all communication. Problems with any dimension of language inhibit competent communication. By understanding the nature of symbols and meaning, by recognizing the various functions of verbal messages, and by realizing the rules by which messages are constructed and stated, you should be able to identify and overcome communication problems. Learning specific verbal skills is essential to creating shared meaning with others.

The following section explains specific skills you can practice and incorporate into your communication repertoire to help overcome problems in verbally expressing your ideas. Even though these skills are primarily oriented toward actions you can take, that is, an action approach, remember that their ultimate use is to cooperatively create shared meanings with others.

Verbal Communication Skills

Understanding the symbolic, syntactic, and pragmatic characteristics of language provides guidelines for learning **verbal communication** skills. You can help others understand your messages by using language that is concrete, vivid, immediate, concise, and appropriate. These skills apply to all contexts; they are equally important in interpersonal, group, interview, and public speaking situations.

Making Language Concrete

As we discussed, language is inherently ambiguous and incomplete. Abstract and ambiguous language is not in itself detrimental to competent communication. Sometimes you want to be abstract, leave out details, and use words that can have several meanings. You may respond to a friend's greeting of "How's it going?" with "It's going good." if you don't want to give details about your physical or emotional well-being. Politicians, lawyers, public relations spokespeople, and union representatives may need to be vague to avoid disclosing details inappropriately. Other times, both people may already know the specific referent and the **abstract language** suffices. For example, if you meet some friends coming out of a movie theater you could ask "How was the show?" and be fairly certain your friends would know you meant the specific movie they just saw. As long as both people recognize the ambiguity, realize its purpose, and understand referents for the symbols, communication proceeds without problems.

Other times, especially when there seems to be actual or potential misunderstanding, you may wish to use more specific or **concrete language.** If you wanted to talk to a friend about how well you did on an exam, you might want to be more specific than "I'm okay," in response to your friend's greeting, "How's it going?" Saying "I just got an *A* on the communication midterm exam," gives your friend specific details about how it is going. Similarly, if you meet your friends on campus and ask them about the "show," they may think you mean a play, or a TV show, or a concert. You might need to be more concrete and ask about the movie they saw by saying "Did you enjoy Rambo IV last night?"

The more abstract the language, the more ambiguous the meaning, and the more likely people are to give the words different denotative meanings than you intend. Concreteness refers to the skill by which we use symbols to refer to small categories with only a few elements. Two ways of making your language concrete are indexing and dating.

Use Indexing

Assume you put all of the letters you ever received in a filing cabinet. You might have a big file labeled Letters, with smaller files labeled letters from friends, letters from family, letters from school, and so on. The file labeled letters from family might contain even smaller files labeled letters from parents, letters from siblings, and letters from aunts and uncles. You might divide the files still further with a file for each specific family member and a file for each specific letter from each specific family member. If you wanted to find a specific letter from your Aunt Mabel in the filing cabinet, you could try to pull out the big thick file labeled letters and try to sort through hundreds of letters to find the one from Aunt Mabel. Or you could sort through the letters from family file, or you could find the file labeled letters from Aunt Mabel. The more specifically you label the files, and the fewer letters in the file, the easier it is to find the specific letter you want.

Similarly, symbols help us categorize things. **Indexing** is the skill of referring to a specific element within a large symbolic category.[8] For example, rather than saying, "I work for a large corporation." (a large category), you could say, "I work for IBM." (a smaller category). You could index your language even more by referring to a specific IBM location, "I work at IBM in Minneapolis." Indexing helps people understand the specific referent you have in mind.

Indexing helps us find specific information in our mental file cabinets.

Use Dating

You can also be concrete by **dating** your language. Most ideas and referents for symbols exist in a specific time frame. People, places, things, and ideas change over time. It is often helpful to say when something happened to help people create an appropriate meaning for the symbol you are using. For example, "The Oakland A's are the best team in baseball." is abstract. To which Oakland A's team are you referring? The 1989 team that won the World Series? The 1990 team that lost the series in four straight? The team that played yesterday? You could index your statement by saying "The Oakland A's team that won the 1989 World Series played better that week than any other team this decade." This would be more concrete and help the other person understand your frame of reference.

Use indexing and dating together to make language more specific and reduce the chances for people misunderstanding your message. Doing so provides the other person with additional information about your ideas, provide a context in which to interpret your symbols, and help her understand what you mean. Others are trying to cooperate with you to share your meanings; you have to help them by making your verbal communication clear.

"Before You Go On"

You should be able to answer the following question:

Why do we use the skills of dating and indexing to make language more concrete?

Making Language Vivid

When people hear the same phrases repeatedly, or listen to the same words describing many different things, they tend to be bored with the verbal description. Vivid language is defined as brilliant, bright, and colorful language that creates a clear and distinctive image. **Vivid language** tends to have more impact than dull, clichéd, ordinary language.

You probably remember people who could tell a story in such a way that you could almost imagine being there. Or, people who could arouse your emotions so strongly you felt like you would burst. Or, people who were just fun to listen to because they said things in unusual and picturesque ways. When you use vivid language you help the other person become interested in your message, help them stay attentive and involved in the interaction, and help them understand your perceptions more clearly. Three ways to make your language vivid are to use description, active voice, and figures of speech.

Use Description

Adjectives and adverbs help us to describe events, things, and ideas with more imagery than simple nouns and verbs by themselves. Consider the following two statements:

- We are in financial trouble on this important project. We must change our production method to incorporate more computer technology.

- This vital project is quickly dying from outdated machinery and antiquated production methods that are bleeding our financial reserves. If we are to avoid financial disaster, we must have an immediate transfusion of innovative computer technology.

The second statement uses **description.** It creates more vivid imagery through the use of adjectives such as vital, outdated, antiquated, immediate, and innovative. They bring a more vivid picture to mind and help the message create more impact.

Use Active Voice

People are more interested when they hear about people, animals, or things doing something rather than when they hear about something happening to them. When you talk about someone or something performing an action, you are using **active voice.** When the subject of a sentence is being acted on, you are using **passive voice.** Consider the following statements:

- I was given a new car by my parents. (passive)
- My parents gave me a new car. (active)

Both sentences describe the same scene. Do these statements give different images of the actions? In the first sentence, the speaker is being acted on by his parents and passively receives the car. In the second statement, the parents are actively giving the speaker the car. Active voice creates a more interesting sense of action and more vivid images than does passive voice.

Create Figures of Speech

Figures of speech are ways to make language more interesting by creating unexpected, unusual, or novel symbolic images. *Metaphors and similes* make comparisons between symbols. For example, "New York: The Big Apple," "My car is a lemon," "You're a turkey," are metaphors comparing the symbol of a city, a car, and a person to that of a sweet fruit, a sour fruit, and a stupid animal. "You're as tough as Rocky Balboa," "The new supervisor is like a big teddy bear," and "Quitting smoking is like losing your best friend," are similes making indirect comparisons between symbols. Metaphors and similes give the first symbol some or all of the characteristics of the second symbol to which it is compared. They help emphasize ideas by making them memorable and helping to create interest in the ideas being expressed.

    Personification creates vivid imagery by treating inanimate or inhuman objects as if they were people. Notice in the earlier description of the business acquiring new computers, the second statement personified the business as an ailing person needing transfusions. The statement described the business (inanimate) using symbols that would normally describe a person. When we talk of a computer thinking or animals talking or a car being obstinate, we are giving the inanimate or inhuman objects attributes of people. Personification can make your ideas more dynamic and interesting.

To increase the interest of your language and make your point with more impact, use **hyperbole,** that is, exaggerate! "You're the best Mom in the whole world," "I feel lower than a snake in a wagon rut," and "He's older than dirt," are examples of hyperbole that can enrich the image you are evoking in the other person's mind. Hyperbole is not intended to mislead or to lie to people, but to make your description more interesting.

Creating figures of speech can make your language vivid. Do not use metaphors, similes, and hyperbole that are trite and overused. To describe your prized Pete Rose rookie baseball card by saying "It's as rare as hens' teeth" is uninteresting; most people have heard this expression so frequently it has little impact. Perhaps a different simile, "It's as rare as a politician telling the truth," or a metaphor, "It's the Hope Diamond of baseball cards," or hyperbole, "It's rarer than the government cutting taxes" will be more unique and have more impact. This skill is called creating figures of speech rather than using figures of speech to emphasize the necessity for fresh, interesting language.

Some people might think that vivid language skills are necessary only in formal public speaking situations. They think if people used metaphors and personification in everyday conversations, others would laugh at them. Vivid language does not mean flowery speech or artificial eloquence. Rather, it means creating fresh and interesting images to help people communicate their denotative and connotative meanings. This is just as important in competent conversations, group discussions, and interviews, as it is in public speaking.

True, not every sentence or conversation requires vivid language, but using appropriate skills for creating vividness can increase competent communication, help both people become involved in the communication, and improve people's ability to share meanings. Deciding when to use language skills of vividness, concreteness, and description is part of the strategy for competent communication.

"Before You Go On"

You should be able to answer the following question:

Why does competent communication require vivid language?

Making Language Immediate

Immediate language is in the here and now. Rather than using symbols referring to people in general or someday, use symbols for specific people in this place, at this time. People pay more attention and become more involved in interactions that directly and immediately concern them. For example, rather than state, "Everyone knows that a college education is good to have," state, "What you learn in today's class will help you create a good impression in your job interview next week." Rather than say in a job interview, "I have skills that will be useful to your company," say, "I can help you write the job descriptions as soon as I start working in your personnel division." Avoid nonimmediate phrases such as everybody, society, someday, and in general. Rather, talk about you or we, discuss today, now, or tomorrow, and refer to people by name. By using verbal symbols referring to the other person directly and referencing the here and now, your message becomes more interesting and creates more impact.

Being Concise

Every symbol you use requires the other person to decipher its meanings. People try to follow syntactical rules and make the words they hear relate to each other. If you fill your message with unnecessary words and redundant statements, you make the listener's job much more difficult. Rather than say "What I wanted to say was that I like your new car," just say, "I like your new car." A common source of confusion occurs when you use verbal fillers throughout your message. Words such as *you know, well, like,* and *stuff like that* add nothing to the meaning of your message and get in the way of what you are trying to get the other person to understand.

Being **concise** does not necessarily mean using few words, but rather using the optimum number of words to create mutual meanings. A long statement may be the most concise way of making your idea clear to another. Being concise requires you to constantly monitor whether others are understanding your message. Be sensitive to people's nonverbal behavior that may indicate understanding (e.g., nodding the head), or boredom (e.g., looking at their watches). Such actions may indicate they understand your message and you have said enough. Repetition can be necessary if you perceive the other person did not understand you the first time. Say enough words to help the other person create the appropriate meaning for your message, but not too many words that merely bore or confuse the other person. Careful analysis of the other person's interest and knowledge about the ideas will provide clues as to how much detail is needed and how much repetition you need.

Using Appropriate Language

Appropriateness refers to the suitability of the verbal message to the people and to the situation. Knowing the rules by which people use language, as well as the purposes and functions of verbal messages, can help you adapt to the needs of the specific communication situation. Your primary focus is the effect your words have on people listening to your message. You want them to cooperate with you in creating shared meaning. If you use jargon they don't understand, words they consider taboo, or language that defines inappropriate relationships, they may be unwilling or unable to understand your message. Imagine beginning a statement to an acquaintance with "Now, now, my dear, it isn't so bad." You may offend the person with condescending language that implies a close relationship. The other person may not want to listen to the rest of your message simply because you called her *dear* which she finds inappropriate to the relationship. It is easy to use language that is familiar and meaningful to ourselves; it takes careful thought to find the words meaningful and appropriate to others.

Considering the purpose of your message and the communication context may suggest the appropriate verbal communication skills. If you are primarily interested in informing people about the facts of a specific incident, you may want to choose highly descriptive, concrete words. If you want to describe the same event for the purposes of entertaining the other person, you may want to use metaphors and figures of speech to create vividness. If you think it unnecessary for the other to know exactly how you are feeling about an unhappy event, you may want to use abstract language with low immediacy. Whatever the purpose of your communication, select language appropriate to the other person's interests, knowledge, and involvement and adapt it to the specific relationship and context.

"Before You Go On"

You should be able to answer the following question:

What is the purpose of using immediate, concise, and appropriate language?

Becoming aware of your use of language and practicing the skills of expressing your ideas is important regardless of the communication situation. We can't assume that because we know what a symbol means to us others will share that same meaning. Clear, vivid, concise, immediate, and appropriate language helps create competent communication. However, communication does not involve just verbal symbols. The next chapter discusses how people use nonverbal communication to create shared meanings.

Responses to *"Before You Go On"* Questions: A Chapter Summary

---

1.   What impact do the symbolic dimensions of language have on communication?

Symbols are inherently arbitrary and ambiguous. There is no direct connection between the symbol and its referent; only through thought can we connect the symbol with what it represents. When we categorize our perceptions into symbols, we leave out information about the referent. Symbols have both agreed-on denotative meanings and personal connotative meanings. Because people give different meanings to symbols, communicators must help each other understand their specific meanings for words.

2.   What are the four pragmatic dimensions of language?

Symbols express our ideas and emotions. We inform people about our perceptions and try to convince them our perceptions are valid. We want to involve others in communication by making our ideas interesting. Symbols also define relationships and identify our membership in groups. We assume that language influences the way we perceive things, so we try to control people's perceptions by controlling the language they use. Euphemisms influence the way people think about taboo topics.

3.   What are syntactic rules of language that communicators use when creating competent communication?

Verbal communication requires agreement on the rules by which we use language. Syntactic rules identify appropriate sequences of words, word choices, and expected responses to language. Appropriate grammar adapted to the specific communication situation helps people make sense of language. The syntactic character of language is most obvious when the rules are intentionally or unintentionally violated.

4.   Why do we use the skills of dating and indexing to make language more concrete?

We improve communication competence through skills that help create mutually shared meanings for verbal messages. When we make language concrete, we attempt to make it less ambiguous through dating and indexing. Indexing narrows the category of referents to which the symbol refers. Dating states a context for interpreting the symbol by indicating when the referent occurred.

5.   Why does competent communication require vivid language?

Language becomes more interesting and clear when we use description, active voice, and figures of speech to help others understand our meanings for symbols. Vivid language involves sensory images and gives impact to ideas to increase people's attention and involvement in the communication.

6.   What is the purpose of using immediate, concise, and appropriate language?

Making language immediate to the here and now and being concise increases the probability that others have similar meanings for the symbols we use. Language appropriate to the communication situation, the syntactic rules, and the functions of the communication enhances competence. People become more involved in the communication when it pertains directly to them and when it will be of immediate benefit.

STUDENT EXERCISES

1.   Coining new words.
Find several advertisements that have created new words for products or use new words to describe their products. Why did the advertisers choose these specific symbols? Explain the specific denotative and connotative dimensions of these new words.

2.   Taboo words and euphemisms.
There are many topics that people feel uncomfortable discussing or that have negative associations. For each of the following topics, write a list of taboo words that you could not use in polite or formal contexts. Then, write a list of euphemisms you could use instead of the taboo words. You may think of additional topics. Compare your lists with a classmate's lists.

Death   Sex   Drunk   Handicaps   Bathroom

3.   Making language concrete.
Identify the ambiguous words in each sentence. Use indexing and dating to re-write each of the following sentences to make them more concrete:

      a. The band was great!
      b. I love you a lot.
      c. Democrats can turn this country around.

4.   Making language vivid.
Clichés do not excite the senses or stimulate thinking. For each of the following sentences, create a new metaphor, simile, personification, or hyperbole to make the meaning of the statement vivid. For example, sentence *a* could be written, "It's as useless as a referee at a professional wrestling match."

      a. It is useless.
      b. I have a great car.
      c. I don't feel well.

5.   Making language immediate.
Immediate language refers to the communicators in the present situation, recent experience, or immediate future. Imagine you are saying each of these statements to a specific friend. Rewrite each of the following statements to make it more immediate.

      a. Everyone should have a good education.
      b. A proper diet is important if you want to perform at your best.
      c. They say the friends you make at college will last your entire life.

GLOSSARY

abstract language Words that can have many meanings because they refer to large categories with many elements.

active voice Making language vivid by making the objects, people, or animals perform an action.

appropriateness A skill for choosing and using language that fits the people and the occasion.

concise language A skill using the optimum number of relevant words to express an idea.

concrete language A skill that uses symbols referring to small categories with few elements; accomplished through indexing and dating.

connotative meaning Personal, idiosyncratic, and emotional meanings for symbols.

dating Creating concrete language by telling when something happened and providing a context for the symbol.

denotative meaning The socially agreed-on referent for a symbol.

description A verbal skill that uses adjectives and adverbs to provide details and create vivid images.

euphemism A socially accepted symbol used as an alternative to taboo words.

hyperbole Exaggeration used to make language more vivid.

immediate language Language that refers to the here-and-now.

indexing A method for creating concrete language by specifying the specific element in the category referred to by a symbol.

language is ambiguous Symbols leave out information about the referent; the word is not all of the thing.

language is arbitrary There is no direct connection between the symbol and the referent; the word is not the thing.

passive voice Language in which the person, animal, or object is acted on by something else.

personification A vividness skill in which inanimate referents are given human characteristics.

pragmatic dimension of language The reasons people use language.

symbolic dimensions of language The meanings people give to symbols.

syntactic dimension of language The rules governing the structure of language.

taboo words A method for controlling thoughts by specifying symbols that are socially unacceptable.

verbal communication The use of written and oral symbols (words) to express ideas and perceptions.

vivid language Brilliant, bright, and colorful language that creates clear and distinctive images in people's minds.

NOTES

1. C. K. Ogden and I. A. Richards, *The Meaning of Meaning,* 3d ed. rev. (New York: Harcourt, Brace, Jovanavich, 1959).

2. John C. Condon, Jr., *Semantics and Communication* (New York: McMillan Co., 1985).

3. Joyce O. Hertzler, *The Sociology of Language* (New York: Random House, 1965).

4. For a discussion and good examples of the relationship between language and perception, see: Condon, *Semantics;* Kenneth Burke, *A Rhetoric of Motives* (Berkeley: University of California Press, 1969); Neil Postman, *Language and Reality* (New York: Holt, Rinehart and Winston, 1967); and Paul Watzlawick, *How Real Is Real? Confusion, Disinformation, Communication* (New York: Vintage Books, 1976).

5. Two good summaries of the work of Edward Sapir and Benjamin Whorf can be found in: John B. Carroll, ed., *Language, Thought and Reality: Selected Writings of Benjamin Lee Whorf* (New York: John Wiley & Sons, 1956); Harry Hoijer, *Language in Culture* (Chicago: University of Chicago Press, 1954).

6. Hertzler, *The Sociology of Language.*

7. For discussions of gender differences in communication, see: Barbara W. Eakins and R. Gene Eakins, *Sex Differences in Human Communication* (Boston: Houghton Mifflin, 1978); Laurie P. Arliss, *Gender Communication* (Englewood Cliffs, N.J.: Prentice Hall, 1990).

8. Skills for being concrete are discussed in: Condon, *Semantics*; Gerard Egan, *You and Me: The Skills of Communicating and Relating to Others* (Monterey, Calif.: Brooks/Cole Publishing Company, 1977).

Skills for Nonverbal Communication

• *I don't believe you. Look me in the eye and say that.*

• *He must like me, he always sits next to me at lunch.*

• *I hate shaking hands; mine are always cold and clammy.*

• *Did you see what she was wearing? What a geek!*

• *You're late again. Don't you care about our date?*

If you've ever heard or said statements like these, you have realized the importance of nonverbal communication in daily communication. Humans use more than just verbal symbols to communicate with each other. Nonverbal communication typically provides more information in a communication situation than what is actually said by the participants. This chapter discusses the nature of nonverbal communication, the types of nonverbal behaviors, and the functions of nonverbal communication.

The Nature of Nonverbal Communication

Nonverbal communication is defined as all nonlanguage aspects of communication behavior. Except for the words you speak, every behavior you use to communicate falls in this category. Nonverbal communication includes body movement, use of space, vocal rate and pitch, eye contact, touching, the use of time, and physical appearance.

Interest in nonverbal communication is by no means new. Research in nonverbal communication has been traced back at least as far as the ancient Greeks. Aristotle, for example, was interested in the information about audience members provided to a speaker by their facial expressions. In 1577, Peacham published *The Garden of Eloquence,* which was concerned with speech delivery. This book was one of the forerunners of the elocutionary movement that advocated the proper use of the body to add meaning to a speech. Charles Darwin made the first scientific investigation of nonverbal behavior in 1872. Darwin focused on facial expressions and their potential effects.[1] In the past forty years, interest in nonverbal communication has increased dramatically. The next sections describe why the study of nonverbal communication is important.

Contributes Significant Meanings

The verbal message is not the only source of meaning in communication. Research has indicated that people typically derive 65 to 93 percent of the meaning they receive in a communication situation from nonverbal behaviors.[2] Most likely, the exact amount of meaning attributed to nonverbal communication depends on the nature of the specific communication situation. In an intellectual or logical discussion, more meaning may be attributed to the verbal communication. On the other hand, if the nature of the conversation concerns emotional messages or is related to relationships or impression formation, more meaning may be taken from the nonverbal. Regardless of the exact percentage, nonverbal communication is a primary source of meaning in people's messages.

Helps Us Evaluate Others

Nonverbal communication provides information people use to make judgments about others. In a large juvenile court system, for example, juvenile defendants received reduced sentences when they looked sorry. Defendants' nonverbal facial expressions, posture, and tone of voice have a significant impact on judges' evaluations and consequent treatment of them.

A person's use of space also gives us some information about him. A person using a lot of space appears aggressive and self-centered. Don't you feel a little irritated when you go to a crowded library to study and one person's books and papers cover a table that should seat four or five students? You evaluate that person by how he uses space.

Is Continuous Communication

Unlike verbal communication that starts and stops, nonverbal communication is continuous. One characteristic of transactional communication is that you cannot not communicate.[3] When you stop speaking, others cannot continue to give meaning to your words. However, you cannot stop behaving. People are able and likely to attribute meaning to anything you are doing or not doing. Not waving at someone on campus can send a message just as clearly as waving. Other people can always attribute meaning to your nonverbal behavior, even if you don't intend to send a message. For this reason, nonverbal communication is continuous.

In many interactions, nonverbal behaviors are the first messages people perceive. Before you say anything, other participants in the communication situation have already attributed meaning to your appearance, posture, promptness, the way you use your space, or other nonverbal behaviors. Thus, nonverbal communication makes your first impression.

Expresses Messages Difficult to Communicate Verbally

Nonverbal communication is important in the definition and development of relationships. Many people have difficulty verbally expressing emotions. Words often seem misleading or inadequate to describe the complexities of emotions or the details of the relationship. At other times, verbal expressions may not be appropriate to the situation or may be embarrassing to the participants. Because emotions are expressed nonverbally, people can sometimes understand the nature of their relationship without ever having to discuss it. The way that they relate to each other through touch, space, eye contact, and other nonverbal behavior says more about their relationship than words.

Is Learned

Nonverbal communication can be conscious or unconscious. Nonverbal communication is often unconscious, that is, we don't seem to think about or plan our nonverbal behaviors. When you are angry with someone, it usually shows on your face. That expression is not carefully planned and structured; it happens spontaneously.

This is not to say, however, that people are born with a repertoire of natural nonverbal behaviors. Much nonverbal behavior is learned rather than innate or instinctive. We have practiced nonverbal communication behaviors and learned their meaning through our interactions with others. Unlike the formal training we receive in reading, writing, and speaking verbal language, we learn nonverbal communication informally. Because we already have nonverbal communication abilities, we can improve these communication skills.

We also consciously use nonverbal behavior to communicate a message. You can nod your head in agreement, purposefully turn your back on someone, open your arms in a warm hug to greet a friend, and carry out a variety of non-spontaneous behaviors. For example, you could wave to a person knocking on your door to come in. You made the gesture consciously and on purpose to signal that person to enter the room. As you executed your planned nonverbal behaviors, you probably were not aware of all the other behaviors you were doing. For instance, did you consciously regulate the amount of space between you and the other person? Were you aware of your facial expression? What messages were your clothes communicating? We selectively attend to some nonverbal behaviors by planning to do some of them at exact times and in specific ways. More often we are not conscious of the number and variety of messages we constantly communicate nonverbally.

Awareness of nonverbal communication is vital to creating competent communication. We constantly communicate messages about our relationships and emotions. We consciously manipulate our nonverbal behavior to create desired messages, and unconsciously communicate many nonverbal messages. Understanding the types of nonverbal communication described next provides insights into the ways we communicate nonverbally.

"Before You Go On"

You should be able to answer the following question:

Why is nonverbal communication an essential element of competent communication?

Types of Nonverbal Communication

By examining various kinds of nonverbal behavior, you begin to understand its use in formal and informal communication situations. Although we discuss each type of nonverbal behavior separately, all nonverbal behaviors are interdependent. They interact with each other and the verbal message to create competent communication.

Eye Contact

Establishing eye contact with others is important for competent communication. Don't you feel uncomfortable when you are talking with people who don't look at you? Do you trust them? Do their messages seem important to you? Do you look at others when you talk to them? If not, you could make them feel strange or make them reluctant to trust you. Being aware of the uses of eye contact can help you avoid such situations. Eye contact serves several functions in communication. Among other things, it opens a channel of communication, shows concern, receives feedback, and reduces anxiety.

Opens a Channel of Communication

You signal that you wish to communicate with people by looking at them. By catching their eye you tell them that you recognize them and want to communicate. Even a brief instant of eye contact opens the channel of communication and makes other messages possible. For example, on seeing someone coming down the hall that you don't want to talk to, you usually look at the floor or the ceiling to close off the channel. When you accidentally make eye contact with a stranger on the street, you may speak or smile or in some way communicate mutual recognition. Eye contact signals a mutual desire to share messages.

Shows Concern

Look into the eyes of others in conversation to demonstrate a concern for them as well as a concern for their understanding of what you are saying. Eye contact also shows that you are sincere and confident in yourself and your message. Avoiding eye contact can signal that you are insecure and not committed to your idea. Looking into the faces of others not only enhances your credibility but also increases your chances for competent communication.

Receives Feedback

To obtain information about others in a conversation, just look into their eyes. If they share the meaning that you intend, they continue to look at you, eyes wide open, as if waiting for more. When others don't understand, they attempt to hide this by diverting their gaze. For example, when giving a public speech, if instead of looking at your audience you look at your notes, over people's heads, at the back wall, or down at the floor, you are passing up a wealth of essential feedback from your audience.

Reduces Anxiety

Look others in the face to actually reduce your anxiety when communicating. When you are anxious, look at the other participants who smile or nod their heads in support. You can do the same for others when they need your support. For example, if in an interview situation with another person you look only at your notes, you could be raising the anxiety levels for both of you. Your lack of eye contact removes the opportunity to get or give supportive feedback. When they notice your anxiety, others usually want to help you. One way to let them help you is to look at them and allow them to give you support through eye contact.[4]

Use eye contact to create competent communication by following three guidelines:

1. *Be direct.* Make sure you look others right in the eye to establish a visual bond with them. You not only have to look at others, they have to perceive that you are looking at them. Glancing at them, looking at them indirectly, or just looking in their vicinity may confuse them; they may wonder whether you truly want to communicate.
2. *Be frequent.* Look at others often. Don't believe that looking at another just once suffices for the entire conversation. Your responsibility is to help others cooperate in the communication event. The consistent diversion of your gaze from those with whom you are communicating creates a barrier to that cooperation.

3.   *Be inclusive.* When communicating with more than one person, look at everyone. It is easy to look at only those listeners who appear interested, who are supportive, or whom you know. However, to communicate with more than one person, you must look at more than one person. You can't cooperate to achieve competence with people whom you're nonverbally excluding.

"Before You Go On"

You should be able to answer the following question:

What is the significance of eye contact in communication?

Kinesics

Ray Birdwhistle coined the term *kinesics;* he was interested in the study of body gestures and movement in communication.[5] Kinesics is defined as the nonverbal communication of the body. As such, the popular press often refers to kinesics as body language. **Kinesics** includes gestures, body movements, and facial expressions.

Gestures

Moving one's arms and hands during communication is natural. Pointing a finger, clenching a fist, describing the size or shape of something, and emphasizing ideas are natural—usually unconscious—behaviors while we speak. Most people find it uncomfortable not to move their arms and hands to support and enrich the meaning of their verbal messages.

Gestures can also distract from the meaning of the verbal communication. Waving hands continually with no purpose or apparent meaning, repeating the same gesture continuously, gluing one's arms to the sides, placing hands permanently in pockets, or always crossing the arms over the chest tend to be distracting.

To create meaningful gestures, use your arms in the most natural way that you can, as a genuine spontaneous response to the ideas you are communicating. Sometimes, you may plan your gestures to illustrate a point or provide emphasis. Guard against overplanning your gestures, so that you do not appear mechanical and uninvolved. Overrehearsed gestures also become a distraction when others begin to pay too much attention to them. If you use too many gestures, they begin to lack meaning. Use gestures to support your message, not to distract from understanding.

Body Movements

Body movement and posture influence the impression that we make on others. For example, you are conducting a job interview and the applicant is slouched in a chair with legs crossed and arms folded. Do you conclude that this person is eager and motivated? Hardly! Another example: An account manager sits on the edge of a table while making a formal presentation at a staff meeting. Is this manager communicating the proper impression to the audience?

Others may interpret posture as a source of information about the self. They may assume your posture reflects your psychological or physiological state. For example, people who hang their heads all the time or do not stand erect could easily be thought to have low self-esteem, to be tired, or uninterested in communicating. Recall that you often make judgments about others based on their nonverbal behavior.

Some popular books, such as *Body Language,* have suggested that the position of the arms and legs sends a definite message.[6] For example, crossed legs and arms indicate that a person does not wish to communicate. A more open position of the arms and legs means that a person wishes to interact. Even though people do attribute meaning to the position of the arms and legs, no general interpretation applies to all people. Note that no movement, by itself, has a precise meaning that can be universally applied to people. Just as we all use symbols in unique ways, each person's body language can evoke different meanings.

Being aware of what your body is doing is important because it has the potential of saying so much about you. Monitor your behavior to some extent and make necessary adjustments without directing too much of your attention to your body language. Otherwise, it draws your focus from the communication itself and becomes a distraction. If you are focused and involved in the communication, your body language should be a natural response.

Facial Expressions

As perhaps your most expressive nonverbal behavior, facial expressions are most commonly credited with communicating emotions.[7] Make some attempt to be aware of what your face is saying to others. Many people are surprised when they view themselves on videotape because they have little idea of how they look. They are especially surprised by their facial expressions.

We do not believe, however, that you should try to control your facial expressions at all times. Such control may be useful when you are playing cards and do not wish to tip your hand (as with the proverbial poker face), but it is not always useful in other communication situations. In fact, if others discover that you are controlling your expression by using too much emotion or by hiding your feelings, they might suspect that you are trying to somehow manipulate them. As you read in chapter 3, if this happens, your attempt at control becomes a distraction for all participants: While you are concentrating on control, the others are becoming defensive, wondering what you're up to.

Monitor your expressions for extreme behaviors or specific expressions that you don't wish to display. Beyond that, allow your face to spontaneously display the emotions you feel.

Use gestures, body movements, and facial expressions to demonstrate sincerity and enthusiasm for your message. You can also use them to accomplish specific purposes:

1. *To Give Emphasis.* As already suggested, you can use nonverbal gestures to emphasize your ideas. You can strategically use gestures, movements, and facial expressions to add meaning and significance to your verbal messages.
2. *To Illustrate or Describe.* You can use kinesics to illustrate size, shape, distance, and motion. For example, when describing a piece of machinery to the service manager, use your hands to illustrate size or shape. Nonverbal behaviors make verbal statements more vivid and descriptive.
3. *To Indicate Emotion.* Kinesics is especially useful for communicating emotion. Even without raising your voice, you can express anger, for example, by tensing your body, pounding your fist, and scowling. Gestures, posture, and facial expression clearly indicate your emotions.

Competent communication seems spontaneous and natural when using kinesics to communicate. However, do not preclude practicing gestures, movement, and posture to improve their use during your communication. After all, nonverbal communication is learned so you can improve the clarity and impact of your nonverbal communication through practice. The key is to make the gestures, body movement, and posture that you plan and practice seem to be spontaneous.

Voice

The use of voice, or paralinguistics, is defined as the use of vocal cues. That is, how you use your voice to accompany the words you speak. How you use your voice communicates information about you and your intended meanings to other participants. The voice has five major characteristics: rate, volume, pitch, articulation and pronunciation, and vocal pauses.

Rate

Rate is the speed with which you say words. Most people's rate is between 140 and 170 words per minute. Talking too slowly bores other participants and boredom encourages their minds to wander. On the other hand, talking too quickly makes others work too hard. Rapid-fire conversation is difficult to listen to and others very easily tune out. Attempt to reach a comfortable speed for yourself and for your listeners.

Rate also communicates emotion or gives emphasis to ideas. For example, a fast rate indicates excitement or anxiety. A slow rate emphasizes an idea by slowing down to call attention to each spoken word.

Volume

Volume is how loudly you talk. Your **volume** level must be appropriate to the specific communication situation. Yelling loudly at a baseball game is appropriate; speaking loudly while at the theater is not. Whispering softly during a private conversation is appropriate; whispering softly during a public speech is not. Consider the situation and the message that you wish to convey, then choose a volume level that seems appropriate. Make sure that all the participants for whom the message is intended can hear you. Don't stick to the same volume level, however. A varied level of volume helps your listeners maintain interest.

Pitch

The pitch of the voice, its relative highness or lowness, communicates and enhances the meaning of verbal messages. A low, deep voice communicates differently than a high-pitched voice. Make an effort to use some variety in the **pitch** of your voice because a repetitive pitch pattern or a single pitch or monotone can be boring. Conversely, avoid using too much variety in pitch as this creates a singsong effect that distracts others. Too much or too little variety creates a distraction; moderate variety creates interest.

As with other nonverbal behaviors, others perceive your meaning and make inferences about the self based partly on the pitch of your voice. A low pitch is more authoritative, while a high squeaky pitch sounds uncertain. Use a low pitch with a slower rate to emphasize an idea or a higher pitch with a more rapid rate to communicate emotional involvement with the message. Use pitch to help emphasize ideas.

Articulation and Pronunciation

In addition to the rate, pitch, and volume of the voice, articulation and pronunciation help give meaning to your verbal message. **Pronunciation** is stating the word with the proper sounds, emphasis, and sequence. Mispronunciations violate one, two, or all three of these elements. If you are unsure of how to pronounce a word, avoid using it until you are able to look it up in the dictionary or can ask others how to use it. Never put yourself in the situation of the person who gave a speech on dominoes, yet continually pronounced the word *donimoes*. Another example is a person who was trying to convince some friends to go to the *cimena* (cinema). Mispronouncing the names of other people is especially embarrassing. Such mispronunciations become a source of distraction for people in the communication situation.

Articulation consists of forming vowel and consonant sounds correctly. Many people are lazy when it comes to articulating the sounds used to communicate. They may slur *s*'s or misstate the *ph* sound. Listed in the following box are some commonly mispronounced words. How many of these do you mispronounce?

> AKS instead of ask
> PIN instead of pen
> DEM instead of them
> DIS instead of this
> NUTTIN instead of nothing
> GITTIN instead of getting
> CAUSE instead of because
> AN instead of and
> WIF instead of with
> KIN instead of can
> PITCHER instead of picture

To help others more easily understand you, be sensitive to your own problems with articulation and pronunciation. Then, strive for clarity, accuracy, and precision.

Vocal Pauses

Another aspect of the voice is the use of vocalized pauses in conversation. Do you use *uhm, you know, well,* or *like* in your communication? These words and sounds often indicate someone stalling for time, trying to think of something to say. Vocal pauses indicate someone trying to fill a given period of time with sound. In a conversation, for example, when one finishes speaking, others may assume that they can take the next speaking turn. The first speaker who doesn't want to give up a turn might use a vocalized pause to keep others from talking, even if he had nothing to say at that moment. Another example is related to public speaking situations. A student has eight minutes to summarize the reasons why the university should add more student parking spaces. She feels the strong need to fill those 480 seconds with sound, so when she has nothing coherent to say, she fills the void with a series of vocalized pauses. Perhaps she doesn't even notice them, but vocalized pauses distract others.

Most vocalized pauses are habitual and serve little purpose in competent communication. By being aware of your speech habits, you can avoid using vocal pauses. Don't think you are required to fill every moment with sound. There is no harm in silence. In fact, you can use silence to create a dramatic effect.

Paralinguistic cues such as vocal pauses, rate, pitch, volume, and articulation and pronunciation all constitute a significant part of the spoken message. Meaning is very often attributed to a message based not so much on what is said but how it is said. An awareness of these cues can go a long way toward communicators helping each other understand the intended meanings of messages.

Can you identify ways in which your voice could be a source of distraction in communication?

Proxemics

Anthropologist Edward T. Hall introduced the study of **proxemics;** he was interested in how people use space in communication.[8] Hall suggested that people unconsciously structure the space around them and that people use space to communicate. Hall divided the study of space into three major areas: fixed-feature space, semifixed-feature space, and informal space.

Fixed-feature Space

Fixed-feature space includes immovable areas that people claim as their territory. **Fixed-feature spaces** are defined by fixed walls, partitions, and doors. The way people design or choose houses, for example, might say something about the kind of people they are. Office sizes indicate status in an organization. The degree to which the fixed territory is defended against intruders also defines a person's power, status, and availability for communication. A corporate president usually has the largest office on the top floor and is protected by several secretaries. Access to the territory is by the president's discretion. On the other hand, a professor who has a door open to the hallway may signal a willingness to communicate with students.

Semifixed-feature Space

Semifixed-feature space involves the use of movable objects such as furniture. The arrangement of furniture either encourages or discourages conversation. Look at the differences in arrangement in the study areas and the social areas of your library. The study rooms have chairs that face a work area; and often they have small dividers between them. This arrangement discourages communication so students can study undisturbed. The social rooms, on the other hand, have couches and chairs that face each other so that the people using them may communicate more easily. Also, people move furniture around to create and define the boundaries and limits of their territory.

*Semifixed feature space
can encourage or
discourage communication.*

Design or choose an environment conducive to your specific communication purpose and context. For example, a circular seating arrangement is usually more conducive to open group communication than a long rectangular table. An interview in which a large desk separates people is more formal than when the people sit next to each other in comfortable chairs.

Informal Space

Informal space is defined as the physical distance between people. Each of us has a territory that travels around with us that we claim as our own. Informal space is a "bubble" that surrounds us into which no others may enter without your permission. Usually, intimate friends can be physically close to you, but strangers must stay farther away.

When someone enters your space without permission, you may view it as a violation of rules or as a discourtesy or even as a threat. At times you let unauthorized people temporarily invade your bubble, such as on a crowded elevator or in a busy hallway. However, you feel uncomfortable in these situations and expect the space invader to move away as soon as possible. Generally, the more intimate and friendly you are with other people, the closer you let them stand to you.

Different cultures have various rules about the use of personal space. Americans, for example, have somewhat larger bubbles surrounding them than many other cultures. In contrast, people from many Arab nations have smaller bubbles and stand very close to one another when communicating. Imagine what happens when Americans and Arabs talk to each other. The Arab would wish to stand close, which the American could easily view as an invasion of space and maybe think that the Arab is being pushy. On the other hand, the American continues to back away from the Arab, which could be interpreted as a signal to go away, even when the American meant no such thing.

Hall identified the average distances that people in the general American culture maintain while communicating with others.[9] As you will see, the distance depends on the relationship between the communicators. The first category is *intimate distance* with a range of zero to eighteen inches. People permitted within this distance include spouses and family members, boyfriends and girlfriends, and close friends. The second category is *personal distance,* ranging from eighteen inches to four feet. This describes the distance at which you would probably communicate with reasonably good friends and people you know fairly well. The third category, *social distance* (four to twelve feet), is the distance at which you might communicate with business associates or people with whom you have a more formal, but less social relationship. The final category, *public distance* (beyond twelve feet), describes the distance at which you would communicate with somebody that you don't know. If you spoke to a stranger on the street, you would normally feel most comfortable at the public distance.

How you use space communicates messages about your relationship to others. It can define the amount of liking, familiarity, power, and trust you have with another. If you stand too close while communicating, you might be regarded as a threat and the other person becomes defensive. On the other hand, if you stand too far away, you might be perceived as distant and unwilling to communicate. Space is a variable in all face-to-face transactional communication. It always exists and thus we are constantly perceiving relationship messages. In communication be aware and sensitive to other participants' feelings about the use of space. If you are, you should be able to cooperate with each other and negotiate the distances between all of you and the configuration of the space to find a situation satisfactory to all.

"Before You Go On"

You should be able to answer the following question:

Why is proxemic behavior significant to nonverbal communication?

Touch

Your use of touch sends messages to others about the kind of relationship that you think you have with them. Touching is generally an indication or expression of closeness or interpersonal involvement.[10] Notice that touch occurs only within the personal or intimate distances of informal space. It can range from a casual handshake or pat on the back to hugs and more intimate touching between romantic partners. You would feel uncomfortable touching or being touched by someone you don't know or that you don't like. On the other hand, it would be hard to imagine never touching your best friend or your romantic partner. Touching is most often a spontaneous behavior, but it can be used purposefully to send relational messages to others.

Time

Americans are preoccupied with **time.** We treat it as a commodity: we use it, save it, and spend it just as if it were money. Because time is so important, how you use it can send messages to others. For example, if you have an 11:00 A.M. appointment with someone and you don't arrive until 11:30, what are you saying to that person? Many would interpret your tardiness as a lack of responsibility or respect. It could say that you think you are too important to be on time for her or that you are not interested in communicating with her. Punctuality, however, would likely be interpreted as an indication of your responsibility, trustworthiness, and interest.

How much time you spend with others can send messages about your relationship with them. You spend more time with someone you like than someone you don't like. Spending time with people may communicate liking.

Appearance

First impressions are often made on appearance cues. Body size and shape, skin color, style and color of clothes, jewelry and accessories, and hairstyle all contribute to the messages we send through our appearances. If people see someone six feet, five inches tall, with an athletic body, and wearing a jogging suit, they may stereotype him as a basketball player. When someone wears an expensive watch, imported shoes, and a custom-tailored pinstripe suit, people may perceive that she is successful in a high-status career. Uniforms and insignia also indicate identity with specific groups.

People spend billions of dollars a year to make sure their complexion is perfect, their hair is the right color, and that they wear the latest fashions. Books such as John Malloy's *Dress for Success* abound with advice on ways to make appearance create a good impression.[11] Expressions such as "dressed to kill," "power suit," and "It's better to look good than to feel good," emphasize people's concern over the messages they send about personality, roles, status, and group memberships.

All of the seven types of nonverbal communication operate interdependently to create shared meaning. Many times the different behaviors occur simultaneously. Although we can selectively perceive them and discuss them separately, we cannot easily separate their effects on our communication competence. Often we are not aware of the messages; other times, we consciously manipulate our behavior for specific functions.

"Before You Go On"

You should be able to answer the following question:

What are some of the uses of nonverbal communication?

Functions of Nonverbal Communication

As with other elements of the communication process, we may view nonverbal communication from the action, reaction, and transaction perspectives. The action perspective addresses ways in which we use nonverbal communication to send a message to another or to add meaning to something expressed verbally. The reaction perspective focuses on ways to use others' nonverbal communication as feedback to better understand their reactions. The transaction perspective combines both the action and reaction perspectives and addresses its use by all participants in a communication situation. The transaction view considers how people use nonverbal behaviors to help each other understand what is happening. It assumes that people must work together to create and share meaning nonverbally. It is through this cooperative effort that we achieve communication competence.

Being familiar with the functions of nonverbal communication increases your ability to understand the nonverbal "language" in a communication situation. As we discuss next, nonverbal communication can communicate emotions, define relationships, reinforce verbal communication, substitute for or replace verbal communication, contradict verbal communication, or regulate an interaction.

Communicates Emotions

You've heard the saying, "A picture is worth a thousand words." One picture or visual image often communicates more than words can describe. The same is true with nonverbal communication. While your emotions might be hard to describe verbally, your nonverbal communication can make your feelings quite clear to others. For example, a smile says a great deal about the way you are feeling. Or, you can sound angry or frustrated. Or, your body can appear to be tense. Although they are expressed fairly clearly through nonverbal communication, these feelings would be much more difficult to represent verbally.

Defines Relationships

When you look at someone and say, "I love you," the information used by the other person to interpret the relationship between you most likely comes not as much from what you said but the way you said it. Saying "I love you" with a warm, pleasant tone of voice and with a smile implies a different relationship than saying it with a straight face and a cold, businesslike tone of voice. How you say something nonverbally often suggests more about your meaning for the relationship than what you say.

Nonverbal behaviors also communicate your feelings about the relationship and about others. If you like them, you smile at them, stand close to them, look at them more, or even touch them. If you don't like them, you maintain a greater distance from them, lean away from them, do not look at them, and do not touch them. All these behaviors provide information to others about the relationship you think you have or would like to have with them.

Reinforces Verbal Communication

Nonverbal behaviors support or agree with the verbal message. For example, when people nod their heads while saying yes, or when they shake their heads while saying no, the verbal and nonverbal messages convey the same meaning. Another example would be saying, "Get out!" while pointing at the door. In each case, the nonverbal message reinforces the verbal message.

If you want others to believe something that you say, the verbal message must be accompanied by appropriate nonverbal behaviors such as a steady voice and a sincere facial expression. These consistent behaviors tell others that you are telling the truth. Or, others can tell you are really excited about something because your verbal message says "I'm excited," as does your grin, wide eyes, loud voice, and jumping up and down.

May Substitute for Verbal Communication

In some situations, the nonverbal message replaces a specific verbal message. For instance, someone enters your room and, saying nothing, you point to a chair. You sent the message, "Sit down," using only a nonverbal gesture. Another illustration: You finally get enough courage to ask that special person to the big dance on campus. As a response to your verbal question, the other person smiles broadly and nods. You understand from just the facial expression and the head nod that the answer is yes.

We also substitute gestures for specific words and phrases; such gestures mean okay, peace, we're number one, or good luck. Thus, taboo gestures substitute for taboo language. When nonverbal gestures substitute for specific verbal symbols, they serve the same functions as language does.

May Contradict Verbal Communication

Nonverbal behavior can send a message contradicting the verbal message. Sarcasm is communicated through the use of a verbal statement and an accompanying nonverbal statement that contradicts the surface or literal meaning of the words. For example, a teacher says "I'm really looking forward to my high school reunion." While he says this, however, he rolls his eyes and shakes his head. His nonverbal behaviors suggest to others that he really is not looking forward to his high school reunion.

At other times, we use inadvertent or unintentional contradiction to send messages that confuse the other person. For example, you enter your friend's room to ask if he wants to go to a movie. Slouched in a chair with his eyes nearly closed, he is surrounded by books and papers piled up as if he had been studying all day. You ask, "Are you too tired to go to the movies?" He responds, "Heck no, I'm not tired. I'm raring to go!" But, your friend doesn't leave his chair. You receive contradictory messages as a response to your request: The verbal message says he wants to go out, but the nonverbal message says that he does not.

When the verbal and nonverbal messages seemingly contradict, people experience a paradox called the **double bind.** They are unsure which message is intended, which meaning they are supposed to perceive, and how to react. People believe nonverbal messages over verbal messages when the two messages are in conflict. They assume that people can manipulate the verbal language but are not aware of (or cannot control) their nonverbal behavior. Even though this is not always the case, people assume the nonverbal message is more genuine, less manipulated, and more accurate. This becomes especially important in trying to determine if someone is deceiving you. For example, you may force a smile when your favorite aunt gives you a set of moose antlers for your birthday. It's not something that you ever wanted, but you say what a wonderful gift it is anyway. That forced smile might be an obvious signal to your aunt that you are not being honest with her. She assumes that your nonverbal smile is a more valid indication of your true feelings than your verbal statement.

Coordinates or Regulates the Flow of Communication

Nonverbal communication can control and coordinate the flow of communication through the use of a **regulator**.[12] If, for example, you are having a conversation with someone who is talking too fast, you are using a regulator when you hold up your hand as if to say slow down.

Nonverbal communication also indicates whose turn it is in a conversation.[13] Nonverbal signals can indicate that you would like to (1) have a speaking turn; (2) give up your speaking turn; (3) keep speaking and not give up your turn; or (4) refuse to take a turn.

Request a Turn

Think of times that you have been involved in a conversation and would like to speak, but somebody else is speaking. How do you get to talk without rudely interrupting the person verbally? In the classroom you might raise your hand and wait to be called on by the teacher. In conversation, you might lean forward and rapidly nod your head to indicate that you want to talk. You could also establish eye contact with the current speaker or you could clear your throat. All these behaviors could show the person whose turn it is that you would like to speak.

Give Up a Turn

If you are the current speaker, you can use nonverbal signals to yield your turn to another participant in the conversation. For example, after you complete your thought, you could sit back in your chair and break eye contact with the others. This signal leaves the floor open and allows anyone to take a turn. You could also establish eye contact with someone after asking a question to indicate the person should respond.

Maintain a Turn

The signal to maintain a turn indicates that you wish to continue speaking when others have requested a turn. A common signal is simply to not acknowledge the request for a turn. Ignoring people is impolite, however, so you could acknowledge the request for a turn with a hand gesture that nonverbally asks them to wait, then continue speaking until you are finished, then use a turn yielding signal. You could also begin to speak more loudly and more quickly to indicate that you do not wish to give up your turn.

Refuse a Turn

Remember being called on in class when you weren't prepared? You used signals indicating you didn't want a speaking turn. You looked down at your notes or at the professor and shook your head. Avoiding eye contact or turning your body away from the other person suggests you want to close the communication channel, that you don't want to communicate.

The perspective of this book is transactional. From this point of view, participants use nonverbal communication to help each other share meanings about their relationships and emotions and the meaning of their verbal messages. For example, if you are speaking too quickly, others in the situation might not be able to follow what you are saying. For all participants to achieve competence together, you should be aware of your own behavior (speaking too fast) and be sensitive to the nonverbal regulators that the others are sending indicating that you should slow down. Perhaps the most important function of nonverbal communication is, therefore, to provide additional messages through which communicators can cooperate to achieve competence.

"Before You Go On"

You should be able to answer the following question:

What role does nonverbal communication play in the creation of meaning?

1.   Why is nonverbal communication an essential element of competent communication?

When communicating transactionally, we constantly and simultaneously perceive each other's nonverbal behaviors because we cannot not behave. Nonverbal behaviors provide a variety of meanings and perform several important functions in communication. Whether they accompany the verbal message or are used alone, awareness of the impact of nonverbal behaviors is necessary for communication competence. Nonverbal communication provides a significant proportion of the meanings in communication. It often expresses ideas and emotions that are difficult to express verbally, and it helps us evaluate others. Nonverbal behaviors are not just innate, inherent reflexes; effective nonverbal communication can be learned.

2.   What is the significance of eye contact in communication?

Eye contact is very significant because it can fulfill so many purposes. Eye contact can establish a conversation or avoid one. Eye contact can display your concern for another person without speaking a single word. Also, it can be very useful for asking for or obtaining feedback from others. Finally, eye contact can reduce anxiety and make you feel more at ease while communicating.

3.   Can you identify ways in which your voice could be a source of distraction in communication?

Your voice can be a source of distraction in many ways. If you speak too quickly or too slowly, the rate draws attention to itself and away from the message. Also, speaking too loudly or softly, or at a constant level can distract. Using an extremely high or low pitch or vocalized pauses also distracts listeners. You want your listeners to pay attention to your message, not your voice.

4.   Why is proxemic behavior significant to nonverbal communication?

Proxemics, or the way we use space, communicates a great deal about us. We use space and objects in the space to send messages about ourselves. We can establish power and create impressions, or establish, define, and maintain relationships. We use fixed-feature space to indicate status or our openness to communication. We use semifixed-feature space to encourage or discourage communication. For example, one can arrange the furniture in a room to encourage other people to drop in. Finally, we can use informal space to define and maintain relationships. By allowing another person to be physically close, we send a nonverbal message of friendship or intimacy.

5.   What are some of the uses of nonverbal communication?

We open and control channels of communication through our direct, frequent, and inclusive eye contact. Proxemics communicates power and relationships through fixed, semifixed, and informal uses of space. People also share meanings of their relationship and emotions through touch. Stereotypes, first impressions, and judgments about people's personalities, interests, and status are often made on the basis of appearance. Natural and spontaneous gestures, movement, and posture communicate interest in the communication and can emphasize and illustrate the verbal message. The way we pronounce and articulate words, and the pitch, volume, rate, and use of vocal pauses helps others interpret the meaning we give to verbal language. How much time we spend with people and our punctuality demonstrates our interest and liking for another person.

6.   What role does nonverbal communication play in the creation of meaning?

The seven types of nonverbal behavior interdependently, and often simultaneously, create the meaning people share in communication. Expressing emotions, defining relationships, and regulating the flow of communication are functions of nonverbal communication. Nonverbal also works with verbal communication by reinforcing, contradicting, or substituting for the verbal message.

S T U D E N T   E X E R C I S E S

---

1.   Design of space.

Visit five places on campus and sketch the design of the rooms and the arrangement of the furniture. What is each room or space designed to do? What sort of message does the space send to you?

2.   Communicating with nonverbal behavior.

Discuss how you might use proxemics, touch, time, or appearance in the following situations:

> *a.* On a date.
> *b.* In your house or dorm room.
> *c.* In your car.
> *d.* In class.
> *e.* At a restaurant.

3.   Specific nonverbal messages.

Discuss how you would use space, touch, time, and appearance to communicate the following:

> *a.* To show affection.
> *b.* To lie to someone.
> *c.* To show status.
> *d.* To show interest.
> *e.* To show attraction.

4.   Time.

In a class group, discuss how you use time. How do you expect others to use it? How does others' use of time affect you? Why?

5.   Functions of nonverbal communication.
What nonverbal behavior could you use to express the following ideas or emotions?

> *a.* We're number 1.
> *b.* Okay.
> *c.* Anger.
> *d.* Time out.
> *e.* Slow down.
> *f.* Victory.
> *g.* Peace.

GLOSSARY

articulation   Forming the vowel and consonant sounds of words correctly.

double bind   Occurs when a verbal and nonverbal message conflict.

fixed-feature space   Territory defined by fixed walls, partitions, or doors.

informal space   Physical distance between people.

kinesics   Study of body movement and gestures in communication.

nonverbal communication   All nonlanguage aspects of communication behavior.

pitch   The relative highness or lowness of the voice.

pronunciation   Speaking words with proper sounds, emphasis, and sequence.

proxemics   Use of space.

rate   The speed at which you say words.

regulator   Nonverbal behavior used to control the flow of communication.

semifixed-feature space   Territory defined by movable objects such as furniture.

time   Category of nonverbal behavior that includes duration and punctuality.

volume   How loudly you speak.

NOTES

1.   See Lane Cooper, *The Rhetoric of Aristotle* (New York: Appleton-Century-Crofts, 1960); Charles Darwin, *The Expressions of Emotions in Man and Animals* (London: Murray, 1872). See also M. Mead, "Review of Darwin and Facial Expression," *Journal of Communication* 25, 209–13.

2.   See Ray Birdwhistle, "Background to Kinesics," *ETC* 13 (1955), 10–18; and A. Mehrabian and S. Ferris, "Inference of Attitudes from Nonverbal Communication in Two Channels," *Journal of Consulting Psychology* 31 (1967), 248–52.

3. Paul Watzlawick, J. Beavin, and D. Jackson, *Pragmatics of Human Communication* (New York: Norton, 1967). See also M. Motley, "On Whether One Can(not) Not Communicate: An Examination Via Traditional Communication Postulates," *Western Journal of Speech Communication* 54 (1990), 1–20.

4. M. Argyle and M. Cook, *Gaze and Mutual Gaze* (Cambridge: Cambridge University Press, 1976).

5. Ray Birdwhistle, *Introduction to Kinesics: An Annotation System for Analysis of Body Motion and Gesture* (Washington, D.C.: Foreign Service Institute, Department of State, 1952). See also Ray Birdwhistle, *Kinesics and Context* (Philadelphia: University of Pennsylvania Press, 1970).

6. Julius Fast, *Body Language* (New York: Evans, 1970).

7. P. Ekman and W. Friesen, *Unmasking the Face* (Englewood Cliffs, N.J.: Prentice Hall, 1975). See also David Matsumoto, "Cultural Influences on Facial Expressions of Emotion," *Southern Communication Journal* 56 (1991), 128–37; M. Motley and C. Camden, "Facial Expression of Emotion: A Comparison of Posed Expressions versus Spontaneous Expressions in an Interpersonal Communication Setting," *Western Journal of Speech Communication* 52 (1988), 1–22; and C. Izard, *The Face of Emotion* (New York: Appleton-Century-Crofts, 1971).

8. Edward Hall, *The Silent Language* (Garden City, N.J.: Doubleday, 1959); and Edward Hall, "A System for the Notation of Proxemic Behavior," *American Anthropologist* 65 (1963), 1003–26.

9. Hall, *The Silent Language* and "A System for the Notation."

10. R. Heslin and T. Alper, "Touch: A Bonding Gesture," in *Nonverbal Interaction,* eds. John Weimann and R. Harrison (Beverly Hills, Calif.: Sage, 1983), 47–75.

11. John Malloy, *Dress for Success* (New York: Warner Books, 1975); and John Malloy, *The Woman's Dress for Success Book* (Chicago: Follett, 1977).

12. P. Ekman, "Movements and Precise Meanings," *Journal of Communication* 26 (1976), 14–26.

13. See John Weimann and Mark Knapp, "Turn Taking and Conversations," *Journal of Communication* 25 (1975), 75–92; H. Sacks, E. Schegloff, and G. Jefferson, "A Simplest Systematics for the Organization of Turn Taking for Conversations," *Language* 50 (1974), 696–735.

8 CHAPTER

Skills for Listening

- *You never listen to a word I say. It just goes in one ear and out the other.*

- *I just told you that. Weren't you listening?*

- *I wish you would turn off the TV when I'm talking to you so that I know you're listening.*

- *I'm sorry. Can you repeat that? I wasn't listening.*

- *He always listens to what I have to say. It makes me feel like he cares what I think.*

We spend most of our waking moments listening, yet we are frequently inept in understanding and remembering what others say. Listening is an essential skill in any communication situation. The first step in improving your listening skills is to understand the nature of listening and the barriers you have to overcome to listen effectively.

Barriers to Effective Listening

Listening is not easy. People are generally poor listeners. Research studies show that people only listen at approximately 25 percent efficiency.[1] One study of students listening to a lecture found that only 45 percent of them were paying attention to the lecture at any one time.[2] Other studies indicate that people remember only about 50 percent of what they hear immediately after listening to a message and a mere 25 percent of the message after two days. People listen even less effectively in informal conversations, remembering only 10 to 33 percent of what they discussed.[3] These findings are disturbing because people spend 40 to 50 percent of their waking moments listening.[4] Several barriers to effective listening hinder our ability to understand and remember messages. Communicators must cooperate to overcome these barriers.

Mind Speed Is Faster than Listening Speed

Most people talk at an average of 140 to 170 words per minute. If you carefully attend to each word spoken, your **listening speed** would be approximately the same rate. Human minds, however, are capable of processing information at rates of 400 to 600 words per minute. Thus, your **mind speed** is faster than your listening speed.[5]

Unfortunately, this extra mental capacity frequently interferes with your concentration on the other person's message. As you listen, you take mental side trips to the past to reminisce or to the future to anticipate an upcoming event. You think about how you are feeling, about food, about your relationships with people, about problems you have, about good things that are happening to you, and about a myriad of topics other than what the other person is saying. The problem continues when you forget to return from these mental side trips often enough to keep up with the other person's message. The difference between mind speed and listening speed becomes a barrier to effective listening when the extra mental words cause inattention to the message.

Distractions Decrease Ability to Focus on the Message

People are easily distracted by events that occur in the communication situation. The transaction model of communication indicates that you simultaneously perceive four sources of information: the environment, the other person's behavior, your own behavior, and your private self. All of these perceptions compete for your attention. Since it is impossible to focus on all of the information at once, you selectively attend to parts of it. As attention focuses on part of the information, all of the other messages and stimuli fade into the background. For example, while you are trying to read your communication text, you may not be able to pay close attention to your roommate explaining a problem with a friend.

If you are interviewing for a job, you may be focusing on your own nervousness so much that you do not listen to the interviewer's questions. When attending the first lecture in a new class, you may be too absorbed in reading the syllabus or looking at other people in the class to listen carefully to the teacher.

Focusing your attention requires work. Because so many elements of the communication situation compete for attention, selecting and maintaining a focus on the other person's behavior requires conscious effort. Paying attention is not a passive activity; rather, it is extremely active. In an effort to achieve communication competence, part of your job is to gather relevant information through observation and analysis of the communication situation. You actively sort the elements of the situation, deciding which are to be observed and which are to be ignored. Maintaining attention is accomplished by discovering and focusing on what both people deem important and ignoring distracting or irrelevant elements of the situation.

The four categories of misinvolvement introduced in chapter 3 indicate some of the major sources of distraction that act as barriers to maintaining focus.[6] Misinvolvement includes external preoccupation, self-preoccupation, conversational preoccupation, and preoccupation with the other person. While these forms of misinvolvement are very common to all communicators, they can be controlled and overcome with practice and determination.

Perceptual Bias Interferes with Accurate Understanding

People do not listen well because they interpret messages according to their personal biases rather than to listen with open minds. As we discussed in chapter 2, **perceptual bias** limits the interpretation of messages in such a manner that the meanings are consistent with what the listener already believes or expects. Individuals tune out messages or refuse to listen to people who express attitudes, values, or beliefs incompatible with their own. People also distort the meaning of a message to make it consistent with what they already believe. For example, a supervisor was listening to a recommendation for an employee eligible for a promotion. The supervisor thought the employee was unworthy of advancement. The recommendation concluded with the statement, "Although the person does not have the college degree which is usually required for promotion, his history of outstanding work indicates we should consider waiving that requirement." The supervisor immediately replied, "I'm glad you agree that we can't promote this person because he lacks a college degree." The supervisor's biases influenced her interpretation of the message so that it was consistent with previous judgments. She ignored the positive statements and distorted the meaning of the message to make it consistent with established knowledge and beliefs. Competent communication occurs only when both people recognize their biases and interpret messages with open minds.

Closure Inhibits Listening to the Complete Message

Problems in listening are also due to the perceptual process of **closure.** As you recall, closure refers to filling in missing information. When messages are abstract or incomplete, the human mind frequently supplies its own information to complete the message. People assume they know what is going to be said and, therefore, add that information to the message whether or not it is actually stated.

For instance, Steve, a marketing manager for an international exporting company, had an appointment to interview a surgeon about a new X-ray machine his company wanted to add to its list of exports. Steve introduced himself to the receptionist, "Good morning. I'm Steve Larson, I have an appointment with Dr. Franks." Seeing his three-piece suit and attaché case, the receptionist switched on the intercom and announced, "Doctor, there's another salesperson here to see you." When Steve corrected her, she looked surprised and said, "I'm sorry, I thought you said you were the sales manager." The receptionist had perceived only a few nonverbal cues of the marketing manager's appearance and had assumed he was another salesperson since, in her experience, salespeople generally wear three-piece suits and carry attaché cases. The receptionist used closure to add information to Steve's message and erroneously thought she heard him say he was the sales manager. She assumed she knew the reason for his appointment without ever asking him. Competent communication occurs when people listen to the complete message, rather than fill in information that isn't there.

Self-Focus Impedes Effective Listening

Another factor inhibiting effective listening is a focus on the self rather than on the ideas of others. People frequently are more concerned with the messages they are sending than carefully listening to the other person. They become overly concerned with their appearance, with what they intend to say next, with formulating arguments against the other's ideas, or with evaluating their own communicative effectiveness.

One college graduate, for example, returned from an employment interview with a rather dejected expression and said, "I was so worried that my palms were sweating and that I wouldn't be able to answer the questions that I kept forgetting to listen. I had to ask the interviewer to repeat questions several times." She had become so concerned with her own nonverbal behavior (blushing, hands sweating, knees shaking, voice trembling) and her verbal message (she thought no one was interested in her ideas, she was afraid she would forget what she wanted to say, she stumbled over the pronunciation of words) that she couldn't focus on the other elements of the communication situation.

When focused on themselves, people lose the ability to maintain attention and to understand the other person's frame of reference. One common mistake among novice interviewers, for example, is to mentally rehearse the phrasing of the next question rather than listening to the interviewee's responses. While it is important to monitor personal behavior during a communication transaction, good listeners try to focus on the other person's message and minimize their concern with the self.

A frequent form of distraction is high communication apprehension. This is a fear of communicating that is most often associated with speaking in public, but it also applies to any communication situation. Apprehension is partly due to the uncertainty of communicating effectively. Although many people associate communication anxiety with the action of sending messages, it also can interfere with effective listening.[7] When your listening apprehension becomes too intense, your mental ability to understand and remember information decreases.[8] You become preoccupied with your own behavior and fail to listen to the other person. (Review chapter 4 for a more detailed discussion of communication apprehension.)

"Before You Go On"

You should be able to answer the following question:

Why is it difficult to listen effectively?

Skills for Overcoming Listening Barriers

With all of the barriers to effective listening, it seems amazing that anyone is able to listen with any degree of effectiveness or certainty. It seems even more unbelievable that most people never receive training in listening. Fortunately, practicing some techniques and skills can help you overcome these barriers to create communication competence. As in all facets of communication, listening can be approached from an action, reaction, or transaction perspective. Each approach provides a different focus and different guidelines for achieving listening competence.

From the action approach, listening is a mental process by which people process information they receive from another's verbal messages. Listening is often considered a receiver-oriented skill. However, from the action model of communication, listening is a mental skill that you perform as you process the other person's message. It requires no behavioral response or feedback to the sender of the message. This type of listening is termed **cognitive listening.**

The primary focus of cognitive listening is on the source and the source's message, rather than on the receiver's feedback. Effectiveness of cognitive listening is measured by the complete and accurate transmission of the sender's message to the receiver. Since the only communication behavior of concern is that of the sender, cognitive listening meets the assumptions of the action model. Competence from this approach would be judged on how well the speaker's message was understood and how much of the information was remembered.

From a reaction perspective, listening is the receiver's response to the message. The reaction model suggests that people take turns sending and receiving messages. The listener is concerned with communicating meaningful feedback to the source of the message. From this approach, competence would be judged on the quality of the feedback. Because listening from the reaction approach is concerned with expressing a response, we call this **expressive listening.**

In the transaction model, however, both people are sending and listening to messages simultaneously and continuously. Communication is the shared responsibility of both people so that listening is an activity that both people create through their mutual behaviors. Through communication, both people help each other understand and remember the messages. Competence in transactional listening would be determined by how well both people understood each other and how well they communicated this understanding. Thus, **transactional listening** includes both cognitive and expressive listening skills. In transactional communication, both types of listening occur simultaneously.

"Before You Go On"

You should be able to answer the following question:

How do the action, reaction, and transaction approaches to listening differ?

Cognitive Listening Skills

People use cognitive listening for two reasons, to understand and to remember information. Cognitive listening is often called *deliberative* or *critical listening.* It is deliberative since you deliberately focus your attention on the message and deliberate about its meaning. You also make critical evaluations of its accuracy and completeness. When you listen to a class lecture, receive instructions about your job, understand directions to a friend's apartment, or learn how to fix your car's brakes, you are concerned with understanding and remembering information. Your focus is primarily on the verbal message and you must listen critically to the information to determine if it is accurate and complete. Your purpose is to make it meaningful to your own frame of reference.

Prepare to Listen

An important step for increasing cognitive listening effectiveness is to prepare to listen. Preparing for communication situations by researching background information on a topic can help you understand ideas more clearly. Students who read assigned material before class are often able to understand and remember the lecture better than students who come to class unprepared. Formulating questions that you want to have answered can also help you focus and remember the information.

Concentrate on the Message

A second skill for improving critical listening is to concentrate on the message. People are easily distracted and must make a conscious effort to focus on the other's statements. Concentration means that you are involved in the communication situation rather than letting your emotions, environmental factors, or extraneous behaviors interfere with your perception of the message. Creating a supportive physical environment can help you increase your communicative involvement. If possible, remove potential distractions from the environment before trying to listen. It takes only a second to close the door, take the phone off the hook, turn off a noisy air conditioner, turn the stereo down, or close the book you're reading. Effective cognitive listening requires that you control the environment, manage your emotions and anxiety, and eliminate distractions before they interfere with reception of the message.

Keep an Open Mind

Perceptual biases reduce the chance that you correctly interpret the speaker's meanings. Awareness of personal biases that influence interpretation and perception of messages is the first step in controlling them. Although it is not possible to completely eliminate all biases, people can succeed in compensating for their influence. Refrain from mental arguments against the other's ideas and suspend judgment about the accuracy or worthiness of the ideas until you are sure that you understand them completely. To increase the possibility of listening with an open mind, try to focus on understanding and remembering what the other is saying, rather than on formulating your own point of view.

Review the Message

The skills for cognitive listening concern methods for increasing comprehension and committing information to memory. An effective cognitive listening skill is to mentally review the messages. In reviewing each message, you are constructively using the extra capacity of the mind to process information. Reviewing includes mentally repeating the main ideas of the message, restating the important facts, and repeatedly summarizing the gist of the message. In essence, the listener stops every few moments to mentally answer the question, "What did I just hear?" Taking written notes can supplement mental review of information.

To learn cognitive listening skills, you must study and practice. As with all communication skills, being prepared to listen increases the chances that the communication will be successful. Good listeners prepare by anticipating listening situations, researching background information on the topic, controlling the environment, adopting an open mind toward the message, and actively concentrating on understanding what the other person is saying.

"Before You Go On"

You should be able to answer the following question:

How can you improve your cognitive listening skills?

Expressive Listening Skills

Expressive listening is a communication skill. When you are listening as a form of communication, you demonstrate to the other person that you are listening. You tell the other person whether the message is clear. Expressive listening involves both verbal and nonverbal behavior communicating to the other person that you are involved in the interaction. You are communicating to them that you care what they are thinking and feeling and that you are willing to expend time and energy to make sure you understand them.

Expressive listening techniques are behavioral skills that help communicate understanding of the other person's emotions, ideas, and frame of reference. This type of listening is sometimes termed *empathic listening*. When you listen to a classmate complain about being overworked, a co-worker happily describing a promotion, or a friend explaining the reasons for missing a date, you are concerned with understanding their emotions, the reasons for their behavior, and the meanings they have for their perceptions. You are trying to put yourself in the other person's place and see things from their perspective, rather than your own. Expressive listening also focuses on nonverbal messages to determine emotions and perceptions of relationships.

Expressive listening differs from cognitive listening in that you are not being judgmental or evaluative. You are not trying to ascertain what the message means to you and your perspective, nor are you primarily concerned with remembering all the details of the message. Rather, your focus is on trying to communicate that you understand the other person's perceptions, emotions, and private self. Therefore, the skills for expressive listening differ somewhat from those for cognitive listening.

Use Restatement

An important step toward improving your expressive listening ability is to keep your focus on what the other person means by words and actions. Don't mistakenly assume that the meanings you give to others' messages are the same meanings they intended. Very often the meanings could be similar, but because of differences in individuals, the meanings are never identical. If you attempt to discover how the other person sees things, you will likely have less trouble creating competent communication.

One of the key skills in expressive listening is to restate the message to determine if you have understood the meaning. The goal of **restatement** is to check the degree to which both people share similar meanings. Consequently, most restatements are in the form of either a direct, or an implied question, which asks, "This is what I heard. Is that correct?" We use restatements at three levels of understanding.

The first level is **repeating the words,** that is, parroting the exact words the other said. At this level, you are asking, "These are the words I heard. Are these the words you said?" Use this skill if you think you may have misunderstood the words, the other person may have misarticulated or mumbled some words, the words you heard don't make initial sense, or you were momentarily distracted and are unsure you heard correctly.

A second level of paraphrasing is to restate the content of the message in your own words. At this level, you are **paraphrasing the content** to determine the meaning of the words you heard. Use this skill when the words could have more than one meaning and you're not sure what the other person meant. At the content level you are asking, "This is what I think you mean, is that right?" You tell them in your own words what you think they meant, and give them a chance to correct your interpretation if necessary.

The third level is **paraphrasing the intent** of the message. Here you are checking your understanding of the motivations for the message. You seem to understand the meaning of the message but are unsure why the person said it or what response they might desire from you. You paraphrase the intent by essentially saying, "This is why I think you said that; am I right?" Often, paraphrasing the intent of the message is the most difficult and most important skill for expressive listening. Understanding intent helps us regulate our interaction with others and understand the other person's frame of reference.

Consider the following example: A friend says to you, "I feel bad." Depending on the situation, you may be unsure whether you accurately perceived the message. You might restate the message in the following ways:

Repeating words:	• Do you feel *bad?*
	• You say you *feel* bad?
Paraphrasing content:	• Do you feel sick?
	• Feeling kind of sad, huh?
	• You seem down in the dumps today. Are you?

Paraphrasing intent:	• You sound like you need a friend. Do you want to talk?
	• You seem tired. Want to lie down?
	• Work is getting to be a hassle, isn't it?

Notice how the example moves from a concern with perceiving the words, to an understanding of the meaning of the words *feel* and *bad,* to an emphasis on knowing the reasons for the statement and the intentions of the person. Notice, restatement does not simply ask a question, such as "What did you say?" or "What do you mean?" or "Why did you say that?" or "What's the matter?" Restatements reflect your interpretations of the message and then try to seek confirmation that you understood correctly.

Use Probing Questions

A second technique to communicate active concern for understanding is using **probing questions.** Probing questions allow the other person to provide additional information about their feelings and perceptions. Probing questions differ from paraphrases in that they ask the person to extend on their original message rather than merely clarify statements already made. A friend who just returned from a trip to Europe may say, "Europe was great! I have never had such a good time." You might ask probing questions such as, "Did you meet any interesting people?" "What sights did you see?" "What was the most exciting thing that you did?" Each of these questions asks your friend to provide more details about the trip. In addition, you could probe into your friend's feelings about the trip: "Were you nervous about being in a strange country?" "Are you glad to be home?" "Would you like to go back again?" "Did you enjoy being on your own?" Effective use of probing questions can elicit more complete information to help increase your understanding of the other's emotions and point of view. Use of appropriate and meaningful questions also expresses an interest in, and concern for, the other person's ideas and feelings.

Demonstrate Involvement

A third technique for developing expressive listening abilities is to show involvement in the communication situation. Expressive listening is not merely an internal, mental concern for the other person, that is, it is not enough to care and want to know the other's point of view. You must be able to communicate that concern and desire to the other person. One way to communicate involvement is to show **attentiveness.** Demonstrate attentiveness through verbal and nonverbal behaviors that show you think the other person's ideas are important. To show attentiveness nonverbally, look directly at persons, face them, move closer, touch them, or lean forward. For instance, when a person comes to the boss's office to talk, the boss can show attentiveness by stopping work on other projects, shaking hands, looking at the employee, and coming from behind the desk to sit next to the person.

People who show attentiveness increase communication involvement.

Demonstrate involvement verbally through short phrases, such as *I see, Go on, I understand,* and *uh huh.* These phrases indicate that you are interested in the message, you are focused on the transaction, and you wish the person to continue communicating. These **continuation remarks** tell the other person you are involved and understand the message.

Paraphrasing, probing questions, and involvement skills not only allow communicators to ascertain the degree of mutual understanding, but they also indicate active concern about the other's point of view. These skills provide feedback to tell the other person whether you are correctly interpreting the message. If your restatement is inaccurate, the other person can rephrase the message to remove ambiguity and clarify its meaning. If you ask probing questions, the other person can assume you understand the message and desire more information.

Expressive listening skills also demonstrate your involvement in the communication situation; this usually increases interest and motivation for effective communication. The key to successful expressive listening is to focus on the other person rather than on yourself or the environment, set aside personal biases, and concentrate on the other's message.

"Before You Go On"

You should be able to answer the following question:

How can you improve your expressive listening skills?

If there are problems understanding someone's message, is it because the message is unclear or because you are not listening effectively? If you understand someone's message, is it because you are a good listener or because they encoded their ideas clearly? From a transaction perspective, listening is a cooperative effort among communicators. A well-constructed, clear message helps people listen; good listening skills make the message understandable.

People must work diligently to attain mutual understanding of their messages. They must help each other to clarify meanings of words, discover the motivations and goals of communication, and determine appropriate responses. Because transactional communication occurs in face-to-face situations, both people are continuously, and simultaneously trying to listen and be listened to, to understand and to be understood.

Therefore, transactional listening involves simultaneous use of both cognitive and expressive listening skills. Even when the primary focus may be on cognitive listening skills, both people are communicating their listening behaviors nonverbally. When the focus is on expressive listening, both people are also trying to remember and understand each other's messages. Transactional listening skills focus on integrating cognitive and expressive skills to create mutual understanding.

Adapt to the Communication Situation

As we discussed in chapters 6 and 7, meanings are not a property of words or nonverbal behavior, but are created by the people using them. Each person's connotative and denotative meanings are unique. To create competent communication, both people must adapt to the meanings that the other person is giving to verbal and nonverbal messages. Analyzing each other's cultural and experiential background, the social and physical context of the communication, and the participants' expectations provide insights into potential sources of misunderstandings. Both people need to communicate in a way that has meaning for the other person, not just for themselves.

One **adaptation** method you can use is to become aware of how you and the other person selectively perceive specific aspects of the message and related information. Discovering the other's values and experiences helps you understand their meaning. Gain other insights by getting to know the others and discovering their interests, priorities, and goals.

Equally important, realize that the other person is trying to adapt to you at the same time. Help him by giving insights into your background, personality, experiences, and attitudes. Self-disclosure helps the other person more accurately understand your meanings. Analysis and adaptation requires cooperation. Competent communication requires that both people are able and willing to adapt to each other.

Discovering another person's interests and values helps you interpret their messages.

Clarify Meanings

Competent communication requires clarity of meaning. Transactionally, both people are responsible to ensure that the messages and meanings are clear. We often assume that others understand our messages without checking to make sure that they do. Lack of shared meaning goes undetected and unnoticed until it is too late and a problem has developed. Use paraphrasing and probing questions to help the other clarify her message. Also, ask the other person to paraphrase your message, or ask if she has questions, to make sure she understands your meaning. Clarity of meaning should not be left to chance. Seeking affirmation from the other person that they are understanding is essential for competent communication.

Clarity also requires the ability to use a variety of communicative behaviors. For example, a person with an extensive vocabulary can more readily choose words that are meaningful to the other than can a person with a limited vocabulary. Using description and concrete language makes your message less ambiguous and helps the other person understand your precise meanings. Being able to organize messages in a variety of ways helps you adapt to the knowledge level of the other person. Being familiar with the impact of nonverbal behaviors, such as personal space and eye contact, can help you create a positive atmosphere and a supportive relationship in which to communicate. Developing a repertoire of behaviors increases your chances of being able to choose the most meaningful words or gestures to share clear meanings.

Create Involvement

Competent communication has impact, that is, it helps to increase involvement in the situation and helps people achieve their communication goals. Both people need to work together to help each other develop and maintain enthusiasm and motivation for effective communication. For example, students and teachers often blame each other for poor classes (or take personal credit for good ones). Teachers sometimes say "I can't do anything with these students. They just won't talk and they seem bored." The students in the same class say, "The teacher is so boring. We just can't get interested when the teacher isn't." Transactional listening means that both are equally responsible for the low involvement and impact of the communication. If the teacher was dynamic, told stories, or used humor that the students found appealing, they would tend to be more alert, attentive, and interactive. On the other hand, if the students would show interest, ask questions, and respond to the teacher more positively, the teacher might increase enthusiasm, be dynamic, try to use vivid and creative teaching techniques, and be more interesting. As the teacher becomes more interesting, the students show more interest, which makes the teacher more motivated, and so on.

As both people work toward achieving competent communication, the process feeds on itself in a positive direction. When both people expect each other to do all the work, the communication process becomes incompetent. The transactional approach to communication suggests that both people work together to create involvement. Using vivid language, dynamic gestures, direct eye contact, and relating directly to each other's interests and experiences can increase the impact and involvement of communication.

Show a Desire to Communicate

Motivation to communicate is essential for competent communication. Your willingness to expend energy, time, and resources is necessary for successful analysis, message construction, and understanding. Your knowledge of how to communicate effectively is not sufficient if you are not willing to use your skills. You also must be willing to help the other person communicate competently. Remember, communication involves showing people what your perceptions are, showing them you are involved in the interaction, and showing them that you want to understand them. Competent communication cannot be accomplished by one person; it requires mutual commitment. You can motivate others by showing them that you are motivated; this, in turn, helps you to maintain and increase your own motivation.

Desire also relates to your motivation to try new behaviors and practice to improve your communication skills. Competent communication does not just happen, it is learned through repeated practice. Success in one situation or one relationship does not mean you have arrived—you are competent. The situation is constantly changing. People are different from day to day, minute to minute. People behave differently in various situations. We have to constantly be alert to the changing requirements of our communication situations. We have to be motivated to communicate effectively. Someone once asked the great golfer Ben Hogan if he was satisfied with his golf ability. When he said no, the reporter asked him, "If you shot a birdie on every hole, would you be satisfied then?" Hogan replied, "No—I would wonder why I didn't shoot an eagle." The point is we should desire to create the best possible communication with others and to continually improve our communication skills.

The transaction approach to listening skills suggests that both people work to create understanding. (Note that the skills spell the acronym A C I D). Both people are **A**dapting to help each other to achieve **C**larity of meaning and increase **I**nvolvement with their communication because of their **D**esire to create competence. Your own communication skills are effective if they help others create effective communication. You can't listen alone, nor can you communicate a message without someone to listen. The way both people listen together determines communication competence.

"Before You Go On"

You should be able to answer the following question:

How can you improve your transactional listening skills?

Listening is part of every face-to-face communication situation. It involves interpretation of verbal and nonverbal behaviors to determine the meaning the other person is giving to messages. The other chapters in this unit discussed analysis, organization, verbal and nonverbal skills that help make meanings clear. The next unit discusses strategies that apply these skills to specific communication situations.

Responses to *"Before You Go On"* Questions: A Chapter Summary

1.   Why is it difficult to listen effectively?
We think faster than we listen. The difference between mind speed and listening speed allows us to think about things other than what the other person is saying. We are also easily distracted. It takes energy to concentrate on the other person's message. Perceptual biases interfere with understanding the other person's meanings as we interpret messages according to our own values, attitudes, and experiences. Through closure we fill in missing information. We incorrectly assume we heard the complete message or we hear information that was not actually said. Self-focus on our emotions, needs, and physical state interferes with our ability to process information. We often concentrate on what we are going to say rather than on listening to the other's message.

2.   How do the action, reaction, and transaction approaches to listening differ?

The action approach focuses on the cognitive ability to understand and remember a message. The accuracy of message transmission from source to receiver determines listening effectiveness. The reaction approach focuses on the feedback of the receiver to the source. Listening focuses on the receiver's communication of understanding, attentiveness, and empathy for the sender's message. Transactional listening involves interdependent people simultaneously sending and receiving messages. People share a responsibility to help each other listen and to help each other send messages that are clearly understood.

3.   How can you improve your cognitive listening skills?

The first step in effective cognitive listening is to adequately prepare for the communication situation. Acquiring background information on the topic and the person, anticipating communication encounters, and practicing listening skills can prepare you to listen. Second, concentrating on the message by minimizing distractions and creating supportive communication environments also improves cognitive listening. Third, keeping an open mind reduces perceptual biases that interfere with listening. Fourth, mental review and organization of the information also increases your ability to remember the message.

4.   How can you improve your expressive listening skills?

Restatement communicates your understanding of the message. Repeating the words, paraphrasing the content, and paraphrasing the intent allow you to check the accuracy with which you heard the words, understood the meanings, and comprehended the intentions of the other person. Probing questions show your understanding and interest in the other person's message by asking for additional information. Demonstrate involvement with the communication by showing attentiveness through eye contact, body orientation, touch, and space. Verbal and nonverbal messages that encourage the other person to continue the message also show involvement with the communication.

5.   How can you improve your transactional listening skills?

Transactional listening requires the cooperation of both people to create understandable and memorable messages. Adapting messages to the other person and the occasion, learning about each other through appropriate self-disclosure, and helping each other overcome listening barriers improves listening. Using language and nonverbal messages that make sense to each other, asking for feedback and restatement, and using description and concrete language helps clarify the message. Creating involvement through vivid language and dynamic nonverbal behaviors increase interest and memorability of the messages. Transactional listening also requires that both people are motivated to communicate and that they demonstrate their desire to communicate to each other.

STUDENT EXERCISES

1.   Listening problems.
Identify three specific occasions when you had difficulty listening. Perhaps it was during a class lecture, when a roommate was discussing an experience, when talking on the telephone, or in a group meeting.

   a. What were the specific listening problems? Understanding the message? Remembering what the other person said? Showing others you were listening?
   b. Try to determine the reasons for your listening difficulties, for example, interest in the message, time of day, distractions in the environment, and so on.
   c. For each problem, identify specific ways you could have overcome the listening barrier and improved the communication.

2.   Approaches to listening.
Consider the statements at the beginning of this chapter. Which approach to listening is represented by each statement? How would the action, reaction, and transaction approaches to listening explain the causes for each statement? How would each approach solve the problem?

3.   Practicing restatement skills.
Statements usually have a variety of meanings. Read the following statements and think of three different ways each could be interpreted. Practice your skills for restatement by writing three different paraphrases of content and intent for each statement.

   a. I really like my classes. They're great!
   b. Nobody likes me anymore.
   c. I can't wait to get my new car this weekend!

Write a probing question for each of the statements. How do your probing questions differ from your paraphrases?

4.   Practicing cognitive listening skills.
Videotape or audiotape a news broadcast or class lecture. Listen to the tape for five minutes without taking notes. Turn off the tape and try to write down all that you can remember. Be as detailed and specific as possible. Review the tape and check the accuracy and completeness of your information. Repeat this procedure using the cognitive listening skills suggested in the chapter.

   How much did you remember? What information did you miss or only partially remember? Why? What barriers affected your listening?

   Try it again for ten minutes. Keep repeating this exercise until you can accurately and completely remember the information you hear.

GLOSSARY

adaptation A transactional listening skill in which people create messages that have meaning for the other and interpret messages according to the other's self.

attentiveness An expressive listening skill in which the listener uses nonverbal behaviors to focus on the other person and decrease distractions.

closure An organizing process which makes perceptions meaningful by filling in missing information.

cognitive listening The mental processes of understanding and remembering another's message.

continuation remarks An expressive listening skill in which the listener shows understanding and encourages the speaker to continue.

expressive listening Communicating to others that we are understanding their messages; communicating involvement with the message.

listening speed The rate at which a person can hear words said by another, closely dependent on the rate the other person talks.

mind speed The ability of the mind to process information.

paraphrase content A restatement skill that checks whether a listener understands the meanings of the words.

paraphrase intent A restatement skill that checks whether a listener understands the reasons and intentions for stating a message.

perceptual bias Limitations on interpretation of information due to physiological, cultural, and attitudinal factors.

probing question An expressive listening skill that asks for additional information to show understanding and interest in another's message.

repeating words A restatement skill that checks whether a listener heard the words correctly.

restatement An expressive listening skill used to check the accuracy of understanding of a message.

transactional listening A combination of cognitive and expressive listening skills in which both people help each other to listen.

NOTES

1. For a summary of listening studies, see Florence Wolff, Nadine Marsnik, William Tacey, and Ralph Nichols, *Perceptive Listening* (New York: Holt, Rinehart and Winston, 1983); J. D. Weinrauch and J. R. Swanda, "Examining the Significance of Listening: An Exploratory Study of Contemporary Management," *Journal of Business Communication* 13 (1975), 25–32.

2.   Paul Cameron and Dorothy Giuntoli, "Consciousness Sampling in the College Classroom: Is Anybody Listening?" *Intellect* 101 (1972), 63–4.

3.   Several studies have investigated conversational listening abilities. See, for example, Alan L. Sillars, Judith Weisberg, Cynthia S. Burggraf, and Paul H. Zeitlow, "Communication and Understanding Revisited: Married Couples' Understanding and Recall of Conversations," *Communication Research* 17 (1990), 500–22; Laura Stafford, Cynthia S. Burggraf, and William F. Sharkey, "Conversational Memory: The Effects of Time, Recall Mode, and Memory Expectancies on Remembrances of Natural Conversation," *Human Communication Research* 14 (1987), 203–29; William J. Benoit and Pamela J. Benoit, "Memory for Conversational Behavior," *The Southern Communication Journal* 56 (1990), 24–34.

4.   Larry Barker, R. Edwards, C. Gaines, K. Gladney, and F. Holley, "An Investigation of Proportional Time Spent in Various Communication Activities by College Students," *Journal of Applied Communication Research* 8 (1980), 101–9. A good summary of the research on the frequency and importance of listening in organizations is found in Andrew D. Wolvin and Carolyn G. Coakley, "A Survey of the Status of Listening Training in Some Fortune 500 Corporations," *Communication Education* 40 (1991), 152–64.

5.   A. Wolvin and C. G. Coakley, *Listening,* 3d ed. (Dubuque, Iowa: Wm. C. Brown, 1988), 208.

6.   Erving Goffman, *Interaction Ritual* (Garden City: N.Y.: Anchor Books, 1967): 117–20.

7.   Two studies that investigated listener apprehension are L. R. Wheeless, "An Investigation of Receiver Apprehension and Social Context Dimensions of Communication Apprehension," *The Speech Teacher* 24 (1975), 258–68; Margaret Fitch-Hauser, Deborah A. Barker, and Adele Hughes, "Receiver Apprehension and Listening Comprehension: A Linear or Curvilinear Relationship?" *The Southern Communication Journal* 56 (1990), 62–71.

8.   Investigations into the role of anxiety on cognitive abilities include Ronald N. Taylor, *Behavioral Decision Making* (Glenview, Ill.: Scott, Foresman and Company, 1984), 20–2; Steven Booth-Butterfield, "Inhibition and Student Recall of Instructional Messages," *Communication Education* 37 (1988), 312–24; John Borhis and Mike Allen, "Meta-Analysis of the Relationship between Communication Apprehension and Cognitive Performance," *Communication Education* 41 (1992), 68–76.

III

U N I T

Strategies for Interpersonal and Group Contexts

Now that you have learned basic communication skills, our discussion turns to the application of those skills to specific communication situations. Although the same set of skills apply to all contexts, each specific context requires a different strategy or application of the skills. This unit examines strategies used in interpersonal and group contexts.

Perhaps the most fundamental situations involve two people communicating with each other. As such, chapter 9 is concerned with interpersonal situations that involve strategies for relationship development and conversation management. Because any interpersonal relationship involves conflict, chapter 10 examines conflict and strategies for its management.

An interview is a form of interpersonal communication; its unique structure sets it apart from other kinds of conversation. Accordingly, chapter 11 discusses strategies for interviewing.

Small groups involve interpersonal communication that is more complex because groups consist of several individuals. Consequently, the strategies for developing and maintaining group relationships, interacting cooperatively, managing group conflict, and achieving group goals are somewhat different than those for interpersonal relationships. Chapter 12 examines strategies for communicating in a group and chapter 13 is concerned with strategies for competent decision making.

In many communication situations, you are likely to encounter an individual from a culture different from your own. This could be a person from another country; from another region of your own country; or from a different ethnic, age, or social group. People from different cultures have different ways of perceiving and understanding the world. Chapter 14 discusses strategies for surmounting cultural differences so that all participants in communication can cooperate to share meaning.

9

CHAPTER

Strategies for Interpersonal Communication

• *The friends you make in college will last your whole life.*

• *I don't know why I don't like him. Just a personality clash, I guess.*

• *Trust is the most important ingredient of a happy marriage.*

• *We just knew when we met that it was love at first sight. I guess we had the right chemistry or something.*

I nterpersonal communication is probably the most frequent context of communication. It involves our one-to-one communication situations at home, at school, on the phone, or at work. Friends, acquaintances, family members, co-workers, lovers, and strangers form just a few of our interpersonal relationships. Our communication in these situations sometimes goes well, while at other times we encounter great difficulty. We are not always sure why our communication works well sometimes and fails at other times. Interpersonal communication is so frequent and common in our lives that we often take it for granted.

This chapter explains the processes and strategies for competent interpersonal communication. Interpersonal relationships are defined by the way you and another person communicate. Indeed, interpersonal communication and interpersonal relationships are virtually synonymous.[1] You can't have a relationship without communication; you can't communicate without developing a relationship. Competent interpersonal communication requires the communication skills you have learned in previous chapters. You use these skills to initiate, maintain, and terminate relationships through the development of attraction and trust, negotiation of power, and reduction of uncertainty.

Communication Processes of Interpersonal Relationships

Interpersonal relationships are the processes by which participants fulfill their needs and goals. The process perspective assumes that relationships are constantly changing and that people are continually negotiating their roles and definitions of the relationship. The processes of interpersonal communication focus on the ways relationships change, how people define their relationships, and how people behave while participating in relationships. We discuss four processes important in developing and maintaining your relationships: uncertainty reduction, attraction, trust, and power.

Uncertainty Reduction

When you first meet someone, your relationship is characterized by uncertainty. You're unsure about what to expect from the other, how the other person will behave, how the other person will interpret your messages, or what the other person's interests and attitudes are. Of course, the other person is just as unsure about you. As you develop your relationships over time, you experience **uncertainty reduction.** You begin to think alike, to know how the person will react to your statements, and to predict the other person's moods and emotions.[2] Even so, no one is completely predictable at all times, on every issue, in every situation. Competent interpersonal communication depends on the following processes for reducing uncertainty.

Categorization

When you first interact with someone, you have little information on which to base your predictions about that person's behavior. Mostly you see the person's appearance, body shape, clothes, hairstyle, and so on. Based on this limited information you place them in a category of similar people you have known in the past. When that category has a socially accepted definition with specific social expectations, it is called a **stereotype.** (You may want to review chapter 2 concerning the processes of perception in forming stereotypes.)

Your first interactions are based on this initial **categorization** and stereotype rather than on the person as a unique human being. This is sometimes called *impersonal communication* because you are interacting with the other as a generalized stereotype or as a generalized role rather than as a unique person.[3] Of course, other people also react to you as a stereotype and generalized other.

Categories and stereotypes are a necessary, inherent function of human perception. Categorization is a process, rather than a static label, of describing, explaining, and predicting communication behavior. Neither good nor bad, categories simply occur. Stereotypes are helpful in providing initial information about the other person; this allows us to reduce our uncertainty about how to act or what to say. For example, someone seeing you wearing a T-shirt with the name of your college on the front can predict you are a college student. This could lead to discussions of your major, the college football team, professors you have for class, or people you may both know at the college. Of all possible topics that you might have discussed, the T-shirt reduced uncertainty by narrowing the topics to those related to college life.

While acting on the basis of categorization processes, realize that the initial category is neither complete nor totally accurate. You must be open to new information that the other person tells you and constantly update your perceptions. Categorization becomes detrimental to interpersonal communication competence when you are unwilling or unable to change your impression of the person

Strategies for Interpersonal Communication

based on your communication. Competent communication requires flexibility; participants modify their perceptions to understand each other as unique individuals.

Even long-standing relationships rely on categorization to reduce uncertainty. Although the categories become more refined—and perhaps more accurate—as you receive more information about the other person, you still categorize to interpret the other's behavior. The categories you use to define another person become evident whenever you try to describe your relationship partner to another person. Your description includes a list of categories with generalized characteristics that you think the other person can understand. Consider how a student, Paul, described what was unique about his fiancée:

> Judy's a small-town gal, raised in Wisconsin, grew up on a farm with
> dairy cows and things. What's neat about her is her sense of humor; it's
> kind of like a cross between Joan Rivers and Roseanne Barr, real sarcastic
> but funny. She's also a pacifist—she never gets mad or yells or anything.
> She's like my mom in some ways. I think it's due to the fact that her Dad
> was a Methodist minister and she was an only child so she didn't have to
> fight with brothers and sisters like I did. She is definitely a unique person.

Notice that even though he intended to show how his fiancée was unique, Paul relied on categories of similar people to describe her. Some of the categories are stereotypes such as small-town gal, from the Midwest, farm girl, pacifist, minister's child, only child. Other categories are more precise and personal, such as Mom, Roseanne Barr, and Joan Rivers. All of these categories help Paul make sense of her behavior and reduce his uncertainty.

As relationships develop, we use categories to organize our perceptions, to give meaning to present behavior, and to predict future behavior. Competent interpersonal communication requires flexibility and openness in changing and modifying these categories. For example, Paul sees similarities between his fiancée and his mom. While this helps him reduce uncertainty about how she will behave, he cannot treat her exactly like his mom. Nor should he be surprised if she isn't always passive and sometimes yells or gets mad or even throws things.

People also have categories and stereotypes of their relationships. When you use phrases such as *boyfriend, best friend, soul mate, wife, companion,* or *roommate,* you are categorizing your relationship as similar to other relationships. Stereotypes of relationships provide information about what is expected or prohibited in the relationship. For example, behavior that is appropriate for a friendship may not be appropriate for a dating relationship. A person who says, "I don't want to go out with you. Can't we just be friends?", is describing more than emotional attachment or interest in you. That person is also describing the limits of permitted behaviors. When people agree on the label describing their relationship, they reduce uncertainty not only about how each party will act but also about what behaviors will mean.

Because relationships are dynamic, continually changing processes, relationship stereotypes must also change. Marriages sometimes become stagnant and uninteresting because the partners never change their perceptions of what their marriage is. Even though the people have changed over the years, they cling to their original category and description of what it means to be married. Other marriages may fail because the stereotype of the relationship is unrealistic and the people can't change their behavior to correspond to their ideal image of what married people should do. In both cases, people use a static, unchanging stereotype of the marriage to explain and predict a dynamic, ever changing relationship. In both cases, the stereotype was not useful to reduce uncertainty since it was unable to explain or predict the people's meaning or behavior.

People in a competent interpersonal relationship are continually negotiating their definition of their relationship. They adapt their categories to changes in people and situations, and they adapt their behavior to the changing stereotype.

"Before You Go On"

You should be able to answer the following question:

What benefits and problems occur when you use categorization to reduce uncertainty?

Rituals

Communication in interpersonal relationships is often based on social rituals that both parties understand. As recognizable patterns of behavior, **rituals** follow an implicitly recognized sequence according to mutually agreed on rules.[4] Greeting rituals, for example, tend to follow mutually understood patterns and rules. People say perfunctory statements such as, "How are you?" or "Nice to meet you." Often a brief handshake, direct eye contact, and a smile follow. Conversation is usually about general topics such as the weather, the communication context, or your home towns. Similarly, other social rituals cover saying good-bye, talking in church, communicating during dinner, giving and accepting compliments, asking for favors, and other common social encounters.

As we discussed in chapter 3, most people are unaware of the rituals unless someone violates the rules. If someone you just met gave you a hug, or looked at the floor all the time, frowned, or asked your opinion about abortion, you would quickly recognize a violation of expected greeting behavior. When rituals are violated, you are uncertain about how to act and what to expect from the other person, making communication more difficult.

Even though social rituals help reduce uncertainty about how to act, the specific ritual may vary according to the situation. For example, when you meet someone, you want to follow the rituals appropriate to the context in which you are communicating. In a formal situation, such as a job interview, you would probably communicate more formally and precisely. At a social gathering or a

Greeting rituals follow mutually understood rules.

party, a formal greeting may be inappropriate. Recognizing and adapting to the expectations of the other person and to the constraints of the situation are important for competent communication.

As relationships continue, the people also develop rituals idiosyncratic to their communication and experiences. They repeat patterns of communication in the same way numerous times. For example, they may greet each other with high fives, trade insults with each other, perform comic routines from movies they have both seen, tell the same stories, or say "I love you" at the end of every phone conversation. One couple always said good-bye to each other by saying the words *love, love, love.* Two friends would perform scenes from *Young Frankenstein* whenever they met at a party. A married couple always read stories from the newspaper to each other during breakfast. You probably perform many rituals with your friends every day. These help you express your relationship to each other in understandable ways, reaffirm your feelings for each other, and reaffirm your perceptions of the situation and each other. Rituals help you reduce uncertainty by performing predictable and familiar patterns of behavior with commonly understood rules and meanings.

Rituals include explicit expressions of relationships such as tokens and markers.[5] **Tokens** are physical objects that tell others about the nature of your relationship. You might wear the same clothes, such as fraternity jackets, uniforms, or school colors. Jewelry may also define your relationship to others, such as identification bracelets, fraternity pins, engagement rings, or badges. During the 1960s, high school girls wore their boyfriends' class rings wrapped in yarn around the band to signify the seriousness of the relationship. Yellow yarn meant we like each other but it's not that serious; blue yarn meant we're going steady; red yarn meant we are really in love—look for an engagement ring in the near future. Ritual tokens have precise meanings that signal the nature of the relationship to both the relationship participants and to outsiders.

Similarly, **markers** signal the nature of the relationship through specific verbal and nonverbal behaviors. Holding hands, gazing into each other's eyes, standing close to each other, and whispering secrets may mark a romantic relationship. Athletes mark their camaraderie by punching each other on the shoulder, slapping each other on the back, and giving high fives. Markers are a ritualized way of expressing and defining the relationship.

We use rituals throughout the duration of a relationship. In the early stages of relationships, communication often occurs through social rituals. As relationships develop, the people develop their own rituals based on their unique, shared experiences and interpretations of the world around them. Relationships are also expressed through the ritual meanings of tokens and markers. Ritualized communication helps reduce uncertainty by establishing familiar patterns of behavior with understood meanings. Competent communication occurs when both people know the rituals and participate in them. When a ritual is not performed according to agreed-on rules, or when people have different meanings for the ritual, competent communication is difficult.

Interpersonal Attraction

We have many commonsense theories to explain why people are attracted to each other such as, opposites attract, you like people who are like yourself, you're attracted to someone who is like your mother or father, people want to marry someone they respect, or absence makes the heart grow fonder. Most of these truisms are supported by neither research nor experience; some of them even contradict each other. You may not even know why you are attracted to one person and not to another. Common sense is not much help in explaining the attraction process.

Interpersonal attraction concerns people of every age and in most situations. Many advertisements promise people will flock to you if you wear the right makeup, use the right cologne, smoke the right cigarette, quit smoking cigarettes, drive the right car, or wear the right clothes. The process by which people develop attraction to each other, and maintain that attraction throughout their relationship, is a critical component of interpersonal relationships.

Proximity

Many relationships develop between people who are physically close to each other, that is, people who find themselves in **proximity.** Strangers assigned to the same dorm room often become close friends because they are physically near each other. Similarly, you are more likely to create friendships with next door neighbors, and co-workers or classmates you sit next to than with people more physically distant. When you are near someone, it is natural to talk to them. As you talk with the person, you tend to find commonalities forming the basis for positive relationships.

We are attracted to people we see frequently.

Accessibility

You also form relationships with people with whom you interact frequently. The person you see at the mailbox every day, a person who jogs the same route as you each morning, or the teacher you see in several classes. Accessibility can be more closely related to attraction than constant physical proximity.[6] For example, although in proximity to your roommate, you may be more attracted to someone you see several times a day in class. Some people remain unattracted to people they work next to every day while becoming good friends with others they see at lunch. Accessibility and proximity often interrelate to increase attraction.

Physical Characteristics

Physical attributes stimulate interpersonal attraction. Research consistently demonstrates that we are more willing to interact with people we find attractive than with unattractive people.[7] **Physical attractiveness** is associated with all non-verbal behaviors including body shape and size, clothes, hairstyle, posture, facial expression, cleanliness, eye contact, and vocal expressiveness. People who are animated in their conversation, who smile and appear friendly, and who show pride in their appearance are often considered more attractive than people who are lethargic and dull in their conversations, who appear dirty or unkempt, and who maintain a stoic, unsmiling facial expression. There is no objective standard for attractiveness; after all, beauty is in the eye of the beholder. No matter how you personally determine physical attractiveness, it influences your choice of the people with whom you form interpersonal relationships.

Similarity

You are also attracted to people similar to yourself. During conversations, you try to determine whether another person has a similar background; likes the same kind of music, sports, or other activities; and has the same attitudes toward current events, religion, education, and other important issues. For example, if you discover someone likes heavy metal music, is a New York Yankees fan, likes to fish, and enjoys science fiction books just as you do, you may be attracted to that person. If you talk with someone and find you have nothing in common, you probably won't be very motivated to develop a close relationship.

Attitude **similarity** has a major effect on the formation and development of interpersonal relationships.[8] As people perceive their attitudes to be similar, interaction increases. Each person assumes the other person understands them because they have similar interests and backgrounds. Each feels less uncertainty in the meaning of the other's messages and more satisfaction in the communication. When people discover a lack of attitude similarity, they attempt to change each other's minds. When no change occurs, the relationship may be discontinued.

The interpersonal partner's attractiveness has a major influence on the initiation and continuation of the relationship. Even though initial interaction may be based on proximity or desirable physical characteristics, relationship development is more a result of attitude similarity. In the movie, *Roxanne,* (a parody of *Cyrano de Bergerac*) the initial relationship between Roxanne (Darryl Hannah) and the handsome fireman was based strictly on physical attractiveness. That relationship ended because there was little similarity between the characters' values, interests, and ability to communicate. Roxanne found she was really in love with Charlie (Steve Martin), the physically unattractive fire chief with the huge nose. Charlie could talk with her, understand her feelings and ideas, and share her attitudes and values. Proximity, accessibility, physical characteristics, and attitude similarity all affect your choices in forming interpersonal relationships.

"Before You Go On"

You should be able to answer the following question:

Which factors influence attractiveness in interpersonal relationships?

Interpersonal Trust

Interacting with others can be risky. In the initial stages of interaction, we are uncertain how another will respond to our ideas. When we tell someone our ideas or disclose information about ourselves, we risk our self-concepts and self-esteem. We are, therefore, usually reluctant to tell new acquaintances or strangers private information that is important and central to our self-concepts or to divulge sensitive information. As we communicate with others, we test their reactions to our statements. If they are supportive of our ideas and of our self-esteem, we perceive that we can trust them. **Trust** is defined as the belief that another person will protect your self.

Generally, trust is necessary for the growth of close relationships.[9] Rarely is trust automatically given to another; rather, the other person has to earn it. Trust develops incrementally as we self-disclose with others.[10] As we risk parts of our private self, we expect others to also risk parts of their private self with us. *Reciprocity* of risk taking increases the level of trust developed in a relationship.

From an action perspective, trust is something the person has or doesn't have. You might say, "I am trustworthy because I can keep a secret." You judge that your actions inherently merit trust. From the action approach, all you have to do to gain trust is to perform trustworthy actions.

From a reaction approach, on the other hand, trust is something given by the receiver. You could say, "I trust my friend not to tell my secret." As a reaction, trust is the judgment you make about another's behavior, or that others make about your behavior. To gain trust, you have to act in a manner that others perceive as trustworthy.

Both of these approaches consider trust as a property of the individual, either possessed by the speaker (action) or given by the receiver (reaction). Loss of trust, therefore, is blamed on the actions of the individual. For instance, saying, "I can't trust you because you broke your promise," places the blame for the loss of trust on the actions of one individual. The one who broke the trust is the only one who has to change; rebuilding trust is that person's responsibility.

FIGURE 9.1

The process of building trust.

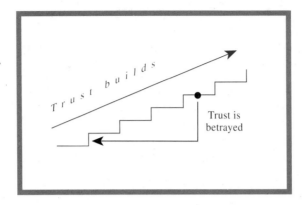

From the transaction approach, trust is part of a relationship. Just as both people simultaneously co-create their communication, they also create a trusting relationship through their mutual behaviors. Trust does not exist outside the relationship. Behaviors are not trustworthy in and of themselves, but only in the context of the relationship. Because both people create the degree of trust in the relationship, loss of trust also results from their actions and the meaning they ascribe to each other's behaviors. When people might say, "We trust each other," they mean they have a trusting relationship. If trust is broken, it changes the relationship. Since both people contributed to the lack of trust, both people have to work at rebuilding the trust.

To conceptualize the development of trust, consider the analogy to a staircase shown in figure 9.1. Just as you climb a flight of stairs one step at a time, a relationship also develops trust in small steps. At each step, the communicators consider whether trust exists. If it does, they may take additional risks and subsequently increase the intimacy of their relationship. Should trust be betrayed at any step along the way, the people don't halt at that particular level, saying "We trust each other this much but no more." Instead, their trust is destroyed at several levels. Rather than just staying at the step where trust was developed earlier, they figuratively fall down the stairs. If the relationship continues, the people must start at a lower step (maybe even at the bottom) and rebuild trust all over again.

Trust is an important process in interpersonal communication. It is a dynamic, constantly changing perception of how much risk you are willing to take in your relationships.

"Before You Go On"

You should be able to answer the following question:

What are the differences among the action, reaction, and transaction approaches to trust?

The constant, dynamic negotiation of power characterizes your interpersonal relationships. As you learned in chapter 2, all communication has both a content and a relationship dimension. As one of the most important dimensions of relationship development, power influences the meaning of communication. Power relationships are often subtle; people rarely recognize the way they negotiate power in the relationship. Usually power becomes important only when one or both people become aware it has been abused. The process through which power is negotiated, exercised, and distributed in the relationship often determines whether you perceive your communication as competent.

We define **power** as the relative amount of perceived influence one person has to change the behavior of another. Notice that power is a relative amount and is a perceived influence. From a transaction approach, both people simultaneously create power. In all situations, both people have some degree of influence over each other. Power occurs when people perceive that one person has relatively more influence than the other. For example, you might say, "I don't care what movie we see—you decide." Your friend, Maria, might then say, "Okay, let's go see *Rocky IV.*" Who has the power? You might say that Maria had the most power since she decided which movie to see. On the other hand, you also showed power in telling her to make the decision. While power was evident in both people's communication, they might perceive that the person who chose the movie was more influential in that situation.

Notice what happens to power if the preceding situation is changed slightly. After you say, "I don't care what movie we see—you decide," Maria responds, "I always have to decide. You make the choice this time." In this case, the power negotiation is about who has to decide, not which movie to see. Your statement was the same power message in both situations (action approach). In the first situation, your power message was implicitly accepted by Maria (reaction approach). The second time, the one who forces the other person to decide may be perceived as having the most power, not the person who makes the choice of the movie. Power, therefore becomes not a property of the person, but a characteristic of the relationship itself. That is, both people's behaviors and perceptions create power in the relationship (transaction approach).

Power Bases

The ability to influence people's behavior in a relationship comes from your mutual dependency on each other for resources you cannot acquire through your own actions. When you depend on another person for desired resources that they control, you are willing to let them influence you in return for the resource. That person has a **power base,** or power resource. Several types of resources are available in relationships and both people negotiate their distribution.[11]

The first power base is the control of **rewards.** When someone can reward you with praise, money, food, grades, or affection, you willingly accept their control to get the reward. For example, your teacher can reward you with an *A* for attending class. Your best friend could reward you with a hug for doing a favor.

People follow advice from perceived experts.

Your parents may reward you with an allowance for doing chores. In all these cases, you are willing to perform behaviors that other persons desire to get rewards they control.

Similarly, people who control **punishments,** the second power base, can influence your behavior. To avoid negative sanctions, you are willing to accept their influence on your behavior. When you threaten to hit your brother if he doesn't loan you his car, when you give the teacher bad course evaluations if your grade isn't changed, and when you tell your roommate to clean the apartment or move out, you are trying to influence their behaviors by giving them punishments.

A third power base is **expertise.** You can often influence others when they perceive you have more knowledge or skills than they do. They follow your advice or directions because they don't have the information or ability to do the task themselves. You may influence your friend to buy a particular CD player if you are perceived as knowledgeable about sound systems. If you think others are more skilled at fishing or sports or sewing or cooking, you will let them tell you how to perform those tasks. Knowledge and skills can be important resources that create power in your relationships.

Legitimate power is derived from the position you have, or the role that you enact, in a group or organization. Being a parent, a boss, a student, a pastor, or a baby-sitter provides a basis of power. For instance, you are willing to complete assignments for your teachers because they have a legitimate authority to evaluate your work. Although more frequently associated with group and organizational situations, legitimate power influences your communication in interpersonal situations as well.

Another basis for influence is **referent power.** When people like you, or want to be like you, you can influence their behavior. People may be willing to let you influence them if they perceive you to possess personal qualities they admire, such as honesty, friendliness, charisma, popularity, and/or attractiveness. Similarly, when people like you and want to be liked by you, they may be willing to be influenced. You are trying to influence others based on referent power if you say,

> C'mon. Do me this favor because I'm your friend.
>
> Go ahead, it's all right to skip class. I wouldn't lie to you.
>
> If you want to be popular (like me), you've got to start going to dances on weekends.

Another type of power resource is **interpersonal linkage.** This power base comes from your access to other people who control desired resources. In a sense, it is indirect power because you do not control the resource yourself, but you control access to people who do have the resources. For example, two brothers were fighting over who had the right to pick the next TV show. When Pete couldn't get his way, he yelled "I'll tell Mom and Dad on you." Pete couldn't punish his brother directly, but he had access to parents who could. Similarly, Betty and Georgia were roommates. Betty liked Georgia's friend, Bob. Georgia told Betty she would fix her up with a date with Bob if Betty would let her use the car for the weekend. Georgia did not directly control affection rewards, but she had access to Bob who did. In all cases, interpersonal linkage power comes from the ability to control access to people who control power resources.

"Before You Go On"

You should be able to answer the following question:

What are the bases of power in an interpersonal relationship?

Power Dependency

Because power, or perceived influence, is created transactionally, the control of resources in and of itself is not sufficient to gain power. The other person must desire the resources. Power bases must fulfill needs or other persons will not be willing to change their behavior to attain them. The more important the base and the more it is desired, the more influence the person has who controls the resources.[12] For example, Joe had tickets to a rock concert. He told his friend George that he would give him one of the tickets if George would wash his car for him. George didn't really like the band and wasn't excited about the concert, and decided not to wash the car. Since the power base Joe controlled was unimportant and undesired, he had no power to influence George to wash the car.

When you are dependent on another person for desired and important resources, you perceive that the other person has power. This creates a **power dependency.** If you decrease the importance or desirability of the resource, the other's perceived power diminishes. Similarly, if you can get the same resources from another person, power diminishes. For instance, Pat had taken excellent notes in class and offered to give them to Chris if Chris would invite her to a sorority party that weekend. Chris desired the notes, and they were important because she needed a good grade, but she also could get the same notes from her friend Jill. Therefore, she was not dependent on Pat for the desired resource, and Pat's perceived power was diminished. The more dependent you are on another person for a desired resource, the more power you perceive that person has. A person who does not control a resource you want is less able to influence your behavior.

Power Balancing

As people negotiate power in their relationships, they become concerned with the relative amount of influence they have over each other. The **power balance** is complementary when one person has power and the other is submissive to the influence. Often referred to as "one-up, one-down" relationships, a **complementary power balance** occurs when one person controls resources and the other person does not.[13] The one-down person depends on the one-up person.

In a **symmetrical power balance,** both people are equally dependent on each other for power resources. They may both have control of the same desired resources or they may control different resources that are equally important. When both people are one up or when both people are one down, they are symmetrical in their power distribution.

Conflict often occurs as a result of power imbalances. When one person has too much or too little power in a relationship, conflict may occur as the relationship partners renegotiate the relative amounts of power each person is perceived to have. A common goal of relationships is to have **power equality,** that is, a symmetrical relationship in which both exert equal amounts of influence. For example, Ray and Joan divorced after being married for seventeen years. Most of their problems were due to conflicts over power equality. Frequently, they fought over spending money. When Joan bought clothes, Ray yelled at her for spending money foolishly on clothes she didn't need. When Ray bought fishing tackle, Joan yelled at him for spending money they needed for rent on a frivolous hobby. The real issue was not whether they needed clothes or fishing tackle, but rather who had control over the money. Both felt the other person was taking too much control over desired resources and perceived that power was imbalanced.

A second way to describe the power balance is to consider **power equity.**[14] Equitable power balance is concerned with the fair distribution of power, not relative amounts of power. When equity is considered rather than equality, the focus is on alternating influence, that is, taking turns in the exercise of influence. You can alternate power over time or by issues. For example, you might choose the movie this week and your date could choose the movie next week. Similarly, you might make the decisions regarding the car because of your expertise in car repair. Your roommate, a good cook, might make the decisions concerning buying groceries. In either case, the power is perceived as equitable because both people enjoy influence at different times or on different issues.

People can perceive power to be finite or infinite. **Finite power** suggests that as you get more power, the other person must get less. The only way you can get more power is to take power away from the other person, and vice versa. Power struggles occur as people try to keep from losing power and at the same time try to diminish the power of others. In contrast, **infinite power** suggests that everyone has power. You can change your power base without necessarily affecting the power you perceive the other person has.[15]

In the previous example of Ray and Joan, the couple perceived power as finite. Every time Joan made a decision to spend money, Ray perceived that his ability to decide what to buy was diminished. Whenever Ray tried to take more control by buying fishing tackle, Joan perceived she had less control over his behavior. Had they considered power as an infinite source, they would have viewed the same situation differently: Purchasing clothes and fishing tackle would be unrelated activities in which both could exercise power without diminishing the other person's ability to make money decisions. Indeed, they could work together to increase their resources rather than fight over the distribution of finite resources. Supporting each other's purchases, rather than fighting about them, could be a way of increasing the reward power of affection that each perceived the other to have. A key to effective power balancing is to consider power as an infinite commodity involving several power bases simultaneously.

The processes we have described occur throughout interpersonal relationships. The processes of uncertainty reduction, attraction, trust, and power are important whenever you are establishing and maintaining competent communication relationships. You never finish building trust or maintaining attraction or negotiating power or reducing uncertainty. There is always more that can be done.

The Development of Interpersonal Relationships

How do interpersonal relationships develop? While each relationship is unique, some theorists suggest that general patterns or stages explain how many relationships develop. These *developmental models of interpersonal relationships* describe a sequence of stages that relationships go through as they move from initial encounters to eventual termination.[16] Figure 9.2 depicts one view of relationship stages characterized by changes in levels of intimacy, self-disclosure, and trust. Although the model suggests that relationships go through a smooth sequence of steps, the relationship can switch from building to declining—and even termination—at any level. For example, you may be unattracted to a person in the initiation step and immediately terminate the relationship. If trust is broken during the experimenting step, you might switch immediately to avoiding. The model in figure 9.2 shows the *possible* sequence of stages a relationship may go through; it does not suggest that all relationships go through every stage or that all relationships develop in exactly the same way.

The specific sequence and number of stages relationships go through have not been empirically identified. More research needs to examine the specific growth patterns and the reasons some relationships develop differently than others. Researchers agree, however, that every continuing relationship evolves through three general stages: initiation, maturation, and termination. Understanding the development of your relationships can be insightful in analyzing and explaining the meaning of each other's behavior.

Strategies for Initiating Relationships

In the **initiation phase,** people are faced with ambiguity and uncertainty about each other. They typically exchange relatively safe demographic information, restrict conversations to socially accepted and standardized rituals, and engage in small talk to find out about each other. They rely heavily on cultural stereotypes as they try to predict what the other person is like and how they should act. That is, they treat each other as social roles rather than as individuals.[17]

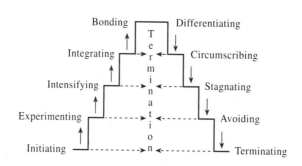

Initiating: starting the relationship; greeting rituals; attraction.

Experimenting: exploring likes and dislikes; self-disclosure; small talk; uncertainty reduction.

Intensifying: expressions of emotional attachment.

Integrating: togetherness; tokens and markers; "we" language.

Bonding: permanence of the relationship; long-term plans.

Differentiating: increased uncertainty; dissimilarities.

Circumscribing: small talk; avoidance of relationship problems.

Stagnating: lack of self-disclosure; assumed certainty of meanings; predictability and repetition of behaviors.

Avoiding: discontinuing contact; reduced communication.

Terminating: separation; passing away; redefinition.

The processes of uncertainty reduction and attraction are primarily important in the initiation phase.[18] Successful negotiation of this phase requires making a good impression on the other person. Maintaining eye contact, smiling, and direct body orientation can signal your interest in the other person. Using vivid language can increase the interest and involvement the other person has in the conversation. Successful initiation of relationships usually requires that you follow acceptable social rituals appropriate to the culture and occasion.

The initiation of relationships also requires that you actively seek information about the other person to reduce your uncertainty. Listening skills such as paraphrasing and probing questions show the other person you are interested

Strategies for Initiating Relationships

- Understand and follow appropriate rituals.
- Disclose safe information about yourself.
- Show attentiveness and focus on the other person.
- Listen expressively and ask probing questions.
- Remember and use the other person's name.
- Continually update your categorization of the other person as you learn more information.
- Let the other person know that you want the relationship to continue (suggest plans for future interaction).
- Help the other person reduce uncertainty about you.
- Find similarities that can increase attractiveness.
- Use vivid language to create interest and involvement.

(see chapter 8). When you listen carefully, you also gain information you can use to alter and refine your stereotype of the other person. People are flattered when you remember their names, their home towns, their majors, their interests, or a story they told. Sincere compliments tell the other person you are attracted to them. Letting the other person know you enjoy talking with them and want the relationship to continue helps make the transition to the next stage of relationship development.

In the initiation phase, both people help to fulfill each other's expectations. Just as you are uncertain about what the other person thinks and feels, the other person is uncertain about you. Just as the other has information you want to know, you also want to tell the other person about yourself. The initiation phase does not require a good opening line, forced and artificial banter, or clichés about the weather. Nor does it demand you play a fabricated role by being someone you're not or monopolize the conversation.

As the relationship continues, people experiment with different behaviors to determine what is acceptable and meaningful. For example, you may tell a joke to see how the other responds to your sense of humor, or you may disclose information to test whether the other person can be trusted. Or, you may ask another to participate in an activity or go on a date to see if that person is interested in you. Successful initiation of a relationship requires a genuine desire to get to know each other, as expressed through appropriate listening, verbal, and nonverbal communication skills. Competent communication in the initiation phase occurs when both people meet each other's needs, show mutual interest, and indicate a desire to continue communicating.

Strategies for Maintaining Interpersonal Relationships

As the relationship becomes more intimate and enters the **maturation phase,** people continue to reduce uncertainty. They self-disclose riskier information and learn more about each other. They might discuss their religious beliefs, tell about embarrassing experiences, talk about their future plans and dreams, and divulge their fears. They are able to treat each other as individuals apart from the roles they play. For example, your neighbor is not just a first year math major from Puerto Rico, he is Juan with a distinct personality, habits, interests, and experiences.

As relationships develop, people use language acknowledging they share a relationship bond. They talk about what *we* want and *our plans* rather than what *I* want and *my plans.* Using we language indicates that they perceive themselves to be together rather than separate individuals.

People also use words that describe and label themselves in the relationship, such as friend, best friend, roommate, steady boyfriend, fiancée, husband. The labels people use to describe relationships are often associated with a stereotype of an ideal relationship. A label of friend carries different expectations or commitment, behaviors, and feelings than best friend. For instance, Fran and Barry had difficulty finding the correct label for their romantic relationship. They had talked about getting married someday, but didn't really consider themselves as engaged. Both were uncomfortable with the long-term expectations of an engagement and the social responsibilities and legal liabilities of marriage. They finally decided that they were going steady forever. In their minds, this was an appropriate label for their level of commitment and the expectations they had for each other's fidelity, without the encumbrances of marriage. The label used to categorize the relationship was their marker for the maturity of the relationship. It signaled to themselves and to others how the relationship was developing.

As a relationship becomes more intimate, people find areas of disagreement. In the initiation phase, people hesitate to offend each other and keep disagreements to a minimum. As people develop mutual trust and disclose more information, disagreements are inevitable. In the maturation phase, however, conflict is healthy and acceptable. Successfully settling a conflict indicates that the people care about each other and that they can work things out. Competent conflict management can actually strengthen a relationship and increase interpersonal bonds.

Strategies for Maintaining Relationships

- Express commitment to the relationship.
- Use we language.
- Talk of future plans.
- Increase the depth and breadth of self-disclosure.
- Develop idiosyncratic relationship rituals.
- Negotiate a label for the relationship.
- Engage in constructive conflict.
- Negotiate power equity.
- Continue to be concerned about being attractive to your partner.
- Adapt to changing conditions and events; keep the relationship new.
- Continue to discover new things about each other; don't be complacent in strategies for reducing uncertainty.

Power distribution becomes a concern in maintaining a relationship. Negotiating power equity or equality is a continuous process throughout the relationship. Two strategies help people maintain a productive power balance: First, be flexible in your need and use of power resources. Understand that both people need to feel they have control over decisions and over the relationship. Second, use metacommunication to discuss problems in power distribution. Talking about how you perceive each other's use of power is an important step in maintaining a mature relationship.

For instance, Laura and Christy were roommates who constantly fought over who had to do the laundry. After one fight, Christy said, "I don't really mind doing laundry, I just hate it when you tell me I have to. You sound like my mom." Laura had not realized she was sounding bossy; she thought she was just making a request. In talking about the problem, they realized that Christy was reacting to a perceived power imbalance rather than the actual task of doing laundry. Discussing the way decisions were made and how they communicated about their division of labor helped them maintain their friendship.

Competent maintenance of a relationship requires both people to recognize that relationships change. Continual attention to attraction, self-disclosure, trust and power helps people develop the relationship. You need to constantly negotiate your roles, work to maintain an appropriate distribution of power, and find ways to reduce uncertainty. *Relationship maintenance* does not mean that you keep the relationship the same, or that the relationship is static. Rather, both people cooperate to adapt to the continual changes that mark the maturation of a competent interpersonal relationship.

Strategies for Terminating Interpersonal Relationships

All relationships ultimately terminate, either by choice or by the death of one of the relationship partners. One or both parties might decide that they are no longer attracted to each other. Or, they may no longer trust each other, be unsatisfied with the power distribution, or find their needs are not being fulfilled. Sometimes, the situation changes and people leave the relationship, such as when people move, change jobs, or finish school. **Termination** of a relationship may take several forms; three of the most common are passing away, sudden death, and redefinition.[19]

Passing Away Strategies

As the term suggests, the relationship dissolves over a period of time. This process of termination is a mirror image of the process of initiation and maintenance. Instead of building trust, the people slowly lose trust in each other. Instead of increasing self-disclosure, the people open up less. Instead of using we when making plans, they revert to referring to I and you. Space, eye contact, touching behavior, and other nonverbal behaviors reflect a growing estrangement. As the relationship steadily weakens, there is less frequent interaction, more superficial small talk, and less dependency on each other for rewards and affection.

 Passing away sometimes occurs without people noticing. Perhaps your relationship with a good friend has slowly passed away. At first, you might not have noticed that you didn't see each other as often or that your talks were more superficial. At some point you might have said, "I don't see Charlie as much as I used to—guess I've been busy." Or, "It's funny, I used to spend ten hours a day with Charlene, but now we hardly even talk." Or, "I think about Ed a lot—I just never seem to get around to writing or giving him a call." The relationship has passed away through lack of attention, effort, or interest.

 Sometimes passing away is intentional. You decide you don't want to be in the relationship, but perhaps you don't want it to just end suddenly because you will hurt another's feelings. You consciously work to disengage yourself from interacting with the other person. Even if that person wants to continue the relationship, you participate less frequently and more superficially until the relationship no longer functions. (See the accompanying box entitled Strategies for Terminating Relationships for a summary of passing away strategies.)

People must constantly work at maintaining their relationship or it will pass away.

Sudden Death Strategies

Some relationships end suddenly, and often painfully for one or both partners. Sometimes a catastrophic event occurs. Perhaps one of the people dies. Perhaps one person found the other cheated on their relationship, or did something dishonest, or betrayed an important trust.

At other times, **sudden death** comes to a relationship when one person just can't take it any more. There is no catastrophic event, just a slow accumulation of negative events and feelings that suddenly burst forth. Perhaps the other person has been continually rude, or lazy, or thoughtless. At some point, the behavior becomes intolerable and one person suddenly decides to leave the relationship.

When sudden death occurs, there is usually no noticeable change in the relationship prior to the termination. The maintenance phase has been occurring for some time and continues right up until the break. Unlike passing away, there is no slow reversal of trust, frequency of interaction, or any of the other variables that comprise the relationship maintenance phase. There is simply the end of the relationship. (See the accompanying box entitled Strategies for Terminating Relationships for a summary of sudden death strategies.)

Redefinition Strategies

Another way in which relationships end is to redefine the relationship in an entirely new way. People may continue interacting, but do so in a brand new relationship. In essence, they start over. Usually the relationship changes from more intimate to less intimate, such as from romantic partners to friends or from friends

Strategies for Interpersonal Communication

Strategies for Terminating Relationships

PASSING AWAY

- Decrease the frequency and length of interactions.
- Ignore the other person's attempts to continue the relationship.
- Decrease the depth and breadth of self-disclosure; rely on small talk.
- Minimize participation in, and importance of, personal rituals; rely on social rituals.
- Find new relationships to replace old ones.
- Refer to own plans and needs rather than relationship; use I rather than we.
- Focus discussions on present activities rather than shared past experiences or mutual future plans.

SUDDEN DEATH

When you end a relationship:
- Discontinue all interaction with the other person.
- Eliminate tokens of the relationship.
- Avoid situations where the other person is present.
- Avoid mutual friends or discussing the other person.

When the other person ends a relationship:
- Engage in activities to fill time normally spent with the other person.
- Find new relationships to replace the old one.
- Talk about your feelings and perceptions to a trusted friend or counselor.
- Don't dwell on reasons for termination or try to place blame; accept the situation as it is and go on with your life.
- Discover appropriate and positive ways of telling others about the relationship's termination. (Don't burden everyone with the sordid details.)

REDEFINITION

- Negotiate a new label for the relationship.
- Discuss what behaviors are permitted and prohibited.
- Change markers and tokens to reflect the new relationship.
- Focus on the present relationship rather than continually discussing the old one.
- Renegotiate power.
- Establish new personal rituals to replace old ones.

to business associates. Sometimes the new relationship is more intimate. People who change from being just good friends to being romantic partners often discover that the relationship is entirely different than it used to be, with new expectations, new meanings for behaviors, and new types of commitment.

For example, Karen and Sam had dated steadily for three years in college and talked about getting married when they graduated. On graduation, however, they realized they could not pursue both careers and stay together. They mutually decided to discontinue their romantic relationship, but to still be good friends. Because they had mutual friends they saw frequently, they continued to interact. They called each other occasionally, sent cards at Christmas and birthdays, and did all the other communication behaviors necessary to maintain their newly defined friendship. They replaced their romantic relationship with a new relationship as friends.

When ending a relationship through **redefinition,** people sometimes try to forget that the other relationship happened. Of course, this is impossible, but they behave as if the new relationship was the only one they had. They often find that they have reverted back to the entry phase as they negotiate new rules for their behavior and try to establish a new kind of trust. They must find new ways to negotiate power distribution, find new ways to express their ideas and feelings, and find new ways to label their relationship. They reduce uncertainty about the meanings of their behavior in light of the new relational definition. (See the accompanying box entitled Strategies for Terminating Relationships for a summary of redefinition strategies.)

Relationships may actually go through several redefinitions during the life of the people involved. Each new relationship is unique. While it has overtones of the previous relationships, it is not just a modification of the existing relationship, but a new definition of how the people communicate with each other.

"Before You Go On"

You should be able to answer the following question:

What are the differences among the termination strategies of passing away, sudden death, and redefinition?

Relationships change and develop over time. Because relationships are inherently defined by communication, relationship development is marked by changes in communication. The processes of and strategies for uncertainty reduction, attraction, trust, and power change in importance and function as relationships develop. Competent interpersonal communication depends on using appropriate strategies for initiating, maintaining, and terminating relationships.

1.   What benefits and problems occur when you use categorization to reduce uncertainty?

Categorizing people and relationships is an inherent function of human perception that allows us to predict and explain people's behavior based on relatively little information. We use categories to predict common interests, determine our strategies for communicating, and even decide whether we will engage in conversation. Categorization creates problems if it is based on inaccurate information or when we maintain a stereotype in light of contradictory information. Stereotypes that are constantly revised and refined to account for new information and changing situations help us reduce uncertainty.

2.   How do rituals reduce uncertainty throughout a relationship?

Rituals are patterns of behavior guided by socially agreed-on rules. When everyone follows the rules, the sequence and meaning of communication behaviors are highly predictable. When rituals are violated, people become confused about how to respond.

As a relationship develops, people not only engage in socially defined rituals but also create their own idiosyncratic rituals. The rituals can reaffirm emotional commitments, remind people of shared past experiences, and define the relationship as special and unique.

Public symbols that define the nature of the relationship are displayed through ritualized tokens and markers. Tokens are objects with specific symbolic meanings indicating the nature of the relationship. Markers are ritualized behaviors indicating how the relational partners define the relationship. Markers and tokens reduce uncertainty about the meaning of the relationship.

3.   What are the differences among the action, reaction, and transaction approaches to trust?

The action approach suggests that trust is based on what a person does. If you act in a trustworthy manner, you should be trusted. Trust is, therefore, a characteristic of the speaker. The reaction approach defines trust as the perception others have of your behavior, that is, people give you their trust. A reaction approach is the response others have toward your actions; it is a characteristic of the receiver. The transaction approach defines trust as created by both people through their communication. The trust is a characteristic of the relationship rather than of an individual. Both people contribute equally to the development of trust between them.

4.   Which factors influence attractiveness in interpersonal relationships?

Attractiveness to another person can be created through proximity, accessibility, physical characteristics, and similarity. We form relationships with people who are physically close to us or with whom we frequently interact. We also like people who have similar values, attitudes, beliefs, and experiences. Similarity helps us predict and understand the other's meanings because we share a common frame of reference. Everyone has different standards, criteria, and perceptions for determining attractive physical characteristics. Whether we create and maintain relationships depends on our awareness and control of the elements of interpersonal attraction.

5. What are the bases of power in an interpersonal relationship?
Power is based on the distribution of resources desired by people in a relationship. Power bases include rewards, punishments, expertise, legitimate roles and positions, referent characteristics, and interpersonal linkages. The relative strength of a power base depends on the importance of the resource and the degree to which it is controlled by one or more people. Dependency can be changed by altering the perceived importance of the resource or by finding other ways of acquiring it.

6. How is power distributed in interpersonal relationships?
When the people control relatively equal amounts of resources, the relationship is symmetrical. If one person controls most of the resources, the relationship is complementary. In relationships where power is perceived as finite, the only way to increase your power is by taking power away from the other person. When power is viewed as infinite, the goal is to increase power resources to allow both people to have power. People in a relationship also negotiate to have equal power (a similar amount of influence) or power equity (a fair distribution of power resources).

7. Which communication strategies initiate a relationship?
Initiation is characterized by high levels of uncertainty. People communicate with each other as generalized social roles rather than as unique individuals. Cognitive and expressive listening skills, vivid and concrete language skills, and appropriate disclosure of feelings and ideas create a climate of trust in which information can be shared. Increasing the amount and quality of information decreases the uncertainty both people have about each other. Both people share the responsibility for creating competent communication by following social rituals, reciprocating appropriate self-disclosure, helping each other understand their meanings, and discovering similarities.

8. Which communication strategies maintain a relationship?
A relationship is continually changing. The processes of attraction, power negotiation, trust, and uncertainty reduction are as important in the maturation phase as they are in the initiation phase. Increased trust allows more intimate and riskier self-disclosure. Power negotiation becomes more critical as people negotiate decision-making responsibilities and the distribution of resources. People develop idiosyncratic rituals to express and reaffirm their relationship.

Maintaining a relationship is helped by metacommunication to discuss the way each person expresses ideas, negotiates power distribution, and displays trust. A primary concern in maintaining relationships is the negotiation of appropriate labels, tokens, and markers. These define the relationship, indicate the appropriateness of behaviors, the level of commitment, and the range of permissible emotions.

9.   What are the differences among the termination strategies of passing away, sudden death, and redefinition?

Passing away is the reverse of relationship growth. Trust, self-disclosure, attraction, and commitment to the relationship decrease. Passing away is characterized by destructive conflict, concern for the individual rather than the relationship, power struggles, changes from personal to social rituals, decreased accessibility, and increased uncertainty.

Sudden death occurs when a relationship faces a catastrophic event, sudden change in the situation, or an accumulation of previously unstated or unrecognized conflicts. Interaction ceases relatively suddenly; thus, there is little chance of re-establishing the relationship or resolving the problems.

Redefinition is a radical change in the definition of the relationship, though interaction between the people continues. The old relationship is ended, though a new and different relationship may be initiated. The people develop new roles, expectations, rituals, and topics of discussion. Tokens and markers of the old relationship are replaced with new ritualized expressions so that other people are aware of the change.

S T U D E N T   E X E R C I S E S

1.   First impressions.

Talk to a classmate or a stranger for five minutes. Immediately after your discussion, write down your impressions.

    a. Describe the other person's physical appearance. What conclusions did you draw from clothing, facial expressions, hairstyle, body shape, gestures, or other nonverbal behaviors?

    b. What topics did you discuss? Why did you discuss these topics rather than all the other possible topics you might have discussed?

    c. How would you describe the other person's personality? Why?

2.   Building trust.

Trust can be defined from the action, reaction, and transaction approaches. Each approach suggests a specific way in which two people build trust.

    a. Describe an experience in which you perceived yourself as trustworthy, but others did not. What did you do to make others trust you?

    b. Describe an experience in which you trusted another person only to be betrayed. Why did you trust the other person? Why did the trust fail? What happened to the relationship?

    c. Describe an experience in which you and another person trusted each other. What did you both do to create that trust?

3. **Power negotiation.**

Power is based on the perceived control of desired resources. Consider this class.

    a. Describe the specific power bases that you, your classmates, and your teacher have. What resources do you each control?

    b. Is the power distributed equally and equitably?

    c. What could be done to change the power distribution in the class?

4. **Rituals.**

We develop rituals that help to define and express our perceptions of our relationships. Describe the following and compare your answers with your classmates' answers.

    a. What rituals does your family have concerning the celebration of Christmas or other holidays? What do these rituals mean to your family?

    b. Describe three different greeting rituals you use when you meet people on campus. Do the rituals differ in the meaning they have for the participants?

    c. Walk around campus for a few minutes. Make a list of the tokens and markers people use to symbolize their relationships. What do the symbols and behavior mean? Is there a common understanding of these meanings?

5. **Development of interpersonal relationships.**

Describe a relationship you experienced that has now terminated. Try to recall the specific sequence of phases it went through. How did the relationship begin? Why did it develop? How did it terminate? Does this relationship follow the development patterns described in the chapter?

G L O S S A R Y

accessibility An element of interpersonal attraction based on the availability and frequency of interaction with another person.

categorization An uncertainty reduction process of labeling people in categories and assuming they have characteristics similar to others in the category.

complementary power balance Power distribution where one person is dominant and the other is submissive; a one-up, one-down relationship.

expertise power Power based on perceived skills or knowledge.

finite power The perspective that power is summative; a person increases power only by taking power away from the other, and vice versa.

infinite power The perspective that people create power together and that power is nonsummative. Increasing one person's power does not necessarily result in a decrease in the other's power.

initiation phase The first stage of a relationship marked by high levels of uncertainty, low levels of trust, reliance on rituals, and communication with another person as a social role.

interpersonal communication One-to-one interaction through verbal and nonverbal behavior with immediate and simultaneous feedback.

interpersonal linkage power Power based on a person's perceived influence with people who control resources.

legitimate power Power based on a person's position or role.

markers Ritualized behaviors that signal the nature of a relationship to the relational partners and to others.

maturation phase The middle phase of relationship development in which the people learn each other's idiosyncratic nature, create relational markers and tokens, and develop a sense of identity through symbolic labels of the relationship.

passing away A strategy for terminating a relationship that reverses the processes of relational growth; trust decreases, conflict becomes destructive, symbols reflect a concern for self rather than the relationship.

physical attractiveness Elements of attraction based on the appeal of nonverbal behaviors, appearance, and mannerisms.

power The relative amount of perceived influence one person has to change the behavior of another.

power balancing The process of distributing power in a relationship; the relative amount of power each person is perceived to have.

power bases The reasons people achieve relative power in a relationship; the resources controlled by one person and desired by the other.

power dependency Desiring important resources controlled by another who is the only source for those resources.

power equality Distribution of power in which both people have the same amount of resources and are equally dependent on each other.

power equity Distribution of power in which people have different power bases but exercise power in fair and reciprocal ways.

proximity An element of attraction in which people are physically close to each other.

punishment power Power based on the control of negative sanctions or the withholding of rewards.

redefinition A strategy for terminating a relationship in which the people continue interacting but relabel the relationship so that it is fundamentally different than the previous relationship.

referent power Power based on liking and personal qualities.

reward power Power based on the control of desired resources or the withholding of punishment.

rituals A pattern of behaviors performed according to specific, though often unstated, rules.

similarity An element of attraction in which people share similar values, attitudes, beliefs, and/or experiences.

stereotype A strategy for reducing uncertainty by categorizing people based on simplistic criteria or superficial characteristics with socially agreed-on interpretations.

sudden death A strategy for terminating relationships in which the communication is terminated quickly due to a catastrophic event or the sudden culmination of heretofore unexpressed conflicts.

symmetrical power balance Power distribution in which both people are equal.

termination phase The stage in which an interpersonal relationship is brought to an end either through noninteraction or through redefinition.

tokens Material artifacts and objects signaling the nature of the relationship both to the relational partners and to others outside the relationship.

trust The belief that another person will protect your private self.

uncertainty reduction The process by which we increase our ability to understand and predict the behaviors and meanings of another person.

NOTES

1. B. Aubrey Fisher, *Interpersonal Communication: Pragmatics of Human Relationships* (New York: Random House, 1987).

2. C. R. Berger and R. Calabrese, "Some Explorations of Initial Interaction and Beyond: Toward a Developmental Theory of Interpersonal Communication," *Human Communication Research* 1 (1975), 99–112.

3. Gerald R. Miller, "Current Status of Theory and Research in Interpersonal Communication," *Human Communication Research* 4 (1978), 164–78.

4. For a discussion of rituals, see Erving Goffman, *The Presentation of Self in Everyday Life* (Garden City, N.Y.: Doubleday, 1959); Erving Goffman, *Interaction Ritual* (New York: Anchor Press, 1967).

5. Erving Goffman, *Relations in Public: Microstudies of the Public Order* (New York: Basic Books, 1971).

6. Fisher, *Interpersonal Communication.*

7. See, for example, L. Zunin and N. Zunin, *Contact: The First Four Minutes* (New York: Ballantine Books, 1972); James C. McCroskey and Thomas A. McCain, "The Measurement of Interpersonal Attraction," *Speech Monographs* 41 (1974), 23–4.

8. The classic treatise on symmetry theory is developed in Theodore M. Newcomb, "An Approach to the Study of Communicative Acts," *Psychological Review* 60 (1953), 393–404.

9. R. Hays, "The Development and Maintenance of Friendship," *Journal of Social and Personal Relationships* 1 (1984), 75–98.

10. See, for example, I. Altman, "Reciprocity of Social Exchange," *Journal for the Theory of Social Behavior* 3 (1973), 249–61; I. Altman and D. A. Taylor, *Social Penetration: The Development of Interpersonal Relationships* (New York: Holt, Rinehart & Winston, 1973).

11. For discussions of power bases, see J. R. P. French, Jr. and B. Raven, "The Bases of Social Power," in *Studies in Social Power,* ed., D. Cartwright (Ann Arbor: University of Michigan Press, 1959), 150–67; Joyce L. Hocker and William W. Wilmot, *Interpersonal Conflict,* 3rd ed. (Dubuque, Iowa: Wm. C. Brown, 1991); A. A. Goldberg, Mary S. Cavanaugh, and C. E. Larson, "The Meaning of Power," *Journal of Applied Communication Research* 11 (1983), 89–108; and D. H. Wrong, *Power: Its Forms, Bases, and Use* (Oxford: Basil Blackwell, 1979).

12. For a discussion of the factors of power dependency, see R. M. Emerson, "Power-Dependence Relations," *American Sociological Review* 27 (1962), 31–41; H. M. Blalock, *Power and Dependency: Toward a General Theory* (Newbury Park, Calif.: Sage, 1989).

13. L. E. Rogers and R. B. Farace, "Relational Communication Analysis: New Measurement Procedures," *Human Communication Research* 1 (1975), 222–39.

14. E. Hatfield, M. K. Utne, and J. Traupmann, "Equity Theory and Intimate Relationships," in *Social Exchange in Developing Relationships,* ed., R. L. Burgess and T. L. Huston (New York: Academic Press, 1979); B. Kabonoff, "Equity, Equality, Power, and Conflict," *Academy of Management Review* 16 (1991), 416–41.

15. Hocker and Wilmot, *Interpersonal Conflict.*

16. See for example A. E. Scheflen, "Quasi-Courtship Behavior in Psychotherapy," in *Interpersonal Dynamics: Essays and Readings on Human Interaction,* ed., W. G. Bennis, E. H. Stein, F. I. Steele, and D. E. Berlew (Homewood, Ill.: Dorsey, 1968); Steve Duck, *Personal Relationships 4: Dissolving Personal Relationships* (New York: Academic Press, 1982); Mark Knapp, *Interpersonal Communication and Human Relationships* (Boston: Allyn & Bacon, 1984); and Fisher, *Interpersonal Communication.*

17. Miller, "Current Status."

18. Berger and Calabrese, "Some Explorations."

19. Fisher, *Interpersonal Communication*; Knapp, *Interpersonal Communication and Human Relationships;* Duck, *Personal Relationships.*

CHAPTER

Strategies for Managing Conflict

• *If people communicated more, there would be a lot less conflict.*

• *Somebody almost always loses in a conflict situation.*

• *Negative feedback should not be given unless it is requested.*

• *I don't think you really love me. We never fight, so you must not care.*

• *Conflict can almost always be resolved if people are just willing to compromise.*

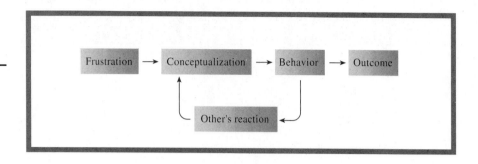

I nterpersonal relationships often encounter conflict. Maybe you've made statements similar to the preceding ones about your own conflict experiences. As some of the statements suggest, many people think that conflict is detrimental to their relationships and should be avoided. Other statements imply conflict can be a positive experience. As we'll see in this chapter, although conflict is inevitable in human relationships, it does not have to be destructive. If managed through appropriate communication strategies, conflict can actually benefit relationships.

This chapter discusses the nature of conflict, describes several models of conflict processes, and suggests some specific strategies for managing conflict constructively.

The Nature of Conflict

People frequently think of conflict as a fight between angry, hostile combatants. They avoid conflict because they perceive it as harmful and unpleasant. However, nothing inherent in conflict supports this view. Conflict is a natural process by which people negotiate their views of reality and try to survive in a complex and uncertain world. A key to effectively managing conflict is to realize that the way you conceptualize conflict influences the way you deal with it.

Approaches to Defining Conflict

Researchers define conflict from three general perspectives: situational, behavioral, and transactional. First, conflict is defined by the situation giving rise to it.

Situational Approach

The **situational approach** assumes that conflict occurs because of competition over scarce resources, perceived threats to attaining personal goals, and/or differences between people's ideas. The situational approach suggests that when the conditions for conflict exist, conflict exists. (For examples, see the accompanying box entitled Situational Definitions of Conflict.) When conflict is defined as arising from the situation, people assess the severity of the conflict by examining the importance of the goals and the degree to which they are incompatible.

- A special case of competition where interference with others' goal attainment occurs.[1]
- A struggle over values and claims to scarce status, power, and resources in which the aims of the opponents are to neutralize, injure, or eliminate the rivals.[2]
- A situation in which incompatible activities occur.[3]
- Conflict is best described as the degree to which people in a common situation have incompatible interests.[4]

The severity, or intensity, of the conflict is directly related to the importance of the goals or resources to the people in the situation and how much they interfere with each other in attaining those goals. For example, two brothers, Bill and Ted, both want to drive the family car on Saturday night. There is only one car and only one brother can have it. This mutually exclusive goal means that if one brother achieves his goal and gets the car, the other brother cannot. According to the situational approach, the intensity of the conflict would increase as the importance of using the car increases and as the interference with reaching the goal increases. If one of the brothers didn't really care that much about using the car, or if they could share the car on Saturday night, the conflict would be less intense than if both brothers wanted the car a great deal and were determined to be the only one using it.

When approaching conflict from a situational perspective, resolution depends on changing the conditions under which conflict started. As long as the goals or resources remain important and exclusive, conflict continues. Conflict is resolved by one or both of the parties changing their perceptions of the importance of the goal or resource, or by deciding which will achieve the exclusive goal and which will not. In the preceding example, Bill could try to resolve the conflict by changing the importance of the goal. He could say, "Go ahead and use the car, I don't really care that much." Bill could also try to change the degree to which the goal is shared by saying, "You can use the car tonight, but I get to use it next Saturday." or "Maybe you and I could double date so we could both use the car." Another way to resolve the situation is for an outside person to decide the distribution of resources for the participants, such as a parent awarding the car to Ted. Despite the resolution strategy used, the focus is on changing the situation to accommodate conflicting goals, scarce resources, or different ideas.

Behavioral Approach

A second way to approach conflict is to focus on people's behavior in the conflict situation. Defining conflict from the **behavioral approach** changes the focus from the situation to the way people communicate about the conflict issues. The behavioral approach suggests the intensity of the behaviors used to express the conflict determines the conflict intensity. (For examples, see the accompanying box

Strategies for Managing Conflict 231

entitled Behavioral Definitions of Conflict.) Conflicts in which people yell, scream, hit, call names, use profanity, or hurt each other physically or psychologically are more intense than conflicts in which people listen empathically, speak calmly, argue rationally, and are supportive of the other person's point of view.

Behavioral Definitions of Conflict

- Conflict can be characterized by the expression of hostility, aggression, and negative attitudes that indicate or result from the perception of contradictory interests.[5]
- A behavior of rivalry and hostility between members of different departments in an organization.[6]
- Conflict is the process in which one or both sides consciously interfere in the goal achievement efforts of the other side. Conflict is an overt struggle. Conflict resolution is the method and manner in which a person attempts to eliminate or minimize a dispute.[7]
- Interpersonal conflict involves two or more people who can only be in conflict through communication, either verbal or nonverbal. Thus, social conflict refers to a particular set of human communication behaviors.[8]

For example, Lois and Judy both want to watch different TV shows at the same time. They have only one TV and it's important to them to watch their favorite shows. From a situational approach this would be a high-conflict situation because the goals are important and mutually exclusive. From a behavioral approach, Judy and Lois determine the intensity of the conflict through their behavior. If they rationally discuss their different needs and goals and cooperate to reach a mutually satisfying solution, their conflict would be less intense than if they screamed at each other, called each other selfish, stormed out of the house, or hit each other.

From the behavioral perspective, conflict management focuses on controlling or changing the way one or both people express the conflict. When conflict behavior is destructive, the focus is on changing the hurtful behavior to make it more supportive. In some cases, people unable to express their feelings and changes might make their behavior more confrontational. From the behavioral perspective, Judy might try to manage the conflict by saying, "Calling me selfish hurts my feelings. Let's try to discuss this without yelling or name calling." The behavioral perspective assumes that people who constructively manage the way they express themselves in a conflict situation have a better chance of achieving productive conflict outcomes than people who communicate destructively. That is, competent communication is prerequisite for effective conflict management.

Transactional Approach

The third approach to conflict combines the situational and behavioral approaches. The **transactional approach** assumes that conflict occurs because of the interaction between perceptions of the situation and perceptions of each other's behavior. (For other examples, see the accompanying box entitled Transactional Definitions of Conflict.) We define conflict as a pattern of communication behaviors between two or more people that, as a whole, express degrees of incompatible perceptions of the context. Our definition emphasizes the interdependence of all elements in the transactional model of communication. To explain the key terms in the definition:

pattern of communication behaviors—Behaviors given meaning by the people involved.

as a whole—Simultaneously created by all parties.

degrees—Various levels of intensity; can change over time.

incompatible perceptions—Disagreement, opposition, negative feelings, negative attitudes, discrepant viewpoints.

of the context—Events, situations, topics, people, environment, self, ideas (includes past, present, and future).

Review the model of transactional communication in chapter 1 and note that communication involves the simultaneous and continuous interaction of people's perceptions of the situation, themselves, and each other's behavior. Each of these factors is interdependent. The perception of the environment or situation is interdependent with the perceptions of the self, our own behavior, and the other person's behavior. Therefore, the transactional approach to conflict requires examining the interdependence of the behavioral and situational approaches.

Transactional Definitions of Conflict

- Manifest conflict is the overt (behavioral) expression of conflict; manifest conflict is part of a conflict episode which evolves through latent, perceived, and felt conflict stages.[9]
- The process which begins when one person perceives that the other has frustrated or is about to frustrate, some concern of his/hers. The process includes the perceptions, emotions, behaviors, and outcomes of the two parties.[10]
- The interaction of interdependent people who perceive opposition of goals, aims, and values and who see the other party as potentially interfering with the realization of these goals.[11]
- A process which is an expressed struggle between at least two interdependent parties who perceive incompatible goals, scarce rewards, and interference from the other party in achieving their goals.[12]

Applying the transactional approach to the previous examples, Bill and Ted would examine not only the distribution of the scarce resources (the car) and their personal goals, but also how they expressed themselves in negotiating the conflict. Lois and Judy would be concerned not only with their communication but also with changing the situation (maybe renting a VCR to tape one show while watching the other). Conflict intensity would be determined by the combination of goal discrepancy, importance, and communication behaviors. If Bill approached conflict from this perspective, he might say, "Let's discuss this calmly and see if we can figure out how we can both go out tonight using just one car." The transactional perspective focuses on using strategies to manage the communication process through which goals and resources are distributed. From a transactional perspective, both people create the conflict together within a specific perceived context. Management of conflict requires a mutual commitment to changing any or all of the behavioral and situational elements that created the conflict.[13]

"Before You Go On"

You should be able to answer the following question:

What are the differences among the situational, behavioral, and transactional approaches to defining conflict?

Productive and Destructive Conflict

A common myth is that conflict is destructive and should be avoided. People often avoid conflict because they dislike the stress and emotions that accompany conflict, fear they will lose the conflict, or think they might hurt the other person. If managed poorly, conflict can be destructive; however, it can also be a constructive process during the development of interpersonal relationships.

Poorly managed conflict escalates to highly intense levels of destructive behavior. It increases feelings of distrust, anger, dislike, and separation from the other person. **Destructive conflict** creates a defensive atmosphere in which people feel compelled to protect their private self from attack or loss. It may promote dishonesty and manipulation as one or more people try to win at the expense of the other.

Constructive conflict helps clarify ideas.

Productive conflict is most likely to occur at moderate intensity, where the parties are motivated enough to engage in the necessary communication but not so emotionally involved that they are unable to clearly process information. Productive conflict can increase the number of viewpoints about a problem, clarify relationship rules, increase understanding of each other's emotions, and provide insight into the self. As people constructively discuss different views by listening cognitively and behaviorally, as they express their own ideas concretely and descriptively, they can better understand and work through a mutual problem. As they try to explain their points of view so that the other person can understand, they also clarify their ideas to themselves.

Productive conflict also motivates people to examine their relationships and ideas. When people always agree, or assume that they agree, there is little motivation to fully examine the situation. Consider your own conversations with a friend about your favorite baseball team, movie, or rock group. If you and your friend both like the same team or group, there is little conversation or exploration of the reasons. But if you disagree, you might have hours of fun conversation trying to explain why your choice is better. In doing so, you may actually learn more about your own choice as well as the other's choice. And, you learn more about your private self and the other person. Thus, a disagreement motivates you to communicate more fully and more specifically about your different ideas.

"Before You Go On"

You should be able to answer the following question:

In which ways can conflict be productive and destructive?

Determining When Conflict Is Productive

Deciding when a conflict is productive or destructive depends on the approach people take to define the conflict. A situational approach focuses on the outcome of the conflict, a behavioral approach focuses on the behaviors during the conflict, while a transactional approach examines both the outcome and the process.

Determining effectiveness by the **conflict outcome** has the intuitive advantage of being easy to measure. You can easily see whether you achieved your goal or not. You can count or measure the resources you control. You can determine whether or not you persuaded the other person to accept your point of view. The situational approach to measuring conflict effectiveness by outcome is called the *win-lose approach*. If you win, you believe the conflict was effective. If you lose, you believe the conflict was negative. Many people advocate that the best approach to conflict resolution is to establish a win-win situation in which all people reach their goals, and the outcome is mutually satisfying to all people.[14]

The outcome approach, however, can be problematic. One problem with using outcome as a measure of effective conflict is the multiple goals in a conflict situation. There are short-term goals, long-term goals, content goals, relationship goals, even goals of which we are not consciously aware or those are not clearly articulated. As chapter 3 suggested, goals often change from prospective, to transactive, to retrospective. Which goal do we use to assess whether we have won or lost the conflict? Consider the following conflict episode:

> Duane and Alison had been dating seriously for six months. In that time, they had many arguments that Duane always won. Duane achieved his goals in every situation, Alison did not. One day, Alison called Duane to say that she had met someone else and didn't want to see him anymore. In a difficult conversation, Alison told Duane the reason she was breaking up with him was because he never listened to her, that he never considered her ideas as valid, and that he had to make all the decisions. She felt useless and stupid when she was with him. Duane was totally surprised. He had no idea she felt this way or even that he had been doing all the decision making. Duane and Alison never saw each other again.

When people focus on conflict outcomes, they are concerned with keeping score to see who wins and loses.

In this situation, Duane would consider each of the specific conflicts with Alison to have constructive outcomes because he won each time. In the long run, however, he lost his goal of being in a relationship with Alison. He had won all of the content conflicts but lost the relationship conflicts. Indeed, he was even unaware of the relationship conflict until it was too late.

Another problem with the outcome approach is that factors other than our decisions also affect outcomes. Other people's behavior, future events beyond our control, even chance occurrences can increase or decrease the effectiveness of our choices. We might get our goals simply because we were lucky; does that mean we won the conflict?

A disadvantage of using outcome as a measure of conflict effectiveness is that we become concerned with the pattern of winning and losing. We keep track of how much each person gets and how frequently we win and lose. When we lose all or part of our goal, even through a mutually agreed compromise, we are often resentful. When we enter into the next conflict, we may be even more determined that we aren't going to lose again. Alison wasn't upset because she lost a few conflicts, but because she always lost. She remembered each loss and the cumulative losses became unbearable. When we use the win-win approach, we have set up competitive thinking. The very phrase, *win-win,* suggests that we measure each person's individual success and that someone is keeping score.

The behavioral approach to conflict management focuses on the process through which the conflict occurs. We focus on what people are doing in the here and now and assess whether it is productive or not. We try to control our behavior as it occurs. Many people have trouble believing that we decide how we will behave and how we will feel. Even though emotions are spontaneous, we decide how to interpret them and how they affect our behavior. In one circumstance, we may receive upsetting news and be depressed or angry. In another situation, we may consciously say to ourselves, "I'm not going to let that ruin my day. I'm determined to be happy today." We don't have to act the way we feel.[15] By focusing on our behavior and the processes of conflict, we learn to be in control of ourselves and to manage conflict constructively.

From the behavioral approach, people also focus on monitoring each other's behavior so they can modify their communication strategies. Other people's behavior causes us to continually redefine and reassess the situation, our goals, and our own communication. From a behavioral approach, conflict management becomes a process of constant assessment and adaptation to each other's behaviors.

The transactional approach combines a concern with outcome and a focus on behavior. It considers that both people are co-creating the conflict situation; therefore, both people are equally responsible for creating the conflict outcome. Conflict exists only within a perceived interpersonal relationship; thus, the relationship goals and the content goals are interdependent. Effectiveness must assess both the content and relationship dimensions of the conflict. Outcome assessment is irrelevant without understanding the process that may have led to the outcome. Similarly, it is difficult to assess the behavior without knowing what outcome the behavior accomplished. Therefore, the transactional view asks the question, "Is what we are doing helping us to reach our goals?" If the answer is no, then it is essential for both people to try a different approach and to communicate differently.

"Before You Go On"

You should be able to answer the following question:

What are the differences between assessing conflict by the outcome and evaluating conflict by the behaviors?

One way to understand the conflict process is to examine a model of how conflict elements interact. Models help us to see the relationships between situation, behavior, and outcome by graphically depicting the conflict process. The next section describes models of conflict and types of conflict to help you understand how conflict works.

Models and Types of Conflict

Conflict always occurs for a reason. Conflict is a process through which people negotiate and adjust their perceptions of the situation, themselves, and each other. Because it occurs over time, the conflict process can be modeled as a series of stages or a conflict episode. An episode begins with the perception of the conflict by one or more people and ends when the communication interaction between the people ceases. The end of a conflict episode does not necessarily mean that the conflict has been resolved, only that the immediate interaction about the conflict has ended. A conflict can continue through several episodes.

Model of the Conflict Episode

The conflict episode model shows how conflict evolves through a series of five interdependent stages.[16] Since people in the same conflict may perceive the situation differently, figure 10.1 shows each person's perspective of the conflict. The episode begins when a person perceives that another person is interfering with the attainment of a goal or a desired resource. The person feels **frustrated** and reacts emotionally to the situation. As the goal frustration and emotions are recognized, the person **conceptualizes** the conflict situation. The person tries to identify possible reasons for the situation, possible strategies to employ to resolve the conflict, and possible consequences of those actions. The first steps of the episode, frustration and conceptualization, are similar to the situational approach to defining conflict.

After conceptualizing the conflict situation, the person enacts a specific **behavior** or communication strategy to resolve the situation and achieve the desired goal. For the first time in the episode, the conflict becomes overt and the other person can realize a conflict exists. Only when the frustration and conceptualization are communicated through verbal and nonverbal behavior can another person become involved in the conflict. This part of the episode reflects the behavioral approach to conflict.

When perceiving the behavior, the other person reacts. That person may agree or disagree, comply or compete, understand or show confusion, be calm or angry, or display other reactions. The other's **reaction** causes the first person to reconceptualize the situation in light of this new behavior. If everything is going as expected, the first person continues with the plan, or changes strategies if the other's reaction was unexpected.

Others become involved in the conflict only when you communicate your frustration and conceptualization.

People may cycle through this conceptualization/behavior-reaction/reconceptualization loop many times before completing the episode. When the people stop interacting, the conflict episode is finished and they have reached the outcome. This does not mean the conflict has been fully resolved, only that the immediate communication, and hence the episode, has ended. The outcome of one episode may be the starting point for the next episode. People may resolve a conflict in one episode or it may continue through episode after episode. Consider the following example:

Helen discovered that her co-worker, Stan, was making more money than she, even though they had identical experience and were doing the same job. She felt *frustrated* that her goal of equal pay was not met and that resources available to Stan were not equally available to her. She became angry. She conceptualized the situation as blatant sex discrimination and decided to confront her boss about the inequity. She thought (*conceptualization*) that she would be aggressive and that her boss would back down when he saw how determined she was. She marched into his office and angrily stated her position, demanding that she receive a raise (*behavior*).

Her boss surprised her by stating he had noticed the discrepancy and had already initiated her pay raise (*reaction*). However, he became angry at her belligerent tone and disrespectful attitude. He began to berate her for insubordination. Helen realized her error (*reconceptualization*), apologized quickly, and left the room (*outcome of episode 1*).

The next day she had to work with her boss on a project. Communication was strained and Helen felt frustrated in her inability to make amends to her boss (*frustration in episode 2*). She rationalized that the hard feelings would pass (*conceptualization of episode 2*) if she would just be nice and pleasant (*behavior episode 2*). Her boss reacted coldly (*reaction to episode 2*). When Helen left the office, she knew it would take time to reestablish the trust and friendly relationship she and her boss had previously shared (*outcome to episode 2 leading to recurring episodes*).

This example illustrates the stages of the conflict and the way the outcome of one episode affects future episodes. Though the situation was changed to resolve the content conflict, the behaviors had created a relationship conflict that became the focus of future episodes. Conflict is a cycle of interrelated episodes and requires continuous management. To paraphrase baseball legend Yogi Berra's well-known "it ain't over 'til it's over," a conflict episode sometimes ain't over even when it's over.

"Before You Go On"

You should be able to answer the following:

What are the stages of the conflict episode model?

Types of Conflict

Identifying the type of conflict can be helpful in deciding which strategy to use in managing a conflict experience. Conflict categories include the topic of the conflict and the rules that govern the conflict episode.

Conflict Topics

The most common topics of conflict are relationship conflict and content conflict.[17] **Relationship conflicts** concern definitions or perceptions of people's interaction patterns. These conflicts center on the definition of the relationship, the distribution of power, the way people communicate, and the emotional involvement of the conflict parties. Statements such as these indicate that the conflict is about the relationship rather than about a specific issue:

> You always get your way.
>
> You don't love me as much as I love you.
>
> You never pay attention to me when we're at a party.
>
> If you were my friend, you would let me have the money.

Content conflicts concern the distribution of resources, achievement of goals, or conflicting ideas. Statements such as these indicate that the conflict is over content:

> I want the dishes washed, and I want them washed now.
>
> Why can't you ever keep your half of the apartment clean?
>
> I want to study and you keep playing the stereo so loud I can't concentrate.
>
> How can you think the president is fair to minorities when he constantly vetoes civil rights legislation?

Sometimes these types of conflict are clearly defined and both people realize that conflict is about the relationship or about a specific content topic. Other times, people confuse the type of conflict occurring and misinterpret its focus. For example, if your roommate says, "You never clean up your share of the dirty dishes," you may interpret the conflict as she doesn't like me any more. You focus on the relational aspects of the conflict while the roommate may simply be trying to gain cooperation in achieving her goal of a clean apartment. Similarly, you may argue with your roommate about trying to study while he plays the stereo too loudly. You may argue about the problem of not being able to achieve your studying goals. You may not realize that you are really upset that your roommate doesn't seem to respect your needs and that you perceive you have little power in the relationship, rather than the loud stereo.

When relationship and content conflicts become confused, the management of the conflict episode becomes more difficult. If you are having a relationship conflict over who has the most power, resolving a specific issue such as playing the stereo does not solve the problem. You will continue to have conflicts over other issues until the power relationship is settled. If you have the same content conflicts over and over, or have conflicts over many issues, the real problem may be a relationship conflict masquerading as a content conflict.[18] Resolving the content issue will have little effect on future conflicts because the underlying relationship conflict has not been addressed.

Since communication inherently involves both content and relationship messages, all conflicts have both content and relationship dimensions. The transactional point of view does not define whether a conflict is due to content or relationship. These categories are not extremes on a continuum so that as you focus more on content you focus less on relationship issues. Conflict involves both content and relationship concerns; focusing solely on one is not effective long-term conflict management. From a transactional perspective, people in conflict situations need to examine the content issues in light of their relationship and to evaluate the impact of their relationship on the content outcomes.

"Before You Go On"

You should be able to answer the following question:

Why is it important to distinguish between relationship and content conflicts?

Conflict Intensity

Conflict can range from low intensity to high intensity. Think of **conflict intensity** as a continuum based on both emotional and behavioral responses to situations. We talk about the low, moderate, and high categories to demonstrate how intensity affects the management of the conflict. We begin with the problems of the low and high extremes and then see how moderate conflict intensity can be most productive.

Low intensity refers to conflicts in which the people feel low levels of frustration, anxiety, stress, anger, or other emotions. Subsequently, the behaviors expressing the conflict are nonconfrontational, neutral, matter of fact, ambiguous, or tentative. Participants have little involvement in the communication and little motivation to engage in managing the conflict.[19]

Extreme emotional arousal and expression of ideas with highly intense language and nonverbal behaviors characterize *high intensity* conflicts. When angry or under extreme stress, people do not process information clearly. They have limited capacity to remember information, are more limited in the way they interpret ideas, and perceive ideas in either-or, all-or-nothing terms. People in highly intense conflicts are less able to listen to and understand other people's perspectives and to verbally express their own ideas. They are also less aware of their own nonverbal behavior.[20] Highly stressed persons react emotionally rather than rationally to the situation and to other's behaviors.

Moderate intensity is potentially the most productive level of conflict. When there is a moderate degree of emotional arousal, people tend to be able to process information clearly. They express their ideas more precisely and with conviction. They have heightened awareness of the situation and their own behavior. When conflict is managed in the moderate level of intensity, there is a greater probability of effective management of the communication process. The people in the conflict are sufficiently aroused and motivated to engage in productive conflict management without being overwhelmed by the intensity of their emotions and behaviors.

"Before You Go On"

You should be able to answer the following question:

How do low, moderate, and highly intense conflicts differ?

The next section suggests several strategies for managing conflicts. The more strategies you learn, the more flexible you can be in handling conflict situations. You should be able to adapt to the situation, to yourself, and to the other person. You can also help the other person communicate productively. Competent communication requires that both people help each other manage their conflict.

Strategies for Conflict Management

A strategy is a pattern of behavior designed to achieve specific content and relationship goals. A strategy is a combination of communication skills that allow you to adapt to the changing situation. For example, your overall goal may be to avoid conflict with your roommates. To achieve this goal, you may use several different strategies such as not being home at the same time they are, not talking to them, giving in to their demands, doing their chores for them, or taking the blame for problems that occur. Similarly, your strategy of cooperation may include using communication skills for transactional listening, using vivid and concrete language, negotiating power, increasing involvement, and creating supportive climates.

Our strategies usually make sense to us. They seem reasonable because, after all, we are behaving naturally. We have learned to use our conflict strategies by watching and modeling our parents, friends, and relatives. We have watched countless conflicts being resolved on television and in the movies. Therefore, we are surprised when other people don't understand what we mean or why we act the way we do. Similarly, we are confused when other people don't act the way we think they should, or in other words, the way we think we would act if we were them. The way to help both people understand each other's behavior is to use metacommunication. Tell them what you are doing and why. Use transactional listening techniques to understand why they are behaving the way they are.

Researchers have developed a wide variety of models and classifications for conflict strategies and styles.[21] Though they use different names for the strategies, most agree on three basic approaches: competition, avoidance, and cooperation.

Competitive Strategies

Conflict occurs when people desire limited resources or perceive interference with attaining their desired goals. By using **competitive strategies,** people gain as many resources and goals as possible for themselves while limiting the gains of others. Sometimes the situation is structured so that specific goals are mutually exclusive. For example, only one person can receive a job promotion or use the car on a given night or receive a bonus for selling the most products during the month. When goals are mutually or partially exclusive and resources cannot be shared, competition becomes a viable strategy.

If productively managed, competitive strategies can be beneficial. (For examples, see the accompanying box entitled Competitive Conflict Strategies.) People use competition when the goals and resources are important to them. The risk of losing something important motivates them to perform at peak level. Competition sparks creativity, heightens mental awareness, and increases physical performance. For instance, businesses use competition to increase job motivation, commitment to decisions, and employee performance.[22] Also note that students competing for scholarships, grades, or acceptance to professional schools work harder. Athletes, debaters, dancers, musicians, and actors often perform better during competition than during practice. Their ability to process information increases under the stress of competition.

Specific strategies for productive competition focus on not only performing at your peak level of ability but also respecting the dignity and self-worth of the other person. You want to achieve your goal because your behavior or ideas are perceived as better than those of the other person. Competition is most productive when both people perform well. Competitive conflicts follow implicit or explicit rules governing the interaction and the means by which the outcome can be achieved. Be sure you understand and follow these rules. If the rules are not clear, discuss them with the other person so that both of you know what tactics are permitted and what behaviors are prohibited.

Focus on the process rather than the outcome as a measure of success. Be assertive in your communication by using the verbal and nonverbal skills discussed in previous chapters. Using descriptive and concrete language, using spontaneous and supportive nonverbal behaviors, and organizing your communication can increase the chances for competent conflict management.

You must also give the other person a turn to express ideas. Listening carefully to these messages by using behavioral and cognitive listening techniques, helps you understand how to better construct your arguments, refute the other's reasoning, and analyze the issues. You never know, the other person might be right!

If you win the competition, acknowledge the efforts of the other person. If you lose, take responsibility for your behavior and learn from the experience so you do better next time. Since the outcome of one conflict sets the stage for future conflicts, being a good winner and loser can make future conflict situations more productive.

Competitive Conflict Strategies

PRODUCTIVE STRATEGIES

- Recognize there are many content and relationship goals in the conflict.
- Understand and follow the rules governing the competition.
- Achieve the goal by doing your best.
- Use assertive behavior.
- Listen carefully to the other person.
- Be a gracious winner and loser.

DESTRUCTIVE STRATEGIES

- Recognize that the most important goal is to win.
- Ignore or bend the rules to your advantage.
- Make the other person perform poorly.
- Use aggressive behavior; withhold rewards or use punishment.
- Focus only on your own strategies, ignore the other person.
- Brag about your success and complain about your defeats.

If performed in a destructive manner, competition can be detrimental to a relationship. Destructive strategies tend to escalate the conflict to high intensity levels and increase the defensiveness of both people. If competition causes you to become overly stressed or anxious, your performance and motivation decrease. Some people use competitive strategies in all situations, even when the goals and resources can be mutually shared. Although competition is concerned with achieving a goal, some people narrowly define the goal as winning. Winning becomes the only goal of the conflict with no concern for the relationship or the means by which the goal is achieved. The specific content goals become secondary and are only a means by which to measure whether you won or lost.

When you use destructive competitive strategies, your concern may be to win at all costs. You use the rules to your advantage and if they interfere with winning, you circumvent or ignore them. Winning is often achieved by making the other person perform poorly rather than by the merits of your own behavior. You become aggressive through name calling, hostile joking, sarcasm, yelling, and psychological and physical violence.[23] You may withhold rewards, affection, or physical contact, or use punishment and threats to make the other person give in. If you keep the focus on your behavior and your own needs, the other person doesn't have a chance to make a case. You interrupt, ignore, and belittle that person's arguments, and maintain power through indifference. When you win, you make sure the other person recognizes your achievement. If you lose, you blame other people, unfair circumstances, or bad luck. You make it clear that you should have won, even though you did not.

Avoidance Strategies

Sometimes it is appropriate to avoid engaging in conflict. As you remember, conflict occurs through communication, hence, if you refuse to communicate about the conflict, you have avoided it. This does not mean that you are unaware of the conflict situation or that you do not feel emotional stress. It simply means that you are not ready or willing to engage in the communicative behaviors that express the conflict.

As shown in the box entitled Conflict Avoidance Strategies, avoidance of conflict can be constructive when you and the other person are unable to engage in productive communication.[24] Perhaps your emotional stress is so intense you can't think clearly. Or perhaps you don't clearly understand the issues involved. In these cases, you may want to avoid the conflict so that you can calm down to a moderate level of intensity. Or you may want time to gather additional information about the situation.

Avoidance strategy can also be appropriate when the situation is not conducive to effective conflict management. Perhaps you are with other people who are not part of the conflict. You might want to wait until you and the other person are alone rather than make a scene in public. In other cases, you may want to postpone the conflict until all parties involved in the issues are present. You might also want to wait to engage in the conflict so that the timing is better. If you're tired or sick or in a bad mood, you may want to wait until you are rested and feeling better before discussing the conflict with the other person.

Similarly, if the conflict is complex and requires lengthy discussion, you don't want to start the discussion five minutes before you have to leave for a meeting, class, or other commitment. An avoidance strategy can prevent nonproductive or insoluble conflicts from escalating. Finding the most productive time to engage in the conflict is an important use of the avoidance strategy.

Constructive avoidance strategies require that you negotiate an appropriate time to discuss the issues with the other person. Suggest that the importance of the conflict requires discussing it at a later time. You may suggest specific actions that can be taken during the delay to make the confrontation more effective when it occurs. For example, both people could gather additional information, check out rumors, validate facts, or invite other interested parties to participate. When negotiating conflict avoidance, discuss the reasons for the postponement, seek agreement that postponement is necessary, and schedule a specific time to discuss the issues. Constructive avoidance merely delays the communication about the issues until a more appropriate time and situation allow constructive confrontation.

Conflict Avoidance Strategies

CONSTRUCTIVE STRATEGIES

- Admit that conflict exists.
- Affirm the importance of confronting the issues.
- Provide reasons for postponing the discussion of conflict.
- Negotiate specific activities to do before confrontation.
- Ensure all the people involved—but only the people involved—are present during the confrontation.
- Schedule a specific time to discuss the conflict situation.

DESTRUCTIVE STRATEGIES

- Deny that conflict exists or that anything is wrong.
- Joke about the conflict and refuse to take it seriously.
- Apologize prematurely or give in quickly.
- Use the silent treatment.
- Avoid the topic.
- Avoid the person or situation.

As shown in the accompanying box entitled Conflict Avoidance Strategies, there are also destructive uses of conflict avoidance. People often avoid conflict because they are afraid of the outcome, dislike the emotional stress that accompanies conflict, perceive conflict as inherently hostile and destructive. They seem to think if they don't talk about the conflict it will go away by itself. Instead of openly confronting the situation, they become defensive and refuse to discuss the issues bothering them.

Unfortunately, conflict situations rarely disappear by themselves. They continue to build in intensity and importance until they can no longer be ignored. When they are finally discussed, the emotions are so intense, and the situation so complex, that there is little chance for productive management. If you avoid conflict in a defensive manner, you run the risk of the conflict escalating at a later time.

You can defensively avoid conflict by simply not talking about it. You can change the subject, employ the silent treatment, or deny anything is wrong. You may joke about the conflict and refuse to take it seriously. You can also issue a quick and usually insincere apology or simply give in to the other's demands. You may avoid bringing up any topics that remind you of the conflict and may even avoid the other person altogether. Defensive avoidance strategies deny the existence of the conflict, refrain from discussing the conflict, treat the conflict as trivial and silly, or escape from the situation entirely.

Cooperative strategies promote interdependence and seek to find mutually satisfying solutions. Since both people co-created the conflict episode, both people must actively engage to create a solution. Compromise, team building, and collaboration are common cooperative strategies; for other examples, see the accompanying box entitled Cooperative Conflict Strategies. All are concerned with working together to achieve the best possible outcomes for all the people involved. When people actively pursue their own personal goals, the personal goals of the other person, and the goals that they share, cooperation can be a constructive conflict management strategy.[25]

Cooperative strategies require that both people actively create a mutually satisfying solution. Cooperation does not necessarily mean that both people achieve all of their goals as is implied by the term *win-win*. Cooperation is not simply additive, that is, counting all the goals you reached and all the goals the other person reached to see if everyone got what they wanted. Rather it is the overall outcome for everyone involved, considered as a whole. For example, a child who wishes to do something dangerous has a conflict with parents who forbid the activity. The parents may prevail in forbidding the child to perform a dangerous activity (the child does not get the goal) but may do so in a cooperative manner resulting in a positive relationship and safety for the family as a whole.

The transactional approach suggests that both the situation and the behavior define the situation so that you could use cooperative behaviors in a competitive situation. Since the conflict situation is co-created by both people, both people's perceptions of the situation and subsequent actions define the conflict. Therefore, both manage the conflict through mutual negotiation and cooperation.

Cooperative strategies help control the conflict at a moderate level of intensity. When people cooperate to reach a mutual decision, they are committed to the content outcome and motivated to make the solution work. They also increase their commitment to their relationship.[26] Mutually derived decisions establish a history of success that has a positive influence on future conflicts. People who have successfully managed previous conflicts are more likely to be motivated to engage constructively in future conflicts.

To cooperate, focus your attention on both your own needs and goals and those of the other person. Effective listening techniques such as paraphrasing, probing questions, and affirmation behaviors are essential cooperative skills. Helping the other person to understand your perspective requires creating supportive climates, concreteness, descriptiveness, and clear organization. Your ability to self-disclose appropriate information and to help the other person disclose helps create an atmosphere of information sharing and trust required of cooperative strategies.

When both people are not committed to cooperating, cooperative strategies often fail to work. It is difficult to compromise if the other person is competing; it is difficult to collaborate with someone who is avoiding the conflict situation. Trying to cooperate in these circumstances is counterproductive.

You cannot make cooperation work without letting the other person know what you are trying to do. Talk to the other person about the conflict strategies you are using. Use metacommunication, talk to each other about communication. We are usually very good at telling others about personal goals we want to accomplish. "I want" is a phrase we learn very early in life to tell others about our content goals. We frequently have difficulty expressing relationship goals such as, "Here is how I feel about you." and "I think of our relationship this way." and "Here's what I'm trying to do to make our relationship work." We have even more trouble communicating about the transactional nature of the relationship as in, "What can we do together to make this situation better?" and "How can we use this situation to make our relationship more satisfying?" Metacommunication is one of the most important strategies you can learn for managing communication from a transactional perspective.

Cooperative Conflict Strategies

CONSTRUCTIVE STRATEGIES

- Discover each other's relationship and content goals.
- Create mutual goals.
- Disclose all relevant information.
- Emphasize commitment to reaching a mutually acceptable solution.
- Emphasize commitment to the relationship regardless of outcome.
- Generate a variety of solutions, brainstorm.
- Be flexible in accepting new ideas and alternative solutions but do not abandon your principles.
- Focus on the process by which you are managing conflict rather than on a specific predetermined outcome.
- Use metacommunication to explain your strategies and how you perceive the other person's behavior.
- Teach each other strategies for conflict management.
- Be involved in the communication and maintain a moderate level of conflict intensity.

DESTRUCTIVE STRATEGIES

- Appear to cooperate only when you know it will fail.
- Cooperate only when you realize you will otherwise lose.
- Cooperate simply to end the conflict.
- Force cooperation even when other strategies are more efficient or more appropriate.

Cooperative strategies are destructive when used inappropriately or for the wrong reason. Some people pretend to cooperate when they know the situation will fail. They justify their subsequent actions by saying, "I tried to cooperate but you wouldn't let me. I have no choice but to be competitive (or withdraw)." Other people might use compromise just to disengage from the conflict situation. They may be tired of the conflict, unmotivated to work hard at finding the best solution, or simply discouraged. Compromising to avoid further conflict or to find a quick solution is ultimately destructive to future content and relationship goals.

Cooperation is not always the best solution. When one person's position is clearly better than another or when one decision will have superior results, compromise is unproductive. Conversely, using elaborate team building techniques in minor conflicts over routine problems easily solved through other means is an inefficient process.

"Before You Go On"

You should be able to answer the following question:

What are the important differences among competitive, avoidance, and cooperative strategies for managing conflict?

Deciding when to use each strategy is an important part of the conflict process. You must learn several strategies so you can employ them appropriately. The conflict episode requires that you conceptualize a strategy based on your perception of the situation. Effective performance of the strategy depends on your analytical, organizational, listening, verbal, and nonverbal communication skills. Being able to adapt your strategies to the other person's reactions and the changing conditions of the conflict episode is essential to competent conflict management.

Responses to *"Before You Go On"* Questions: A Chapter Summary

---

1.   What are the differences among the situational, behavioral, and transactional approaches to defining conflict?
The situational approach defines conflict as the inability to reach our goals or acquire resources due to the interference of other people. From this perspective, conflict becomes more intense as the goals and resources become more important. Conflict resolution focuses on changing the situation.

The behavioral approach defines conflict by the way people communicate about the conflict. Intensity of conflict depends on the intensity of the behaviors used to express the conflict. Conflict management focuses on changing the behaviors of the people involved in the conflict.

The transactional approach to conflict examines the interdependence of the situation and the people's behavior. Both people create conflict through their communication that reflects their perceptions of the situation. Conflict management requires focus on both the situation and the behavior because changing one element of the context affects all of the elements.

2.   In which ways can conflict can be productive and destructive?
Conflict can be productive if managed constructively. Conflict helps stimulate thinking by providing different viewpoints; it also helps us clarify our own perceptions and better understand others. Conflict can often strengthen a relationship by increasing commitment, self-disclosure, and trust.

Conflict is destructive if the participants try to hurt each other to gain their own goals, or if they avoid conflict to prevent losing their goals. Poorly managed conflict may result in reduced trust, destruction of the relationship, and emotional stress.

3.   What are the differences between assessing conflict by the outcome and evaluating conflict by the behaviors?
Outcome provides an easily assessed measure of goal achievement. Since conflicts involve multiple goals, it is problematic to determine which goal to use as the criteria for effectiveness. Although it is assumed to be the result of our behavior, goal attainment might be due to external factors such as luck or other people's actions. A successful outcome, therefore, does not necessarily mean that the conflict was productively handled.

The behavioral approach focuses on emotional responses to the behaviors and how well we model appropriate conflict strategies. Even though we lost, we might believe the conflict was productive if we are satisfied we did all we could. Since behavior can be learned, people can be trained to create productive conflicts.

The transactional approach assesses both the situational and behavioral outcomes. The focus is not only on the goals and resources the people achieve, but also the way in which the conflict is conducted by both people simultaneously.

4.   What are the stages of the conflict episode model?
Frustration is the first stage. It occurs when a person perceives someone interfering with their efforts to attain personal goals and/or objectives. Experiences frustration usually results in an emotional response. Think of a situation where you have felt frustrated as a result of someone else's action. You probably reacted emotionally and tried to conceive of a way to reduce your emotions and frustration.

As you became frustrated, you probably began to **conceptualize** the conflict situation—the second stage in the model of a conflict episode. You began to think of why you were frustrated, what or who was causing your frustration, and how you should react with your frustration. The third stage in the model begins when you adopt **behaviors** in reaction to and in attempt to reduce or eliminate the conflict and achieve desired goals and objectives. As a result of your behaviors (reactions to the conflict), the other person **reacts** to the situation which causes you to re-conceptualize the conflict situation and adopt a new or additional behaviors. In a conflict episode, the individuals may remain in the cycle of **conceptualization-behaviors-other's reaction-reconceptualization-behaviors-other's reaction,** etc. for a long period of time. The final stage, **outcomes,** occurs when the individuals stop interacting. This does not mean, however, that the conflict has been resolved. For example, you may have become so frustrated with the conflict episode that you stop talking about it—an outcome. However, the conflict was not resolved. Therefore, the outcome may be the starting point for a new conflict episode which begins with the first stage—**frustration.**

5. Why it is important to distinguish between relationship and content conflicts?

Relationship conflicts concern how people interact and feel about each other. Power distribution, affection, and personalities are topics of relational conflicts. Content conflicts concern issues related to the situation. Values, attitudes, beliefs, ideas, resources, and goals are content issues.

One reason to distinguish between the topics of conflict is to adopt appropriate strategies. A second reason is to keep one type of conflict from becoming the other. Confusing one type of conflict for another and transferring content and relationship conflicts are detrimental to competent conflict management.

6. How do low, moderate, and high intensity conflicts differ?

Low intensity conflict represents one extreme in which there is little involvement or concern with the process or outcome of the conflict. Motivation to seek information or communicate about the conflict is low. Cognitive processing capabilities are diminished.

High intensity conflict is the other extreme in which emotional responses are high. Highly intense behavior distracts the participants from clearly analyzing the conflict. While motivation to engage in conflict may be high, cognitive ability to process information is decreased.

Moderate conflict intensity provides sufficient motivation to engage in the conflict without being overwhelmed by the emotional and behavioral responses. Cognitive ability is at its peak allowing increased creativity and problem-solving ability.

7. What are the important differences among competitive, avoidance, and cooperative strategies for managing conflict?

Competitive tactics assume a win-lose situation. Competition can be productive when both parties understand and follow the rules and when both the winner and loser accept the outcomes of the conflict graciously. Destructive competition occurs when winning becomes so important that participants try to destroy each other, break the rules, fight unethically, gloat over their victories, or seek revenge for their defeats.

Avoidance is a strategy that seeks to disengage from the conflict. Constructive use of avoidance strategies ignores trivial issues. It also postpones the conflict until more information is gathered, people have achieved a moderate intensity level, all people involved in the situation are present, people not involved in the conflict are absent, and there is sufficient time to discuss the conflict. Destructive avoidance tactics deny that conflict exists, give in too quickly or insincerely, or avoid communication necessary to resolve the situation.

Cooperative strategies work to help all people gain their goals. The important consideration is not whether everyone got all they wanted, but whether the situation and relationship is better than it was. Working for the maximum gain for the relationship may entail compromise, collaboration, and even accommodation.

S T U D E N T   E X E R C I S E S

1.   Approaches to conflict.

Think of the conflicts you had last week. Write a list of the main reasons for each of the conflicts. Now examine your list of reasons. Which approach to defining conflict did you use in your experiences? Did you perceive conflict to be about the situation, the behaviors, or both situation and behavior?

Now think about the solution to your conflicts. What did you change? Did you change the elements of the situation, or focus on changing the way people expressed conflict, or change both the situation and behavior? Is this consistent with your perceptions of the reasons for the conflict?

2.   Conflict between heroes and villains.

TV shows and movies are often based on conflict. Which character in a movie or TV show best epitomizes the ideal handler of conflict? In other words, who handles conflict like you think you should? Why?

Which character on TV or in the movies handles conflict badly? Why?

3.   Attitudes about conflict.

Do you agree or disagree with the following statements? Why? How do your attitudes compare to your classmates' and friends' attitudes?

a. If people communicated more there would be a lot less conflict.
b. The most important variable in dealing with conflict is to approach it rationally and objectively.
c. Somebody almost always loses in a conflict situation.
d. Negative feedback should not be given unless it is requested.
e. Most people avoid openly discussing conflict situations.

How do your answers relate to this text's assertion that the way you think about conflict affects how you manage it?

4.   Conflict strategies.

Consider each of the following situations. How do you typically react in each conflict situation? Do you typically avoid it? Are you competitive? Are you cooperative?

   a. Conflicts with your parents or guardians.
   b. Conflicts with your roommate.
   c. Conflicts with your boss or teacher.
   d. Conflicts with friends.
   e. Conflicts with people you don't like.

What patterns do you see? Are you the same in each situation? Is this appropriate? Are you different in each situation? What elements of the situation make a difference in your strategies?

G L O S S A R Y

avoidance strategies Strategies designed to avoid communication about the conflict issues.

behavioral approach to conflict Defining and perceiving conflict as it is expressed through the behaviors of the participants. Conflict is resolved by changing the behaviors used to express it.

behavior phase The third phase of the conflict episode model in which the person communicates feelings and ideas about the conflict situation to another person.

competitive strategies Strategies designed to attain personal goals while interfering with others' attainment of their goals; a win-lose strategy.

conceptualization phase The second stage of the conflict episode model in which the person defines the conflict, assumes causes of the conflict, considers strategies, predicts other's behaviors, and conceptualizes goals.

conflict intensity The severity of the conflict determined by the importance and incompatibility of goals and/or the intensity of the verbal and nonverbal behaviors used to express the conflict. Intensity varies from low to high conflict with moderate conflict being the most productive.

conflict outcome The final stage of the conflict episode that is the result of previous communication. The outcome of one conflict episode can become the first stage of subsequent conflict episodes. Outcome is often used as a measurement for the success of the conflict communication.

content conflict Conflict over specific issues, goals, resources, procedures, decisions, values, beliefs, or other topics. Conflict related to the elements comprising and defining the situation.

cooperative strategy A conflict management strategy which recognizes mutually interdependent goals and works with the other person to arrive at the most beneficial solution for the relationship. Cooperation focuses on mutual benefit rather than on the gains or losses of the individuals.

destructive conflict Conflict in which one or both parties lose important resources or goals and which damages the relationship between the parties.

frustration phase First phase of the conflict episode model in which the person perceives that goals are not being met or resources are not being attained due to the actions of others. The emotional response to the situation first occurs during this phase.

productive conflict Conflict which benefits all people in the situation and which is conducted in such a manner as to maintain or enhance the relationship.

reaction phase The fourth stage of the conflict episode in which the person's behavior is reacted to by others.

relationship conflict Conflict concerning elements of the relationship between the participants including power, affection, decision making, personalities, and commitment.

situational approach to conflict The approach to defining and perceiving conflict according to the importance of goals and resources and the degree of interference with their attainment. Conflict resolution requires changes in the situation.

transactional approach to conflict The approach to defining and perceiving conflict as the interdependent interaction of the situation and people's behavior. Since behavior and situation are interdependent, the management of conflict requires changes in both situation and behaviors.

N O T E S

1.   Kenneth Boulding, *Conflict and Defense: A General Theory* (New York: Harper Torchbooks, 1962).

2.   L. A. Coser, *Continuities in the Study of Social Conflict* (New York: Free Press, 1967).

3.   M. Deutsch, "Conflicts: Productive and Destructive," in *Conflict Resolution through Communication,* ed., Fred E. Jandt (New York: Harper and Row, 1973).

4.   Sara Kiesler, *Interpersonal Processes in Groups and Organizations* (Arlington Heights, Ill.: Harlan Davidson, 1978).

5.   E. Rhenman, L. Stromberg, and G. Westerlunch, *Conflict and Cooperation in Business Organizations* (New York: John Wiley & Sons, 1970).

6.   C. Reeser, *Management: Functions and Modern Concepts* (Glenview, IL: Scott, Foresman and Company, 1973), 503.

7.   J. F. Brynes, "Connecting Organizational Politics and Conflict Resolution," *Personnel Administrator* (1986) 47–50.

8.   Fred E. Jandt, ed., *Conflict Resolution through Communication* (New York: Harper and Row, 1973).

9.   L. Pondy, "Organizational Conflict: Concepts and Models," *Administration Science Quarterly* 12 (1967), 296–320.

10. R. Kilmann and K. Thomas, "Interpersonal Conflict-Handling Behavior as Reflections of Jungian Personality Dimensions," *Psychology Reports* 37 (1975), 971–80.

11. Linda L. Putnam and M. Scott Poole, "Conflict and Negotiation," in *Handbook of Organizational Communication: An Interdisciplinary Perspective,* ed., Frederic M. Jablin, Linda L. Putnam, Karlene H. Roberts, and Lyman W. Porter (Newbury Park, Calif.: Sage Publications, 1987).

12. Joyce L. Hocker and William W. Wilmot, *Interpersonal Conflict,* 3rd ed. (Dubuque, Iowa: Wm. C. Brown, 1991).

13. C. D. Mortenson, "A Transactional Paradigm of Verbalized Social Conflict," in *Perspectives on Communication in Social Conflict,* ed., G. R. Miller and H. W. Simons (Englewood Cliffs, N.J.: Prentice Hall, 1974), 90–124.

14. Roger Fisher and William Ury, *Getting to Yes: Negotiating Agreement Without Giving In* (New York: Penguin Books, 1981).

15. Hocker and Wilmot, *Interpersonal Conflict.*

16. K. Thomas, "Conflict and Conflict Management," in *Handbook of Organizational Psychology,* ed., M. D. Dunnette (Chicago: Rand McNally, 1976).

17. William W. Wilmot, *Dyadic Communication,* 3rd ed. (New York: McGraw-Hill, 1987).

18. Hocker and Wilmot, *Interpersonal Conflict.*

19. L. D. Brown, *Managing Conflict at Organizational Interfaces* (Reading, Mass.: Addison-Wesley Publishing, 1983).

20. Ronald N. Taylor, *Behavioral Decision Making* (Glenview, Ill.: Scott, Foresman, 1984).

21. Kilman and Thomas, "Interpersonal Conflict"; Linda L. Putnam and C. E. Wilson, "Communicative Strategies in Organizational Conflicts: Reliability and Validity of a Measurement Scale," in *Communication Yearbook 6,* ed., Michael Burgoon (Beverly Hills, Calif.: Sage Publications-International Communication Association, 1982); Hocker and Wilmot, *Interpersonal Conflicts.*

22. Kilman and Thomas, "Interpersonal Conflict."

23. Descriptions of tactics can be found in George R. Bach and Peter Wyden, *The Intimate Enemy: How to Fight Fair in Love and Marriage* (New York: Avon Books, 1968); A. Filley, *Interpersonal Conflict Resolution* (Glenview, Ill.: Scott, Foresman, 1975); M. Fitzpatrick and J. Winke, "You Always Hurt the One You Love: Strategies and Tactics in Interpersonal Conflict," *Communication Quarterly* 27 (1979), 3–11.

24. E. Van de Vliert, "Escalative Intervention in Small Group Conflicts," *Journal of Applied Behavioral Science* 21 (1985), 19–36.

25. Victor D. Wall, Jr. and Gloria Galanes, "The SYMLOG Dimensions and Small Group Conflict," *Central States Speech Journal* 37 (1986) 61–78; Alan L. Sillars, 1980 "Attributions and Communication in Roommate Conflicts," *Communication Monographs* 47 (1980), 180–200.

26. F. Tutzauer and M. E. Roloff, "Communication Processes Leading to Integrative Agreements: Three Paths to Joint Benefits," *Communication Research* 15 (1988), 360–80.

11

Strategies for Interviewing

- *A reporter asks the president of General Motors about the economic future of the company.*

- *A talk show host questions a celebrity about an upcoming movie.*

- *A police investigator interrogates a witness to a crime.*

- *A potential employer asks you questions about your job skills and qualifications.*

- *A salesperson tries to convince you to buy a life insurance policy.*

When you think of an interview, what images come to mind? If you thought of any of the preceding situations, you are correct; these are all interview situations. Interviews are more common and happen more often than many people might think.

Imagine you had a question for your professor that you weren't able to ask in class. You don't want to wait until the next class, so you go to the professor's office. You knock on the door, stick your head in and ask: "Do you have a few minutes to answer a question for me?" You receive a nod from the professor, take a seat, and spend the next few minutes asking questions and receiving answers. You then thank the professor and go on your way. You probably didn't realize it, but you just conducted an interview!

Other common interview situations include asking directions at a gas station, trying to find out about your roommate's date last night, getting class registration advice from your academic advisor, or getting a job evaluation from your boss. Taking a phone survey, answering a pollster's questionnaire, seeing a counselor for advice or help with a problem, or asking new acquaintances about their lives and experiences are also examples of interviews.

The Nature of Interviewing

Interviewing is a specific type of interpersonal communication. Even though an interview involves conversation, all conversations are not interviews. One difference between interviews and normal conversation is that at least one person usually has a deliberate or premeditated goal to achieve. The goal of an interview can be to obtain information, seek advice, make a sale, create an impression, or get a job. Another characteristic of most interviews, even very informal ones, is the asking and answering of questions. When you ask your academic advisor for advice, you ask questions and expect answers. Your advisor might also ask questions of you, to better understand your goals and interests in an effort to give you good advice.

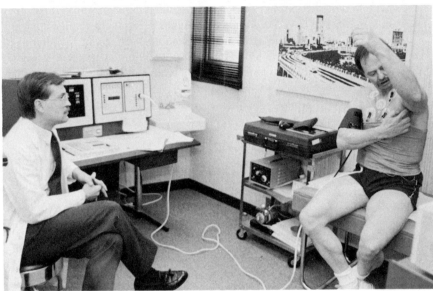

Definition

Perhaps the best way to define the **interview** is to examine these definitions of communication scholars:

> A particular form of interpersonal communication in which two persons interact largely through a question and answer format for the purpose of achieving specific goals.[1]

> A specialized form of oral, face-to-face communication between people in an interpersonal relationship that is entered into for a task-related purpose associated with a particular subject matter.[2]

> A process of dyadic, relational communication with a predetermined and serious purpose designed to interchange behavior and involving the asking and answering of questions.[3]

Note that at least four common elements appear in these definitions: interpersonal communication, two people, specific purpose or goals, and questions.

Strategies for Interviewing 259

Interpersonal Communication

As mentioned earlier, interpersonal communication can certainly take place in an interview, but whether it does or does not depends on the context, the number of people, and the immediacy of face-to-face interaction. Other contexts such as telephone interviews, mail questionnaires, group interviews or forums, panel interviews, and press conferences are not discussed in this text. We focus on those interviews capitalizing on the characteristics and processes by which two people form a relationship in an immediate face-to-face setting.

Two People

Most definitions suggest that two people are involved in interviews. In many cases, that is true. However, the roles people play in an interview are greater than the exact number of people. Rather than two people, it is more accurate to consider an interview consisting of two parties—an *interviewer* and an *interviewee*.[4] In reality, each party can be one or more persons.

Specific Purpose

One distinguishing feature of an interview is that at least one of the parties has a specific goal to accomplish. As a consequence, that person usually has a pre-planned strategy for the interaction that is related to the goal.

Questions

The primary format of most interviews is the asking and answering of goal-related questions. An interview, therefore, has a fairly specific structure. Thus, the purpose and structure of the interview define and separate it from other kinds of conversation.

"Before You Go On"

You should be able to answer the following question:

Which four elements are common to the definitions of an interview?

Types of Interviews

Information Interview

Information interviews are either information giving or information gathering. An *information giving* interview is designed to give information to an interviewee. Some typical examples are a company representative explaining rules and regulations to an employee, and a physician explaining the nature of an illness to a patient. Other examples include a personnel manager training someone to do a job and an instructor commenting on the work of a student.

An *information gathering* interview is designed to get information from the interviewee. Examples include a journalist looking for information for a story, a public opinion pollster, and a marketing survey taken. Other examples include a student looking for information about the parking policies on campus, or a TV talk show host questioning a rock star about an upcoming MTV video.

Employment Interview

In an **employment interview** employers (interviewers) evaluate and select employees (interviewees) and employment seekers evaluate and select employment. Both parties act as persuaders as well as providing and receiving information. In order to be hired, the applicants attempt to impress employers with qualifications, personality, attitudes, and energy. On the other hand, the employers attempt to impress the applicants with the quality of the company, available opportunities, and potential job satisfaction to convince them to accept employment.

In many companies, an applicant must pass through several levels and types of interviews before a hiring decision is made. For example, a company might begin with a screening interview. The personnel department usually conducts this primarily information-seeking interview. To create a pool of qualified candidates for the available position, the personnel interviewer screens applicants, looking for the necessary qualifications. Those who meet the requirements go on to the competence or qualifications interview. The purpose of this interview is to rank order the applicants based on how well they perform a specific task. From this point, successful applicants go to formal selection interviews conducted by the actual people with whom they might be working. Since the interviewers know that the applicant can perform the job, the purpose of this interview is to determine how well each applicant fits the organization. The applicant who has the best fit receives the position.

Assessment Interview

The primary objective of an **assessment interview** is the exchange of information to improve the performance of the employee. This kind of interview is also referred to as an evaluation interview. Business organizations and schools use it to evaluate the performance of an employee or a student. The interviewer might ask questions about how well the interviewee likes the job or classes, about particular problems, and about improvement. Just as these evaluations help employers make decisions about promotion and retention, they help teachers make decisions about performance and grades. Assessment interviews discover problems, indicate corrective action, and encourage the further development of the interviewee.

People use persuasive interviews to sell products.

Assessment interviews provide feedback to an employee or student. For instance, suppose your academic advisor discovers that you have a problem studying, that you are working too many hours per week at your job, or that you spend too much time at parties. The advisor might suggest attending a study clinic or cutting down your nonacademic activities. Assessment interviews let you know how you're doing on the job or in class in a way not available through other communication channels. This interview also gives the interviewee an opportunity to supply feedback to the interviewer in the form of criticism or suggestions for improvement.

Persuasive Interview

The **persuasive interview** is designed to change the attitudes or behaviors of the interviewee. The interviewer attempts to convince the interviewee to adopt an attitude or a particular course of action. Some examples of a persuasive interview include selling a product or service, raising funds for charities, trying to motivate an employee, or trying to get someone to quit smoking or start exercising. For instance, when purchasing an automobile, both you and the auto salesperson have particular goals to achieve through the interaction. This interaction is largely made up of questions and answers. You ask questions about the car, the service, and the price, while the salesperson asks you questions about your transportation needs and budget. You are trying to persuade the salesperson to sell you the best car for your needs for the best price. The salesperson tries to persuade you to purchase a car at a price yielding a good commission and to convince you to come back the next time you need a car. In many situations such as this, both parties achieve their persuasive goals.

Counseling/Helping Interview

The **counseling interview** is designed to provide personal advice or guidance to the interviewee. A trained interviewer such as a psychologist, psychiatrist, or other specialist concerned with the personal well-being of the interviewee conducts this interview. Its goal is to help the individual understand and manage problems or to adapt to situations. In organizations, managers wishing to help subordinates resolve personal or work-related problems also conduct counseling interviews. Other interviewers who conduct counseling interviews include social workers, academic counselors, marriage and family counselors, legal advisors, drug counselors, religious counselors, and placement counselors.

"Before You Go On"

You should be able to answer the following question:

What are five kinds of interviews?

Planning an Interview

Every interview involves the pursuit of a goal through the use of communication skills and strategies. As such, it is important to plan your interview in advance. This section considers four aspects of planning: goals, questions, the interview guide, and structure.

Goals

By definition, at least one of the parties in an interview enters the situation with a goal in mind. (At this point, you may want to review chapter 4's discussion of general and specific goals.) Before beginning any kind of interview as either the interviewer or the interviewee, define your *general goals* for the interaction. Are you looking for advice, information, employment, attitude change, motivation, instructions, or problem solution?

After determining your general goals, define your *specific goals*. Do you want help with a certain part of your job? Do you want advice on whether to take another communication class? Do you want career information? The more specific you can be while conceiving these goals, the easier it is to plan your interview. The goal of an interview defines the purpose of the interaction, determines the kinds of questions asked and the structure used, and, ultimately, determines the success or failure of the interview.

"Before You Go On"

You should be able to answer the following question:

What is the function of the goal of an interview?

Questions

Because you obtain your goals through asking and answering questions, it is important to understand the kinds of questions you can use. Questions fall on a continuum from open to closed.

Open Questions

With an **open question,** the interviewee has a great deal of freedom related to the way the question may be answered. An open question often asks for very broad or general information, with very little direction given by the interviewer as to the desired response. Some examples of open questions follow:

> Tell me about yourself.
>
> What do you know about the university?
>
> Tell me what happened.

Open questions have both advantages and disadvantages. Open questions allow the interviewer to discover the interviewee's frame of reference, priorities, or depth of knowledge about a topic. They are useful when the interviewer knows little about the topic or the interviewee. Open questions are useful for covering a topic in depth, because the interviewee can talk about any topic for any length of time. However, open questions take time to answer and require that the interviewer have good listening skills. Responses to open questions must be managed by the interviewer to keep the interviewee from wandering off the desired topic. Open questions are not useful for covering a wide variety of topics because of the time required for the interviewee to answer each question.

Moderately Open Questions

Moderately open questions are in the middle of the open-closed continuum. When using questions that are less open, the interviewer slightly restricts the way the interviewee may respond to the question. The interviewer supplies a little more direction related to the desired response. Some examples:

> How do you feel about the president's position on drug abuse?
> How would you evaluate the local news media?
> What is your reaction to this statement?

These questions still give the interviewer more ability to control the topics addressed in the answer. Since the topics are somewhat restricted, the interviewer can restrict the duration of the answers as well. With all open questions, the interviewer must be well-trained to listen and ask probing questions.

Closed Questions

By asking closed questions, the interviewer specifically limits the possible answers the interviewee can give. Examples include:

> What kind of car do you drive?
> Where did you attend college?
> In what city do you live?

Closed questions allow greater control of the interview and require more precise and specific answers to reach interview goals. Interviewers can use several types of closed questions for specific purposes.

Multiple Choice Questions   Multiple choice questions are one type of closed question. A multiple choice question restricts the interviewee's response options. Public opinion polls and job interviews often use this type of question. Some examples are:

> To which political party do you belong?
> *a.* Republican
> *b.* Democratic
> *c.* Libertarian
> *d.* Communist
> *e.* Other

What is your approximate salary?
  a. Below $20,000 per year
  b. $20,000 to $30,000 per year
  c. More than $30,000 per year
Would you rather work in Atlanta, Dallas, or Seattle?

By using multiple choice questions, interviewers can gather very specific information in a fairly short time. That information is easy to compare and interpret because the answers are in the same form. And, since the questions and answers are predetermined, the level of interviewer training does not have to be high. Interviewees face the problem of fitting the answers they want to make to the responses provided by the interviewers.

For example, in a marketing interview surveying consumer reactions to a new antacid, the interviewer asked how frequently the consumer used the product. The consumer used the product for two days during the month trial period. However, the possible answers were once a week, twice per week, three times per week, or more than three times per week. Having not used the antacid every week, the consumer's experience did not fit the responses provided. Multiple choice questions provide little flexibility for reporting specific information the interviewee wants to share.

A **bi-polar question** is a closed question requiring a yes/no answer or some other two-option answer. Examples of bi-polar questions are:

> Are you satisfied or dissatisfied with your education?
> Did you read the chapter assigned for today's class?
> Do you agree or disagree with this proposal?

Although these questions are easy to ask and answer, they reveal little information beyond that which the interviewer specifically requests.

Closed questions have advantages and disadvantages. On one hand, they give the interviewer an opportunity to direct the conversation and cover specific information about a variety of topics. Closed questions take less time than open questions and require less interviewer skill. Closed questions are normally useful for covering many topics in a short time. On the other hand, closed questions limit depth of response because of the restrictive nature of the question and possible answers. Closed questions do not always get the most useful or complete information.

Biased Questions Some questions bias the interviewee's responses. Biased questions are normally avoided since the answer is not what the interviewee really thinks. One type of biased question is the **leading question** that directs the interviewee toward the answer desired by the interviewer. Some examples are:

> Everyone knows that people should recycle their waste. Do you recycle your newspapers and cans?
> Thirty-five miles to the gallon is pretty good gas mileage, don't you think?
> Aren't these great seats?

Leading questions bias the response of the interviewee in the direction desired by the interviewer or require the interviewee to give the socially correct and acceptable response. Salespeople commonly use leading questions to convince customers to purchase a product or service.

Loaded questions lead interviewees to give different answers than they might have otherwise. These questions contain assumptions that often provoke an emotional response, give equally unattractive alternative answers, or place the person in a paradox where any answer is unacceptable. Loaded questions create a defensive climate in the interview and rarely get good results. Some examples of loaded questions are:

Have you recovered from your drinking problem?

Did you cheat on your exams again?

How do you feel about losing the election so badly?

Primary and Secondary Questions

Two additional kinds of questions are primary and secondary questions.[5] The function of a **primary question** is to introduce topics or new areas of discussion. A primary question is easily identified because it can stand alone, out of context, and still make sense. Primary questions range from being very open to very closed, as these examples show:

Where were you employed during the last five years?

What do you think of the company's new no smoking policy?

When did you turn in your report on the Davidson contract?

A **secondary** or probing question usually does not make much sense when used out of context. This question encourages an interviewee to keep talking, to provide additional information, or to clarify a previous answer. When the interviewee hasn't answered a question satisfactorily, the interviewer might ask for more information with additional open or closed questions. Secondary questions can be preplanned or asked spontaneously during the interview. Examples of secondary questions that might be asked to probe responses to the preceding primary questions might include:

Which job did you like best? (preplanned follow-up question)

Does that mean you agree or disagree with the policy? (spontaneous clarification question)

Why was it late? (spontaneous probe for additional information)

"Before You Go On"

You should be able to answer the following question:

Describe open and closed questions; what are their respective advantages and disadvantages?

The Interview Guide

The next step in the planning process is to decide on your general approach to the interview and prepare an interview guide. An interview guide outlines your plan for the interview; it contains topic areas for discussion and the sequence of specific questions. The format of the guide changes with the general approach to the interview. Guides can vary along a continuum between directed and nondirected approaches.

In the **directed interview** approach, the interviewer controls the topics covered and the flow of the conversation. With this approach, questions usually fall toward the closed end of the scale. In the **nondirected interview,** the interviewee controls the flow of the interview and the topics covered. The nondirected interview normally employs open questions. A **limited direction interview** approach falls somewhere in the middle of the continuum.

The approach you take should depend on the goals you have for the specific interview you are about to undertake. If you want to explore the psyche of the interviewee and discover that individual's perspective on life, then the nondirected approach might be more useful. If however, you are gathering information on a wide range of topics from large number of people, perhaps the directed approach is appropriate. The more nondirected the interview, the more skill required of the interviewer because of the constant need to adapt. The box entitled Strategies for Selecting Interview Guides shows how different types of interviews use different guides.

Strategies for Selecting Interview Guides

Goal	Type
Counseling	Nondirected
Information gathering (on broad subject area)	Nondirected
Information gathering	Limited direction
Employment	Limited direction
Assessment	Limited direction
Survey (information gathering)	Directed or Standardized

Nondirected Interview Guide

The nondirected interview guide might consist of only suggested topics to be covered. In this situation, the interviewer exerts minimum control over topics and responses of the interviewee. The interviewer begins by asking open questions to get the conversation started, then asks more questions as they fit into the conversation. This interview approach is useful when the interviewer isn't sure what information is relevant or if the subject area is broad because it offers the opportunity to probe answers and investigate different content areas. The interviewer must be skilled to adapt to the different directions in which the conversation might proceed. Counseling interviews and some types of information gathering interviews follow this approach.

Limited Direction Interview Guide

With the limited direction interview guide, the interviewer exerts a little more control than with a nondirected interview guide. This guide lists central or primary questions as well as possible probing questions that direct the interviewee to the information desired. An example follows:

> What is your biggest concern about life after college?
> - How about getting a job?
> - Would you like to raise a family?
> - What contributions would you like to make to society?

The limited direction approach uses mostly open questions sometimes followed up by more directive or closed questions. Interviewers use this approach for information gathering, employment, and appraisal interviews.

Directed Interview Guide

In the directed interview guide approach, the interviewer exerts a good deal of control over responses and the topics covered. Interviewers use this approach for information gathering interviews such as market surveys or opinion polls, where a large number of people must be interviewed. Each interviewee answers questions that are usually closed, asked in the same order, and worded the same way. Interviewers ask the questions in the same way so that the results of each interview may be compared to all the others.

"Before You Go On"

You should be able to answer the following question:

What is the difference between directed and nondirected interviews?

Structure of an Interview

As discussed in chapter 5, all communication contexts require organization and structure. An interview has a recognizable structure much like that of a public speech. As do other organized messages, the interview has three main parts: the introduction, the body, and the conclusion.

Introduction

Also referred to as the *opening,* the introduction is a very important part of the interview, yet it often receives little attention during the planning stages. The introduction serves three main functions. The first is to *establish a positive relationship* between the interview parties. Whatever occurs in the introduction sets the tone for the remainder of the interview. Many interviewing experts recommend that some self-disclosure be used here, but that should be decided case by case based on the individuals involved and the purpose of the interview. The second function of the introduction is to *motivate* the other party to participate fully in the interaction. You can use encouragement, offer a reward, show respect for the other, or stress the importance of the information to be exchanged. The important thing is to let the other party know that you wish full participation. The final function of the introduction is to *give orientation.* The interviewer should explain the purpose and main topic areas of the interview, how the interview will proceed, and what is expected of the interviewee. In most interviews, the interviewer should mention how the information is used after the interview. When the introduction is completed, the interviewer should make a smooth transition into the body of the interview.

Body

The body is the central part of the interview. In this section, most of the information is exchanged and your goals are primarily accomplished. The body contains the majority of your planned questions and interview guide. Regardless of the kind of interview you are planning, the topics to be discussed in the body must be in a logical order. Use a smooth progression of topics so that neither party gets confused or distracted. (Chapter 4 discusses organizational patterns in detail.)

Conclusion

The conclusion is another important part of the interview which, like the introduction, is often overlooked. As a result of poor or no planning, many interviewers try to rush the conclusion. For example, when the interviewer's only goal is to acquire information, once the information is received, the interview is over. The interviewer just says "Thanks" and leaves, not considering the relationship with the other person. This does not leave the other person with a good impression and would not motivate the other to cooperate again should the interviewer need more help.

The conclusion of the interview serves at least three functions. The first is that the interviewer *provides closure* by indicating clearly that the conversation is finished. For instance, summarize the content of the interview or exhibit some verbal or nonverbal leave taking behavior. The second function is that the interviewer makes every effort to *maintain the relationship* established through the interview. The relationship should remain positive, especially if the two parties will be working together after the interview or if the interviewer will need further cooperation from the interviewee. The final function of the conclusion is that the interviewer *shows appreciation* for the interviewee's help. This does not mean prolonged goodbyes or effusive thank you's. Simply offer a sincere thank you and leave. If the interviewer might need further information at some later time, the interviewee should be motivated to cooperate. Showing appreciation also gives the interviewee a sense of satisfaction related to knowing that the time in the interview was well spent.

Conducting an Interview

Now that you know how to plan the interview, know the goal, the kind of interview approach to take, the kinds of questions to ask, and the logical arrangement of topics, you are almost ready to begin an interview. During an interview, you must accomplish some additional tasks: build a relationship, create a supportive climate, maintain involvement, and record information.

Build the Relationship

Relationships between people in interviewing situations develop in much the same way as relationships between people in other contexts. When the parties first meet, communication is largely superficial and based on broad generalizations made by each party about the other's behavior and intentions. At this level, each person attempts to become acquainted to find out if the other may be trusted with more intimate information. As the parties interact, if they begin to build trust more and more self-disclosure takes place and the relationship helps the participants achieve their goals.

Many interviewing experts suggest that better interpersonal relationships between the parties creates a freer exchange of information. You will more likely achieve your goals for the interview if you can build an effective interpersonal relationship. It might not be possible to move into a highly trusting interpersonal relationship in just one interview.[6] Even so, make every effort to build rapport and make the relationship as positive and friendly as the situation allows or requires.

Two of the many ways to build a relationship between parties in an interview are to create a supportive climate and to be involved in the interaction.

Supportive Climate

A **supportive climate** is one in which neither party feels threatened. As we mentioned in chapter 3, the perception of threat creates a climate of defensiveness causing one party to suspect ulterior motives and manipulation by the other. As the result of this climate, the parties perceive meanings and intentions inaccurately. Information is never freely exchanged in a defensive climate. To prevent the creation of a defensive climate, use the strategies in the accompanying box entitled Strategies for a Supportive Climate.[7]

Specifically, avoid loaded or leading questions that create a strategic defensive climate. Be careful to use appropriate language that is inoffensive to the interviewee. Be honest in your stated purpose for the interview and what you plan to do with the responses you receive. Sales interviews, for example, are often initially disguised by persons who claim they just want to get some information. Interviewees who discover that the information interview is really a sales interview feel manipulated and defensive. Show respect for the other person by being punctual and taking only the amount of time originally agreed on. Showing you respect the other person and being candid in your approach to the interview helps create a supportive climate conducive to competent communication.

Recording Information

In many interviews, you want a record of the responses you receive to your questions. With all the barriers to effective listening and the lack of success people have in remembering conversations, don't rely only on your cognitive listening skills and selective memory. Instead, find a nondistracting and reliable method for recording the interview.

An efficient way to record complete and accurate information is to use a tape recorder. You must get the interviewee's permission to tape the interview. Make the recorder as inconspicuous as possible so it doesn't disrupt either party's involvement in the communication.

Strategies for Interviewing   271

You can also take notes during the interview. Have several pens or pencils ready, plenty of paper, and a firm place to write. Even while taking notes, it is essential to maintain eye contact with the interviewee. Don't let note taking interfere with listening carefully to the answers. Simply jot down brief notes. Immediately after the interview, take time to clarify your notes and fill in information you could not write down during the interview. Note taking can (and usually should) accompany tape recording. If the recorder fails, you will at least have some notes to remind you of what was discussed.

Strategies for a Supportive Climate

Use descriptive rather than evaluative statements.

Maintain a problem orientation rather than exerting control over the situation.

Maintain an honest, spontaneous approach to the situation rather than giving the impression you have hidden motives or are trying to manipulate the interviewee.

Show concern for and interest in the other party rather than a cold detachment.

Maintain an atmosphere of equality rather than trying to exert superiority.

Keep an open mind rather than maintaining a biased viewpoint.

Involvement

Perhaps the most important thing you can do to build and maintain a relationship with an interview partner is to be involved. Being involved means to participate fully in an interaction without being distracted by elements not related to the interaction. **Involvement** not only helps you accomplish your specific goals in the interview but it also communicates an interest in the interviewee and the topic. As others find that you are genuinely interested and involved in what is happening, they become more involved as well. Therefore, the result of your involvement is the increased commitment of all participants to the free exchange of information and to the ultimate success of the interview.

"Before You Go On"

You should be able to answer the following question:

What are two ways to build the relationship in an interview situation?

Chapter 11

1.   Which four elements are common to the definitions of an interview?
The definitions of an interview in many textbooks have at least four common elements. The definitions suggest that interviews are interpersonal communication situations; they involve two parties; an interviewer and an interviewee; they have a specific purpose; and they are conducted primarily through questions and answers.

2.   What are five kinds of interviews?
The five types of interviews described in this chapter are (1) information interviews that include both information giving and gathering; (2) employment interviews in which employers evaluate and select potential employees and in which employees evaluate and select potential employers; (3) assessment interviews usually designed to evaluate the performance of the interviewee; (4) persuasive interviews designed to change the attitudes or behaviors of the interviewees; (5) and counseling interviews designed to provide help or guidance to the interviewee.

3.   What is the function of the goal of an interview?
The goal of an interview defines the purpose of the interaction, determines the kinds of questions that will be asked and the structure to be used, and it ultimately determines the success or failure of the interview.

4.   Describe open and closed questions; what are their respective advantages and disadvantages?
An open question is usually a general question that allows the interviewee a wide range of possible responses. This kind of question helps the interviewer to understand the interviewee's point of view and priorities. It is very useful when trying to cover a topic in depth. Open questions often take a lot of time to answer, generally do not allow a wide variety of topics to be discussed in a limited time, and require a fairly high level of interviewer skill to conduct.

Closed questions allow the interviewer to control the responses of the interviewee. These questions take less time, allow more precise answers to questions, require little skill on the part of the interviewer, and can be used to cover a wide variety of topics in a limited time. Closed questions are not very useful for covering a topic in significant depth and do not always obtain complete information.

5.   What is the difference between directed and nondirected interviews?
The interviewer controls the topics and the conversation flow in a directed interview. Often interviewers use this interview for gathering information from large numbers of people. The questions are usually closed to allow the responses to be compared. In a nondirected interview, the interviewer has little control over the conversation flow and topics covered by the interviewee. Frequently, interviewers use this interview when the subject area is broad. It allows the interviewer to ask probing questions to obtain more in-depth answers.

6. What are two ways to build the relationship in an interview situation?
Two ways to build the relationship between parties in an interview are to create and maintain a supportive climate and to be involved. A supportive climate helps all participants relax and focus on the conversation. Nonsupportive climates make participants defensive. Defensiveness distracts the attention of the participants from the conversation itself and inhibits accurate perception of the communication of others. Involvement in the conversation means to focus on the conversation itself and not to be distracted by extraneous factors. It also shows the other participants that you think they and the conversation are important enough to expend the energy necessary to pay attention.

S T U D E N T   E X E R C I S E S

1. Interview guide selection.
Select the kind of interview guide that you would use in each situation:

- *a.* An investigative reporter looking for facts in a story.
- *b.* A soft drink company doing taste tests.
- *c.* An attorney interrogating a witness in court.
- *d.* Your academic advisor trying to help you choose a major.
- *e.* A final examination for a class of 400 students.

2. Question identification.
For each of the following, identify the type of question:

- *a.* What is your dog's name?
- *b.* Is your dog a good dog or a bad dog?
- *c.* When did your dog stop eating the furniture?
- *d.* Tell me about your dog.
- *e.* How do you feel about the current trend in favor of laws prohibiting vicious dogs?
- *f.* How much does your dog weigh? (*a*) 1 pound or less; (*b*) 1 to 10 pounds; (*c*) 10 to 50 pounds; (*d*) over 50 pounds.
- *g.* You like dogs more than you like people, don't you?
- *h.* How do your friends like your dog?
- *i.* Ten years is a pretty long life for a dog, isn't it?
- *j.* Are you allowed to have pets in your apartment?

3. Type of interview.
For each of the following, identify the type of interview described:

- *a.* Convincing a person to vote for a political candidate or issue.
- *b.* Seeking advice on how to solve your financial problems.
- *c.* Asking a teacher how you are doing in class.
- *d.* A physician trying to convince a patient to continue a prescribed treatment.

e. A public relations representative of a large company introducing a new product.

f. Teaching a new employee how to operate the cash register.

g. Parents trying to find out how their children are doing in school.

h. Asking your boss for a raise.

GLOSSARY

assessment interview An exchange of information designed to improve the performance of the interviewee, often an employee in an organization.

bi-polar question A type of closed question that requires choosing between two alternatives.

closed question A question in which the interviewer restricts the possible responses by the interviewee.

counseling/helping interview An interview designed to provide advice or guidance to the interviewee.

directed interview An interviewer controls the topics covered and the flow of conversation.

employment interview An interview in which employers evaluate and select employees and in which employees evaluate and select employers.

information interview An interview designed to give information to an interviewee or obtain information from an interviewee.

interview A form of conversation between two parties that has predetermined goals and involves the asking and answering of questions.

involvement To participate fully in an interview or communication situation without being distracted by elements not related to the interaction.

leading question A question designed to direct the response toward the answer desired by the interviewer.

limited direction interview The interviewer and the interviewee share control of the topics and the flow of the interview.

loaded question A question that places interviewees in a bind by restricting responses to those that do not necessarily reflect the intention of the interviewee.

nondirected interview The interviewee controls the topics covered and the flow of the interview.

open question A question asking for very broad or general information and providing little indication of the desired response.

persuasive interview An interview designed to change the attitudes or behaviors of the interviewee.

primary question A question designed to introduce topics or new elements of discussion.

secondary question A question designed to probe an answer or to encourage the interviewee to elaborate.

supportive climate A communication environment in which neither party feels threatened by the other.

N O T E S

1. J. DeVito, *Human Communication: The Basic Course* (New York: Harper & Row, 1988), 291.

2. C. Downs, G. Smeyak, and E. Martin, *Professional Interviewing* (New York: Harper & Row, 1980), 5.

3. Charles Stewart and W. Cash, *Interviewing: Principles and Practices* (Dubuque: Wm. C. Brown, 1991), 7.

4. Stewart and Cash, *Interviewing*.

5. Ibid.

6. Ibid.

7. Jack Gibb, "Defensive Communication," *Journal of Communication* 11 (1961), 141–48.

CHAPTER

Strategies for Group Communication

E ver since there have been enough people around to form them, groups have been in existence. We all belong to a variety of groups including families, work groups, peer groups, civic groups, and social groups. Membership in groups helps us define our self-concepts and learn appropriate rules and behaviors for functioning in society. Most major decisions of governments, large and small corporations, families, and even individuals are made in groups. The purpose of this chapter is to investigate and define small groups and examine some of the major aspects that influence a group's behavior and productivity.

The Nature of Small Groups

Scholars have investigated small groups for many years. However, the study of groups only became popular among social science scholars in the middle 1940s, when World War II ended. Since that time, groups have become a focus of research because of the particular development of the American culture. Due to the war, economic prosperity, and especially advances in industrial technology, people and jobs are more individualized and more specialized.[1] As a result, they are interdependent. A consequence of interdependence is that many problems must be solved by a group. This focus on interdependence in business and industry has spilled over into nearly every other aspect of the culture. Now we approach most tasks and decisions as group problems.

Groups Make Better Decisions

Most decisions made in families, business, or government, are made in groups. Groups tend to make better quality decisions than individuals working alone for a variety of reasons.[2] For example, instead of just depending on the resources, knowledge, or expertise of one person, the resources of all group members are combined. Another reason is human error. People are going to make mistakes whether they are working alone or in groups. However, in a group, errors that might go unobserved by an individual have a much greater chance of being noticed and corrected. Another reason groups make better decisions is that group discussion stimulates ideas in group members that might not occur to an individual working alone. A final reason is that the presence of other people improves the quality of an individual's work. Having other people depending on and working with you often increases your motivation to perform well.

The small group situation is interpersonal in nature but somewhat more complex. People communicate within the context of a relationship; instead of managing a relationship with just one other person, they balance several relationships simultaneously. To further complicate matters, it is unlikely that your relationships with all the members of the group exist at the same level. You might know one or two people better than the others, you might work with some members more often or better than others, or perhaps you don't get along with someone in the group. You can have different relationships with various members of the group at the same time. Eventually, however, a group relationship is negotiated and group goals and rules for appropriate behavior are established. At this point, the group members become more comfortable and productive.

Many problems can only be solved by people working interdependently in groups.

"Before You Go On"

You should be able to answer the following question:

Why do groups make better decisions than individuals working alone?

Definition of a Small Group

A **small group** can be defined as an integrated collection of persons engaged in a cooperative, goal-oriented interaction; they are aware of their own and others' participation and get some satisfaction from participating in the activities of the group. This section examines the elements of this definition.

Integrated collection of persons engaged in a cooperative, goal-oriented interaction. The whole of a small group is greater than the sum of its parts because of the integration or interdependence of it members. A group is not just an assembly of individuals, but a dynamic combination of people working together to accomplish some goal. The term *interaction* suggests communication. Communication among members is the major element that separates small groups from random collections of people and is responsible for groups' ability to solve problems.

They are each aware of their own and others' participation. Members of a small group perceive themselves to be members of the group.[3] They know who belongs in the group and who does not. Over time, the members of the group begin to use words and phrases that only have meaning to them; a nonmember would not know what they were talking about. They also develop relationships that allow them to know who can be trusted and who can be counted on to be committed to the goals of the group. If individuals do not perceive themselves to be members, they are not likely to participate in creating and achieving the goals of the group.

Getting some satisfaction from participation. A common observation is that people join groups to fulfill or satisfy some personal need.[4] For example, a business person might join a group to make contacts with other business people, or a new college student might join a Greek organization to meet new people and to feel included in the college environment. Whatever the need, you usually remain a member of a group as long as the group is satisfying some need. A group that does not meet the needs of its members either disintegrates or its members redefine their needs or the direction of the group.

"Before You Go On"

You should be able to answer the following question:

What is a small group?

Major Concepts in the Study of Small Groups

Six major concepts related to small group communication are group culture, cohesiveness, roles, leadership, conflict, and conformity. Decision making is the most common function of small groups. Decisions are the product of group effort and related directly to the purpose of the group's existence. We devote the next chapter to a detailed look at decision making. This chapter focuses on the processes of group communication affecting group decisions.

Group Culture

Members of groups cooperate not only to accomplish some task but also to create a **group culture** different from the larger culture.[5] Over time and through the use of communication, the group negotiates a collective personality and a group point of view. This view is comprised of attitudes and values concerning the group, the task, and all elements of the group environment. Much like the worldview of an individual, this perspective influences the behavior of group members by setting standards for appropriate behavior. The end result is that the group point of view affects the way decisions are made by the group and the group product.

For example, a group of executives working for a large computer manufacturer was having difficulty making good decisions. Theoretically, this group should not have made such poor decisions because each member was very competent and experienced. On investigation, a communication consultant discovered that the group had created a competitive group culture. That is, instead of sharing information and working with each other to make a good group decision, the members withheld information. They tried to steal information from one another so each one might make a decision and take individual credit for it. Instead of cooperating for the good of the group, members were competing in an effort to score points with the boss and increase their chances for promotion. If they had negotiated a group culture of cooperation, they would have had much less difficulty making good decisions.

Similarly, groups in which you interact have developed their own unique cultures. Fraternities and sororities, dorms, classes, clubs, and other social groups to which you belong have each negotiated a unique view of reality. The rules governing your interaction with other group members, your interpretation of events, and the meaning you give to jargon and specialized phrases differ from group to group. The culture of the group provides a frame of reference indicating how group members should behave and interpret each other's behavior.

A primary result of the group's culture is the establishment of norms. **Norms** are shared guidelines for beliefs and behavior.[6] Norms develop as the members of the group come to agree that certain beliefs are true and that certain behaviors are appropriate. Just as individuals do, groups tend to develop idiosyncratic rules and behaviors as well as a unique set of meanings for certain symbols. Despite some deviance within each group, norms help establish the group identity and become a significant influence on the behavior of the group members. (A later section on conformity discusses deviance further.)

The Group Consultant

PROBLEM:

If your group has a competitive climate, it very often represents a basic incompatibility between individual and group goals.[7]

STRATEGY:

Create a cooperative climate. Instead of allowing the competitiveness to intensify and further stifle the group, try to find something on which everyone can agree. Even if the other members of the group don't go along with you, finding opportunities to agree should help move the climate to a more cooperative one.[8] Agreement is reinforcing; sooner or later, those with whom you agree are inclined to pay you back with some cooperation. Over time, the group should become more cooperative.

In attempting to analyze a group to understand its performance, examine the group culture. Just as insight into the self-concept of an individual can help explain much of the individual's behavior, understanding the culture of a group can provide reasons for a group's behavior. For example, a professor teaching an honors class was puzzled by a lack of class participation. He thought that honor students were smart and should have something to say in class. It wasn't until his relationship with the class developed that he learned why they were quiet. As the group relationship developed, members of this class came to believe that speaking in class was just a way of showing off for the professor. As honor students, they thought that they didn't have to behave that way, so class participation came to be regarded as inappropriate behavior. Armed with this insight, he began to help them slowly redefine the group culture and the class performed well. Understanding the cultural reasons for the behavior can help solve problems.

Cohesiveness

Have you ever wondered why some groups work very well together and some groups just can't get along? One possible answer to this question is that some groups are more cohesive than others. **Cohesiveness** is another word for group loyalty or esprit de corps.[9] It is the "resultant of all the forces acting on the members to remain in the group."[10] Cohesiveness could also be called groupness as it describes a situation in which all group members work together to achieve a common goal.[11] Members of cohesive groups tend to make the group's goals their own, very often resulting in a group that is more productive and satisfied than noncohesive groups.[12]

Cohesive groups are more productive because their members care about the goals of the group and about each other. They talk extensively, they are not afraid to disagree with each other, and they are more relaxed and informal. Noncohesive groups, on the other hand, are more formal and polite; they often feel too socially inhibited to openly argue about task issues.[13] The consequence of the interplay within cohesive groups is that the group discusses more points of view and considers more potential solutions to problems.

A group can be too cohesive, however. Some groups get caught up in being social and friendly and ignore the task. Also, because the members feel loyal to the group, highly cohesive groups sometimes experience groupthink (discussed in chapter 13). When groupthink occurs, productivity declines because members do not want to seem disloyal to the group by disagreeing. As a result, the group does not consider as many alternatives and the outcome is a lower-quality decision.[14]

Cohesiveness often increases when the group makes progress toward a goal. Satisfaction with the task helps to create satisfaction with the group. To encourage cohesiveness in a group, make other members feel secure and valued, develop relationships with them, create realistic group goals that serve the interests of the members, and encourage cooperation among members rather than competition.

Roles in the Small Group

Everyone assumes several social roles in the course of a daily routine. The same person can assume the role of parent, student, worker, and child all in one day. Each of these roles requires the individual to adopt a different set of behaviors. A **role,** therefore, is a set of behaviors enacted or expected by people within a specific context. Playing a role in the wrong context, or one that violates the others' expectations of the role, can have unfortunate results. While you might sometimes be able to exhibit childish behavior in the company of your parents, chances are very good that your boss won't appreciate such behavior on the job. Similarly, when you enact a democratic leadership style and group members expect you to take an authoritative, autocratic approach, your role enactments contradict their role expectations. It takes a constant reassessment of the context to understand which behaviors are appropriate and which are not.

Functional Roles

The notion of functional roles has been a popular approach to the study of small group communication. A functional role is a role related to the operation of a small group. Members assume three basic types of functional roles in a small group: group task roles, group maintenance roles, and individual centered roles.[15]

Persons who adopt **group task roles** orient their participation toward completing the task in which the group is engaged. Their purpose is to direct and coordinate group effort in the selection and definition of a problem and its solution. For several examples of group task roles, see the accompanying box entitled Group Task Roles.

Group Task Roles

Initiator-contributor	Coordinator
Information seeker	Orienter
Information giver	Evaluator-critic
Opinion seeker	Energizer
Opinion giver	Procedural technician
Elaborator	Recorder

The behaviors in the **group maintenance roles** category help the group function as a group. Persons playing these roles are more interested in the group functioning smoothly as a social system than in the group solving problems. As such, these roles are not usually directly related to the task. The job of a maintenance person is to help manage conflicts, provide encouragement to group members, and try to maintain the group's positive attitude. For some examples of group maintenance roles, see the accompanying box entitled Group Maintenance Roles.

Group Maintenance Roles

Encourager	Standard setter
Harmonizer	Compromiser
Observer and commentator	Follower
Gatekeeper and expediter	Tension reliever

The final category is **individual centered roles.** Other members view group members who assume individual centered roles as nonproductive persons. Members taking these roles are interested only in satisfying their own individual needs. The purpose of their participation is a private goal relevant to neither the group task nor the maintenance of the group as a social system. Individual role behavior can be detrimental to the productivity and the motivation of the group as a whole. For some examples of these roles, see the accompanying box entitled Individual Centered Roles.

Functional roles usually develop over time through a pattern of positive reinforcement. If a member exhibits a particular behavior and the group responds positively to it, that member is likely to continue the behavior. If, however, the group responds in a negative way to a member's behavior, the member will discontinue the behavior. As such, the group slowly decides which behaviors or

Individual Centered Roles

Aggressor	Joker
Blocker	Dominator
Recognition seeker	Help seeker
Self-confessor	Special interest pleader

roles are appropriate. The forms that roles take are also influenced by the individual member's own desire to perform in a certain way. Some members would probably rather leave the group than submit to group pressure to take on a particular role. Finally, the member's own ability may determine whether a certain role is played.

Propositions on Functional Roles

Next we consider several propositions related to functional role behavior. The first is that *an individual member may perform more than one role* in the same group. Members are not limited to one specific set of behaviors. An individual may play task and maintenance roles, several different task roles, and so on. The same person may even play individual centered roles along with task and/or maintenance roles. This probably will not happen for an extended period of time because the group will bring pressure on the person to suppress the individual centered roles.

A second proposition is that *several members of the same group may perform the same role.* Within a group, having one person exhibit a particular set of behaviors does not prevent others from doing the same. For example, there can easily be more than one harmonizer or initiator-contributor in the same group.

A third proposition is that *no role is universally present in all groups.* Just because a role is on the list doesn't mean that it exists in every group. If a group is very fortunate, for example, it will not have any members playing individual centered roles.

A final proposition is that *the role played by an individual in one group may be quite different from the role played by that same individual in another group.* As the context changes, competent communicators know that expected or appropriate behaviors change as well. As a competent communicator, you should be able to adapt to changing situations and to cooperate with other participants.

Roles influence patterns of communication in social systems, and these patterns have a significant impact on the problem-solving ability of a small group.

Another role function that has a substantial effect on the communication patterns and productivity of a small group is leadership. In this approach to groups, leadership is a role to be played just like any of the others discussed. As such, all the ideas related to functional roles would apply to leadership.

Leadership

Leadership may be defined as the ability to influence the behavior of others. The influence that one person has over others depends on the relationship among the people in a specific context. If the context changes, the new context could require a change in the relationship among the people so that the influence shifts to another person or persons.

Our perspective is that leadership is not inherent in a particular person. People are not born leaders. No genetic trait makes a person a natural leader. Leadership is given or attributed to a person by the people over whom the leader has influence. An employee, for example, attributes leadership to an employer because the employer controls rewards that are desired by the employee. The influence is based on the perceived power that followers are willing to attribute to a leader. Chapter 9 discusses several specific power bases in detail.

Many small groups do not have appointed leaders; however, a leader usually emerges over time. If your group does have an appointed leader, note that this person might not always have the most influence. For example, if your group has a member who is an expert in the topic area, the expert could have more influence on group members than the appointed leader. If this is the case, conflict could arise over a claim for leadership.

Realize that leadership is not the sole possession of the leader. Other members of the group could provide leadership or have influence in different areas as the group progresses through a decision. For example, if your group is working on a project related to environmental protection, even though you might not be the leader, you might be influential in decision making because you know a lot or are interested in environmental matters. When you influence the course the group takes, you have provided leadership.

"Before You Go On"

You should be able to answer the following question:

What is leadership?

Functions of Leadership

Leadership is a role function similar to any other member role. As such, the functions of leaders fall into two categories: task and maintenance.

The interests of the *task leader* are the same as the task role functions described earlier. The primary focus of the task leader is the completion of the job or solution of the problem. Some general propositions can be made about task leaders. First, they are considered to be the uncontested leaders in their groups. Second, although not necessarily well-liked, task leaders are respected by group members. They often pass judgment on the value of a group member's behavior and members look to them for approval or disapproval. Task leaders are not always unpopular, but popularity isn't a prerequisite for this role. Finally, task leaders usually emerge from the group over time. The group essentially auditions different leaders until one is chosen. This leader is usually the one who can control the sources of power the group perceives as important.

Task leaders also affect the flow of communication in a group. For example, research indicates that task leaders interact more than other group members in discussions and that they have more communication directed toward them.[16] They send and receive more messages than other members and they get more attention paid to their ideas. If you are interested in learning who is the task leader of the group, one way to gather evidence is to listen to the conversation and count the number of messages sent and received by members. In most cases, the task leader should have the highest number. Research also suggests that the presence of a leader in a group is related to the group spending more time on a specific topic. That is, groups with leaders have longer attention spans than groups without leaders.

The Group Consultant

If you want to take a leadership position in a small group, you can gain some insight from research.[17] Reports indicate that a process of elimination of possible contenders for leadership takes place in the early meetings of the group. If you want to contribute to the goals of the group and become a leader:

Be informed: being uninformed is a negative trait that eliminates most contenders.

Participate: groups often judge quiet types as nonparticipative and therefore unsuitable.

Be flexible: remain open to new ideas or methods, especially when your ideas or methods are in conflict with group norms or goals.

Encourage: encourage others to participate; don't try to make all the decisions yourself.

The function of *maintenance leadership* is consistent with the maintenance roles discussed earlier. The maintenance leaders tend to be group members who are the best at performing maintenance functions. Because they primarily reward and encourage group members, maintenance leaders are usually the best-liked in the group. Maintenance leaders try to build and maintain the morale of the group. They relieve tension, try to resolve conflicts and build solidarity among group members. The group thinks of maintenance leaders as the task leader's first assistants; they are rarely in conflict with the task leader. Maintenance leaders emerge in a group over time in much the same way as task leaders.

Styles of Leadership

The style of a leader, or the way the leader decides to exercise influence over group members, is related to the leader's assumptions about followers. These assumptions are based on either Theory X or Theory Y.[18]

Theory X assumes that people are basically lazy and don't want to work; people don't want responsibility; people are not creative in problem solving; people are only motivated by basic needs for survival, food, and money; and people must be closely supervised and controlled.

Nearly the opposite of Theory X, Theory Y assumes that people like to work; work comes as naturally to them as play; people want self-control and responsibility; people are creative in problem solving and like to make decisions; people are motivated by needs for self-esteem, social acceptance, and for self-actualization; and people can be self-directed and self-monitoring.

In effect, we can place leadership styles on a continuum based on leaders' assumptions. The styles are the traditional style, the human relations style, and the human resources style.

Traditional Leaders using the traditional style follow Theory X assumptions about group members. These task-oriented leaders see their function as supervising and controlling followers to make sure that the task is being accomplished. In the traditional style, leaders make all the decisions. The leaders' power base is primarily legitimate, but often includes coercive power and power to reward basic needs of followers. The communication patterns in groups under the traditional style of leadership are fairly simple. Most communication from these leaders comes as instructions to the followers who communicate with their leaders when they ask task-related questions or provide feedback to their leaders' questions.

Human Relations Leaders who use the human relations style make assumptions about followers that combine Theory X and Theory Y. Because leaders assume people are motivated by needs such as self-esteem, they see their function as making people feel useful by consulting with them on task decisions. These leaders believe that when followers feel like they are contributing to the process, they have higher satisfaction and are motivated to work hard. However, the leaders make all the important decisions and allow the followers to make only routine decisions. So, while the followers are consulted in decision making, their participation is limited. With the human relations style, the leaders' power bases are primarily legitimate, reward, or coercion for important decisions and referent and expert for routine decisions.

Human Resources Leaders using the human resources style follow mostly Theory Y assumptions about followers. Because the followers are assumed to be creative and motivated, leaders see their function as creating the proper environment to promote creativity and productivity. In this situation, members make all the decisions with the leader having an equal voice. The power bases of the leaders are primarily reward, referent, and expert. The communication patterns are completely different from groups with traditional leaders. Most communication takes place among the members and there is little directive communication between leaders and followers. In this situation, group members view the leader as just another member, so the leader's role is not dominant.

The Group Consultant

PROBLEM:

How should you respond when you believe that the group leader is moving the group away from group goals?
Often, group members privately oppose their leaders if they sense their group is moving away from its goals. However, instead of voicing this opposition, they remain silent.

STRATEGY:

One way to begin to move the group back toward its goals is to resist the leader in a nonthreatening way. For example, you could ask that the leader or the whole group to clarify or review group goals. After the goals have been stated, it should be obvious to the leader that the group is moving in the wrong direction. If not, you could suggest some alternatives that more clearly relate to the goals. You can accomplish this without directly challenging the leader.[19]

No one style of leadership is best for all situations. Conversely, all leadership styles are useful in specific contexts. The traditional style of leadership may be appropriate in situations in which quantity of output is the primary concern, when group members do not have high commitment to the group goals, and when they have limited knowledge and expertise in performing their tasks.

On the other hand, the human resources style of leadership is appropriate in situations in which the decision requires the collective expertise and creativity of all group members. The traditional approach would fail here because it is difficult to order someone to be creative. When group members are highly motivated, have expertise and experience doing the task, and are committed to the group's goals, human resources leadership may be most appropriate.

In summary, Theory X groups produce a higher quantity of output in a short amount of time and they make fewer mistakes than Theory Y groups. However, the level of member satisfaction in Theory X groups is much lower than Theory Y groups. Theory Y groups produce a higher quality output than Theory X groups, but it takes more time. Theory Y groups have high morale and satisfaction with decisions. They also have greater cohesiveness and higher levels of independent and creative behavior.

"Before You Go On"

You should be able to answer the following question:

What are the differences among traditional, human relations, and human resources leaders?

Conflict

Anytime more than one person works on solving a problem, the potential for conflict exists. Because everyone has a unique worldview and a unique way of interpreting experience, there is a lot of room for disagreement or misunderstanding. In other words, conflict is inevitable. (Chapter 10 provides a detailed look at conflict in interpersonal relationships.) In the context of group decision making, **conflict** is a disagreement over alternative choices that a group can make. Since our culture operates on a basis of politeness, you might think that conflict is always bad and that it should be avoided if at all possible. Note, however, that conflict can be quite beneficial and is often central to group problem solving.

If there were no source of conflict, there would be no problem for the group to solve. Also, one of the benefits of solving problems in a group is having access to the members' alternative points of view. Since each person sees the problem from a slightly different perspective, there should be a number of possible solutions. Conflict can easily get out of control, however, and must be carefully regulated. Although conflict is not to be avoided, it must be managed by the group to work well.

Conflict also serves maintenance functions. First, it provides a vent for hostilities building up between group members. Even the most friendly and cohesive groups get hot under the collar now and then; conflict provides an outlet

Conflict encourages sharing of different perspectives on group problems.

for those feelings. Second, conflict facilitates a close examination of the relationships in a group. Sometimes, you really get to know another person only through conflict. When conflict is managed well, it can be productive on both task and maintenance levels.

Two types of conflict are important to the study of small groups: conflict intrinsic to the task and conflict extrinsic to the task.

Intrinsic Conflict

Conflict intrinsic to the task usually centers around disagreements relative to issues, procedures, values, goals, and opinions. This positive and highly beneficial form of conflict should be managed and not discouraged in a group. Task-related conflict is a primary reason for the existence of a problem-solving group. As such, **intrinsic conflict** should be best handled by the group. When intrinsic conflict is not managed well, it takes time away from the task and could get out of control, leading to extrinsic conflict.

Extrinsic Conflict

When most people think of conflict, they probably think of extrinsic conflict. This affective conflict is not related to the task at hand. Rather, **extrinsic conflict** is related to the personalities and relationships of group members. This conflict arises when you just don't like somebody. As stated before, extrinsic conflict can serve a useful maintenance function. However, unmanaged extrinsic conflict can be harmful to the group. Minor extrinsic conflicts can easily turn into a major problem. Conflicts that go unresolved or unmanaged over time do not usually go away. After a time, the minor conflicts explode and the group cannot go about the business of making decisions because it is crippled by destructive conflict.

There are several causes of extrinsic conflict. First, remember that all communication implies an interdependence among people. When interdependence is more competitive than cooperative, the potential for conflict is high. Second, the use of abrasive influence strategies, such as threats and punishments by leaders or other members, can lead to extrinsic conflict. Third, extrinsic conflict frequently arises when individuals fail to understand the reasons for the behaviors of others. If the reasons are not understood, then the behaviors can easily be misinterpreted and lead to resentment. Fourth, sometimes extrinsic conflict arises from the communication itself. Sometimes it is not what you say but how you say it; (i.e., the metacommunication) that creates the problem. If the communication makes another member defensive, then conflict is likely. The final cause of extrinsic conflict is a struggle over roles. For example, there can be a struggle for leadership. As mentioned before, sometimes a group member gains more influence over the group than an appointed leader or some other individual who desires control. If this happens, there can be a conflict over who should direct the group. Since this struggle involves member relationships, it is extrinsic conflict.

PROBLEM:

Extrinsic conflict can lead to low member satisfaction, a lack of agreement, the loss of the cooperative climate, and even the disintegration of the group. What do you do when you see escalating extrinsic conflict?

STRATEGY:

Individual group members can successfully counteract extrinsic conflict by trying to turn disruptive acts that would normally escalate the conflict into constructive contributions. This can help defuse the situation and refocus the attention of the group to the task at hand.[20]

For example, if a group member complains, "Steve is always late for our meetings. He says we meet too far from his house. That really burns me up. Let's throw him out of the group!" You could turn that expression of anger into a constructive suggestion by saying: "Let's meet at Steve's house. That way, he can't be late! Besides, he has a computer we can use and his refrigerator is always full of food!"

While intrinsic conflict can be very helpful for the group, extrinsic conflict is sometimes detrimental. By distracting the group from its task, extrinsic conflict could cause the disintegration of the group. If managed properly, however, extrinsic conflict can be quite beneficial because it allows the venting of hostilities, relationship clarification, and ultimately, some tension relief. Whatever the kind of conflict that arises in your group, the key to making it work for you is management.

Strategies you can use to manage extrinsic conflict include encouraging cooperation among group members; encouraging participation among all members, including the leader; not hiding your intentions; maintaining a supportive climate; and, perhaps most important, keeping the group goals as a priority over your own individual goals. These behaviors should go a long way toward reducing the occurrence of extrinsic conflict and allowing the group to concentrate on the task at hand.

"Before You Go On"

You should be able to answer the following questions:

What are the advantages and disadvantages of conflict for a small group?

Conformity

Conformity is defined as a rigid adherence to norms.[21] In the 1950s a group of people called beatniks tried to be nonconformists. They wore different clothes and listened to poetry and jazz. In the 1960s and 1970s, the job of the beatniks was taken over by the hippies who also had long hair and promoted peace, love, and sexual promiscuity. The 1980s had punks who had their own set of habits. Surely similar groups will emerge in the 1990s. The point is that each one of these groups deviated from the societal norms and each group was pressured by the larger society to shape up, or conform. The result of nonconformity is rejection. This phenomenon occurs because group norms often imply an obligation for members to go along with a decision or the will of the group. In short, whether they are small or large, groups tend to force agreement.

Pressure to Conform

Groups exert different amounts of pressure on members to adhere to their norms. In a problem-solving group, pressure to conform increases as individual members become less certain that a decision is right or correct. This level of certainty varies with the type of problem faced by the group. When dealing with an unclear or vague problem, members are more likely to conform. However, if a problem is clear and a concrete or correct answer exists, group members are less likely to conform. If you don't know where you're going (vague problem), then any direction seems acceptable. If you do know where you are going (clear problem), only certain directions are acceptable to you.

The problem with pressure to conform is that it can decrease the quality of the decision-making process in a group. High pressure to conform creates problems. First, it inhibits the expression of true feelings. Anyone with something to contribute that is not consistent with the decision made by the group feels pressure not to express it. Second, the pressure to agree with the decision minimizes alternative points of view from the group. Since the real value of group decision making is difference of opinion, pressure to conform effectively undermines the process. Such pressure may prevent the group from finding the best solution to the problem.

All pressure to conform is not necessarily bad, however. For a group to accomplish anything at all, there has to be some agreement among members. The complete lack of conformity in a group would lead to confusion and disorder. Only when the pressure to conform inhibits the complete participation of members does it become detrimental to the group.

Deviance

Occasionally some member of the group refuses to agree or go along, no matter what. The failure of a group member to conform is often a source of extrinsic conflict. Deviance studies indicate that a four-stage cycle occurs when someone refuses to conform.[22]

Stage One: communication toward the deviant increases. The rest of the group tries to convince the person to agree.

Stage Two: solidarity increases among the conforming members of the group. The members of the group are now becoming polarized against the deviant.

Stage Three: communication ends between the deviant and the rest of the group. By now, it is clear that the deviant is not going to agree, and the rest of the group is tired of arguing. The group ignores the deviant and continues with the business at hand.

Stage Four: the conforming majority punishes the deviant. Punishment usually entails receiving undesirable jobs to perform or complete ostracism from the group. However the group handles deviance, the nonconformist is usually considered the least productive and the least liked.

"Before You Go On"

You should be able to answer the following question:

What are the effects of conformity on a small group?

Groups that make the best decisions have several common characteristics: First, the group members joined the group because they have certain needs to satisfy. As such, members of the best groups are committed to accomplishing the goals of the group. Second, the most successful groups have members who actively participate and who are involved in the group's activities. Finally, groups that make the best decisions tend to make the time and expend the energy to work on task completion and to work on the development of the group as a social system. These groups pay adequate attention to task and maintenance functions.

After reading this chapter, you should understand that the small group is a complex social phenomenon. The abilities of the most competent communicators can be taxed to the limit while trying to manage relationships with other group members and attempting to accomplish a task. Even though the group is more complex than interpersonal communication between two people, the same criteria defines competent communication in a group. The primary focus should be on involvement with the social situation. Involvement includes attention to and accurate assessment of self and environmental factors, the formulation of appropriate goal-related strategies, cooperation with other participants, and the use of appropriate communication skills. In the next chapter, we discuss the central purpose of a task-oriented small group: decision making.

Responses to *"Before You Go On"* Questions: A Chapter Summary

---

1.   Why do groups make better decisions than individuals working alone?
Groups make better decisions than individuals working alone for several reasons: the resources of all the members are combined; errors that might occur by chance have a greater likelihood of being noticed and corrected in a group; members may stimulate ideas in other members and play off the ideas of others to create new ideas; and the presence of other people might motivate some members to work harder toward making a high-quality decision.

2.   What is a small group?
A small group is a collection of persons who come together to satisfy needs and achieve goals. A small group is distinct from a random assembly of people because it shares a common purpose and is held together by communication. A small group has become the primary decision-making tool in our culture.

3.   What are functional roles?
A role is a set of behaviors that you exhibit in a particular situation. You must choose the behaviors that you think are appropriate for that situation and avoid those that seem inappropriate.

A functional role is a set of behaviors exhibited in a small group related to the operation of the group. Group task and maintenance roles are constructive and contribute to good decision making. Individual centered roles are usually destructive and impede the ability of a group to make good decisions or achieve goals.

4.   What is leadership?

Leadership is the ability to influence the behavior of other group members. Leadership is based on the group members' perceptions of a person's coercive, reward, referent, legitimate, and expert power. Leadership can be exhibited by any member of the group. If you have influence over some aspect of the group's activities, then you have exhibited leadership.

5.   What are the differences among traditional, human relations, and human resources leaders?

Traditional leaders follow the assumptions of Theory X in guiding group members. These members need to be controlled and supervised because they do not like to work and are not interested in taking responsibility for the group goal. Human relations leaders emphasize the social dimensions of the group interaction and try to build members' self-esteem. They assume both Theory X and Theory Y are partially correct. The leader still controls major decisions and supervises group members to make sure they are performing the task, but consults with them and tries to give them some minor decision-making responsibility. Human resources leaders follow the assumptions of Theory Y in guiding group members. These members are motivated, skilled, and want to perform to the best of their ability. Close supervision is unnecessary. The emphasis of the human resource leader is to coordinate and promote cooperative behavior while helping the members reach their full potentials.

6.   What are the advantages and disadvantages of conflict for a small group?

Conflict has several advantages for a small group. The most critical benefit is probably that it provides alternative points of view. However, conflict also allows a vent for hostilities that build up among group members and it can facilitate an examination of the relationships in the group. Disadvantages of poorly managed conflict include a distraction of the group from its task and possibly even the disintegration of the group.

7.   What are the effects of conformity in a small group?

A group needs to have some conformity among members to get anything accomplished. If there were no conformity, there would be no agreement. When conformity pressures are too strong, the quality of decision making is harmed because expression of true feelings is inhibited and the expression of alternative points of view is minimized.

S T U D E N T   E X E R C I S E S

1.   Leadership style.

You have probably had some experience as a leader of a group. Discuss with other members of your class how you chose a style of leadership. Was your choice a conscious one? Was it influenced by your own goals or personality? Was it influenced by the personalities of the group members? Was it influenced by the goals of the group? Was your style useful in helping the group accomplish its goals?

2. **A small group model.**

How would you change the model of communication presented in chapter 1 to make it more appropriate to the small group? Are the concepts the same? How does the presence of more than two people change the process of communication?

3. **Satisfaction with membership.**

Make a list of all the small groups to which you belong. Discuss with your class-mates why you joined those groups and why you remain a member of those groups. Have the goals of any of the groups changed while you have been a member? If so, discuss why you think they have changed. What effect do you think a change in goals has had on the groups?

4. **Conflict.**

Are the following situations examples of intrinsic or extrinsic conflict?

    a. A debate over where to have a group meeting.
    b. A conflict over who should control the group.
    c. Phillip threatens to quit because Don always gets his way.
    d. Lynn has missed three meetings in a row.
    e. Stan didn't complete his last assignment.

GLOSSARY

cohesiveness An esprit de corps or the extent to which a group sticks together.

conflict Disagreement over alternative choices that a group can make.

conformity A strict or rigid adherence to the norms of a group.

extrinsic conflict Conflict based on personality clashes among members of a group.

group culture A collective personality and a group point of view that is negotiated by the members of the group.

group maintenance role Behaviors oriented toward the group operating smoothly as a social system.

group task role Behaviors oriented toward accomplishing the goals of the group (i.e., completing the task).

individual centered roles Behaviors oriented toward the satisfaction of the individual needs of a single member. These behaviors are most often counterproductive to the group's goals.

intrinsic conflict Conflict that centers around procedures, opinions, issues, values, and goals related to the task of a small group.

leadership The ability to influence the behavior of others.

norms Shared guidelines for beliefs and behavior that are negotiated and enforced by the group.

role A set of behaviors enacted by people within a specific context.

small group A small group is an integrated collection of persons engaged in a cooperative, goal-oriented interaction; they are aware of their own and others' participation and get some satisfaction from participation in the activities of the group.

N O T E S

1. Alvin Toffler, *The Third Wave* (New York: Morrow, 1980).

2. See B. A. Fisher and D. Ellis, *Small Group Decision Making: Communication and the Group Process* (New York: McGraw-Hill, 1990); I. Janis and L. Mann, *Decision Making: A Psychological Analysis of Conflict, Choice, and Commitment* (New York: Free Press, 1977); and M. Zeev, "The Decision to Raid Entebbe: Decision Analysis Applied to Crisis Behavior," *Journal of Conflict Resolution* 25 (1981), 677–708.

3. John Brilhart and Gloria Galanes, *Effective Group Discussion* (Dubuque, Iowa: Wm. C. Brown, 1989).

4. J. Thibaut and H. Kelley, *The Social Psychology of Groups* (New York: John Wiley & Sons, 1959). Also, see W. Schutz, *The Interpersonal Underworld* (Palo Alto, Calif.: Science and Behavior Books, 1966).

5. Robert F. Bales, *Personality and Interpersonal Behavior* (New York: Holt, Rinehart and Winston, 1970). See also E. Bormann, "Symbolic Convergence Theory and Communication in Group Decision-Making," in *Communication and Group Decision Making,* ed., R. Hirokawa and M. S. Poole (Beverly Hills, Calif.: Sage, 1986).

6. Sara Kiesler, *Interpersonal Processes in Groups and Organizations* (Arlington Heights, Ill.: Harlan-Davidson, 1978).

7. Dennis S. Gouran, "Principles of Counteractive Influence in Decision-Making and Problem-Solving Groups," in *Small Group Communication: A Reader,* ed., R. S. Cathcart and L. Samovar (Dubuque, Iowa: Wm. C. Brown, 1988).

8. Ibid.

9. E. Bormann, *Small Group Communication: Theory and Practice* (New York: Harper & Row, 1990).

10. Leon Festinger, "Informal Social Communication," *Psychological Review* 57 (1950), 271–82.

11. D. Cartwright and A. Zandar, "Group Cohesiveness: Introduction," in *Group Dynamics: Research and Theory,* D. Cartwright and A. Zandar (Evanston, Ill.: Row, Peterson, 1960).

12. Bormann, *Small Group Communication;* and M. Shaw, "Group Composition and Group Cohesiveness," in *Small Groups and Social Interaction,* ed., H. Blumberg, A. P. Hare, V. Kent, and M. Davies (London: John Wiley & Sons, 1983).

13. Bormann, *Small Group Communication.*

14. I. L. Janis, *Groupthink: Psychological Studies of Foreign Policy Decisions and Fiascoes* (Boston: Houghton Mifflin, 1983).

15. K. Benne and P. Sheats, "Functional Roles of Group Members," *Journal of Social Issues* 4 (1948), 41–9.

16. C. Larson, "The Verbal Response of Groups to the Absence or Presence of Leadership," *Speech Monographs* 38 (1971), 177–81.

17. J. C. Geier, "A Trait Approach to the Study of Leadership in Small Groups," *Journal of Communication* 17 (1967), 316–23.

18. D. McGregor, *The Human Side of Enterprise* (New York: McGraw-Hill, 1960).

19. Gouran, "Principles of Counteractive Influence."

20. Ibid.

21. Kiesler, *Interpersonal Processes.*

22. Stanley Schacter, "Deviation, Rejection, and Communication," *Journal of Abnormal and Social Psychology* 46 (1951), 190–207.

Strategies for Group Decision Making

P erhaps the most significant consideration in the study of groups is the way decisions are made. No matter what task the group attempts to accomplish, decisions must always be made. The group must decide what the nature of the task is, what the goals of the group are, how the labor should be divided, and what solution is best for the current problem. They even have to decide how to make the decision!

We have already discussed that one of the advantages of working in a small group is access to several alternative points of view. These multiple points of view and the new ideas that they stimulate in group members make the small group a very powerful decision-making tool. Because of this, scholars have paid much attention to the study of decision making in small groups. This chapter describes group decision making, discusses the major theoretical and practical approaches to decision making, and suggests strategies for improving your own decision making in a group.

The Nature of Decision Making

A group decision requires that at least four circumstances exist: choice, action, consequences, and commitment. First, some *choice* must exist. Without a reasonable choice among realistic alternatives, there really is no decision to be made. The second circumstance is *action*. Group decisions require that a course of action implements a decision. Without action, there is no real decision to be made; the group is merely expressing opinions. The third circumstance concerns *consequences*. After the group has made a decision and taken action to implement it, consequences result. The action has an effect on the group and its environment requiring that subsequent decisions be made. The final implied circumstance is that decisions require *commitment*. Group decisions commit the group to a given course of action. As such, the group members must be willing to follow through on their decisions even despite initial negative feedback.

Another important element of group decision making is that groups do not operate apart from their environment. Rather, they function in an open system that continually interacts with the physical and social environment. As discussed in chapter 2, because individuals are components of a social system, their behavior is affected by and affects the environment. Groups are also components (or subsystems) of larger systems. As such, the decisions made by a group affect the group's environment and are affected by it.

Current decisions affect future decisions made by the group because past decisions become part of the context for future decisions. A similar process happens in law. Legal decisions are made by citing precedent. The way legal decisions have been made in the past provides a model for making current decisions that, in turn, provide models for making future decisions. The same tends to hold true for decisions made by groups.

Basic Model of Decision Making

A simple way of looking at any decision is illustrated by a model consisting of five components (see figure 13.1):[1]

1. The **history** is all the events leading to the current situation or the past occurrences of the problem.
2. The **present situation** is the status quo or the way things are right now.
3. The **goal** is the desired future state that the group wants to reach; it may or may not be compatible with the present situation. This is the reason for the group to make a decision.
4. The **obstacles** are those factors or constraints preventing movement from the present situation to the goal.
5. Finally, the **solution** is the course of action that eliminates or modifies the barriers allowing the group to reach the goal.

For example, assume your group is assigned a class presentation on conflict in small groups. You examine your *history* to see what you know about conflict, small groups, and making class presentations. Your *present situation* is that you have the assignment as a member of a group. Your group *goal* is to receive a grade of *A* on the presentation, but you have no information or plan for reaching the goal. As such, the present situation is not compatible with your goal of getting an *A*. To reach that goal, you must find a way to circumvent the *obstacles* to your goal: there is a lack of information, you have no ideas for examples, and your group is unorganized and needs practice. Your *solution* consists of visits to

FIGURE 13.1

Basic model of decision making.

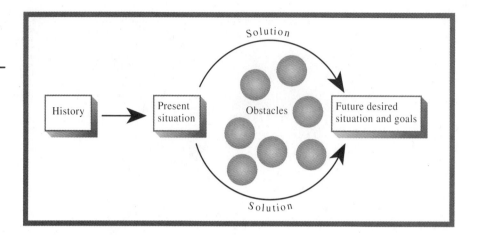

the library, some brainstorming sessions during which you create examples, and some meetings during which you organize and practice your presentation. After you have reached this point, your goals and current situation are compatible, and you have solved your problem. Although this is a simple model, it is a very useful tool for breaking down a problem to basic parts and understanding how best to solve it.

"Before You Go On"

You should be able to answer the following question:

What circumstances must exist for a group decision to be made?

Individual versus Group Decision Making

You can understand how complex group decision making is if you compare it to the decision-making process of an individual working alone.[2] When individuals make decisions, they only need to be concerned with the task at hand and with making up their own minds. When the same task is given to a group, however, the nature of the task itself changes. Since a group has several members, they must share resources and information so the group can assess its strengths, abilities, and goals. Also, a group has to decide how the task is to be approached. In effect, they have to decide how to decide to solve the problem. Finally, the group must come to some agreement or reach consensus on the best solution. Consensus does not necessarily mean complete or total agreement; it means the group members agree enough to accept the decision and commit themselves to its implementation.[3] The issue here is that groups have an extra social dimension that individuals working alone do not.

Advantages

There are definite advantages to making a decision in a group. As discussed in the previous chapter, one advantage is that groups tend to make better quality decisions than individuals. Most important, more persons working on a problem means more alternative points of view and the added advantage of the group members stimulating ideas in other members.

Disadvantages

There are some disadvantages to making a decision in a group. For example, groups often take more time to solve problems. There may also be difficulties in arranging meeting times. Some people may work faster than others and be idle while others catch up. Time is wasted coordinating the different work rates. In addition, some of the group's time is spent on social interaction that may interfere with the task. An individual working alone could have spent all that time working on the task itself.

The pressure to conform is another disadvantage to group decision making. Because of this pressure, groups make hasty decisions and aren't careful about making the best decision. When conformity pressures are high, the group forces agreement just to have the task completed.

An extreme case of conformity pressure is **groupthink.**[4] Groupthink can be defined as the tendency of a group to get stuck on one idea and not be able to move beyond it. If the group concludes that one particular solution is reasonable, members screen out further information and divergent points of view. Pressure to conform is high, so the group becomes fairly closed minded and does not tolerate other points of view. As discussed in chapter 12, groupthink occurs when groups are highly cohesive. If there is strong agreement on a topic, the positions of individual group members often change to conform to the group position and avoid conflict. The typical consequence is that the group overlooks other parts of the problem and other (possibly better) solutions. In addition, the group develops a sense of infallibility and invulnerability. The participants believe that they can make any kind of decision they wish, that they won't be mistaken, and that no costs will result from a poor decision. Groups involved in groupthink usually make faulty decisions inferior to groups not involved in groupthink.

The members of a group bring different points of view to the problem, which is usually an advantage in making quality decisions. However, it can also be a disadvantage. Differing points of view contribute to the potential for conflict. Resolving conflict takes time. If not managed properly and constructively, conflict may lead to the disintegration of the group.

The Group Consultant

PROBLEM:

Your group is displaying some of the symptoms of groupthink (i.e., alternative points of view are not encouraged, a feeling of invulnerability, a concern with justifying outcomes, strong pressure to conform to decisions). What steps can you take to guide your group out of groupthink?

STRATEGY:

Take the following steps to counteract groupthink, provided, of course, that you are aware it is happening.[5]

1. *Independent thinking should be encouraged.* You and/or the group leader must try to discourage immediate, noncritical agreement.

2. *Evaluate the quality of an idea on its own merit.* Don't let another's status or your relationship with the person making the suggestion or proposal bias your opinion. Agree or disagree with an idea, not a person.

3. *Invite an outsider to evaluate the decision-making process in your group.* Often a person who is not a member of your group can identify problems more clearly than someone who is.

4. *Appoint a devil's advocate* or play the role yourself. If you provide the group with a fairly consistent source of constructive disagreement, it will consider more possible alternatives or solutions.

5. *Subdivide the group to evaluate proposed solutions.* There could be less pressure to conform and members could be more likely to express their true feelings and concerns when they are not the center of the group's attention.

In spite of the disadvantages, the product of group decision making is still typically better than the product of an individual working alone. Although social interaction can sometimes get in the way, the product of the social interaction is the strong point of the most groups.

"Before You Go On"

You should be able to answer the following question:

How can groupthink affect the decision-making process?

Another interesting difference between group and individual decision making is **progressive modification.**[6] With little interference, an individual decision maker can evaluate an idea and decide if it will solve the problem. However, a group member's ideas are subject to the collective mind of the group. After an individual group member generates and contributes an idea, it is modified or changed by the group. The idea is modified again and again until it corresponds with the cumulative point of view of the group. If an individual were working alone, the original idea would remain fairly intact.

Risk

Groups make decisions involving more risk than an individual is likely to take. **Risk** can be defined as taking a course of action that has a high possible payoff but a low probability of occurrence. The main reason groups are likely to make decisions involving more risk is that the risks will be diffused throughout the group. More than just one member accepts the responsibility. Individuals working alone are normally less likely to take such risks. The amount of risk groups take varies with the personalities of the members and the context of the decision.

Suitability

Some tasks or decisions are suitable for groups, while others are more suitable for individuals.[7] An individual problem has one best or correct answer that can be validated by an outside source. An example would be a highly technical problem requiring the attention of an expert. In such a case, the decision of a group would not make the solution to the problem any more right, as the group could probably do no better than the efforts of its most expert member.

A task suited for a group, on the other hand, is one that requires the consensus and commitment of a group to implement the decision. This type of problem would not have a best or correct answer, and the answer would not be externally verifiable. In such a case, the group has to decide how to handle the situation and then commit itself to implementing the solution. Also, some problems require the processing of more information than an individual might be capable of processing. So the group has a larger capacity to handle information. The group is also better able to handle decision-related stress than an individual working alone. As such, the group could face large amounts of stress and continue to function when the same amount of stress could incapacitate an individual.

Theoretical Approaches to Decision Making

There are two major approaches to the discussion of decision making. The logic-based prescriptive approach is concerned with how decisions should be made. Prescriptive models usually consist of a set of instructions that, if followed correctly, should lead to a quality decision. The experience-based descriptive approach is concerned with how people actually make decisions. Experience based means that information has been collected about decision making by watching and describing how people actually make decisions. Included in this section are the assumptions and weaknesses of both approaches as well as examples of each.

Prescriptive Approaches

Prescriptive models of decision making are based on these six assumptions about the decision-making process:

1. There is one best way for structuring the decision-making process. That best way depends on the decision you are making.
2. The decision-making process is primarily linear or sequential across time. Groups should follow the steps of the model exactly and not skip around.
3. Failure to follow the correct sequence of steps can result in inferior decisions.
4. Groups operate in a **closed system** in which all outcomes can be known or predicted. Decision makers can reason out and predict all possible contingencies of a decision.
5. Emotional behavior is disruptive to decision making, which should be a logical enterprise. People are capable of the detachment required to make superior decisions.
6. Decision making is a rational process that implies people are unbiased and capable of processing large amounts of information.

You might have noticed some difficulties with the assumptions of the prescriptive approach. Perhaps the most obvious is the assumption of rationality. While you may like to think that humans are totally rational beings, you would have some difficulty living up to this particular expectation. Humans do experience emotions. We have discussed the interdependence between the task and maintenance functions of groups and it seems difficult to separate the two. Humans don't have the capacity to know all the alternatives and outcomes for most situations. We know only some of the alternatives and outcomes due to a lack of information or insufficient time for thorough search. Even with all the information available and the help of computers, the human mind could not process all of the data or do so without bias. Another difficulty with the prescriptive approach is the assumption that small groups function in a closed system. This text assumes that groups operate in an **open system** interacting with its environment. This means that there is no end to the availability and search for information, that groups must continually adapt to changing conditions, and that predictions of consequences can never be exact.

Two examples of prescriptive approaches are the reflective thinking model and the ideal solution model.[8] (See the accompanying boxes entitled Reflective Thinking Model and Ideal Solution Model.)

The reflective thinking model is based on the assumption that the group must adequately understand the problem. This understanding creates the criteria for evaluating the quality of a solution.

Reflective Thinking Model

1. Define and limit the problem.
2. Analyze the problem: causes, present situation, consequences, solutions, goals, obstacles.
3. Suggest solutions.
4. Evaluate and select the best solution.
5. Implement and evaluate the consequences of the solution.

Source: J. Dewey, *How We Think* (Boston: D.C. Heath, 1910).

The second prescriptive model is the ideal solution model, which also has five steps. This model assumes that an adequate understanding of what the group wants the solution to do provides the criteria for the evaluation of the solution.

Ideal Solution Model

1. Agree on the specific nature of the problem.
2. Determine the ideal solution as if there were no constraints or obstacles.
3. Determine which parts of the present condition can be changed to create the ideal solution.
4. Find the solution actually available that best approximates the ideal solution.
5. Implement and evaluate the solution.

Source: A. A. Goldberg and C. E. Larson, *Group Communication: Discussion Processes and Applications* (Englewood Cliffs, N.J.: Prentice Hall, 1975).

The ideal solution model helps groups more clearly establish goals. By temporarily ignoring possible constraints on their behavior, group members increase their ability to examine a problem without bias. Rather than focusing on what cannot be accomplished, they focus on what can be done.

Notice how the assumptions of sequential order and rationality function in the models. Each starts with a definition of the problem. However, the reflective thinking model indicates the group should suggest solutions in accordance with the criteria and constraints discovered during analysis of the problem. On the other hand, the ideal solution model suggests that the group should ignore constraints until after the best solution is determined. Following one model precludes following the other. Each of the models might be good for different problems and different groups. However, the assumption that there is a best way to make decisions causes a dilemma concerning which model to use for which problem.

In spite of what appear to be serious problems with their assumptions, many of the prescriptive models have proven quite useful. When used as a guide for organizing group discussions, they can improve a group's ability to make quality decisions.

"Before You Go On"

You should be able to answer the following question:

What are the primary assumptions made by the prescriptive models of decision making?

Descriptive Approaches

The **descriptive models of decision making** are based on how groups actually make decisions. While prescriptive models provide more of a cookbook set of task-related instructions, descriptive models combine task and social functions to create a broad picture of how groups progress through decisions. The descriptive approach is based on four assumptions:

1. Decision making is not necessarily a linear or sequential process.
2. Groups make decisions naturally and don't require a prescribed procedure to be imposed on them.
3. Decision making involves an interdependence of task and social dimensions.
4. External constraints (such as time and resources) are minimal.

The first three assumptions almost directly contradict the assumptions made by the prescriptive approach. The final assumption is a weakness of the approach. For some models to function properly, the group should have as much time, energy, money, and other resources as it needs to solve a problem. However, groups operate as parts of other systems with frequent constraints. Lack of time is usually a constraint, especially in business-related decision making. Another weakness of early descriptive models is the data on which they are based. Much of the data came from college students making decisions in classrooms without real-world constraints. As such, some of the models are not as realistic as they could be.

We discuss two examples of descriptive models. Instead of a sequence of steps to be followed, these models provide descriptions of phases through which groups move while making a decision. (See the accompanying boxes entitled Three Phase Model and Decision Emergence Model.)[9]

In the three phase model, much task-related activity does not occur until the third phase. Most of the activity before the final phase relates to group members finding out about each other and deciding what the problem is about. Also, problems of individual differences, often minor extrinsic or intrinsic conflicts, are constantly being solved by the group. The decision emergence model confronts the task earlier than the three phase model, but it takes time in the final phase to reinforce the decision and to build cohesion.

Three Phase Model

PHASE ONE: ORIENTATION

a.   Group agrees on a common definition of the situation.
b.   Group members build expectations.
c.   Group solves problems of individual differences in orientation.

PHASE TWO: EVALUATION

a.   Group sets standards for success.
b.   Group generates norms and values to guide them.
c.   Group solves problems of individual differences in evaluation.

PHASE THREE: CONTROL

a.   Group establishes division of labor.
b.   Group establishes status hierarchy.
c.   Group establishes leadership.
d.   Group solves problems of individual differences in control.

Source: R. F. Bales and F. Strodbeck, "Phases in Group Problem Solving," *Journal of Abnormal and Social Psychology* 46.

Note the similarity between the two descriptive models. The descriptive approaches generally recognize that groups experience a period of orientation followed by conflict. The conflict stage is where much of the task is accomplished. The final stages bolster or reinforce the decision and promote group members' satisfaction with the decision. While the prescriptive models provide organization and direction, they don't acknowledge the social dimensions of group decision making. While the descriptive models acknowledge the social and emotional dimensions, they don't provide specific instructions for problem solving. In brief, both approaches are useful but incomplete explanations of the decision-making processes that groups experience. A more useful model accounts for human limitations yet provides enough task direction to help a group to make a decision when it is unsure about how to proceed. The conflict model fits both these criteria. We examine this model in the following section.

Decision Emergence Model

PHASE ONE: ORIENTATION

a. Getting acquainted.
b. Neutral nonevaluative statements exchanged.
c. Members' attitudes explored.
d. Mostly agreement.

PHASE TWO: CONFLICT

a. Argument and disagreement.
b. Statements unfavorable to decision proposal.
c. Members' attitudes polarize.

PHASE THREE: DECISION EMERGENCE

a. Primarily interpretive statements.
b. Attitudes converge on decisions.
c. Dissent modifies.
d. Neutral statements begin to be reinforced.

PHASE FOUR: REINFORCEMENT

a. Dissent minimized or disappears.
b. Favorable interpretive comments.
c. Reinforcement of the decision.
d. Cohesion and satisfaction builds.
e. Group unity affirmed.

Source: B. A. Fisher, "Decision Emergence: Phases in Group Decision Making," *Speech Monographs* 37.

"Before You Go On"

You should be able to answer the following question:

What are the primary assumptions made by the descriptive models of decision making?

The conflict model of decision making is oriented more toward individuals than groups.[10] As such, it doesn't attempt to account for the various phases of social orientation and reinforcement like the descriptive models. However, the model does assume that a human will be making the decisions rather than a completely rational machine. One major assumption made by the model is that decisions are made under conditions of uncertainty with the goal of reducing the uncertainty. That is, a decision maker can never be absolutely sure of a decision's outcome. Another assumption is that the way groups examine available information and possible choices affects their ability to make decisions.

The result of functioning under conditions of uncertainty is **anxiety** which impairs the ability to make decisions. How much the decision making is impaired or how the group handles it depends on the extent of the anxiety. Too much anxiety can completely disable most people. Sometimes you can get so worried about the outcome of a decision that you just can't function. Too little anxiety, on the other hand, does not promote good decision making because you are not sufficiently motivated to take the proper or necessary action.

A strength of the conflict model is that it is a combination of prescriptive and descriptive approaches to decision making. The model combines the logical prescription to problem solving while taking into account that emotional humans are making the decisions. To address both these areas, the model has two parts: coping patterns and decision steps.

Coping Patterns

We assume that humans who experience anxiety will attempt to find a way to reduce it. Stating that decisions are made under conditions of anxiety, the model suggests several ways that decisions are treated in the face of anxiety. These are **coping patterns:**

1. **Unconflicted adherence:** This method of coping indicates little or no anxiety related to a decision. The present condition is compatible with the goal (or the barriers are not thought to be serious) and there is no risk involved with continuing the current course of action. In effect, this is a decision to do nothing.

2. **Unconflicted change:** This coping pattern indicates very little anxiety. The present condition is not compatible with the goal. The group sees a need for some action and adopts the first alternative coming to mind that has no apparent negative aspects and meets the requirements of the goal. This strategy does not entail an adequate search and evaluation of possible solutions to the problem. As such, the best

solution is probably never found. Unfortunately, many personal as well as public decisions are made this way. For example, assume your group scheduled a speaker to talk to your class. Some time before the class was to meet, the person canceled. Instead of going through the decision-making process again to select a new speaker, your group simply finds somebody else who is available to speak. It might not be the best person for the job, but at least you have a speaker.

3. **Defensive avoidance:** The defensive avoidance coping pattern involves moderate to high anxiety. The present condition is not compatible with the goal and the group sees a need to take some action. The problem is that the only available alternatives have negative or unattractive consequences. In this case, the group responds by distorting information, procrastinating, attempting to pass responsibility to someone else, and avoiding thinking or talking about the problem. A group stuck in the defensive avoidance coping pattern creates excuses why it cannot deal with the problem. It could get involved in an extrinsic conflict episode that threatens the existence of the group just to avoid the problem.

4. **Hypervigilance:** Hypervigilance involves high anxiety. The present condition is not compatible with the goal, so the group sees a need to take action. A good solution exists to the problem, but there is insufficient time to search for and evaluate alternatives. As such, the group perceives that it must make a snap decision. The group responds to this pressure by quickly and indiscriminately examining as much information as possible. Information overload occurs and the group operates in a state of panic resulting in inadequate evaluation of information. For example, imagine a person trying to escape from a burning building. When he first notices the fire, it is not very serious. He has several escape routes and sufficient time to decide which one to take. However, the longer he thinks about it, the more the fire spreads, closing off the possible routes of escape. With no time left to decide, the decision maker is in a state of panic which reduces his chances of making a good decision (i.e., escaping from the fire).

5. **Vigilance:** For many important decisions, the vigilant coping pattern is the best of all possible strategies. The present condition is not compatible with the goal, so there is a need for action. The level of anxiety is high enough to motivate a thorough search for alternatives but not high enough to impair decision making. The group has adequate time to search for and evaluate solutions. This coping pattern is the only one that promotes a quality decision because the group is able to and does progress through all the steps necessary for good decision making.

If possible, decision-making groups should function under this ideal condition of vigilance. There are defects in the decision-making strategies of groups functioning under the other coping patterns. The group needs to assess its coping pattern and make adjustments to get as close to the vigilant condition as possible.

Five-Step Plan

The second part of the conflict model of decision making is a five-step plan for the task dimension of the problem. The five steps are as follows:

Step 1. Appraise the challenge: At this point, the group finds that some opportunity has arisen or some information has been made available indicating it must make a change in the current course of action. The group then asks the central question for this step: "Are the risks serious if we don't change the course of action?" If the answer to that question is no, then most likely the group will adopt the unconflicted adherence coping pattern and take no action. If the answer to the question is yes, the decision process moves to step 2.

Step 2. Survey the alternatives: Since it is apparent that something must be done, the group begins to collect and make a preliminary evaluation of all available alternatives. Those judged unacceptable are discarded. The remaining alternatives are further evaluated in step 3. Some groups, however, have a tendency to skip step 3 and adopt the first reasonable sounding alternative that comes to mind. This leads to the unconflicted change coping pattern.

Step 3. Weigh Alternatives: The group conducts a further search for and evaluation of consequences of alternatives. After a thorough examination of consequences, the group chooses what appears to be the best alternative. They ask "Will this alternative meet the essential requirements of the goal?" If the answer is no, the group returns to step 2 to survey more alternatives. If the answer is yes, the group can move to step 4. At any time during steps 2 and 3, if the group decides that all possible alternatives are unattractive or negative, it could get caught in the defensive avoidance coping pattern.

Step 4. Deliberate about commitment: When the group deliberates about commitment, it is really trying to project into the future to see if it can live with the decision it has made. The group tries to anticipate the consequences of the decision and formulate strategies to cope with possible negative feedback. If the group thinks it can cope with the consequences of its decision, it adopts the course of action and allows others to know about it. Should the group decide it can't cope with the consequences of the decision, it must return to either step 3 or step 2 in search of new alternatives. The box entitled Methods for Increasing Commitment indicates how different types of decisions affect commitments.

After deliberation, a group commits to its chosen course of action.

Step 5. Adhere despite negative feedback: Commitment to the course of action selected by the group depends on the quality of the process used to make the decision. A group that does a good job of anticipating the consequences of its decision, builds in a kind of invulnerability to negative feedback concerning the decision. As such, the group should have no trouble coping with the consequences. For a group that did not adequately examine the consequences and risks of implementing the solution, however, the negative feedback comes as a surprise. At this point, the model reverts back to step 1 and the group is confronted with appraising a challenge to the current decision. Suppose the new challenge is serious enough that the answer to the question, "Are the risks serious if we don't change?" is yes. Then, the group begins the process of making a new decision and proceeds through the model once again.

Methods for Increasing Commitment

GOOD: VOTING

The objective of voting is closure or resolution of the problem. Decisions are made when a majority (or some other predetermined number) support the conclusion. Unless the vote is unanimous, there will be winners and losers and, as such, different levels of commitment to carrying out the decision. The winners will be satisfied and should be strongly committed to adhering to the decision. The losers will feel far less commitment and would probably be the first to abandon the decision in the face of negative consequences.

BETTER: COMPROMISE

Compromise is the result of negotiation. This method reaches a decision by means of mutual concessions from all group members. The result is that no member is completely satisfied, but no member is completely frustrated as all have partially achieved their goals. Commitment to the decision is balanced, often reluctant, but generally sufficient to stick to the decision.

BEST: CONSENSUS

As well as it can be done, a consensus decision reflects the desires of all members of the group. Consensus is reached by groups whose members tend to place group goals ahead of personal goals and operate as a team. Decisions reached by consensus tend to be moderate. Because the views of all members are, at least to some extent, represented in the decision, commitment to the decision should be strong even in the face of negative consequences.

Source: J. Wood, "Alternative Methods of Group Decision Making," in *Emergent Issues in Human Decision Making,* ed. G. Phillips and J. Wood (Carbondale: Southern Illinois University Press, 1984).

"Before You Go On"

You should be able to answer the following question:

What are the major assumptions of the conflict model of decision making?

Obstacles to a Quality Decision

The major obstacles to making a good decision are task obstacles and social obstacles. *Task obstacles* include lack of information, biased evaluation of information, inadequate definition of the decision model (history, present situation, goal, obstacles, solution), and a lack of time for adequate search and appraisal of alternatives. The *social obstacles* include a lack of cohesiveness, extrinsic conflict and/or deficient conflict resolution strategies, pressure toward conformity that limits alternative points of view, anxiety, and role rigidity. Perhaps the most important social barrier is the lack of involvement and motivation of the group members. Members who are not involved aren't going to be thorough in the search for alternatives; nor are they going to be firmly committed to any decision made by the group.

Strategies for Improving Decision Making

Your group can improve its decision making by implementing one or all of the following suggestions:

Become sensitive to the group's and individual's maintenance needs. Just being aware of the interdependence of the task and social aspects of decision making should improve your performance. Also, members of the group can enhance their communication skills. Improved listening skills, using supportive statements that do not arouse defensiveness, and stating ideas clearly and concretely can decrease misunderstanding and enhance supportive climates.

Increase the participation of group members. Allowing and encouraging every member to participate in the group's activities improves individual satisfaction with the group and increases involvement and commitment. Also, increased participation ensures that valuable information and viewpoints are not lost because of members' silence. Developing a supportive climate and following established agendas and turn-taking rules ensure that everyone can contribute ideas.

Try to reach agreements often during discussion. This suggestion serves a number of purposes: Reaching agreement can help the group members keep up with the current thinking of the group and clarify information. It also pinpoints areas of disagreement that might otherwise go unnoticed by the group.

Focus on the entire decision model to promote vigilance. The group should make every attempt to remain in the vigilance coping pattern to avoid defective decisions. This can be done if the group stays aware of time constraints and deadlines to avoid hypervigilance. Also, the group should try to reach consensus on desired goals before trying to identify obstacles and possible solutions to problems.

"Before You Go On"

You should be able to answer the following question:

What strategies can you use to improve decision making?

Responses to *"Before You Go On"* Questions: A Chapter Summary

1.   What circumstances must exist for a group decision to be made?
The group must have a realistic choice between or among alternatives; some course of action must be taken to implement the decision; the decision involves consequences that affect the group; and the group must have the commitment to follow through on the decision.

2.   How can groupthink affect the decision-making process?
Groupthink inhibits the decision-making process because it restricts alternative points of view. Group members agree with the position without entertaining other perspectives. The group also reinforces the decision and creates a sense of invulnerability against possible negative consequences of the decision. The typical result of groupthink is an inferior decision.

3.   What are the primary assumptions made by the prescriptive models of decision making?
The prescriptive models assume that there is a best way to make decisions; that the decision-making process is linear and sequential; that the failure of a group to follow the sequence can result in inferior decisions; that all possible outcomes of a decision can be known and predicted; that emotions are disruptive to decision making; and that humans are rational decision makers.

4.   What are the primary assumptions made by the descriptive models of decision making?
The descriptive models assume that decision making is a process; that groups make decisions naturally and do not need a prescribed procedure; that decision making involves both task and social dimensions; and that external constraints are at a minimum.

5.   What are the major assumptions of the conflict model of decision making?

The conflict model assumes that decisions are made under conditions of uncertainty. You can never be absolutely sure of the outcome of a decision. How you cope with the anxiety created by uncertainty that you can make the best choice influences how you make the decision. The quality of decision making is also related to the manner in which groups examine information.

6.   What strategies can you use to improve decision making?

You can improve decision making by being sensitive to the needs of people in the group and by striving to maintain a supportive climate. You can also gain the commitment of members by encouraging every member to participate in the discussion, by reaching agreements often, and by trying your best to remain in the vigilance coping pattern.

S T U D E N T   E X E R C I S E S

1.   Design a group project.

Design a class project to be carried out by your group. Specify the group goals, the method of decision making, the method of gathering information, the method of presenting the information, and the method of grading the presentation.

2.   Suitable projects.

Discuss with your group the kinds of projects or decisions that seem appropriate for a small group. What criteria will you use to judge the appropriateness of the problem for the group?

3.   Effects of anxiety on decision making.

Think of a time you made an important decision while experiencing anxiety. How do you feel emotionally and physically when you are anxious? How do you think anxiety affected your ability to make a decision? How did you cope with it? What was the outcome? How could you have improved the outcome?

4.   Coping with groupthink.

Recall a time when you participated in groupthink. How do you know it was groupthink? What behaviors make you believe this? Did you know something was wrong at the time? What could you do about it?

anxiety The result of functioning under conditions of uncertainty.

closed system A system that does not interact with its environment.

coping pattern A way in which a decision is made in the presence of anxiety.

defensive avoidance Avoiding making a decision because all the available alternatives are undesirable.

descriptive model of decision making A data-based model that characterizes how groups actually make decisions.

goal A desired future state or condition that a group wants to achieve.

groupthink The tendency of a group to get stuck on one idea and refuse to challenge it or move beyond it.

history All of the past events leading to the current situation or past occurrences of the problem.

hypervigilance Panic when a decision must be made quickly with no time for search and appraisal.

obstacles Those factors preventing movement from a group's present situation to its goal.

open system A system that interacts with its environment.

prescriptive model of decision making A logic-based model consisting of a set of instructions that dictate how decisions should be made.

present situation The status quo; the current condition of a group.

progressive modification An idea is changed again and again by the group until it corresponds with the group's cumulative point of view.

risk Taking a course of action that has a high possible payoff but a low probability of occurrence.

solution A course of action that eliminates obstacles and allows a group to achieve its goal.

unconflicted adherence A decision to do nothing; to take no action.

unconflicted change Adoption of the first alternative that comes to the attention of the decision maker that meets minimum criteria.

vigilance A decision maker has adequate time and resources for a thorough search and appraisal resulting in a quality decision.

N O T E S

1. K. MacCrimmon and R. Taylor, "Decision Making and Problem Solving," in *Handbook of Industrial and Organizational Psychology,* ed., M. Dunnette (Chicago: Rand McNally, 1976).

2. Sara Kiesler, *Interpersonal Processes in Groups and Organizations* (Arlington Heights, Ill.: Harlan-Davidson, 1978).

3. J. Wood, "Alternative Methods of Group Decision Making," in *Emergent Issues in Human Decision Making,* ed., G. Phillips and J. Wood (Carbondale: Southern Illinois University Press, 1984).

4. I. L. Janis, *Groupthink: Psychological Studies of Foreign Policy Decisions and Fiascoes* (Boston: Houghton Mifflin, 1983).

5. S. Beebe and J. Masterson, *Communicating in Small Groups: Principles and Practices* (Glenview, Ill.: Scott, Foresman, 1990).

6. T. Scheidel and L. Crowell, "Idea Development in Small Discussion Groups," *Quarterly Journal of Speech* 50 (1964), 140–45; see also B. A. Fisher, "The Process of Decision Modification in Small Discussion Groups," *Journal of Communication* 20 (1970) 51–64; and D. Gouran and R. Kirokawa, "Small Group Communication in the 1980s." Paper presented at the annual meeting of the Speech Communication Association, New Orleans, November 4, 1988.

7. B. A. Fisher and D. Ellis, *Small Group Decision Making: Communication and the Group Process* (New York: McGraw-Hill, 1990).

8. J. Dewey, *How We Think* (Boston: D. C. Heath, 1910); A. A. Goldberg and C. E. Larson, *Group Communication: Discussion Processes and Applications* (Englewood Cliffs, N.J.: Prentice Hall, 1975).

9. R. F. Bales and F. Strodbeck, "Phases in Group Problem Solving," *Journal of Abnormal and Social Psychology* 46 (1951), 485–95; B. A. Fisher, "Decision Emergence: Phases in Group Decision Making," *Speech Monographs* 37 (1970), 53–66.

10. I. L. Janis and L. Mann, *Decision Making: A Psychological Analysis of Choice, Conflict, and Commitment* (New York: Free Press, 1977).

C H A P T E R

Strategies for Intercultural Communication

I was staying in a rented house in Mexico City while I was working

there. My boss had transferred me to that location for a short time to

reorganize our local office. About one week after moving into the house, the

water heater died leaving me with only cold water. I called the landlord and explained the problem. He understood, and said that he would come over

mañana to replace it. I thought it would be an inconvenience, but I could take

a cold shower the next morning and survive. It would be fixed tomorrow.

Tomorrow came and went, but I never saw the landlord. I called him

the next day and reminded him of the problem. He seemed a little surprised

that I was irritated, but was very nice and said he would attend to it mañana.

Okay! I figured I had his attention and he would soon be fixing the water

heater. I could survive one more cold shower. After all, he would be there

tomorrow.

Tomorrow came and went, and, once again, there was no hot water.

Now really irritated, I called the landlord and complained. He became angry

and said he couldn't believe how impatient and pushy Americans were. He

said he would come that evening around five o'clock.

At nine o'clock the next morning, the landlord pulled up with a new

water heater. He didn't apologize for being late or making me take so many

cold showers. As a matter of fact, he was still angry with me for being a

pushy American. You would think that a guy as irresponsible as that would

never make a good landlord. I never did figure out what his problem was.

Fortunately, I didn't have to rent from him for very long.

T his story illustrates a misunderstanding based on differences in the way people view the world; that is, differences in the cultures of the communicators. People in the United States assume that mañana means the same thing as tomorrow. As such, the person in the example assumed that the water heater would be repaired in roughly twenty-four hours. People in the United States also assume that when you say you will do something at a certain time, you will do it at that exact time. However, to people from Mexico and other Central American cultures, mañana does not mean tomorrow; it means an indefinite time in the future. So the American tenant was irritated when the Mexican landlord did not repair the water heater in twenty-four hours, and the landlord was provoked when the tenant complained about the lack of service. As far as the landlord was concerned, the promise of service was not broken, so the tenant had no reason to complain. The conflict was based on the difference in interpretation of a single word. If the participants shared a similar meaning for mañana, most likely there would have been no conflict.

You might have the idea that cultural differences only exist between people of different countries. If you do, you are not alone. Many discussions of intercultural communication focus only on clear differences between people from different countries. For example, Arab cultures use personal space differently than Americans. During a conversation, Americans are inclined to stand farther apart than Arabs, who stand almost toe to toe. When an American and an Arab have a conversation, the Arab tries to stand close and the American considers the Arab pushy and feels uncomfortable. In contrast, the Arab sees the American as cold and aloof because of the distance between them. Many textbooks mention differences such as this, while ignoring less obvious, more subtle cultural differences in the same country.

Strategies for Intercultural Communication   325

The Nature of Intercultural Communication

Intercultural communication is not only communication between residents of different countries. Cultural differences exist between people in the same country, the same city, and the same neighborhood. They even exist between people in the same house. They exist between different racial, ethnic, and religious groups. They also exist between parents and children, men and women, physicians and patients, professors and students, biology majors and communication majors, college seniors and college freshmen, younger people and older people, Democrats and Republicans, and a virtually endless list of others.

All that is really required for intercultural differences to exist is a dissimilarity between the way that two groups of people see the world. This *worldview* is influenced in a significant way by the society in which the group lives. As such, the focus of this chapter is culture. We begin by examining the nature of culture and intercultural communication.

"Before You Go On"

You should be able to answer the following question:

Is the study of intercultural communication limited to the investigation of communication between people of different nationalities?

Culture

There are many ways to define culture. *Webster's Ninth New Collegiate Dictionary* defines culture as an "integrated pattern of human behavior that includes thought, speech, action, and artifacts and depends on (human) capacity for learning and transmitting knowledge to succeeding generations." Another definition is "that complex whole which includes knowledge, belief, art, morals, law, custom, and any other capabilities and habits acquired by man as a member of society."[1]

Perhaps a less complicated way to view **culture** is as the collective beliefs or principles on which a community or a part of a community is based. Shared by the members of the community, these beliefs or principles are passed from generation to generation. This worldview provides a common frame of reference through which the community understands its experiences.

Culture includes a group's set of expectations about what is or what ought to be, and it defines what you take for granted about yourself and your environment. These expectations include your beliefs, your language, what meanings you should give to the behavior of others, and what you expect to see in the world around you. If everything seems normal to you, that means everything fits your expectations about what is or what ought to be.

Enculturation

Culture is not something with which you are born. You didn't bring culture home from the hospital with you. It's not a biological gift from your parents. You are, however, born into a culture, so from the time of your birth your culture surrounds you. It's something that you learn and keep learning. Your experiences within and outside of your culture shapes, adds to, and changes your expectations. Culture is passed from generation to generation in a community through communication. This process of learning the culture is referred to as **enculturation** and occurs through parents, siblings, friends, schools, religious groups, the mass media, language, and many other sources. If you try to explain some of your behaviors or beliefs, your investigation will, most likely, lead you back to these sources.

For example, you learn about your culture in school. You learn the history of your community, the community beliefs and values, and the laws that describe appropriate behaviors for those living in your community. You learn about heroes and villains and myths that depict the accepted values and goals of the community.

Culture is also learned and passed on through **rituals,** or behaviors associated with particular occasions. For example, a birthday party is a ritual in our culture that celebrates becoming one year older. We have birthday parties because we have always had birthday parties. Your parents or friends had birthday parties for you, you will have birthday parties for your children, and your children will have birthday parties for their children. We do it because it was done for us, and because we think it is appropriate. It is part of our culture. Not every culture celebrates birthdays the way we do; some don't celebrate them at all. You may find it strange if someone doesn't understand your concern for sending cards or having parties.

Sapir-Whorf Hypothesis

Culture is also transmitted and maintained by means of language. Things are identified or labeled through the use of language. Some linguists suggest that we cannot think of something for which we have no label. According to this approach, referred to as the **Sapir-Whorf hypothesis,** the criteria for whether something exists in a particular culture is the existence of an appropriate label or name for it.[2] Language, then, determines the behavior, habits, and way of thinking in a particular culture. (See chapter 6 for a detailed discussion of how language influences thought.)

Different cultures, by virtue of their different symbol systems, constitute different worldviews or realities. The English language, for example, is based on the relationship of nouns to each other. Things are prominent in importance. Speakers of the language conceive of objects in stasis, that is, in terms of how they are. Some American Indian languages, however, are based on the verb. An object is a thing in motion. To talk about a ball, for instance, Indian languages require that you know what the ball is doing. There are different ways of referring to a ball rolling across the ground or thrown through the air. Language not only transmits culture from generation to generation but also affects the way people within the culture think.[3] Because language shapes the way we think, making changes in the way we talk about something should change the way we think about it. For instance, as we mentioned in chapter 6, one way to get people to perceive equality between sexes is to get them to use gender-neutral language that supports equality.

Your culture can help shape the way you perceive or interpret experience. If you observe something that is different from your normal expectations, chances are good that you will distort it somehow to fit with your expectation of what ought to be. Culture also allows you to fill in details missing and not readily available. Your cultural expectations make a kind of perceptual filter or terministic screen that helps you try to make sense of your experiences and tends to distort experience in favor of the familiar. Unless you are concentrating very hard on what is really there, your perceptual filter will probably help you see what you expect to see.

For example, Mike recently traveled by air to a vacation spot. Unknown to him, the pilot of the airplane was a woman. During the course of the flight, the pilot made a few announcements over the intercom concerning flight time, weather conditions, and points of interest. When he exited the plane, Mike shook hands with the woman who was standing in the cockpit door and thanked her for a pleasant flight and a smooth landing. After picking up luggage, his wife, Sonja commented that she had never been on an airplane with a female pilot. Mike objected, saying "You still haven't. Women don't fly airplanes for major airlines. A man flew our plane. That woman was a stewardess." Even though Mike heard the pilot's voice, saw her pilot's insignia on her uniform, shook her hand as she stood where the pilot stands, his expectation of a male flying the airplane did not allow him to see the female as the pilot. Had he been a little more aware, he could have moved beyond his cultural expectations and seen what was really there.

Intercultural Communication

Cultural expectations have a profound effect on communication. When you communicate using verbal and nonverbal behaviors, you expect those with whom you are communicating to give those behaviors meanings similar to the meanings that you gave them. You might expect that the others who receive your message perceive the world in much the same way that you do. But what happens when they do not? What happens when you are trying to communicate with a person from a foreign country or different geographic area, or of a different race, ethnic background, gender, or profession? In such cases, your expectation that others will attribute meanings to your communication behaviors similar to yours is probably not valid. How do you help the other person understand? How can you understand the other person? This is the challenge of intercultural communication. We define **intercultural communication** as communication between people or groups that have different shared beliefs or principles on which their communities are based. It is communication between people from dissimilar cultures. Research suggests intercultural communication "occurs whenever a message produced in one culture must be processed in another culture."[4]

Communication across cultural boundaries has usually been attempted by learning where the culturally different person was coming from. This approach assumed that if you could empathize with the other's experiences, you could try to explain what your message means in the other person's own terms. Intercultural communication was based on translating meanings from one language to another.

Intercultural communication is frequently taught from the perspective of empathy. That is, you need to be able to see the world as a culturally different person sees it and be able to feel what the culturally different person feels. This perspective assumes that only when that empathy is achieved can you completely understand another's culturally defined meaning.

At times, such an approach is neither practical, reasonable, nor possible. It is often very difficult to comprehend the behavior of another person because you don't have the background, education, or experiences with that culture. If this is the case, do you simply throw up your hands and say "We're not going to get anywhere?" Of course not! There are communication strategies for managing such situations and the balance of this chapter describes and explains them.

Barriers to Intercultural Communication

The basic theme of this book is that participants in communication cooperate to create competent communication. They work together to create mutual meaning out of verbal symbols, nonverbal behaviors, and the context of the encounter. The most important point you should understand about intercultural communication is that intercultural communication is actually not very different from any other communication situation. The same communication skills necessary for competent communication in other contexts are also necessary to create competent intercultural communication.

One difference is that the overlap of experience and cultural expectations is not as great as in most of the other situations we discuss. Ethnocentrism, cultural stereotyping, and the myth that merely learning the language is learning the culture are all barriers to intercultural communication.

Ethnocentrism

As mentioned earlier, we are inclined to view the world through perceptual filters shaped by the culture in which we live. These perceptual filters work well for managing day-to-day life within our own culture. Difficulties occur, however, when we use those same perceptual filters to interpret the communication behavior of someone from a different culture. This is a very common tendency because all of us, to some degree, are ethnocentric. **Ethnocentrism** is the tendency to assume that your own culture is universal or natural, that it makes more sense, and that it is more reasonable than the cultures of other people. This perspective makes it very difficult to understand the culture of another because you cannot—or will not—see that culture outside of the context of your own.

An assumption related to ethnocentrism is that the other cultures should make an effort to adapt to yours. After all, yours is clearly the superior and more reasonable culture! For example, Americans have a reputation for expecting people of other cultures to treat them as they would be treated in the United States. A student who recently visited England complained that the restaurants there were too cheap to put ice in soft drinks. He expected ice in his diet soda and was offended when he received none. When he complained at the restaurants, he was considered rude and was, on at least one occasion, chastised by a waiter for making unreasonable requests. He couldn't understand how the English could enjoy drinking soft drinks at room temperature. He was unwilling to accept any cultural values or standards as equal to his own.

Similarly, some American entrepreneurs become upset with the slow progress of business discussions they encounter in some Japanese cultures. They expect their hosts to adapt to their busy schedules and not waste time with rituals and sight-seeing. During the Persian Gulf War, Americans were angered that the Saudis demanded that American soldiers abide by their customs concerning proper dress and the role of women. In both cases, the Americans assumed that their culture was correct and became upset when asked to abide by the norms of a host culture they perceived as backward and unenlightened.

Competent intercultural communication accepts another person's cultural behavior as reasonable.

The point is that the tendency toward ethnocentrism inhibits your ability to consider the culture of the other as equal to or as reasonable as your own. Competent communication with culturally different others dictates an effort by all participants to consider the culture of others as plausible alternatives to their own.

Cultural Stereotyping

When you are communicating with a person from a different culture, remember that you are communicating with an individual. You are not communicating with the culture or all members of the culture, but an individual person who is a member of that culture. Take a look at five of your friends who are members of your culture. Even though they share many characteristics attributed to their culture, each person is different from the other. You would not think of treating each of them exactly the same as the others. They are all individuals and have differences.

When you meet an individual from a culture different from your own, it's easy to assume that the person shares the characteristics that are typical of the culture. This is referred to as **cultural stereotyping.** It means you know something about the culture, so you make a generalization that all members of the culture fit into that category. Cultural stereotypes are problematic for two reasons: First, the stereotype is probably an inaccurate and incomplete representation of the culture. It oversimplifies the rich experiences of the culture and is often based on false interpretations, outdated information, and/or generalized myths. For example, many Europeans have the stereotype that Americans are all cowboys, live in huge houses, and make lots of money. Does this describe the United States? Similarly, you might assume that all British people are stuffy, that all French are arrogant, that all older people drive big cars very slowly, that all college students are lazy and drink too much, or that all Japanese are extremely polite. Stereotypes are inaccurate representations of the actual culture.

Second, the cultural stereotype does not accurately describe an individual in the culture. In the same way as your five friends are all different, members of other cultures are different as well. When you first encounter a culturally different person, basic cultural information may be all you have to work with. However, as you interact, try to be sensitive to individual characteristics and begin to communicate on a more personal level. Difficulties arise when intercultural communicators fail to recognize each other as individuals and assume that the other is a stereotypical member of a group.

Culture Is Language

A common myth is that merely learning the language of a culture allows you to understand the culture. Although it is true that language affects the thinking of members of the culture, learning the language is usually limited to learning denotative meanings that can be translated into your native language. As an outsider to the culture, you still would not have access to the rituals, experiences, unwritten rules, and other elements of the culture that cannot be found in dictionaries and form the connotative meanings of language.

Strategies for Intercultural Communication

When you are speaking a language that is foreign to you, it seems natural that your sensitivity to alternative meanings and cultural differences would be heightened. You have to bring all your attention to focus on the meanings of words and sentences, because the language is different than your own. Because it is different, you are more sensitive to the possibility of multiple interpretations.

However, speaking the same language strengthens the assumption that knowing the language is knowing the culture. To speak the same language as a culturally different person can certainly be advantageous because you share a basic symbol system allowing you to share some ideas. The result, however, is that sensitivity of the participants to cultural differences is reduced because you assume that all interpretations will be similar.

For example, a student described an incident in a New Orleans restaurant. She was having dinner with some friends, one of whom was native to the area. The friend from the area ordered dinner and assured the others that they would approve. After the food arrived, everybody at the table was commenting about how delicious the main course was, but they couldn't identify it. The person who ordered waited until everybody was nearly finished before revealing what they were eating. One of the diners, a friend from the East Coast, was especially taken with the meal and couldn't wait to find out what it was. "It's some kind of Cajun chicken, right?" he asked. "This is the best I've ever had!" When he found out that the main course was alligator, he spit out the bite in his mouth and ran into the restroom. Angry at his friend for not telling him earlier what he was eating, he couldn't understand how people could actually eat that stuff. He indicated that there must be something wrong with people who would eat it. The student telling the story also indicated that her friend was not inclined to taste the rattlesnake stew.

A summary of strategies for overcoming barriers to intercultural communication appears in the accompanying box.

Strategies for Overcoming Barriers to Intercultural Communication

1. Communicate with the individual person, not the culture. Don't allow cultural stereotypes to bias your perceptions of others.

2. Strive to adapt to each of the other participants. Don't assume that your own culture is superior to others and expect the other participants to adapt to you.

3. Be sensitive and open to alternative denotative and connotative meanings for familiar words. Don't assume that a common language means common interpretations.

Strategies for Competent Intercultural Communication

The following discussion of strategies for achieving competent intercultural communication focuses on three distinct but related questions: What do I mean?, What do they mean?, and What do we mean?

What Do I Mean?

This question asks what you can do, within yourself, to prepare for an intercultural encounter. It assumes an action approach to communication. Probably the most important step you can take is to make yourself aware that your vision is filtered or biased by your cultural expectations. The more that you can be conscious of this bias, the better you are able to see beyond it and be open to new and different meanings.

Baseball legend Yogi Berra reportedly once said, "You can observe a lot by watching." Even though you can't really see culture, one way to observe your own cultural expectations is to note violations. When your expectations are violated, they are much easier to see. For example, you might not notice that you expect someone to shake your hand when you extend it. However, when you extend your hand and the other does not shake it, this violates your expectation and draws your attention. Noting violations of your cultural expectations highlights the differences that you have with a culturally different other. This makes your own, taken-for-granted expectations more obvious to you.

Another step you can take to prepare yourself for an encounter with a culturally different person is to bring your consciousness and attention to bear and focus on the communication situation. This is not the sort of circumstance that you can walk through in that mindless, unaware state with which you handle the mundane patterns or rituals of everyday communication. In this case, you need to be especially conscious of your own behavior to ensure that it reflects what you mean. Explain your meaning to the other person, rather than just assuming that person knows what you mean.

What Do You Mean?

This question assumes a reaction approach and asks you to focus on the other participants in communication situations. A key aspect of preparing for communication with a culturally different person is awareness that the other has cultural expectations that could be much different than your own. As such, the other does not give the same meaning to symbols and behaviors that you do.

You should listen very carefully. In everyday encounters, you might be able to rely somewhat on your perceptual filter to fill in things that you miss or did not hear. However, because that filter is made up of your own cultural expectations, it will not help you in a situation with a culturally different person. Listen for what is really there as opposed to hearing what you want to hear. We often incorrectly assume that if we heard the words correctly, we know what the other person means. Paraphrasing the intent and content of messages helps ensure we have the same meaning for the words and understand the other's motives. This kind of listening, as discussed in chapter 8, takes a great deal of concentration and energy.

If you have the opportunity, make an attempt to understand the cultural background of the other person. By appreciating what motivates the behavior of a culturally different person, you improve your chances of reaching some understanding. Be aware, however, that this appreciation might not always be possible. You might not have the preparation time or the background necessary to fully understand the culture of another. At best, you might gain only superficial insights into the other's experiences. Concentrating too much effort on understanding where someone else is coming from could become a barrier to communication because it shifts the focus from the communication itself to a cultural psychoanalysis of the other participant.

For example, a restaurant owner from India commented that American history only goes back about 500 years, while India has endured for 5,000 years. An American might understand his point intellectually and achieve a superficial understanding of the historical and philosophical differences. However, it is impossible to internalize a philosophy of endurance created by 5,000 years of cultural history that the American can never experience. Similarly, men might intellectually understand the trials and joys of giving birth, but there is no way they can actually experience it. At best, understanding of cross-cultural differences is superficial.

What Do We Mean?

The focus of this text has been on the transaction approach to communication. Consistent with that perspective, perhaps the best way to treat communication encounters with culturally different people is to engage in a transaction in which the participants cooperate to create meaning.

Because the participants might not have the ability to communicate in a competent way from the perspective of either culture, they must create a new

and different culture where both can operate.[5] The culturally different participants in the interaction might be able to merge perspectives or cultural expectations rather than adopt either one or the other contrasting perspectives. In this way, they create a **third culture** based on the specific participants, their two cultures, and the context of the communication situation.

In the context of this third culture, the participants do not have to be bound totally by either their own cultures or the cultures of the others. Certainly, the cultural backgrounds of the participants affect the interaction, but they do not have to dominate it. The idea is for the participants to cooperate with each other to create meanings from the interaction. Meaning, then, would be a product of the communication interaction itself and not something that was exclusively brought to the conversation or reproduced from an analysis of the cultures of the participants.

In an earlier example, we mentioned making language gender neutral. Notice that the change is not to masculine language or feminist language. We are not trying to impose or adopt one cultural perspective or the other. Instead, we are using language to create a third culture, one based on gender-neutral meanings. From this perspective, *chairwoman* is as equally unacceptable as *chairman*. The third culture allows the participants to create meanings that bridge cultures and create a new way of thinking, a new frame of reference in which they all share common meanings.

In this kind of situation, the participants do not have to focus solely on the similarities between their cultures to find a source of meaning. Instead, the

Strategies for Intercultural Communication

third culture and the meanings produced from it can be a celebration of the differences in cultures. Their backgrounds can become less important because meaning is created by the conversation and not brought to it totally by the participants.[6]

"Before You Go On"

You should be able to answer the following question:

What is a third culture?

In theory, creating a third culture sounds like a good idea. In practice, however, it's much more easily said than done. The following suggestions should help create a third culture.[7]

Climate

One of the prerequisites that appear necessary for the creation of a third culture is the willingness to participate. It's essential for you and a culturally different person to create an environment or climate that encourages cooperation. A defensive climate, as described in chapter 3, frustrates cooperation. For example, if one of the participants is strongly ethnocentric, and communicates that her culture is superior, the other participant might well become defensive. On the other hand, the development of a supportive climate should go a long way toward encouraging the creation of a third culture. Messages that indicate a willingness to cooperate and to be open-minded should contribute to the supportive climate.

Open Mind

An open mind is another element necessary for the creation of a third culture. You and the culturally different person should be open to new meanings and possibilities. To do this, you must be willing to consider alternative meanings. Focus your full attention on the interaction because your involvement is necessary to respond to the changing demands of the situation. Do not allow your perceptual filter to take over and automatically make sense of things for you in this situation.

Preoccupation with Self

Move beyond a preoccupation with yourself and your culture. It's very difficult to do this, but you should at least try to understand how your own preconceptions and previous understandings influence your behavior and the meanings you attribute to the behavior of others. Also, do not be ethnocentric. See yourself as part of a relationship with a culturally different person. This establishes a climate of cooperation and openness.

Preoccupation with the Other Person

On the other hand, don't try to put aside yourself and become one with the other person. It's not possible and is a distraction from the interaction itself. Instead, integrate your cultural outlook with the other person's to form understandings. It is more productive to focus on building understanding from the mutual communication of shared meanings than endlessly trying to determine where the other participant is coming from. Your concern should be with the communication and the co-creation of a shared reality.

Emphasize a Dialogic Attitude

Four steps for achieving the necessary attitude and climate for creating and maintaining a third culture include:

1. Be willing to put forth the effort necessary to work through differences. Your assurance that you are not going to give up on the encounter will motivate others to work along with you.
2. Demonstrate commitment to the encounter that is necessary to overcome possible conflict situations. It's not always going to be smiles and friendly cooperation.
3. Be willing and able to explore alternative meanings. This might take some practice, but it will be well worth the effort. Ask questions or paraphrase what others say to reduce uncertainty and increase understanding.
4. Be willing and able to participate in the jointly creative venture that is involved in the evolution of a third culture.

A summary of strategies for creating a third culture appears in the accompanying box.

Strategies for Creating a Third Culture

1. Create a climate of cooperation.
2. Keep an open mind to new meanings and possibilities.
3. Move beyond a preoccupation with yourself and your own culture.
4. Move beyond a preoccupation with the other person's culture.
5. Emphasize a dialogic attitude.

Source: B. J. Broome, "Building Shared Meaning: Implications of a Relational Approach to Empathy for Teaching Intercultural Communication," *Communication Education* 40.

1.   Is the study of intercultural communication limited to the investigation of communication between people of different nationalities?
No. Intercultural communication can take place between members of any groups or communities that have dissimilar worldviews. Intercultural communication can occur between men and women, physicians and patients, members of different racial and ethnic groups, parents and children, and many others.

2.   What is culture?
Culture is the collective beliefs or principles on which a community is based. These beliefs or principles are shared by all members of the community and provide a worldview or frame of reference from which the community organizes and makes sense of its experience. Culture provides expectations about what is normal in a particular environment.

3.   What is enculturation?
Enculturation is the process through which culture is passed from generation to generation in a community through communication. It refers to the process of learning a culture from schools, parents and family, peers, and other sources.

4.   What are barriers to intercultural communication?
Three barriers to intercultural communication are ethnocentrism (the tendency to assume that one's own culture is superior or more natural than the culture of another), cultural stereotyping (the assumption that all members of a particular culture are similar and can be placed into the same categories), and the myth that understanding the language is the same as understanding the culture.

5.   What is a third culture?
A third culture can be created when members of different cultures are able to merge their perspectives rather than contrast them. Because participants might not have the ability to communicate in a competent way from the perspective of either culture, they create a new, different culture in which they are both able to communicate.

S T U D E N T   E X E R C I S E S

1.   Personal experience: misunderstandings.
Discuss some misunderstandings that you personally have had that can be attributed to differences in culture. Did you ever reach an understanding with a culturally different person? If you did, how did you do it? What strategies did you use? If you did not reach an understanding, what prevented it?

2.   Personal experience: cultural differences.
Identify people you know who are members of groups or communities different from your own. How is the culture of each group different from yours? Discuss differences in the language used in each group. What communication problems have these differences created for you and a member of another group?

3.   Personal experience: international contact.
With a group of students from your class, talk about trips you have taken to other countries. Was there a language barrier? Did you have difficulty understanding the local culture? What communication problems did you have? How did you overcome them?

4.   Personal experience: cultural awareness.
Describe your own culture. What are some generally held myths or stories that everyone knows? What do these stories and myths say about your culture's values? How do the myths and stories suggest you should behave? What goals do they suggest are appropriate and worthwhile?

G L O S S A R Y

cultural stereotyping The assumption that all members of a particular culture share the same characteristics.

culture The collective beliefs or principles on which a community or part of a community is grounded or based.

enculturation The process of transmitting or passing on culture from generation to generation within a community.

ethnocentrism The tendency to assume that your own culture is universal or natural and that it is more reasonable than the cultures of others.

intercultural communication Communication between people or groups that have different beliefs or principles on which their communities are based.

ritual Behaviors associated with particular occasions.

Sapir-Whorf hypothesis Language determines the behavior and habits of thinking in a particular culture.

third culture A mutual creation of meanings and a frame of reference that supersedes each individual's culture.

N O T E S

1.   E. B. Tylor, *Primitive Culture* (New York: Bretanos, 1924).

2.   E. Sapir, *Language: An Introduction to the Study of Speech* (New York: Harcourt, Brace, & World, 1921); B. L. Whorf, *Language, Thought, and Reality* (New York: John Wiley & Sons, 1956).

3.   G. Ruth and S. P. Wallace, "'Waiter, There's a Fly in my Soup!' or How Does Your Phenomenal Feel?" in *Small Group Communication: Selected Readings,* ed., V. D. Wall (Columbus, Ohio: Collegiate, 1978).

4.   R. Porter and L. Samovar, "Basic Principles of Intercultural Communication," in *Intercultural Communication: A Reader,* ed., R. Porter and L. Samovar (Belmont, Calif.: Wadsworth, 1991).

5.   F. Casmir, "Introduction: Culture, Communication, and Education," *Communication Education* 40 (1991), 229–34; F. Casmir, *Intercultural and International Communication* (Washington, D.C.: University Press of America, 1978); B. J. Broome, "Building Shared Meaning: Implications of a Relational Approach to Empathy for Teaching Intercultural Communication," *Communication Education* 40 (1991), 235–49.

6.   Broome, "Building Shared Meaning"; J. Stewart, "Interpretive Listening: An Alternative to Empathy," *Communication Education* 32 (1983), 379–91.

7.   Broome, "Building Shared Meaning."

IV

Strategies for Public Speaking

A s in all communication situations, public speaking involves a transaction process through which people come to share meanings. The same skills that you have learned in previous chapters also apply to public speaking situations. However, when you speak to an audience of several people, you use different strategies for creating competent communication with your listeners.

In public communication, the speaker has the primary message responsibility. Therefore, the speaker has to carefully plan the best way to make the message understandable and believable. Chapter 15 examines how you can prepare for competent public communication by selecting and narrowing your topic, formulating precise ideas, and organizing your message to help your listeners understand your ideas. Chapter 16 discusses strategies for using nonverbal communication to enhance the audience's understanding of your verbal message.

Chapter 17 presents ways to share meanings through definitions and supporting materials, and methods to help listeners remember your information by using mnemonic devices, visual aids, and audience involvement in the communication. Chapter 18 develops strategies for convincing your audience that they should believe your ideas, change their attitudes, or change their behaviors. We also discuss strategies for overcoming resistance to your persuasive messages and for reinforcing your audience's beliefs.

Public speaking is similar to many other communication situations because your audience is comprised of individual people. You try to develop a relationship with each listener by adapting to your audience's culture, needs, experiences, and knowledge. Your goal in public speaking is to help the audience to help you create shared meanings for ideas. Competent public communication depends on creating shared meanings with each member of the audience.

15 CHAPTER

Strategies for Planning and Developing Public Communication

OUTLINE

• *I have to give a speech in class next week. I just don't know what to talk about. I can't put it off until the last minute, but I just don't know where to start.*

• *I would really like to talk about my hobby of quilting, but I don't think the class would be interested. How can I make them as excited about quilting as I am?*

• *I think it will be fun to give a speech—I've never had a real opportunity to do this before. And I have enough time to put together some really creative visual aids.*

• *I have to give a speech next week on campus facilities for physically disadvantaged students during the student government meeting. I know a lot about the topic. If I spend some time putting my thoughts together for the speech, and practice what I am going to say, it should go pretty well.*

These statements are all from students anticipating a speech assignment or speaking opportunity. Maybe you have had similar thoughts. Do you view a public speech as an undesirable chore, or as an opportunity to share your ideas and information with others? As in all face-to-face communication, public speaking is a transaction process, created through the mutual efforts of the speaker and the audience. By employing appropriate strategies in preparing your messages, you help yourself and the audience create competent public communication. When you are prepared, public communication becomes an opportunity to talk with others about something that interests you—something that is also interesting to them. This chapter discusses strategies to help you prepare public speeches.

Strategies for Planning the Message

Preparing a speech is best understood as a series of steps similar to the ones you would follow in putting a simple bookcase together. When assembling something, you should start by reading all of the instructions. Once you understand the concept of the overall assembly process, you get out the pieces, gather any needed tools, and begin putting the bookcase together. In principle, preparing a speech follows a similar process. You begin by selecting a topic, then choose a specific purpose, and finally gather and organize information into a recognizable form.[1]

Selecting and Narrowing a Topic

The **topic** area is a general subject for your speech. It is a label for an entire category of data, opinions, and information. For example, you might want to talk about coaching or hunting or job harassment or equal rights or other broad categories of information and ideas. When beginning to prepare a speech, selecting a topic gives you a general direction to follow.

Broad topics are difficult to cover thoroughly in a short time so frequently you need to narrow the topic. A narrow topic develops a specific focus within the broad topic area; one you can talk about in the time you have. For example, you might narrow down the subject of coaching to the following topics:

> Coaching young athletes.
>
> Coaching skills to young athletes.
>
> Coaching soccer skills to young athletes.
>
> Understanding the nutritional needs of your athletes.
>
> Coaching and working with athletes' parents.

Each of these topics is a subcategory of information about coaching and provides a specific focus for your speech.

During the preparation process, you may actually have to narrow your topic several times. You make these decisions as you assess the available information, change your perceptions of your audience, and/or change your interest in particular areas related to your general topic. For example, the subjects of space travel and soccer are abstract and broad enough to include a range of specific topics as depicted in the accompanying box entitled Narrowing Your Topic. Whether abstract or concrete, each topic labels a category of information. As you narrow the topic, you focus on a smaller area of information with a more limited range of ideas to discuss. In most public speaking situations, it is better to provide detail on one or two smaller topics than to cover the entire topic superficially.

While you are selecting and narrowing a topic, ask yourself these questions:

About the audience:
1. What might the audience be interested in listening to?
2. What does the audience already know something about?
3. What does the audience want to know more information about?

Narrowing Your Topic

Broad Topic:	Space travel Space travel history Space travel in the 1960s United States space travel in the 1960s
More Narrow:	United States manned space travel in the 1960s United States manned space travel to the moon in the 1960s Cost of U.S. space travel to the moon in the 1960s Benefits of U.S. space travel to the moon in the 1960s
Narrow Topic:	Medical benefits of U.S. space travel to the moon in the 1960s
Broad Topic:	Soccer in the United States The United States' participation in the World Cup Indoor soccer in the United States
More Narrow:	The history of soccer in the United States The development of the United States Soccer Federation The selection of teams for the World Cup Tournament The development of professional soccer in the United States The history of collegiate soccer competition in the United States
Narrow Topic:	The changes in rules for intercollegiate soccer competition during the 1990s

About yourself:
   4. What am I interested in talking about?
   5. What do I already know something about?
About the occasion:
   6. What topics are expected in this occasion?
   7. How much time do I have to speak?
   8. Are other people also speaking in this occasion?

We recommend making a list of ten to fifteen topics for each of the first five questions. After completing these lists, look for similarities across them. Look for a topic or several topics that appear on all the lists. When you find some, you have one or several topics to think about developing for your speech.

If one topic area does not appear on all the lists, go back and keep adding topics to each list. Look for similar ideas that might be combined to develop into a speech. For example, you might be able to combine your interest in the federal deficit with your perceptions of your audience's interest in controlling inflation. Or you might be able to combine your interest in equal rights with the audience's interest in freedom of speech. Take a look at the Selecting a Topic box for a sample set of lists developed for a speech in a beginning communication course.

Selecting a Topic

1. *What might the audience be interested in listening to?*

Car maintenance	Equal rights
Space travel	Financial aid
Graduate school	Intercollegiate athletics
Federal deficit	Touring Europe
Crime prevention	Self-defense

2. *What does the audience already know something about?*

Crime prevention	Self-defense
Travel	Space travel
Graduate school	Career development
Inner-city crime	Drug abuse
Abortion	Gun control

3. *What does the audience want to know more information about?*

Gun control	Crime prevention
Federal deficit	US-Japan relations
Space travel	Drug cartels
Retirement planning	Health care
Organ donations	Pawn shops

4. *What am I interested in speaking about?*

Gun control	Space travel
Federal deficit	Soccer
Plagiarism	Apartheid
Equal rights	Corporate ethics
Violence on TV	Drug control

5. *What do I already know something about?*

Violence on TV	Intercollegiate athletics
Space travel	Pornography
Ethics	Equal rights
Military spending	Soccer
Car maintenance	Construction

The occasion also affects your choice of a speech topic.[2] Occasions such as a high school graduation, an orientation for new employees, a banquet honoring a renowned citizen, a sermon, a classroom, or a political rally naturally limit the appropriate topics. The amount of time you have to speak also limits the breadth of the topics you can choose. If your topic is too narrow, you could

Strategies for Planning and Developing Public Communication

The occasion influences the choice of speech topic.

have difficulty fulfilling your message responsibility; if it is too broad, your time will be up before you finish. If other speakers are also addressing the same audience, your specific topic cannot overlap theirs. An audience quickly becomes disinterested when listening to redundant ideas.

All of the preceding questions are important in selecting a speech topic. Once you have found topics that answer questions about your audience and yourself, check them against the answers to questions 6 to 8 to be sure they are appropriate for the occasion.[3] Ignoring the audience's interests and knowledge makes competent communication difficult. Similarly, speaking about a topic that does not interest you or about which you have little knowledge makes it difficult to become involved in the communication.

For example, Andre needed a topic for a ten-minute speech for her communication class assignment. She prepared a set of topics for each of the questions. She wanted to talk about the entertainment value of professional wrestling, but could not honestly put this topic on any list in response to questions about the intended audience. However, she told herself she would be all right because she really liked this topic and she already knew something about wrestling. Still, she believed that most of the audience probably would not be interested. She found a lot of information and tried to tell the audience everything she knew about the topic. In delivering the speech to the class, she took twenty minutes to cover all of her material. Needless to say, Andre's speech was not well received. To summarize, select a topic that interests both the audience and the speaker, one appropriate for the occasion.

This does not mean you can never discuss a topic in which the audience has no interest. Sometimes you are assigned a topic or the occasion demands that a specific topic be addressed. At other times, you want the audience to know information, or hear a persuasive speech, about a topic they need to consider. One of the most difficult tasks for a public speaker is talking with listeners who have little initial interest in the topic. We discuss strategies for creating interest later in this chapter.

"Before You Go On"

You should be able to answer the following question:

What are the questions a public speaker should ask when selecting a topic?

Developing Your Proposition or Core Idea

At this point, you have selected a specific topic appropriate to the situation and the audience. However, a topic—no matter how narrow—does not make a statement. It merely provides a label for a category of information. Now you need to decide your purpose and to create a **proposition** statement about your topic.

Determining Your Purpose

Everyone communicates for a specific reason; this is especially true for public speakers. There are three primary **purposes** for a public speech:

A *persuasive message* attempts to change listeners' beliefs, values, attitudes, opinions, and/or behaviors. When you use emotional appeals or logical arguments to convince the audience to adopt a new behavior, to discontinue current practices, to change their minds about a topic, or to increase their motivation to do an action, you are trying to persuade them.

An *informative message* attempts to increase the audience's understanding of a topic and help them remember ideas. When you show how to do something, explain something with greater detail, teach a new concept, or heighten awareness, you are informing the audience.

Entertainment is often considered to have the narrow purpose of increasing an audience's enjoyment through humor, telling stories, jokes, and anecdotes. We define the entertainment purpose more broadly to include any attempt to increase audience interest and involvement in the communication. When you use dynamic delivery, vivid and immediate language, and personal examples, you increase the involvement of the audience so that they enjoy the communication.

All speeches inherently involve all three purposes—to inform and persuade and entertain. All speakers want their audiences to understand and remember information and ideas. All try to convince audiences that ideas and information are valid and try to involve audiences in the communication. However, a speech may focus primarily on one specific purpose, that is, it may be primarily persuasive, or primarily informative, or primarily entertaining. For example, you could want the audience to understand the reasons for the depletion of the ozone layer, without asking them to perform specific actions to solve the ozone problem. On the other hand, you could inform them about the problems, but be dissatisfied unless you could also persuade them to sign your petition against the manufacture of chlorofluorocarbons and other harmful chemicals.

Unless you are told the specific purpose for your speech, you have to select the purpose that best suits the occasion, yourself, and the audience.

"Before You Go On"

You should be able to answer the following question:

What are the differences between the three purposes for a public speech?

Stating Your Proposition

A proposition statement is an assertion that summarizes the topic and the speaker's purpose. Information presented during the speech supports the proposition statement. It is a statement, not a question. The **core proposition** is the overall theme of your speech, similar to the thesis statement for an English paper. You develop the core proposition through narrower supporting propositions that make more specific assertions about the core statement. Proposition statements fall into three categories.

A *proposition of fact* is a statement that is either true or false based on empirical or observable data. For example, these are all propositions of fact:
- The Civil War was caused by economic issues, not the moral injustice of slavery.
- President John Kennedy was assassinated as a result of a conspiracy.
- Bridge is a game anyone can learn to play.

Propositions of fact are either true or false, depending on the verifiable evidence supporting them.

A *proposition of value* is a statement comparing facts and observations against moral, ethical, aesthetic, or social standards. The proposition of value does not compare facts directly, but rather establishes their compatibility with a stated or implied value system. For example, these propositions are based on aesthetics, justice, morality, or ethics:

- Abortion is morally wrong.
- XXX movies are pornographic.
- The president of the United States is honest.
- The grading system employed at our university is unfair.
- Elvis was a gifted musician.

They imply no objective truth or falsity that we can simply discover with enough facts. They cannot be verified or observed in the world around us. They are judgments made according to ethical, social, moral and/or aesthetic standards.

A *proposition of policy* calls for specific actions to be taken or prohibited. The proposition of policy typically includes words such as *should, shall,* or *must.* For example, these propositions are calling for action:

- Our university should increase the number of computers available to its students.
- No student shall enter the university library without a student ID.
- We must ban smoking in all campus buildings.

Listeners perceive the policy statement in terms of whether the action should be adopted or not.

Even though all three propositions are different, they become interrelated when developing the speech. A core proposition of policy may rely on **supporting propositions** of fact and value to justify the desirability of its suggested actions. For example, using the proposition of policy that we must ban smoking in all campus buildings as a thesis, we might develop the message with one or all of the following supporting propositions:

Propositions of fact:

- People who smoke have a high likelihood of suffering from cancer in their lifetimes.

- Students and faculty who smoke are less productive than students and faculty who don't.
- People inhaling sidestream or second-hand smoke experience allergic reactions and blurred vision; they have an increased risk of cancer.

Propositions of value:

- Smoking is a violation of a person's right to a clean learning and work environment.
- The university has a moral obligation to protect the welfare of its students, faculty, and staff.

Propositions are necessary to develop the topic into a speech. The core proposition is the overall point the speaker is trying to make for the audience, developed through supporting propositions and documented with available information.

"Before You Go On"

You should be able to answer the following question:

What are the differences among propositions of value, fact, and policy?

Strategies for Developing Ideas

After developing a core proposition with supporting propositions for your speech, you are ready to create and flesh out the speech. The rest of the speech should relate to your general purpose and your propositions. Once you identify which ideas to develop in support of your proposition, you are ready to begin collecting information.

Gathering information requires time; however, it is a crucial step in the speech preparation process. Look for materials in books, magazines, newspapers, electronic data bases, scholarly journals, trade publications, television programs, and a variety of other sources. Also, collect relevant information directly from people who have knowledge about the topic. Focus your search on information and ideas that are useful in supporting your propositions.

Choosing Supporting Materials

Search for materials that not only support your propositions but also can be accepted by listeners as believable. Four types of supporting materials help sell your propositions.

Explanation

Explanations provide facts, definitions, and/or descriptions of your topic. For example, assume you are discussing this proposition of fact: The use of outdated steel production equipment caused the collapse of the steel industry in the United States. You might describe the machinery used, explain the history of the equipment, discuss the current state-of-the-art technologies in steel production, and compare the cost of operating the outdated equipment versus modern equipment. These facts and explanations would support your proposition and increase the likelihood that others understand the topic.

Testimony

A second frequently used supporting material is **testimony.** Testimony is *direct* when you quote a specific source in your speech, such as:

- According to *Time Magazine,*
- George Bush stated
- In Studs Terkel's book, *Working,* he reported that
- According to a *USA Today* survey,

Testimony is *indirect* when you quote someone else's recollections of a direct quotation, such as:

- Walter Cronkite quoted George Bush as saying
- Reporters for *The New York Times* quoted the chairman of General Motors as stating

- The witnesses in the Iran-Contra hearings stated they heard Oliver North say

Testimony can be verbatim or close and accurate paraphrases of others' ideas. Whenever you borrow words from other sources, give the person with the original idea credit for it by using an oral footnote.

Oral footnotes serve the same purpose as term paper footnotes or citations. They give credit to the person whose ideas you are borrowing for your speech and tell when the statement was made. The key to effective use of testimony in a speech is to make certain that the material pertains directly to the proposition and that your audience perceives the source of the information as believable.

Examples

Use examples to support propositions. **Examples** can be either real or hypothetical. *Hypothetical examples* did not really occur, but could have occurred. They must appear realistic to your listeners. For example, in a training session for new employees, the company's safety officer could illustrate the importance of safety on the job by examples of plausible accidents that could happen to employees. Hypothetical examples are effective when discussing the future or explaining sensitive issues or if real examples are not available.

Use *real examples* whenever possible because others believe your ideas if you can demonstrate that your examples actually occurred. For example, if your proposition is that employees are sexually harassed on the job in 40 percent of the Fortune 500 companies, several actual cases may be more effective than a hypothetical example that merely implies this could happen.

Personal examples are effective in establishing the strength or amount of believability of your proposition. Listeners are usually involved with you as a person when you speak to them, and they can feel the experiences that you describe. Think about your reactions to experiences that happen to friends compared with experiences that happen to people you don't know. Personal examples are powerful supporting materials.

Be ethical in describing examples. In a speech class, one student advocated that the university spend additional funds to increase police and security protection after dark. To support her proposition, she described in considerable detail the night she was attacked on campus. Listeners' emotional levels were extremely high as they empathized with her as she described her experiences that night. After the speech, one of the members of the class asked what happened to the person who attacked her. She replied, "Oh, I made up that story. The instructor said we should use personal examples to support our propositions, and I thought I would fib a little to get a better grade." The point is that we can be easily tempted to fabricate stories or exaggerate personal experiences to make our supporting materials more dramatic. Truthfulness in giving examples or presenting any other type of supporting material is necessary for competent communication.

"Before You Go On"

You should be able to answer the following question:

What is the value of using real and/or hypothetical examples in a speech?

Statistics

Use **statistics** to provide specific and concrete data to support propositions.[4] Many people believe numbers more than they believe other information. Advertisers in the United States realize this and quantify support for products. For instance, these are examples of media advertisers' statistical support for their products:

- This deodorant is 33 percent drier than before.
- Our car gets 49 miles per gallon.
- Four out of five dentists recommend our toothpaste.
- This antacid absorbs twenty-seven times its weight in excess stomach acid.
- Nine out of ten car owners prefer this particular car.
- Cooking oils are 99.9 percent cholesterol free.

Statistics used by speakers are generally one of three types: magnitudes, averages, and trends. **Magnitude** refers to the raw amount of something and is expressed as a total or percentage. Magnitudes impress others with the importance of the data. For example, in describing the role of the goalie to a group of new coaches, a soccer goalie may state, "I've played this position in more than 200 games." Or, a representative from the local electric company may support a proposal to increase rates for residential electric users by stating, "Our costs for obtaining coal to produce electricity rose 24 percent in the last decade." In each example, a number expresses a specific quantity or magnitude of something.

A second type of statistics often used to support propositions is the **average.** The average is simply the total magnitude of the activity, event, or object divided by the number of objects, events, or activities considered. These statements use averages to support propositions:

- Our team allowed only 0.7 goals per game over the past soccer season.
- The average number of absences in elementary schools has increased to 17.6 days per student each academic year.

The third major type of statistics used in communication is the **trend.** When numerical information is compared over a period of time, trends or tendencies can describe or project the future, or they can describe the past. For example, a government representative might state, "Inflation has been increasing at a rate of one-half of 1 percent for the past twelve months and we expect this rate will

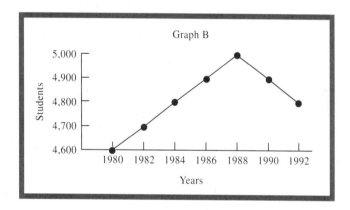

FIGURE 15.1
Trends in enrollment.

continue for the next twelve to sixteen months." Trend statements suggest that the trend is a continuous and regularly developing series of events during the time period indicated.

When using trends to support propositions, be certain that you analyze the data accurately. For example, look at the two graphs in figure 15.1. Graph A predicts that the enrollment trend is increasing. Graph B, however, indicates that the years between 1980 and 1992 are important in understanding the nature of the trend. Analysis of Graph B indicates the enrollment trend is decreasing. Although trends are useful in describing a series of numerical data, be careful when interpreting and presenting trends during a speech.

"Before You Go On"

You should be able to answer the following question:

In which situations would you use trend, magnitude, or average statistics in a speech?

Regardless of the type of evidence they use to support propositions, speakers must be sure the information is clear, accurate, and meaningful to the audience. Speakers must also use evidence that is current, unbiased, specific, and believable. The key to effective use of supporting materials is to select information that the listeners believe and that directly supports your proposition. Test each bit of information to see if it makes your proposition more believable. If you are not convinced, your listeners won't be either. The information you gather to support your proposition either helps others accept your proposition or causes them to reject it.[5]

Organizing Ideas

In chapter 5 we talked about various ways to organize messages; specifically, (1) the sequential pattern, (2) the spatial pattern, (3) the cause-effect pattern, (4) the topical pattern, and (5) the problem-solution pattern. See the accompanying box for a summary of these organizational patterns. Note that each organizational pattern creates a different relationship among the ideas.[6]

Organizational Patterns

Sequential—Ideas are related by when they occur.

Spatial—Ideas are related by where they are located.

Cause-effect—Ideas are related by the reasons for specific events or actions.

Topical—Ideas are related according to the similarities among categories of information; these categories are organized according to their familiarity or importance.

Problem-Solution—Ideas are related to show how a specific action can fulfill a particular need.

Choose an Organizational Pattern that Fits Your Purpose and Proposition

Some speech topics are more easily developed by one organizational pattern than another. Also, your proposition may imply a particular relationship among your ideas. For example, an informative discussion of the history of mountain bicycle racing or the procedures for assembling a mountain bike naturally follow a sequential pattern. A discussion of the potential effects of the recent NCAA rules governing student-athlete recruitment or an analysis of the reasons why one particular basketball team dominates the NBA require a cause-effect organizational pattern. A persuasive message to convince a potential sponsor to purchase needed equipment and supplies for a shelter for the homeless suggests a problem-solution pattern. To determine the appropriate pattern, examine the purpose of your message and your propositions.

More than one organizational pattern can support a specific proposition. For instance, the proposition that my trip to Europe was exciting could be developed chronologically (the sequence of the countries you visited), spatially (the geographical location of the countries), or topically (your activities during the trip). In this case, you must decide which relationship among your ideas you want the listeners to understand. Is it more important that the listeners remember where you went, the sequence of your trip, or the activities you enjoyed? The goal that you select determines your organizational pattern.

Careful analysis of the topic and the purpose suggests which pattern is most useful for a specific speech. The accompanying box entitled Differing Organizational Patterns illustrates how various patterns could be used for a single topic. Notice the different focus each pattern provides for the speaker and the audience.

Differing Organizational Patterns: Same Topic

Topic: Space travel

Topical pattern:
Proposition: The United States should invest the necessary money to travel to Mars.
   I.   Pursue new knowledge.
   II.   New technologies.
   III. Costs and revenues.

Problem-Solution pattern:
Proposition: The United States needs to invest more monies into spaced exploration through the development of a space station.
   I.   A space station is critical to the economic and political future of the United States.
   II.   There is not enough money invested into the NASA space program to finance a space station.
   III. Divert money from military expenditures to support research and development of the space station.

Sequential (Chronological) pattern:
Proposition: The evolution of the space shuttle fleet began in the 1950s.
   I.   Unmanned space flights
   II.   The *Mercury* program
   III. The *Gemini* program
   IV.   The *Apollo* program
   V.   The space shuttle

Choose an Organizational Pattern that Increases Others' Involvement

A second consideration in following a specific organizational pattern in a speech is the degree of involvement others have with the topic and purpose of the speech. The degree to which your listeners are knowledgeable on the topic, their interest levels and attitudes toward the topic, and their willingness to listen influence your choice of organizational patterns. For example, if your audience knows little about your topic, use a familiar-to-unfamiliar topical pattern rather than a climactic topical pattern. If others already agree on the necessity for change, the problem-solution pattern may not be appropriate. It isn't necessary to spend time developing a need that others already recognize. Instead, use the cause-effect pattern to focus on the effects the solution could have or use a sequential pattern to visualize the results of the plan over the next five years. The knowledge and insight gained through communication analysis techniques described in chapter 4 can help you determine others' involvement with the topic.

The point is that you should not predetermine an organizational pattern or patterns without taking into account your specific purpose, your propositions, and the information you have collected. In addition, constantly examine and reexamine the available organizational patterns because as you are preparing your speech, you may discover that another pattern would be better than the one you originally selected.

Choose a Consistent Organizational Pattern

After taking into account everything previously mentioned, you may decide to select and use one organizational pattern for your entire speech. In some cases, because of your analysis of the propositions and/or your information, the organizational pattern chosen for the main ideas in your speech may differ from the pattern selected for supporting ideas. For example, the main ideas could be sequential and the supporting ideas, topical. In discussing your trip to Europe, you might use a chronological pattern to indicate the order in which you visited each country. The supporting ideas might be organized topically as you discuss the educational, historical, and entertainment activities you enjoyed in each of the countries you visited. (See the accompanying box entitled Using Different Organizational Patterns within the Same Speech.)

In this speech, the main propositions (I, II, III, and IV) are organized in a problem-solution pattern. The supporting propositions (A, B, and C under each topic) are organized according to a spatial pattern.

Choosing an organizational pattern to facilitate your purpose and help others understand the relationship among ideas is a skill that you can develop with appropriate study and practice. Proper arrangement of materials and ideas helps others understand your message as intended, increasing the likelihood of competent communication. Careful thought and planning should precede every attempt at competent communication in public speaking situations.

Topic: Reorganization of sales districts

Proposition: Sales districts should be reorganized.

I. The distribution of population centers has changed causing an imbalance in market needs.
    A. Eastern district populations have decreased 15 percent because of migration to the country.
    B. Central districts have increased in population by 6 percent due to immigration from the East and increased birthrates.
    C. Western districts have increased by 10 percent due to the growth of large cities and immigration from Far Eastern countries.

II. Efficient and cost-effective transportation is less available which increases the overhead of each district.
    A. The closing of railway lines has hindered efficient transportation of goods in the East.
    B. Increased road tariffs and road-use taxes in the central district have increased the costs of trucking.
    C. The strike by dock workers on the West Coast has bottlenecked shipping in the western district.

III. A proposal that may solve these problems calls for reorganization of the sales districts.
    A. The boundaries of the eastern district should be expanded to include all states east of the Mississippi River.
    B. The boundaries of the central district should be from the Mississippi River to the eastern edge of the Rocky Mountains.
    C. The western district should be divided into two districts: mountain states and coastal states.

IV. The location of service centers in each district should be changed.
    A. The eastern service center should be in Atlanta to take advantage of the railway routes that converge there.
    B. The central service center should be in Omaha to capitalize on its central location and railway facilities to supplement trucking.
    C. The western service center should be in San Francisco for the coastal states and in Las Vegas for the mountain states.

"Before You Go On"

You should be able to answer the following question:

What criteria should you use to select an organizational pattern?

Beginning and Ending the Speech

In chapter 5 we discussed how to begin and end messages. The same ideas we discussed in that chapter are appropriate for beginning and ending public speeches. See the accompanying box for a summary of the skills necessary for beginning and ending messages.

Beginning and Ending a Speech

Beginning a Speech
- A. Gaining attention
  - 1. Questions
  - 2. Dramatic illustrations
  - 3. Humorous statements
  - 4. Startling statements
  - 5. Quotations
- B. Establishing your credibility
- C. Relating the message to the listeners
- D. Previewing the main ideas

Concluding the Speech
- A. Summarizing the main ideas
- B. Relating the message to the listeners
- C. Providing closure

Beginning the Speech

The four primary goals during the beginning or introduction to any public speech are to (1) gain the interest of others, (2) establish your credibility, (3) relate the topic to the listeners, and (4) introduce and preview the topic.

It is essential to gain your audience's interest during the beginning of your speech. Give them reasons to listen to you. Get them involved in what you want to accomplish. For instance, if you are discussing the importance of wearing seat belts, use a startling statement such as, "Last year 1,000 people died unnecessarily in the United States because they failed to wear seat belts." Or, tell your audience about the latest changes in the tax laws and how they affected a local family that lost more income to taxes as a result. Or, select a quotation from Lee Iacocca if you are discussing the import policies of the United States pertaining to goods from Japan.

These opening remarks use startling statements and thought-provoking quotations to gain immediate interest in the topic of the speech:

- David Roderick, former president of USX Corporation, began a speech by saying, "The message I would bring you today is not new nor is it original. It is not the words of a wise man to wiser men. You know the words, you are well aware of the themes and you and I share the problems, if not solutions."

- Rebecca Johnston, a college senior addressing a group of freshman physics students, started her speech by saying, "Einstein said it best, 'Concern for man himself must always constitute the chief objectives of all technical effort—concern for the big unsolved problems of how to organize human work—to assure that results of our scientific thinking may be a blessing to mankind and not a curse.' "

Of the many options available to you, choose one that creates interest and gets the audience thinking about your topic.

Next, establish your credibility to talk about the topic. In other words, tell others why they should listen to you and why they should believe you. In a speech about defense spending legislation you might say,

- My uncle is a member of the Pentagon and has talked with me at great length about the topic (if this is true).
- I have spent the last several weeks studying trends in defense spending over the last twenty years by the United States government.
- I have read the recent congressional testimony on defense spending and have some interesting conclusions.

Each statement makes what you are about to say more believable.

John Bryan, chief executive officer of Sara Lee Corporation, began a speech to a group of new employees by stating, "It was about thirty years ago that I was a new hire. That seems a long time ago. I get my thirty-year pin this year, because I haven't job-hopped an awful lot since then. About half the time since then, I've been stuck in the same job that I've got in Chicago. I haven't had a promotion in fifteen years. It happens to some of us. But my assignment this evening is to tell you about Sara Lee." With thirty years of experience, the new employees are likely to believe his view of Sara Lee.

The introduction also relates the topic to the audience. As you learned in chapter 8, people are self-focused; they listen to messages that directly affect them. Early in the speech, tell the audience how the topic relates to them personally. Use immediate language to show the topic's relevance to each individual. For example, a speaker wants to inform a class about word processing on a personal computer. The speaker might say, "You all have term papers due next week. I can show you how to save four hours of work, write a more creative paper, and have fewer errors. Word processing lets you get more done in less time." The audience is now eager to listen to information they can use immediately to benefit themselves. You can also use hypothetical questions, responsive questions, and personal examples to help the audience relate the topic to themselves. Although you adapt your topic to the audience throughout your speech, by telling them how the topic relates to them in the introduction, you motivate them to listen from the outset.

Usually, the introduction also lets others know what your speech covers. This **preview** should include your proposition statement and the major ideas. This can be as obvious as stating, "I'm going to talk about the three approaches to take when asking your boss for a raise," or "In the next seven to ten minutes, I want to help you understand the importance of writing your congressperson about proposed legislation in defense spending." The point is to let others know what you hope to accomplish in your speech.

This is your first opportunity to tell the audience what you are going to tell them in your speech. For example, in a speech with the proposition statement advocating legislation to increase military expenditures in the United States, you might say, "The proposed legislation does not allow our military to adequately prepare for—much less fight—a conventional war; it does not raise salaries adequately to compete with salaries in the private sector; and it does not reflect the sentiment of the majority of American taxpayers." Robert W. Mahoney, chief executive officer of Diebold, Incorporated, offered the following preview of a speech he delivered to company managers: "The banking and financial services field has become a free-for-all. And with competition heating up, efficiency is at a premium. When it comes to serving the massive consumer market, there are basically two approaches, upscale and broadscale." Such a preview statement tells others what you are going to talk about in your speech.

Ending the Speech

Just as important as the introduction is ending the speech. Your three goals as you end your speech are to (1) summarize what you have said, (2) relate the information to the listener, and (3) provide closure.

The ending to your speech should include a summary of the major ideas in your speech. This can be as obvious as stating, "Today we've talked about," or it can be more creative, "This speech was my attempt to explain the following." The summary is more than merely restating the main topics covered in your speech. The summary gives listeners an additional opportunity to hear the main ideas in your speech and should help them remember your propositions.

Your goal in public speaking is to have others understand and remember what you have said. People remember information better when it directly relates to themselves. Therefore, relate the topic to your audience during the conclusion. Remind them how the information you have presented will benefit them or how they can use it immediately or how it directly applies to a situation they are facing. For example, to relate information from your speech on personal safety to your audience, tell them how they can use some of your ideas as they walk to their cars after class or work. These strategies can help others remember your speech.

To provide closure to your speech, let others know that the speech is over. Refer to the skills we talked about in chapter 5 for ending messages. For example, if you were using a startling statement to conclude your speech on seat belts, you could say, "So don't be one of the 1,000 people who die unnecessarily this year because you forgot to put on your seat belt." This strategy reinforces your major points and lets others know you are ending your speech. William W. Boeschenstein, when addressing a management council meeting of Owens/Corning Fiberglass, ended his speech by saying, "To sum up: This message is not just a pep talk. It contains the very essence of what all of us, together, must concentrate on in the coming transition period."

Strategies for Preparing Visual Aids

People remember information they see and hear almost four times better than information that they just see or hear.[7] One method for increasing the sensory input in your speech is to use **visual aids** to supplement or complement your verbal message. (Visual aids never substitute for the verbal message.) Examine your message carefully to determine which specific information you want your audience to remember and devise a strategy for using visual aids to reinforce that information. Visual aids take a variety of forms.

Types of Visual Aids

Visual aids include any object, chart, graph, or demonstration that contains visual information related to the verbal message.[8]

Verbal Charts

Lists can highlight important key words or phrases you want others to remember. Verbal charts can also list specific steps in a procedure or define key terms.

Graphs

Pie charts and line and/or bar graphs present statistical information in graphic form. Pie charts show specific percentages of the total. Line graphs show trends over time, while bar charts illustrate statistical comparisons. Look at figure 15.2 for examples of a bar graph, a line graph, and a pie chart.

Pictures and Photographs

Pictures and photographs show representations of objects, animals, or people. They are especially useful to show the minute details or coloring of a larger object when the actual object is too large to display, or for increasing the visibility of minute objects. In preparing to use pictures and photographs, remember that everyone in the room must be able to see them. If the pictures and photographs are small and hard to see from a distance, use an opaque projector to enlarge them on a screen.

FIGURE 15.2
Sample graphs and charts.

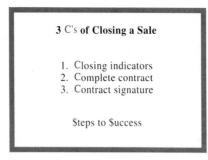

Sample Chart

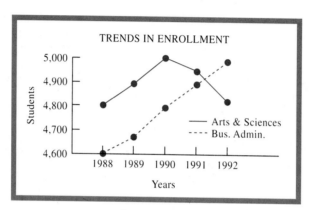

Sample Line Graph

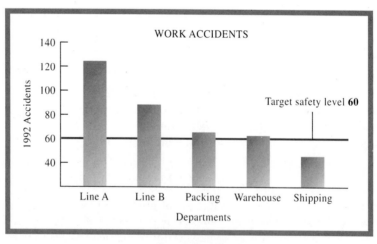

Sample Bar Graph

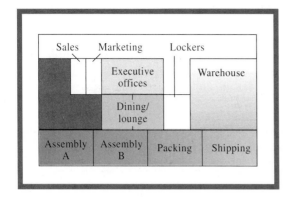

Sample Diagram

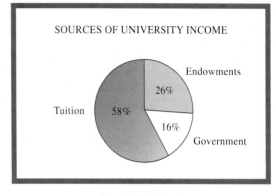

Sample Pie Chart

Maps and Diagrams

Diagrams illustrate the specific details of an object or the steps in a complicated process. Obviously, maps show geographic locations or routes to places or distances between places.

Objects and Models

Models show the dimensions or scale of an object. It is better whenever possible to bring the actual object instead of a model. However, sometimes this is simply not possible or advisable. Both actual objects and models can help you show how something works.

Time Lines

To show the chronology of events or the steps in a process use a time line. It is especially helpful when trying to illustrate the development of an idea or concept over time.

Demonstrations

Demonstrations show how something works by actually doing the process in the speech. For example, if you are talking about mixing paints to create different colors, one of the visual aids you can plan is a demonstration of mixing the colors as you talk about them. You might also use a demonstration when you want to show others how to perform some specific action or activity.

The specific visual aid you select depends on the type of information you present and the situation in which the speech occurs. Whether the visual aid is a chart, graph, object, or demonstration, your message becomes more understandable and memorable if others can both see and hear the information. (See figure 15.3 for examples of visual aids.)

Designing Visual Aids

As with other supporting material, visual aids can greatly enhance the effectiveness of your speech when you carefully plan, neatly construct, and skillfully use them. The suggestions in the accompanying box entitled Guidelines for Effective Visual Aids should help you select, design, and prepare visual aids.

Guidelines for Effective Visual Aids

USE VISUAL AIDS WHEN:

1. The topics or ideas are complex.
2. You need to talk about statistics—especially proportions, trends, large sequences of numbers or dates, or comparisons of numerical facts.
3. When describing an event, object, place, or idea that you want the audience to visualize.
4. When demonstrating how something works.

DO NOT USE VISUAL AIDS:

1. Merely for decoration, as background, or to add atmosphere to the speech.
2. To list topics or points in your speech that can be as easily understood from the verbal message.
3. To substitute for the verbal message.

CONSTRUCT VISUAL AIDS BY:

1. Making the visual aid simple—use only one idea on each chart, graph, or illustration.
2. Making the visual aid neat and professional looking. Show the audience that you spent as much time on the visual as you did on the rest of the speech.
3. Using dark contrasting colors on a light background so the visual aid is seen easily.
4. Using broad lines and making the details large enough to be seen from the back of the audience.
5. Using colors or illustrations to emphasize important ideas—make them memorable.
6. Printing in plain block letters (not script) and in straight lines (use stencils and a ruler if you need to).
7. Avoiding excessive detail. Include only easily and quickly understood information that is necessary to make your point.

To condense the guidelines into four principles:

Necessary

The visual message should reinforce your verbal message and be relevant to the information presented verbally. Avoid using visual aids unrelated to the verbal message or as a frill to decorate your speech. These visuals actually distract the audience's attention from your verbal message. Ask yourself if your message would be just as clear and memorable without the visual aid. If the answer is yes, do not use a visual aid. Conversely, if the answer is no, a visual aid is required to make the information easier to understand or remember. Then, you must take the time and give the necessary effort to design and use the visual aid.

Impact

Visual aids with impact are memorable, creative, and add emphasis to the verbal ideas. Visual aids that have high impact increase your credibility as a speaker. The impact of a visual aid comes from its creative design, clear and memorable organization of material, vivid and meaningful colors, and its overall quality and appearance. A sloppily drawn or lettered visual aid with unimaginative black lettering on white poster board, and an uncreative layout has little positive impact on others. In this scenario, listeners focus their attention on the sloppy letters or the lack of organization in the visual aid rather than its message. Using bright colors, creative and innovative designs, and professional quality artwork and lettering increases the impact of the visual aid in supporting your verbal message. This careful preparation helps your listeners focus their attention on the messages and become more involved with the ideas.

Clarity

The visual aid must be understood easily. Realize that when your listeners are looking at the visual aid, they are splitting their attention between you, your verbal message, and your visual aid. If they take a long time to understand a complicated visual aid, they are less likely to fully understand the content of the verbal message. Keep each visual aid simple and try to present only one major idea. Presenting complex graphs or tables of numbers from which you use only one or two statistics confuses your audience. Instead, present only the information the audience needs to know on the visual aid. Keep it simple!

Easily Seen

To be sure that everyone can see your visual aids, make the lines and letters dark, large, and thick. The presentation of visual aids also affects how easily they can be seen by everyone in your audience. (We discuss how to use the visual aids in chapter 16). If you stand in front of the visual aid, if the visual aid is not in everyone's line-of-sight, or if it is too small to be seen, you have violated this principle. Never introduce visual aids with the statement, "I know those of you in the back can't see this, but. . ." If the visual aid cannot be seen by everyone, then don't use it!

Criteria for N-I-C-E Visual Aids:

Necessary	They increase *understanding* and *retention* of information.
Impact	They give *emphasis* to ideas and create *interest*.
Clarity	They are easily and quickly *understood*.
Easily Seen	They *can be seen* by everyone.

If you follow all of the guidelines for effective construction and use of visual aids, your visual materials are *Necessary,* have *Impact,* are *Clear,* and are *Easily* seen. In essence, following these guidelines ensures that you have a **NICE** visual aid. Notice how the use of color and organization emphasize the mnemonic N-I-C-E and gave the material visual impact. This example should make it easier for you to remember the guidelines for designing and ultimately using visual aids. The examples in figure 15.3 show poor and effective visual aids.

"Before You Go On"

You should be able to answer the following question:

What are four criteria for effective visual aids?

Responses to *"Before You Go On"* Questions: A Chapter Summary

1. What questions should a public speaker ask when selecting a topic?
When beginning to prepare a public speech, ask and answer each of these questions: (*a*) What might the audience be interested in listening to? (*b*) What does the audience already know something about? (*c*) What does the audience want more information about? (*d*) What am I interested in talking about? (*e*) What

FIGURE 15.3

Poor visual aid; effective visual aid.

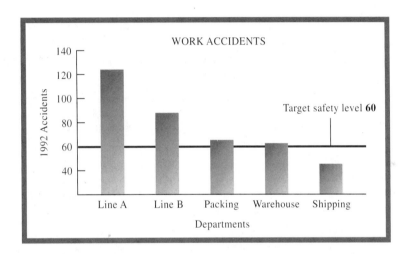

do I already know something about? (*f*) What topics are expected on this occasion? (*g*) How much time do I have to speak? (*h*) Are other people also speaking on this occasion?

In responding to these questions, generate a list of topics or ideas for each. Generally, the most frequent topics on the lists are the ones you should consider for your speaking topic.

2. What are the differences between the three purposes for a public speech?

The three purposes of communicating are also the three major purposes for a public speech. They are to inform, to persuade, and to entertain. When trying to inform, you are helping listeners understand and remember information, how to do something, or the steps in a process. When persuading your listeners, you are trying to change their attitudes, beliefs, values, opinions, and/or behaviors. To accomplish this, provide emotional and logical supporting materials that illustrate the reasons why they should change. Entertaining speeches are attempts to involve the audience in the topic and occasion and to make the speech enjoyable through humor, explanations, anecdotes, stories, dynamic delivery, and immediate and vivid language. All speakers try to accomplish all three purposes, though there may be a primary emphasis on a specific purpose.

3.   What are the differences between propositions of fact, value, and policy?
A proposition of fact is a statement that is either true or false based on objective, verifiable evidence. A proposition of value is a question of what is right or wrong, good or bad. The proposition of value is a comparison with moral, ethical, or aesthetic standards. The proposition of policy encourages changes in attitudes or actions.

4.   What is the value of using real and/or hypothetical examples in a speech?
Preferably, use real examples whenever possible to provide support for your ideas. If you do not have a convenient or useful real example, then a hypothetical example is an appropriate strategy. The hypothetical example should appear realistic to your listeners. Examples, whether real or hypothetical, provide powerful support for your propositions.

5.   In which situations would you use trend, magnitude, or average statistics in a speech?
Magnitudes are raw amounts expressed as whole numbers or percentages. Speakers use them to impress others with the importance of the numbers used. *Averages* are the mean of a set of numbers. Averages allow the expression of numbers for comparison purposes. *Trends* allow the tracking of a set of data over a period or allow the prediction of data in the future. Trends are usually viewed as a set of continuous events over a specified period of time.

6.   What criteria should you use to select an organizational pattern?
Speeches often can be developed using several organizational strategies. Select a strategy that fits your communication purpose and proposition. It should show the relationship among ideas that you want to emphasize. Your organizational pattern also should increase listeners' involvement. Adapting to listeners' knowledge and attitudes helps them focus on your ideas. A consistent organizational pattern helps listeners understand and remember your ideas.

7.   What strategies are used to begin and end a speech?
The introduction gains the audience's interest, establishes the speaker's credibility, relates the topic to the listeners, and previews the main ideas of the speech. Using immediate and vivid language, clear personal examples, and dynamic delivery helps the audience get ready to listen to you speak. Stating the core proposition and previewing your intended development of the proposition helps the audience anticipate how the upcoming information fits together.

8.   What are four criteria for effective visual aids?
Visual aids should be N-I-C-E. Only use visual aids that are necessary to clarify or emphasize the verbal message. Visual aids should have impact through creative design and professional appearance. Clear visual aids have only one main idea and avoid confusing or distracting clutter. Visual aids must be large and handled properly so that the audience can easily see the information.

STUDENT EXERCISES

1.   Assessing others' interests.
Spend some time talking with others about things they would like to have someone tell them. Keep track of the topics or ideas they bring up. Talk with eight to ten people and, after completing your lists, see where the lists are similar and see where they are different. Keep these lists for future reference as you prepare your speeches for class.

2.   Assessing your interests.
Take fifteen minutes and write down every topic or idea that you would like to talk about with a group of people. What things would you enjoy talking about with others? Keep this list for future reference as you prepare your speeches for class.

3.   Communication purposes and the media.
For three evenings concentrate on the commercials you watch on television. Are they solely persuasive? Are they solely informative? Are they solely entertaining? Are they a combination of the three purposes?

Keep a log of the commercials—record about thirty to forty of them. Write down the product being advertised and its communication purpose. Do you notice any trends?

4.   Using C-SPAN to review propositions.
Watch a House of Representatives' session on C-SPAN when there are special orders for the members of Congress. Listen to each member speak and keep track of the major propositions and supporting propositions. Make a check list of the propositions discussed in this chapter and determine which types members use most frequently.

5.   Computing statistics.
Using the following weekly sales from three vending machines on campus, decide which is better for the owner. Machine A's sales totals are $55, $80, $77, $92, $60, $86 and $101. Machine B's sales totals are $76, $77, $78, $78, $78, $76 and $78. Machine C's sales totals are $101, $44, $100, $56, $100, $66, and $98. Compute the averages for each of the machines. Draw a chart illustrating the sales for each of the machines. Decide which machine is a better sales opportunity for the owner. Be prepared to defend your choice in class discussions.

GLOSSARY

average   The total magnitude of the activity, event, or object divided by the number of objects, events, or activities considered.

core proposition   The overall theme of the speech or the central idea about the topic that you want your audience to believe.

example Illustrative situations that support major or supporting propositions. Examples may be real or hypothetical. Usually the best examples are personal examples that occurred to the speaker.

explanation Providing facts, definitions, and/or descriptions to support major and supporting propositions.

magnitude A statistic expressing the raw amount of something as a number or a percentage.

preview Includes the speaker's major and supporting propositions (major ideas) of the speech.

proposition A statement summarizing the topic selected for the speech and the speaker's purpose.

purpose The three reasons for communicating: to inform, to persuade, and to entertain.

statistics Numbers representing occurrences and events that provide specific and concrete data to document a speaker's major and supporting propositions.

supporting proposition A proposition that develops or explains the core proposition.

testimony Direct or indirect quotations, or close and accurate paraphrases of others' ideas. The sources of testimony must be revealed through oral footnotes in the speech.

topic The general subject or idea for the speech.

trends Numerical information compared over a period of time. Trends can be used for future projections of descriptions of past events.

visual aids Anything used by a speaker containing visual information related to a verbal message.

NOTES

1. D. O'Neill and L. Hugenberg, "Teaching the Critical Issues Speech Course," *Ohio Speech Journal* 26, 2 (1989), 23–6.

2. For lengthy discussions of the importance of the occasion for public speaking, see L. Bitzer, "The Rhetorical Situation," *Philosophy and Rhetoric* 1, (1968), 1–15; K. Burke, "Dramatism," *The International Encyclopedia of the Social Sciences* (New York: Macmillan, 1968), 445–51.

3. J. W. Wenzel and D. J. Hample, "Categories and Dimensions of Value Propositions: Exploratory Studies," *The Journal of the American Forensic Association* 11, (1975), 121–30.

4. D. Huff, *How to Lie with Statistics* (New York: W. W. Norton, 1954).

5. T. D. Daniels and R. F. Whitman, "The Effects of Message Introduction, Message Structure, and Verbal Organizing Ability upon Learning of Message Information," *Human Communication Research* 7, (1981), 147–60.

6. D. Ausubel, "The Uses of Advance Organizers in the Learning and Retention of Meaningful Material," *Journal of Educational Psychology* 51, (1960), 267–72.

7. E. P. Zayas-Baras, "Instructional Media in the Total Learning Picture," *International Journal of Instructional Media* 5, (1977–1978), 145–50.

8. For an extended discussion of visual aids and their use, see T. Pont, *Developing Effective Training Skills* (New York: McGraw Hill, 1991), 91–7; or G. Mitchell, *The Trainer's Handbook* (New York: American Management Association, 1987), 216–65.

CHAPTER

Strategies for Presenting Public Communication

• I liked his ideas, but he was so monotonous.

• She seemed really in control and so calm.

• He stated his ideas with so much conviction, I knew he was telling

me something important.

• She said everything so well, but I cannot remember what she said.

• He was so nervous he was distracting; I cannot think of one thing he

told us during the speech.

After organizing your ideas and selecting appropriate supporting material to develop your ideas, you have to deliver your message. Good delivery enhances the work you completed in each of these preceding steps. Poor delivery jeopardizes all that previous work. This is why you must place equal emphasis on both the content of the speech and its delivery. In this chapter, we suggest strategies to improve your public speaking delivery.

Strategies for Choosing Appropriate Delivery Styles

What is good delivery? People use four guidelines to judge your delivery as a public speaker:

1. Was the speaker natural?
2. Was the speaker spontaneous?
3. Was the speaker in control?
4. Was the speaker responsive?

Being natural implies that you use the same communication skills you use in other communication situations. In essence, be yourself.

The audience should believe your speech is spontaneous, that you created it for them and that particular speaking occasion. Do not give the impression that your speech is manipulative or artificially contrived. And make sure that the audience does not notice any insincerity in your delivery.

Obviously, you want to appear in control. If you appear overly anxious, listeners remember that you were nervous rather than the content of your speech. If you let distractions interrupt your flow of thought, if you are so relaxed the audience thinks you don't care, or if you become incensed and rant and yell at the audience, you are not perceived as in control. Being able to adapt to situational events such as the lights blinking on and off, the overhead projector not working, or noise in the hallway demonstrates control of the speaking situation.

Finally, by demonstrating that you are responsive to the audience in communicating your message, you involve your listeners in the communication; that helps them remember more of your speech. Adapting your speech when people do not appear to understand, or answering questions, or acknowledging applause and laughter at a joke is important in creating competent public communication.

"Before You Go On"

You should be able to answer the following question:

Which four guidelines do people use in judging a public speaker?

Evaluating Delivery Styles

When preparing to deliver a speech, you can deliver the message in any of four styles.[1] The accompanying box entitled Strategies for Delivering Public Speeches summarizes the strategies for each type of delivery that we discuss in this section.

Manuscript Delivery

A speaker might consider this delivery in situations where specific words in the speech are so important that to miss one might cause the message to be misunderstood. For example, the president of the United States uses **manuscript delivery** to allow little room for misinterpretation of the message. A corporate executive might consider using a manuscript if exactly the same message must be given in a number of situations or when exact wording is important. Examples include company statements of policy or verbal press releases on corporate or environmental issues. A scientist might use a manuscript to deliver a technical report on her experiments because there is no way to remember all the precise data she wants to report.

People are seldom asked to speak using a manuscript. Manuscript delivery inhibits deviation from the prepared text during delivery. A person delivering a message from a manuscript may note that members of the audience are having some difficulty understanding the speech. What should the speaker do? All that is available to work with is the manuscript. This is all the speaker is familiar with; this is what was used for practicing the speech. How can the speech be changed to make it clearer to others?

One of the biggest problems with the manuscript form of delivery is the difference between written style and speaking style. We write differently than we speak, and written language often sounds artificial and contrived when read aloud. The success of manuscript delivery depends on the speaker's ability to read.

Strategies for Delivering Public Speeches

MANUSCRIPT DELIVERY

- Use large type.
- Use double or triple spacing.
- Put the manuscript on stiff paper or use a folder.
- Write in an oral style.
- Practice to become familiar with the script.
- Maintain eye contact as much as possible.

MEMORIZED DELIVERY

- Memorize the speech in blocks or chunks of material.
- Use mnemonics and key words in transitions to stimulate memory of the next section.
- Create a bail out strategy in case you lose your train of thought or forget part of your speech.
- Practice aloud, not just through mental rehearsal.

EXTEMPORANEOUS DELIVERY

- Focus on learning a sequence of ideas rather than precise sequence of words.
- Practice from a full sentence outline before practicing from speaking notes.
- Write speaking notes on easily handled note cards.
- Establish eye contact with the audience rather than looking at note cards or visuals.

IMPROMPTU DELIVERY

- Anticipate opportunities when you will be asked to speak.
- Prepare for possible questions.
- Think before you speak.
- Use a preview of one or two limited ideas.
- Be concise and avoid vocal pauses.
- Organize your ideas with a beginning, middle, and end.
- Avoid the temptation to add unnecessary details and irrelevant ideas just to fill time.
- Look at everyone, not just the questioner.

Manuscript delivery also inhibits eye contact with the audience. Because of the lack of eye contact, the speaker observes only limited feedback from the audience. Having a written style and reading to the audience increases your control over the content of the speech, but inhibits a natural and spontaneous delivery and the ability to adapt to the audience.

If you deem it necessary to deliver a manuscript speech, write in an oral style that sounds natural when you read it. When preparing the manuscript, use large type and triple space the manuscript. Use a highlighter to emphasize key words. Use a folder or stiff paper backing for the manuscript rather than loose paper that could flutter and be difficult to manage. Above all, practice extensively to become familiar with the words so you can look at the audience as much as possible.

An inaugural address requires a manuscript delivery style.

Memorized Delivery

Almost everyone has been forced to memorize something such as Lincoln's Gettysburg Address, the preamble to the Declaration of Independence, or your fifth-grade teacher's favorite poem. Or, you may have memorized the lines of a play so you realize that memorizing a lengthy message is not easy. A lot of time and energy go into the memorization process and not to other delivery skills. The major premise when memorizing anything is that you must remember words and phrases in a proper sequence. That is, *A* is followed by *B* which is followed by *C*, and so on. Your concern is focused on which word or phrase comes next in the sequence. **Memorized delivery** causes a communicator to focus attention on sequences of words rather than on ideas.

Imagine you were addressing your student government about a major change in requirements for students to qualify for financial aid on campus and you confuse the sequencing of your ideas. All of a sudden, *C* follows *D* which follows *B*, and *B* follows *G* and you've forgotten *A* entirely. What are you going to do? It will be difficult to adapt the message and salvage the proposal. All you have is the memorized sequence of ideas that you are having difficulty remembering.

Because you have to write the speech to memorize it, the memorized delivery mode suffers from the same problems of written language as manuscript mode. In addition, the memorized mode reduces your ability to adapt to the listeners who do not understand what is being said and to problems that occur during the speech. Being natural, spontaneous, and responsive is difficult when your focus is on remembering words rather than communicating ideas.

When you use memorized delivery for all of your speech or for parts of it, memorize the speech in small chunks or blocks, rather than the entire speech as a whole. Then, should you forget a small block of information, you can go to the next block without destroying the entire sequence of ideas. Effective transitions that use mnemonics or key words to trigger your recall of the next idea are helpful. When you finish one section, the transition reminds you of the next block or idea. Lastly, devise a bail out plan to use if you totally lose your train of thought or get confused. The bail out can be a statement that lets you introduce information you forgot to say earlier. It can be a transition that moves you into the next major section of the speech, or an alternative conclusion that lets you exit gracefully.

Extemporaneous Delivery

The type of delivery most often advocated in public speaking classes is the extemporaneous mode. The goal of extemporaneous speaking is to be sufficiently familiar with the information of the speech so that all you need is a few key words and/or phrases jotted on a note card to jolt your memory of what you intend to say. **Extemporaneous delivery** permits use of prepared materials, organized and rehearsed for the speech. Through practicing, the speaker becomes familiar with ideas and not specific words. This mode of delivery permits adaptation to others as well as to the occasion as the speech progresses. If a speaker perceives that someone is not comprehending a particular part of the speech, the extemporaneous mode is flexible enough to allow repetition or rephrasing of ideas to make them clearer.

Extemporaneous delivery appears spontaneous and natural. Although planned and rehearsed, the language comes across to the audience as spontaneous. In the extemporaneous mode, the speaker is more likely to talk as if the speech is a conversation. The speaker focuses on talking about ideas rather than reading or reciting words. The nonverbal components of delivery arise from a natural involvement with the message and also appear spontaneous. There is a perception that the message was created at that instant for that audience. If the speech is given a second time, the message is different because of the necessary adaptation to the specific audience and the occasion, even though the speaker may have used the same notes and talked for about the same amount of time. This is why the extemporaneous mode of delivery is preferred. It enables you to prepare, to organize the message, and to practice and rehearse, while also providing sufficient flexibility to adapt to most situational variables likely to be encountered.

Impromptu Delivery

Impromptu delivery offers a person little time to prepare to speak. These public speaking situations occur frequently. For example, when you are called on to answer a question in class or when you are unexpectedly asked to introduce a guest speaker. Other examples include when you are asked to comment to an audience about recent changes in a union agreement, or in local school board meetings when the audience asks questions to find out more about your ideas. The key to competent impromptu communication is to spend what little time you have on organizing your thoughts into a coherent pattern, thinking of the best way to say what you have to say and then saying it.

Seldom are you asked to give a long impromptu speech; more likely, you are asked a question about a topic and have to formulate a brief response right then. Thus, you should be familiar with information on topics that you might be asked to discuss. An important strategy for impromptu speaking is to anticipate speaking opportunities and think ahead to what you might say. President John Kennedy practiced for hours for impromptu press conferences by having his staff give him practice questions that reporters might ask. It is acceptable to take a brief pause to formulate a response to a specific question and even jot down brief notes beforehand.

As in all messages, the impromptu speech follows the principles of organization; your message needs a beginning, a middle, and an end. A brief preview of your ideas in the introduction can help you mentally organize what you are about to say. Limit your remarks to one or two concisely stated ideas. If the audience wants more information, they can ask additional questions.

Be aware of your delivery in impromptu situations. The tendency is to just look at the person who asked you the question or the person you are addressing. Realize that the comments have significance for everyone in the group and that everyone is interested in your information.

Fluency is another communication skill difficult to incorporate into the impromptu delivery mode because of the lack of rehearsal time. Overusing vocal pauses such as *uhm, you know, like, and so,* and *okay* make you appear less credible, less informed, and less confident. Although people tolerate lapses in delivery in impromptu situations, they also appreciate confident, fluent, animated, and direct delivery styles. Improve your chances of success by improving your ability to think on your feet and express ideas coherently in an impromptu situation.

"Before You Go On"

You should be able to answer the following question:

What are the advantages and disadvantages of the four types of delivery for a public speech?

Adapting Delivery Styles

Deciding which mode of delivery is most appropriate is influenced by several factors: your purpose in speaking; the amount of prior preparation available; the complexity of the information; your verbal message responsibility; and the interests, goals, and knowledge of the intended audience. The amount of influence these factors have changes from situation to situation, from speech to speech, and from topic to topic.

Speakers using manuscripts have difficulty conveying involvement with their ideas.

If you present numerous facts and complex details in a speech, you need to have more things written on note cards so that you are accurate. However, if you are using emotional appeals in a persuasive speech to change attitudes on a particular issue, you can likely convey the information using fewer notes during delivery. Conveying your own commitment to your ideas is difficult if you are reading or reciting your speech.

We recommend extemporaneous delivery for almost all purposes, whether in your class, your career, or your community. This mode of delivery allows you to prepare and practice the speech while maintaining flexibility to adapt to the audience to accomplish your speaking goals.

Your audience also influences your selection of a delivery mode. For example, in a speaking situation where the audience is interested solely in information and its accuracy, you might appropriately use a manuscript. When listeners expect to actively participate in the speech through questions and sharing ideas, extemporaneous or impromptu styles might be more appropriate. Formal speaking situations may allow more extensive use of written materials than informal speeches.

In most public speaking situations, the relationship between the speaker and the audience is important. The best way to create this relationship is to use extemporaneous delivery. Members of an audience are usually supportive and want a public speaker to do well. Extemporaneous delivery helps to build on this good will because the speaker talks with the audience rather than reading or reciting to the audience.

Each of these factors influences your selection of delivery modes in every speaking situation.[2] These delivery styles are not mutually exclusive. In some speeches, you use one primary delivery style but may include one, two, or all of the other modes as well. For example, while focusing on the extemporaneous delivery style, you might memorize one or two quotations (memorized delivery mode). And you may write down an entire list of dates, events, or statistics (manuscript delivery style), and have to add information to make the ideas clearer (impromptu delivery mode) during the speech. Even though your focus remained on the extemporaneous style, you used each of the other three delivery modes during the speech. We strongly urge you to keep the extemporaneous mode of delivery as your primary delivery style.

Strategies for Effective Nonverbal Delivery

Regardless of your delivery style, be aware of the nonverbal aspects of your delivery. Eye contact, gestures, movements and facial expressions, your voice, and personal appearance influence how listeners perceive you and your message.[3] Remember that actions speak louder than words, because people believe nonverbal communication when it contradicts the verbal message. People perceive that you control nonverbal messages less than your verbal messages. Therefore, spontaneous and natural delivery enhances your message when it supports your verbal message. Conversely, delivery weakens your communication when it is perceived as artificial, contrived, or incongruous with your verbal statements.[4]

Chapter 7 discusses the skills for creating nonverbal messages. We suggest you review that chapter before proceeding. Rather than repeating the characteristics of nonverbal communication or the dimensions of meaning associated with nonverbal behavior, this chapter focuses on how to use nonverbal behavior to create competent public communication. We discuss specific strategies for delivering your public speech based on your understanding of the functions and characteristics of nonverbal communication.

Creating Interest and Maintaining Attention

As discussed in chapter 2, people have short attention spans and are constantly seeking new stimuli. A speaker who presents the same visual picture or creates monotony in vocal delivery quickly loses the audience's attention. Nonverbal delivery that is varied and interesting keeps the listeners selectively attending to the speaker.

One way to create variety in the visual picture is to use movement. A speaker who constantly stands in one place provides a static picture to which the listeners quickly become accustomed. On the other hand, aimless and repetitive pacing is distracting. Controlled and purposeful movement keeps the audience's attention. Occasionally moving toward and away from the audience, as well as from side to side, changes the audience's visual picture.

A second strategy is using gestures to make your visual image more interesting for the audience. Moving your hands and arms while talking is natural. Without gestures, the audience sees the same static picture. Avoid habitual, constant, and redundant gestures that are monotonous. Instead, use spontaneous, purposeful gestures to create interest in the message.

A third strategy for keeping attention is to vary the auditory stimuli, that is, your voice. Most important is variety in pitch. A monotone quickly loses the audience's attention, as does the repetition of a sing-song voice. Changing the rate and volume also keep the audience's attention.

Last, maintain attention through direct, frequent, and inclusive eye contact. People want to pay attention when they think you are talking directly to them. If you stare at the wall, merely glance at people, or talk to only one part of the audience, you lose audience interest. Effective eye contact makes the listeners feel that you are having a one-to-one conversation with each individual, not an impersonal speech to a general audience.

Enhancing Credibility

Credibility is the listeners' belief that you are trustworthy and knowledgeable. Their judgments of your credibility derive mostly from your nonverbal communication. A critical basis for their judgments is your appearance. During a public speech, your appearance can influence your credibility either positively or negatively. That is, your appearance can make you look like you know what you are talking about. How you look influences the audience's initial impressions of you.

Your appearance influences the likelihood of communication competence. For example, a local business leader attended a meeting of a campus honorary society to talk about career development opportunities. The speaker's very casual attire—jeans and a sweatshirt—offended some members of the audience. They felt the speaker didn't take the situation or the students seriously. Obviously, they were paying a great deal of attention to the appearance of the speaker, not the topic of the speech.

Direct eye contact also increases your trustworthiness. Comments such as, "Look me in the eye and say that," and "You can't trust him; he has shifty eyes," and "I knew she was lying, she couldn't even look at me," indicate that eye contact has a strong influence on people's perceptions of trustworthiness. To enhance your credibility, establish frequent and direct eye contact with all members of the audience.

Natural and spontaneous movements also increase people's perceptions that you are trustworthy and competent. A person who speaks very rapidly, uses numerous vocal pauses, lacks fluency, or uses rapid and repetitive gestures may be perceived as nervous and unprepared. Similarly, a person who uses obviously preplanned, rehearsed, and artificial movements and gestures appears ingenuine and insincere. Dynamic, animated gestures and movements arising from your involvement and desire to communicate your ideas enhance the audience's perception that you are confident, knowledgeable, and sincere.

Creating Involvement

Competent communication requires that both the speaker and the audience are involved. Distractions from the speaker or the environment, however, create barriers to involvement. Controlling distractions helps increase involvement for yourself and your listeners. (See chapter 3 for a discussion of involvement and distractions.)

Controlling the physical surroundings to create a supportive environment increases involvement. Often you can arrange a semifixed-feature space so that everyone is comfortable and can easily see you. Choosing an appropriate time of day for the speech, moving chairs together, controlling the room's temperature and lighting, and minimizing extraneous noise also decreases distractions.

Facial expression helps create involvement with your message.

People become more involved in communication that is important to them. When the speaker seems interested and enthusiastic about the message, the listeners are likely to perceive that the message is important. Your facial expressions are a prime indicator of your own involvement in the message and your desire to share your ideas. For example, if you say, "I am glad to be here," or "I am excited about this idea," with a blank facial expression, the audience is less likely to believe your enthusiasm. Your facial expression should be responsive to your own desire to share your ideas.

Again, eye contact increases the importance of the message for listeners. Everyone likes to feel part of the situation. When you look at your listeners, you tell them that your message is important for each one of them. Reading from note cards for too long or looking at your visual aid instead of your audience creates an unnecessary barrier and closes an important communication channel.

The key to creating involvement is to understand that communication is reflexive, that is, people reflect each other's behaviors. Eye contact also helps you obtain feedback from the audience. As you look at the listeners, you can monitor their reactions to your message. If they look uninvolved, you know you have to adapt your delivery to create interest. When they look interested and supportive of your ideas, it encourages you and you become more involved as well. If you are excited, enthusiastic, and involved, the audience reflects your involvement. As in all communication, public speaking is a transaction process in which people help each other to create competent communication.

Supporting the Verbal Message

You can use gestures, body movements, facial expressions, and voice to give meaning to your verbal messages. Repetitive or random behaviors lack meaning. Using the same gesture or facial expression over and over again probably won't support your verbal message. Nonverbal behaviors that are a natural response to your ideas and closely related and synchronized to the verbal message, however, illustrate and emphasize the verbal message.

For Emphasis By using gestures, you can emphasize ideas when delivering a speech. Appropriate pointing, clenching your fist, and quick hand movements indicate the importance of an idea. Moving toward the audience signals that they should listen to your idea. Taking a few steps to the side during a transition highlights the change to a new topic area. Strategically using gestures, movements, and facial expressions adds significance to verbal messages.

Similarly, your vocal expression tells listeners that an idea is important. An increase in volume, a whisper, a more rapid rate, or a dramatic pause focuses attention on the idea, making it stand out in the minds of the audience.

To Illustrate or Describe Use gestures to illustrate size, shape, distance, motion, and so on. For example, use your hands to describe the sizes of different breeds of dogs, the shapes of different brands of stereo speakers, the motion of a kite, or the speed of your car. Obviously, you should not pantomime everything you talk about. You can, however, selectively use gestures to supplement and complement your verbal message. Nonverbal behaviors make verbal statements more vivid and/or descriptive.

Helping the Audience Listen

Realize that as you speak, your audience is trying to overcome all of the listening barriers we discussed in chapter 8. Help them by making your message easy to listen to and clear. By controlling your rate and articulation you increase the ability of the audience to listen to and understand your message.

Rate is the speed with which you deliver your speech. Most people talk between 150 and 170 words per minute. Talking too slowly bores others, and their minds wander. Talking too fast makes them work too hard to perceive and interpret the message. Reach a comfortable speed for you and your audience. As a natural reaction to the anxiety felt when delivering a speech, your rate of delivery may increase. In preparing for your speech, be aware of this tendency so you can plan to slow down. Monitor your delivery during the speech and make a conscious effort to keep the rate under control. Write a reminder to go slow on your speaking notes and use pauses during transitions to help control your rate.

Volume is the loudness with which you speak to make certain everyone hears you. You must decide on a volume level sufficient to convey the message to others and to make certain that all listeners hear you. This is especially difficult in a large room where electronically assisted amplifiers and microphones aren't used. Make sure the persons in the back of the room can hear you; then the people in the front can hear you, too.

Pronunciation is stating each word correctly with the proper sounds, emphases, and sequence. Mispronunciation violates one, two, or all three of these elements. For instance, when one student read a quotation in which she mispronounced *misled* as "missled," her audience lost the meaning of the statement entirely.

Speakers often mispronounce people's names and technical words making the meaning of their messages unclear. If you are unsure of how to pronounce a word, ask someone or look it up in a dictionary, and then practice until you become familiar with saying it. Mispronunciation detracts from the chance for co-creating communication competence during a speech because it violates the audience's expectations, may illustrate a lack of preparation on your part, and may change the meaning of the statements you are making.

Articulation consists of forming the vowel and consonant sounds correctly. Many people are lazy about articulating many sounds used to communicate. (Remember the sample list of these problems from chapter 7?) For instance, a speaker was talking to a faculty group in Iowa about the reasons teachers voted against the contract her union had negotiated for a school in Georgia. She wanted to say, "We asked all faculty who voted against the contract and they said they didn't like the way the administration treated them." What she actually said was, "We 'axed' the faculty who voted against the contract" which the Iowa faculty understood to mean they had fired the uncooperative faculty. Mispronouncing asked communicated a totally different message than she intended. As a public speaker concerned with competent communication, you should understand the common problems associated with articulation and pronunciation, then strive for accuracy, clarity, and precision.

Vocal pauses are another aspect of the voice. Do you utter sounds such as *uhm, you know, well'm,* or *like* when speaking? Speakers use vocal pauses when they need to fill a given period of time with some type of sound. Used too frequently, vocal pauses distract from your message and make it difficult for the audience to listen. Vocal pauses also make it difficult for the audience to attend to the important words you are speaking and understand the continuity of your message. Strategies for effective nonverbal delivery are summarized in the accompanying box.

Strategies for Effective Nonverbal Delivery

CREATING INTEREST AND MAINTAINING ATTENTION

- Create interest in the audio message by varying your volume, rate, and pitch.
- Create interest in the visual message through movements, gestures, and facial expressions.
- Use direct, frequent, and inclusive eye contact to signal that the message is important to each member of the audience.

ENHANCING CREDIBILITY

- Adapt your appearance to fit the expectations of the audience and the occasion.
- Look at people directly to enhance trustworthiness.
- Control movement, gestures, and voice to demonstrate you are confident and in control of the message and situation.
- Use a dynamic, spontaneous, and natural delivery style.

CREATING INVOLVEMENT

- Use an animated and appropriate facial expression to show involvement with the verbal message.
- Control environmental distractions and create supportive physical surroundings.
- Look at the audience to make them feel part of the situation.
- Use audience feedback to help you increase your own involvement in the communication.

SUPPORTING THE VERBAL MESSAGE

- Use gestures to illustrate the meaning of the verbal message.
- Use volume, rate, and dramatic pause to emphasize ideas.
- Use emphatic gestures to make ideas stand out.
- Use movement to signal a change in topic areas.
- Move toward the audience to increase the importance of the message.
- Use facial expression to communicate the emotional meaning of the message.

HELPING THE AUDIENCE LISTEN

- Minimize extraneous noise that distracts listeners.
- Use a comfortable rate that neither overworks nor bores the audience.
- Speak loudly enough that people can easily hear your message.
- Pronounce words correctly.
- Articulate words clearly and precisely.
- Avoid excessive vocal pauses and other nonfluencies that distract from the verbal message.

"Before You Go On"

You should be able to answer the following question:

Which nonverbal strategies can you use to create competent communication when delivering a public speech?

Strategies for Effective Context Management

During your speech, you may have to handle specific materials or adapt to unexpected occurrences. This section provides insights into managing these oftentimes difficult situations. You need to be prepared to respond to anything that occurs. Your ability to handle unexpected circumstances increases your chances for creating competent communication with your audience.

Managing the Environment

Many times you can choose the environments in which you communicate. When you can, select an environment conducive to achieving competence through your speech. For example, company sales representatives and spokespersons often arrange for a good environment that best suits their communication purpose. Many representatives arrange their presentations in fancy hotel meeting rooms, hoping the environment has a positive effect on their audiences.

Other ways to control the environment are as important as the selection of the location. If the room is too cold or too warm, too dark or too light, if the seats are too hard or too soft, if it is too early in the day or too late, your chances of attaining your speaking purpose are diminished. Adjust the thermostat, close the blinds, turn off distracting lights, move tables and/or chairs around, and choose a time of day that assists you in achieving your speaking purpose. Each of these factors influence the co-creation of public communication competence. You have to control the environment; don't let the environment control you.

Managing Media and Visual Aids

Speakers often use visual aids and media aids in public speaking. Despite their benefits, be aware of their potential problems and practice using them when preparing your speech.[5]

Media Aids

Two common **media aids** for speakers are the lectern and the microphone. These are not available in all speaking situations; be prepared, however, to use them correctly when they are necessary or available.

The *lectern* has one primary purpose—to hold your speaking notes. Using the lectern correctly calls for some basic common sense. Its purpose is not to hold you up nor hide your knocking knees or shaking feet. The lectern is not a barrier to inhibit communication between you and others.

Some situations require the use of a *microphone* to amplify your voice. Talk normally and let the amplification system do the rest of the work. You do not have to scream to make sure everyone can hear you. When facing a microphone, generally you can talk more quietly than you would talking to someone ten to fifteen feet away from you. Don't let the microphone frighten you. The only purpose it serves is to help everyone hear your speech by amplifying it to all parts of the room. By the way, it's a good idea to check the sound level of the mike before the audience arrives, rather than testing it as you begin your speech.

If the microphone is attached to the lectern, stay near enough to the microphone so your voice is amplified. Moving too far away makes the mike useless. For instance, during an orientation session for new students, while discussing registration policies the dean of admissions walked away from the microphone. As a result, only the students in the first couple of rows heard the policies. If you wear a lavaliere microphone around your neck or attach a portable microphone to your clothing, you have more freedom to move around when speaking because the microphone comes with you.

Visual Aids

Suppose your speech centers on a visual aid that suddenly is not available. What would you do? Regardless of how much time you spend preparing visual aids, something can, and usually does, go wrong. By preparing for the unexpected, however, you can remedy the situation. For example, the light bulb suddenly burns out in the overhead projector, but you are prepared because you brought a replacement bulb with you. The easel breaks but you have duct tape to strap it back together. The slide projector jams but you brought a spare. Someone yanked

Strategies for Presenting Public Communication

the screen from the wall when pulling it down, so you show the slides or overheads on a blank wall. All of these situations have actually occurred at one time or another during speeches. The key to surviving such an occurrence is to be adaptable.

The extemporaneous style of delivery is more conducive to bad luck with visual aids than are the other modes. The extemporaneous mode gives you more flexibility to make necessary adjustments to problems while delivering your speech. Be sufficiently familiar with the material on the visual aid that you can present the information verbally even if the aid is not available. The speech would be different had the visual aids cooperated, but you have to adapt and make the best of the situation and deliver the best speech you can. After all, this might be the only opportunity you have to get this information across to others. You have to be able to make a good impression and accomplish your speaking goals without your visual aids if necessary. Some guidelines for the use of your visual aids appear in the accompanying box.

Guidelines for Using Visual Aids

1. Keep the visual aid out of sight until you need it—then remove it from the audience's view when you are finished with it.
2. Put the visual aid close to the audience and to one side of you, the speaker. Don't stand behind or in front of the visual aid.
3. Use a pointer rather than your finger or hand to refer to specific parts of the visual aid.
4. Do not talk to your visual aid—maintain eye contact with the audience.
5. Do not pass objects or papers around the audience while you are speaking.
6. Do not draw your visual aids during the speech, e.g., such as listing ideas on a chalkboard.
7. Practice and practice with your visual aids while you learn your speech.

Managing Your Speaking Notes

Speaking from a manuscript means you have the entire written speech before you. On most extemporaneous speaking occasions, you use notes typed or clearly printed on file cards. Avoid using loose sheets of notebook paper that are difficult to handle and distract the audience. Also avoid crowding too much material on one note card which makes it difficult to find the information you need. When using speaking notes for extemporaneous speaking, the fewer the notes and the more familiar you are with the content of your speech, the better the communication flow.

There are several approaches to using note cards during the speech. One approach is to lay the cards in an inconspicuous place so listeners do not focus their attention on them. For example, if using a lectern, lay the note cards there. If seated at a table for the speech, lay the cards directly in front of you. Another approach is to hold the cards in your hand assuming that once people become accustomed to seeing them, they forget about their presence. Never wave your cards in the air as you speak as they may become a distraction to everyone in the room.

To avoid having people focus attention on your note cards, write the information on only one side of each card. Therefore, you will not have to turn cards over as you progress through the speech. And, be sure to number your cards appropriately. If you drop them, you'll want to make sure they are back in the correct order for your speech.

Managing the Audience

What do you do when you experience an unexpected response from people? Perhaps, you have analyzed everyone as carefully and as thoroughly as you can. You are in the middle of your speech and they are not responding as you anticipated. In fact, some people are bored; others have come in late, and some are getting ready to leave. If you are delivering your speech from a manuscript or have memorized the speech, there is little you can do. However, if you are delivering your speech extemporaneously, you can adapt and alter your speech to make it more appealing to the listeners. This might be as obvious as stating, "I had prepared to go on to a new idea, but, I have noticed that there are confused faces in the audience. So we are going to spend a little more time talking about this subject."

Being flexible is the key to dealing with the unexpected behavior from people. Tolerate their idiosyncracies and realize that people do yawn, look around, stretch, fiddle in their seats, and do a variety of things simply because they are people. There is no use focusing undue attention on these behaviors. Tolerate these behaviors and make sure you are doing all you can to make your speech interesting and involving. As discussed in chapter 8, listeners have a responsibility to give the communicator a chance to get the message and the intended meaning across to them.

When you are speaking to a large group, avoid altering the speech too much to accommodate an individual or small group of people in the audience. You don't want to bore the majority of the audience while you try to clarify one person's confusion. You don't have to start the speech over or repeat ideas for each late arrival. Anticipate that people who arrive late for your speech will understand your ideas differently, but also expect them to catch up with someone else or ask questions at the completion of your speech.

As a public speaker, you should analyze everyone carefully, be tolerant of their idiosyncratic behaviors, and be flexible in communicating to achieve your communication purpose. With these strategies in mind, you can adapt to unexpected behaviors during your speech.

MANAGING MEDIA AIDS

- Speak directly into the microphone.
- Talk normally and let the microphone amplify your voice.
- Use the lectern to hold your notes, not your body.
- Use the lectern to facilitate your use of notes, not as a barrier between you and the audience.

MANAGING THE ENVIRONMENT

- Control distractions (temperature, lighting, noise, etc.).
- Try to speak at a time when people are ready to listen.
- Create a supportive environment through manipulation of semifixed-feature space.
- Control the environment, don't let it control you.

MANAGING THE AUDIENCE

- Adapt to the audience's needs and level of understanding.
- Tolerate idiosyncratic and unintentional movements and noises.
- In large groups, focus on the majority of people's responses rather than those of a few confused persons.

MANAGING SPEAKING NOTES

- Use notes limited to key words and phrases.
- Use as few note cards as possible.
- Write clearly on one side of the card.
- Limit the amount of information on each note card.
- Number your note cards, if using several.
- If possible, place the note cards in an inconspicuous place.
- If holding note cards, keep them still so they don't distract the audience's attention.
- Glance at the notes only when you need them.

MANAGING QUESTION-AND-ANSWER SESSIONS

- Repeat the question so everyone can hear it and to assure that you understand the question.
- Answer the question concisely and clearly.
- Don't bluff or make up information; admit when you don't know, and tell the questioner you will find out.
- Don't disclose sensitive or inappropriate information; simply indicate you have no comment to make on that issue.
- State your answer clearly and then stop; don't debate or argue with the audience.

Managing the Question-and-Answer Session

Although impromptu in nature, the question-and-answer session is an extension of the speech you have just completed. During the question-and-answer period you can elaborate on material that you may not have had time to explain previously. Therefore, be prepared to deal with the questions people ask. Even though you can't anticipate every possible question, you can prepare possible responses to probable questions. Practice organizing all of your messages with a beginning, a middle, and an end. Think before responding in the question-and-answer period. Take time to prepare an articulate and organized response, and then answer the question clearly and concisely.

When asked a question you are ill-prepared to answer, don't try to make up an answer or try to bluff the questioner. Instead, simply say that you are not prepared to answer, but that you will find out the information for the person who asked the question. This approach is certainly better than answering the question in a haphazard manner and finding out that you were incorrect. Admit that you are not all-knowing, and respond to questions accordingly.

When asked a question you have been told not to answer, simply tell the questioner that you cannot answer that question. For example, the public information officer for the United States Department of State was asked about secret information during Desert Shield. During the beginning stages, when troops were sent to the Middle East, the media asked about the deployment of the United States and allied troops, their mission in Saudi Arabia, and their safety. Frequently, the response to journalists was, "We have no official comment at this time." Not responding to a question is the best communication strategy in some instances. Don't overuse this no comment statement, but don't feel obligated to answer each question posed either.

These additional skills may prove useful when you are involved in a question-and-answer period:

- Repeat the question to check your understanding of the person's intent. This repetition also helps ensure that everyone else in the situation heard the original question.
- Answer the question directly, concisely, and as specifically as you are able.
- When answering a question, look at everyone in the situation, not just the person who asked you the question. This relates to our earlier discussion of the importance of eye contact with others when you are talking.
- After completing your response, check to see if the questioner understood your answer and if there is any follow-up material needed.
- After you have answered the question to the best of your abilities, don't argue or debate your response. You've already given it your best shot; there is no need to pursue that area or topic any more.

Answering people's questions completely and competently, with clarity and conviction is essential to your successful handling of the question-and-answer period. (For a summary, see the accompanying box entitled Strategies for Managing Communication Situations.)

"Before You Go On"

You should be able to answer the following question:

What strategies can you use to manage the communication situation?

Responses to *"Before You Go On"* **Questions: A Chapter Summary**

1.   Which four guidelines do people use in judging a public speaker's delivery skills?

People judge a public speaker's delivery skills using the following criteria: (1) how natural was the delivery style of the speaker, (2) how spontaneous did the speaker's delivery appear, (3) how much in control was the speaker, and (4) how responsive was the speaker to the audience and the occasion.

The relative importance of each of these criteria varies depending on the audience. For example, it may be extremely important for one member of the audience that the speaker appear relaxed; yet for another listener it may be most important that the speaker be natural or conversational while delivering the speech.

2.   What are the advantages and disadvantages of the four types of delivery for a public speech?

Manuscript delivery gives the speaker the entire speech written out word for word. Disadvantages of this type of delivery include the written verbal style, the importance placed on the reading skills of the speaker, inflexibility in adapting to listeners, loss of eye contact, loss of movement, and a loss of spontaneity. The greatest advantage of manuscript delivery is the fact that the speaker has the exact words and phrases to read to the listeners.

Memorized delivery is not adaptable to the listeners' needs because it relies on the speaker's skills at reciting a message. It focuses on remembering sequences of words rather than ideas. An advantage is that the speaker can work without notes, establish eye contact with the listeners, and move about.

Extemporaneous delivery enables the speaker to be flexible and adaptable during the delivery of the speech to help the listeners better understand. The speaker appears more spontaneous and natural. In situations where exact wording must be repeated over and over, the extemporaneous delivery style might not be the best choice for the speaker.

Impromptu delivery calls for the speaker to give a quick, unrehearsed statement or a response to a question. With little time for preparation, the speaker organizes a message on the spur of the moment. While highly flexible, the obvious disadvantage to impromptu delivery is the fact that the speaker cannot thoroughly prepare the specific message.

3. Which nonverbal strategies can you use to create competent communication when delivering a public speech?

The speaker can create interest, maintain attention, and create involvement through movement, gestures, and eye contact. Dynamic delivery, eye contact, and appearance enhances credibility. Nonverbal delivery illustrates and emphasizes the verbal message and helps the audience to listen through vocal and visual variety.

4. Which strategies can you use to manage the communication situation?

Strategies include practicing with visual and media aids and developing alternative plans if they malfunction. Control the environment; make the physical surroundings supportive and free of distractions. Anticipate unexpected responses from your audience and don't be distracted by normal reactions to the environment and your speech. Keep your speaking notes easily visible to you yet unobtrusive to the audience. Answer questions concisely and honestly. Tell the audience if you do not know the answer or are not allowed to give specific information.

S T U D E N T   E X E R C I S E S

1. Evaluating a speaker's delivery mode.

Select two or three public speaking situations, either live or on television, and examine the different types of delivery. Was the delivery mode manuscript, memorized, extemporaneous, or impromptu? Was it the appropriate style for the situation and the message? How well did the speakers use each delivery style? What differences did you notice in their specific strategies for using each style? Would a different style have changed the effects of the speech? What implications do your answers have for the delivery style you will use in your next speaking opportunity?

2. Logging your impromptu speaking situations.

For a week keep a daily log of the impromptu speaking situations you find yourself in at school, at work, and at home. Indicate how many of these were planned and how many were unexpected. Reflect on each of them at the end of each day and label them as successful, unsuccessful, or neither. Be consistent in recording your comments and evaluations of the situations. After the week is over, discuss your observations with the people who participated in the impromptu situations.

How do your conclusions compare with the conclusions of the other people? What are your strengths and weaknesses in dealing with the impromptu situations?

3. Impromptu speeches.

With your classmates, write down twenty to twenty-five proposition statements you would like to hear someone give a speech on. Use one 3 × 5 note card for each proposition. Place the propositions in a sack and, one at a time, pick the cards. Take no more than one minute to prepare your impromptu speech meeting any criteria specified in the proposition. Talk on your topic for two to three minutes.

4.   Communicating with facial expressions.

Pick up one or two weekly news magazines. Page through each looking at people's faces in each picture and advertisement. Make a list of the messages they are communicating solely with their facial expressions.

After you have a list of emotions being communicated in the pictures, take the list to a mirror in your room. Using the list, communicate the same emotion you have listed using facial expressions. Concentrate on the mirror so you can see how your face looks communicating the same emotion.

5.   Listening to your speaking voice.

Talk into a tape recorder for four or five minutes; then play it back. See how rapidly you talk; is it difficult for you to follow? Are you talking loudly enough for others to hear you? Listen carefully to your articulation and pronunciation. Do you hear any problems?

Next, read a written text into the tape recorder for four to five minutes. Compare your reading with your speaking. What differences and similarities do you notice?

G L O S S A R Y

articulation   The way we form individual vowel and consonant sounds when we speak.

extemporaneous delivery   Planned, practiced, and rehearsed communication of a message. Requires the use of speaking notes with only a few key words and phrases during delivery. Encourages adaptability and visual relationship building with the listeners.

impromptu delivery   Spur-of-the-moment communication the speaker has little time to prepare or rehearse. Often used when unexpectedly called on to make a statement or respond to questions.

manuscript delivery   Using a word-for-word, written document and reading your speech to listeners. Emphasizes your abilities to read to others. Used often when exact word choice and phrasing is important.

media aids   Any device which facilitates the audio delivery of the speech. Two common examples are the lectern and a microphone.

memorized delivery   Using a word-for-word document and remembering each word and phrase in a sequence for delivery at a later date. Emphasizes your abilities to recite the speech to your listeners. Can be helpful for remembering statistics or short testimony in your speech.

pitch The relative highness or lowness of your voice. Extreme examples are a monotone when the pitch does not vary or the sing-song pitch when the pitch varies too much in a repetitive pattern.

pronunciation A communicator's ability to say words correctly with the correct emphasis, the proper sounds, and in the correct sequence.

rate The speed of your delivery. The average person talks at a rate of approximately 150 words per minute.

visual aid Anything used by a speaker containing visual information related to a verbal message.

volume The loudness of your voice when speaking. It is important that you speak loudly enough so that everyone in the room can hear you deliver your speech.

NOTES

1. For additional discussions on the types of delivery, see S. A. Beebe and S. J. Beebe, *Public Speaking: An Audience-Centered Approach* (Englewood Cliffs, N.J.: Prentice Hall, 1991); or M. Osborn and S. Osborn, *Public Speaking,* 2nd ed. (Boston: Houghton Mifflin, 1991).

2. For a history of theories related to delivery, see L. Thonssen and A. C. Baird, *Speech Criticism: The Development of Standards for Rhetorical Appraisal* (New York: Ronald Press, 1948).

3. T. G. Hengstrom, "Message Impact: What Percentage is Nonverbal?" *Western Journal of Speech Communication* 43, (1979), 134–42.

4. R. Ailes, "You Are the Message," *Executive Communications* (1988), 1.

5. W. L. Haynes, "Public Speaking Pedagogy in the Media Age," *Communication Education* 38, (1990), 89–102.

17

C H A P T E R

Strategies for Giving Information

- *I know a lot about how to size a business suit; I wish I knew how to*

  tell others.

- *My grandparents have a lot to tell us about our family history. I*

  hope they are able to do that at our family reunion.

- *I wish I could express my ideas more clearly when I talk with*

  this group.

- *She did an excellent job of explaining things to us. How did she*

  do it?

E veryone needs information. Suppose you want to talk about your university's class registration process to a group of new students and their parents. You already know something about that process because of your personal experience. You begin looking for information on the topic; once you have the information, you put it in a form that you can communicate with others. This is the challenge of informative speaking. This chapter explains how to share information with others during a speech.

The strategies for sharing information depend on your specific purpose, the characteristics of your listeners, and the variables within the communication context. Although messages are primarily informative, they also must persuade the audience to believe the information and entertain the audience by creating interest and involving them in the communication.

Strategies for sharing information in a speech incorporate two related purposes: others must understand the meaning of the message and others must be able to remember what you told them. You want others not only to understand your message but also to use the information at a later date. For instance, the director of the university computer center wants students to understand the procedures for operating the word processing equipment and to use that information later in completing their work. Instructors want students to understand course policies regarding absenteeism, tardiness, and class participation as well as to use that information by coming to class and participating in discussions. Corporate personnel directors want employees to understand the details of the retirement program and to use that information in making intelligent decisions regarding saving and investing for retirement. Keep in mind the dual purposes of understanding and remembering information when designing your informative speeches.

"Before You Go On"

You should be able to answer the following question:

What are the two primary purposes of sharing information during a speech?

This chapter examines strategies for sharing information which are useful when developing an informative speech. The strategies assume you have already developed effective communication skills. These include analyzing the communication situation, selecting a topic, writing a proposition, deciding on supporting propositions and main ideas, organizing information, choosing appropriate language, and delivering the speech. Information-sharing strategies are plans of action or techniques for developing ideas that meet your specific purposes. Information-sharing strategies are distinct from communication skills in the same way a person's typing skills at a computer keyboard are distinct from the strategies of computer programming or designing computer graphics. Strategies for sharing information help others understand and remember information.

Strategies for Helping Others Understand Information

To increase others' understanding, you may decide to use all the available strategies in your speech or choose to use only one or two. Base your choice of strategies on your analysis of the communication situation and the audience. Strategies are effective only to the extent that they enhance others' understanding.[1] Therefore, message strategies must be adapted to the specific characteristics of the listeners as well as their involvement in the topic you have selected. Strategies for increasing understanding are concerned with focusing others' attention on your message, developing shared meanings for your message, and delivering your message.

Focusing Others' Attention on the Speech

Effective perception of information requires that others focus their attention on your message. If they do not, the information you are sharing is likely to be misunderstood.[2] In every speaking situation, your speech is only one of several sources of information competing for everyone's attention. Noises in the environment, the physical state and mood of each participant, distractions from other audience members, and your own extraneous behaviors are sources of distraction that decrease audience attention and involvement with your message. You must devise specific strategies to capture the attention of others and ensure that they listen to your message.

Controlling the Environment

As the transaction communication model illustrates, people are bombarded with messages from the environment at the same time they are trying to comprehend and respond to your verbal and nonverbal messages. An important communication strategy is to reduce the number of distractions for the audience. Select and arrange the communication environment to help you accomplish this. Creating supportive physical surroundings makes it easier for the audience to focus on your message.

The following example illustrates how a speaker can control the environment to facilitate communication competence. The local chamber of commerce held weekly meetings from 4:00 to 5:00 on Thursday afternoon. Each week, the president of the chamber arranged for a different speaker to talk about business and social developments in the city. These meetings were important to chamber members because they received new information. For the most part, however, the speakers were ineffective because chamber members failed to listen to or understand the important information delivered in each speech. Often, they would call speakers the next day to ask them questions about their speeches. The problem occurred because there were too many environmental distractions to the speaker's message. The room was usually hot and fairly noisy. The time of day also caused a lack of attention; members had already worked a full day and were thinking of going home. The president of the chamber of commerce finally realized that the environment had to be controlled to reduce the number of distractions during their meetings.

The president changed to an early morning meeting rather than the late afternoon meeting. The president arranged for coffee and donuts to be served at each of these meetings to establish a more comfortable environment for the guest speakers and the membership. When attending a morning meeting, the members were much more ready to listen to the speakers. They were not tired from a day's work and actually looked forward to hearing each speaker. They were able to listen to the message more carefully because the competing messages from the environment were reduced.

Speakers have to help others focus their attention and energies on the message by carefully selecting and arranging a supportive climate for others to listen to the speech.

Controlling Any Extraneous Messages You Send

Speakers must control their behaviors to eliminate **extraneous messages** irrelevant to the ideas they want others to understand. Excessive shifting of weight from leg to leg, overly repetitive gestures and movements, poor eye contact, and/or nervous pacing are nonverbal messages that distract from a speech. Verbal distractions such as nonfluency, misusing words, mispronouncing words, excessive vocal pauses, and/or imprecise and inconcise language can also distract or confuse people listening to your speech. When you ramble by taking verbal side trips to irrelevant information in your speech or use incorrect terminology, others have difficulty in focusing on the ideas you want them to remember. Once they discover they have devoted their energies to selectively attend to irrelevant or contradictory messages from you, they are less likely to listen to and understand your information.

Controlling Distractions from Other People

Probably the most difficult problem you face when communicating is controlling distractions from people listening to you. When they are hungry, tired, nervous, or angry, they are less likely to carefully attend to your speech. Sometimes, people will even talk to each other when you are speaking with them. You must recognize the importance of these distractions and try to minimize their influence.

One method is to deliver your speech when these internal distractions can be minimized. For example, speaking in mid-morning or mid-afternoon minimizes the chances that others are hungry or tired. Speaking about important information can be done early in the week so people are not thinking about their weekend activities instead of listening to the speech.

Speakers also need to help others overcome any emotional biases in their perception of the messages. Emotions often affect which information we hear and how we interpret it. If some listeners are angry, for example, you might decide to wait until their anger subsides before trying to give them important information. If people are bored, you must work hard to motivate them to pay attention by showing them the importance and relevance of the information.

For example, a speech teacher conducting a class on public speaking at the local community college realized that most of the students were nervous about speaking to the group. The teacher knew that they were probably thinking about the upcoming speech assignment instead of listening to the explanation of the techniques for constructing effective visual aids. Rather than delivering this important information to people who were not paying close attention, the teacher began the class session with a discussion of speech apprehension (anxiety). After about twenty minutes of discussions and class exercises, the students had relaxed sufficiently that they could focus on the information concerning visual aids. The teacher's strategy was to reduce the competing messages induced by the students' nerves to help them focus on the content of the message. Speakers must be flexible and adapt messages to the specific needs of others to help them focus their attention on the speech.

"Before You Go On"

You should be able to answer the following question:

What are three concerns when creating strategies for increasing understanding?

Creating Shared Meanings

Competent communication occurs when both the speaker and the listener work hard to reach shared meaning from the speech. In making an informative speech, the speaker is concerned with helping the others understand the message. And, the listener is concerned with co-creating shared meaning with the speaker. The speaker can do several things to help: define words and ideas, compare and contrast ideas, use examples, and use statistics.

Defining Words and Ideas

As we pointed out in chapter 6, words can be given numerous denotative and connotative meanings. To ensure accurate understanding, be sure that everyone gives a similar meaning to each word you use. One method for improving understanding of important words is to define them by using synonyms, examples, or analogies. Which specific words you define depends on your audience's knowledge about the topic and their familiarity with any jargon or technical terms.

Speakers may define terms in their speeches by quoting dictionaries or noted authorities concerning the meanings of the words. You may also give examples illustrating the use of the term or its application. Analogies to familiar concepts also increase people's understanding of terms. For example, the term *corporate image* may be defined by a speaker discussing public relations by using each of the following techniques:

Quoting an Authoritative Source:	John Clancy Williams III, director of public relations at ABC Toy Company, described corporate image as "the attitudes the public has toward the company and its products."
Giving an Example:	"When a person says they admire the company, agree with its policies, or would like to work for it, they are describing their perception of the corporate image."
Using an Analogy:	"The corporate image is similar to a mental picture the consumer has about the company. The picture may be large or small, brightly colored or black and white, clear or fuzzy, depending on the consumers' knowledge of the corporation, their emotional reactions to its operations, and the strengths of their attitudes."

Each technique helps clarify the meaning of corporate image so members of the audience understand what the speaker means.

Using Comparison and Contrast

Informative messages are often easier to understand if we can relate unfamiliar information to familiar knowledge. One way to clarify unfamiliar information is to compare or contrast it to previous experiences or knowledge. **Comparisons** tell others that the new information is similar to information already known. For example, we have used several comparisons in this text to relate new information about speaking skills and strategies to previously understood images concerning developing skills in athletics and computer operation. Likewise, you may find it helpful to compare new information to others' understanding of common events, familiar objects, frequent or common experiences, or well-known ideas.

For instance, at a conference of authors, editors of publishing firms explained their marketing strategies for selling college textbooks. One editor compared textbook marketing and selling strategies to the strategies of a military campaign. These included defending strategic ground, scouting enemy forces, and mounting a charge with well-armed troops. Drawing from the audience's previous knowledge of these basic strategies of war, the editor clearly explained the company's strategies for textbook acquisitions, market research, and sales campaigns. By relating marketing strategies with well-known principles of war, the editor not only captured the audience's interest but also assisted everyone in understanding the intricacies of effective textbook marketing and sales strategies.

Speakers may also **contrast** new information with existing images. Through contrasting, people better understand how the information differs from their current knowledge of the subject. For example, an encyclopedia salesperson may explain the advantages of *Encyclopaedia Britannica* by contrasting its characteristics with those of the more familiar *World Book Encyclopedia*. The prospective client can readily understand the differences between the encyclopedias through direct contrast of the salesperson's encyclopedias and the other kinds.

Using Examples

Examples are specific instances, models, specimens, or representations of an idea. Examples, as explained in chapter 15, can either be real or hypothetical. Hypothetical examples are fictitious situations or instances that could be true. Real examples are actual events or situations that previously occurred or presently exist. People have a better chance of understanding your information if you use examples. Explanations of new registration procedures at your college or university may be more clearly understood if you show actual examples demonstrating the new procedures for registering. Similarly, new sales techniques can be clarified by giving examples of actual salespersons using the techniques on their sales calls. Whether you use real or hypothetical examples, it is important to draw conclusions from them.

Each example should relate to the main idea of your speech so the audience understands its meaning. Examples can help clarify material by adding concrete details, personalizing the information, or showing applications.[3] George Fisher of Motorola, Incorporated, used the following example to add detail in one of his speeches on the development of new technology: "In Arlington Heights, for example, we completely changed the way we make cellular phones. Our semiconductor engineers designed application specific integrated circuits to help reduce the component count from 1,655 on the earlier model to 723 on the new Mini-TAC, which is three times smaller."

Using Statistics

Many number-oriented people favor information explained in numerical quantities. They understand statistical data more easily than abstract concepts, qualitative assessments, and/or general statements. Many decisions we make are based on information provided through statistical analysis. For example, when you decide to buy a new car, your decision is not solely based on a general feeling that "I will look great in this car; I have to have it." Rather, you will likely examine automobile ratings, owner satisfaction surveys, the miles per gallon rating by the government, the car's repair record as reported in *Consumer Reports,* and estimate how much it will cost you to operate this car for the next several years. All of these data, plus the specific data in the box, may be necessary for you to know before making the decision to purchase a particular car.[4]

FORD FESTIVA

Body type:	3-door hatchback
Passive Restraint:	Motorized front shoulder belts
Wheelbase:	90.2″
Overall length:	140.5″
Overall width:	63.2″
Overall height:	55.3″
Curb weight:	1785 lbs.
Track, f/r:	55.1″/54.5″
Passengers:	4
Head room, f/r:	38.6″/37.4″
Leg room, f/r:	40.6″/35.7″
Shoulder room, f/r:	51.9″/50.9″
Cargo volume:	11.7 cu. ft.
Engine type:	I-4
Displacement:	1.3 liter
Horsepower:	63 @5000
Torque:	73 @ 3000
Transmission:	5 sp. manual, 3 sp. auto
Drive:	Front
Steering:	Rack and pinion, manual

Brakes, f/r:	Disc/drum, power
Tires:	14/12 (L), 165/70–12 (GL)
Fuel capacity:	10.0 gal.
Mileage:	31/33, 35/41

1991 PRICES

| L 3-door hatchback | $6,620 |
| GL 3-door hatchback | $7,460 |

FORD THUNDERBIRD

Body type:	2-door coupe
Passive Restraint:	Motorized front shoulder belts
Wheelbase:	113.0″
Overall length:	198.7″
Overall width:	72.7″
Overall height:	52.7″
Curb weight:	3550 lbs. (base)
Track, f/r:	61.6″/60.2″
Passengers:	5
Head room, f/r:	38.1″/37.5″
Leg room, f/r:	42.5″/35.8″
Shoulder room, f/r:	59.1″/69.1″
Cargo volume:	14.7 cu. ft.
Engine type:	V-6, V-6 supercharged, V-8
Displacement:	3.8, 3.8, 5.0 liter
Horsepower:	140 @ 3800, 210 @ 4000, 200 @ 4000
Torque:	215 @ 2400, 315 @ 2600, 275 @ 3000
Transmission:	4 sp. auto, 5 sp. manual
Drive:	Rear
Steering:	Rack and pinion, power
Brakes, f/r:	Disc/drum, power; disc/disc, power, anti-lock (Super Coupe)
Tires:	205/70–15 (Standard/LX), 225/60–16 (Super Coupe)
Fuel capacity:	19.0 gal.
Mileage:	17/23–19/27

1991 PRICES

Base	$15,318
LX	$17,734
Super Coupe	$20,999

Which statistics you use to increase the understanding of your idea depends on the nature of the topic, the knowledge listeners have about statistics, and the point you are trying to make. Statistics are often more easily understood if the speaker employs strategies of definition, analogy, and comparison when presenting the data. Numbers are meaningless in isolation. Is $12 million a lot of money or not? Compared to most people's yearly salaries, $12 million is a staggering sum; compared to the national deficit of the United States government, $12 million is a drop in the bucket. Making numbers meaningful to your audience is an important strategy when using statistics in a speech. Consider the following two statements explaining the statistical data related to a proposed new marketing strategy designed to increase enrollment at a major university:

Statement A: "The new strategy for marketing our university will result in a 10.2 percent increase in enrollment. Our faculty hiring must also increase 5.6 percent during the first two years and 8.4 percent in the last three years of this plan. In the fifth year of this plan, the faculty-to-student ratio will be within one standard deviation of current acceptable national figures."

Statement B: "The new marketing strategy for our university will result in a 10.2 percent increase in student enrollment over the next five years. This means we will have a tenth more students— approximately 1,800 more students will be attending our university. In addition, this projected increase in student enrollment will increase our revenues by more than $1 million annually—a substantial increase in our operating budget. If these projections are correct, we must increase the number of faculty over the next five years to keep a faculty-to-student ratio within national norms. The 5 percent increase the first two years and the 8 percent increase the last three years in the size of our faculty will mean specific departments can grow while others will be less dependent on part-time faculty to teach many of their introductory courses."

Notice that in Statement B, the percentages were related to the total enrollment at the university and a total revenue figure was projected. Statement B also:

- Expressed numerical data both as specific percentages and as approximations (e.g., 10.2 percent versus a tenth more).
- Rounded complex numbers to simpler forms, (e.g., 5.6% to 5%).
- Avoided statistics jargon that the audience may not understand (e.g., standard deviation).
- Indicated total amounts as well as percentages (e.g., 10.2% equals 1,800 students).
- Interpreted the meaning of the statistics in human terms (reduce part-time faculty).

These strategies make statistical support more understandable. Figure 17.1 shows some direct comparisons between isolated and confusing statistics and ways to express numerical data more meaningfully during a speech.

FIGURE 17.1
Isolated and meaningful statistics.

Isolated Statistics	Meaningful Statistics
a. 25% of the houses	1/4 of the 350 houses
b. 12,335,194 people	12 million people
c. $12 million	$12 million or 5 times our annual revenue
d. 15% increase in enrollment	1,200 additional students
e. 0.27% of the time	less than once out of 300 times
f. 35% of accidents involve impaired drivers	1 in 3 accidents involve impaired drivers

Examples A and D in figure 17.1 make percentages more meaningful by providing the total number. Examples B, E, and F use approximations to make complex or abstract numbers easier to understand. Example C provides a point of reference so the audience can more easily grasp the magnitude of the number.

Numerical data often help clarify ideas and make the abstract more concrete. Use caution in presenting numbers so they are easily perceived and understood by the audience. You might find it helpful to graphically display statistical data with visual aids. People understand complex numerical relationships better if they can see the numbers as they listen to the explanation.

"Before You Go On"

You should be able to answer the following question:

What four strategies can you use to help develop shared meanings with your listeners?

Establishing the Believability of Information

Information must be believable for the audience before they remember it. If the information comes from a source they respect, people tend to pay closer attention to it and more readily accept its validity. The credibility of your sources is a judgment the audience makes. You can increase the believability of information by citing its source and by choosing current information from sources others respect.

The sources you use may also affect your own credibility during your speech. For example, if you use sources that others find credible or believable, the credibility they place in the source of the information is also granted to you. As a result, they are more likely to understand your message and be more motivated to remember it. On the other hand, if you use sources people find hard to believe, it affects your credibility negatively.

All the strategies discussed thus far in this chapter are useful for increasing the audience's understanding of your informative messages. Focusing others' attention, defining words, using comparison and contrast techniques, employing examples and statistics, and establishing the believability of your information help others pay attention to your information and understand it. The selection of suitable strategies and the precise wording and construction of the message depend on careful analysis of everyone in the communication situation and your creativity. Understanding is one primary goal of sharing information; a second goal is to help listeners remember it.

Strategies for Helping Others Remember Information

Memory is our ability to recall information as needed. You probably have had the experience of knowing that you have heard something but simply cannot remember it. As discussed in chapter 2, our memories are selective. We remember information better when it is important to us, when we have clear labels for the information, when we use or mentally rehearse the information, and when it is associated with multiple memories. To help others remember information, use the following strategies to develop information that is easy for them to recall.

Highlight Important Ideas

People remember information better if speakers let them know which ideas they are supposed to remember. Obviously, the major ideas of your speech are ideas that you want others to remember. You need to highlight these ideas to make them stand out from the rest of the speech. The goal of this strategy is to place emphasis on the upcoming idea or to direct others' attention to a specific statement. **Highlighting** says to your listeners, "Pay attention to what I'm going to say next." Thus, the listeners are ready to concentrate on remembering your next idea.

Highlighting can be accomplished through verbal statements. You may specifically tell others that your next statement is important. Design each statement to catch people's attention, focus their attention on the next statement, and prepare them to remember an important idea. When you have helped the audience anticipate your next statement, they are more likely to concentrate on receiving and remembering the information.

Also highlight important ideas nonverbally through delivery strategies such as vocal emphasis, dramatic pauses, gestures, and changes in volume and rate (see chapter 16). When you have been speaking at a rapid pace, saying something more slowly adds emphasis. If you have been speaking in a loud and forceful tone, stating an important idea more softly may give it added importance. Emphatic gestures and movement can signal the beginning of important statements. To make your ideas more easy to remember, signal others to pay close attention.

Repeat Important Ideas and Information

You can help others understand and remember your information by repeating major ideas and by restating important information. Repetition and restatement affect other's ability to remember information in two ways.

Repetition Ensures Perception of Information

People have to listen to information to remember it. One of the barriers to effective listening discussed in chapter 8 was the difference between listening speed and mind speed. Because your listeners think three to four times faster than you can talk, they let their thoughts wander. Be sure that others don't miss important ideas in your speech; repeat your main ideas so they have several chances to hear them. Even though their thoughts are wandering when you state the idea the first time, chances are they will be paying attention when you repeat the idea.

During an informative speech, you can state major ideas during the introduction (the preview), during the body of the speech (main points), and in the conclusion (the summary). In addition, each idea may be restated during transitions from one point to another. To avoid boring others by repeating the exact same sentences each time, vary the wording of each restatement in the speech. At the same time, maintain consistency among your statements by using key words that are the same in each restatement. For example, a department store manager training new employees to sell major appliances may have the following main ideas:

I.   Listen carefully for closing indicators, that is, remarks indicating the customer is ready to buy the item.
II.   Record the sales information to complete the order form as you explain the purchase agreement.
III. Ask for a signature on the sales contract immediately upon its completion.

The new employees, soon to be salespersons, must understand these three steps to close a sale. As stated, however, the ideas may be difficult to repeat without boring others. The manager should select key words from each idea to be repeated while varying the exact wording of each sentence. The key words in these three ideas may be:

I.   Closing indicators
II.   Complete the order
III. Contract signature

The manager could repeat these key phrases while maintaining variety in the introduction, body, and conclusion of the speech. Possible variations in repeating the ideas follow:

Introduction (*Preview*):   To successfully close a sale, you must remember to watch for *closing indicators, complete the order form,* and obtain a *contract signature.*

Body (*Main Ideas*):

    I. You must listen carefully for the *closing indicators* that tell you the customer is ready to buy the appliance.

    II. You must have a *complete order* filled out as you discuss the details of the purchase agreement.

    III. You must clearly ask for a *contract signature* after you complete the order form.

Conclusion:

In sales you must be sure to close, close, close! Closing a sale is easy if you remember and understand the three steps. If you listen carefully for *closing indicators*, if you have shown the customer a *complete order*, and if you have clearly asked for a *contract signature*, you can be sure you will close the sale.

Notice that each part of the speech repeats the same phrases to ensure that the listeners have at least three chances to listen to and remember the speaker's key ideas.

Restatement Encourages Appropriate Memories

In chapter 2, we compared memory to a filing system. We associate new information with that already stored in our memories. As we selectively attend to stimuli, we file it in our memories. We put it in a mental folder and label the folder so that we can find it again. When we want to retrieve information, we think of the label that stimulates recall of the information.

Understanding is the incorporation of information into appropriate files or memories. You want people listening to your speech to create, modify, or reinforce specific memories. When listeners relate the information to the wrong or an inappropriate memory, they misfile the information and understanding has not occurred. In the previous example, the appliance store manager wanted the information concerning closing a sale to be incorporated into the employees' memories correctly. New employees who placed the information from the manager's speech into memories related to opening a sales interview or into memories regarding designing advertisements for the appliance, misunderstood the message.

Restating and rephrasing ideas help listeners remember information. As we pointed out in chapter 6, language is ambiguous and words have numerous denotative and/or connotative meanings. Therefore, using different words to express the same idea ensures listeners' comprehension. By restating the idea in two or three different ways, the speaker helps ensure that the audience places the information in the appropriate memory. A speaker can also clarify the meaning of the ideas by telling which ideas are not related to the information. For example, in the explanation of closing techniques, the manager could explain:

I'm *not* going to tell you about ways to open a sales interview, methods for explaining the advantages of our appliances, or strategies for persuading your customers to make the purchase. I want you to focus on the closing of the sales interview. The closing or conclusion of the sales presentation can be the most important part of the sales pitch since it is where you finalize the deal. Think about the last few minutes of a selling situation you have been involved in recently. What did the salesperson do to get you to sign the purchase agreement?

Notice the different ways the manager restated and rephrased the term *closing*: as the *conclusion, where you finalize the deal,* and *the last few minutes of a selling situation.*

Notice also how the manager specifically told the new employees which memories are inappropriate. The manager helped them create the correct memory by asking them to "think about the last few minutes of a recent selling situation," rather than the opening of a sales interview or persuasion techniques. Rephrasing ideas by using words that evoke appropriate memories and specifically referring to ideas related to the information increases the likelihood of competent communication.

"Before You Go On"

You should be able to answer the following question:

What is accomplished by repeating ideas during a speech?

Create Immediacy of Information

People who are told that the information they are listening to will be needed immediately or in the near future listen more carefully. In addition, they expend the extra effort to remember it. Teachers use the **immediacy of information** in classes merely by stating this information will be covered on the next test. If others know the information applies directly to them, they are more motivated to remember it. The example of techniques for closing the sale could be made more immediate if the manager stated, "We know these steps for closing the sale will increase your sales effectiveness. We expect you to use these steps with the *next* customer you talk with. To make sure you remember each of these steps, we want you to practice the procedures in an exercise immediately at the conclusion of my comments." Create and maintain a sense of immediacy throughout the speech so that your listeners are attentive.

To accomplish this in the introduction, relate the topic to your audience. For example, refer to you rather than people, address your listeners by name, refer to the immediate situation or the near future, avoid overgeneralizations, and tell your listeners how to personally use the information.

Involving the audience in physical application of your ideas makes information memorable.

Create Involvement in the Speech

People remember information better if they are actively involved in its acquisition and application. Passively listening to a speech decreases attention to the information and reduces the strength of any memories created. Involvement can be either through mental rehearsal of the information or through physical activities requiring people to apply the information to a specific task. In either case, involvement strengthens the relationship between the new information and established memories. Strategies for increasing involvement include asking questions and practicing or applying the information.

Asking Questions

By using questions throughout the speech, you can encourage others to engage in active mental associations between the new information and their knowledge, experiences, and attitudes. For example, you might ask, "How many of you have had difficulty starting your car in the cold weather?" The question mentally prepares others for upcoming information they can directly relate to personal experiences with their cars.

Use these two types of questions: The first is a **rhetorical question** that does not require a direct response but suggests the audience think of responses to themselves. The second is a **responsive question** that seeks a direct behavioral or verbal response. Questions, whether rhetorical or responsive, cause others to be actively involved with the communication and with applying the information to their own experiences.

"Before You Go On"

You should be able to answer the following question:

How do rhetorical and responsive questions help listeners remember information?

Practicing or Applying the Information

Information is easier to remember when the speaker provides an immediate opportunity to apply the information.[5] Exercises used in training seminars, discussions of important concepts in staff meetings, and tests of knowledge and skills used after giving instructions all require immediate application of information. For instance, a teacher may explain a math concept and then ask a student to show how to complete a math formula on the chalkboard. The student asked to complete the formula learns the information more completely and quickly because the information is retrieved from his or her memory immediately. This strengthens the bond between the information and the student's memory. Application also allows you to check the accuracy of others' understanding of your information.

Create Memorable Units and Phrases

When presenting new information, realize that the audience is probably relying on you to help them remember important information. You can help improve their memories of your message by supplying words or phrases that are easy for them to remember.

Mnemonic Devices

Mnemonic devices are words, phrases, abbreviations, initials, or acronyms used to recall complex information. The simple statement used to recall the number of days in each month (Thirty days has September, April, June and November) is a mnemonic device. The sentence used to recall the musical notes of the treble clef (*Every Good Boy Does Fine*) is another mnemonic device that aids memory of information. Indeed, we have used several mnemonic devices in this text, such as the transaction listening skills A-C-I-D and the N-I-C-E visual aid.

Review the example of repetition illustrated earlier in this chapter. When discussing the techniques for closing the sale, the speech included three key phrases: Closing indicators, Completing the order, and Contract signature. Notice that each of these key phrases must be remembered if the new salesperson is to effectively close the sale. Each of the three key phrases begins with the letter *C*. The manager could aid retention of the key phrases by referring to them as the three *C*'s of closing the sale. When subsequently retrieving the information, the salesperson might think, I need to close the sale. *Close* starts with a *C*—oh yes, the three *C*'s of closing the sale. The letter *C* evokes the information from the salesperson's memory, and the short phrases should come to mind easily. D. V. Fites of Caterpillar Corporation used this strategy during a speech to the Pacific Logging Congress by stating: "In my remarks, I talked about four key issues facing the forest products industry. I called them the Four *P*'s . . . *p*roductivity, *p*rofitability, *p*olitics, and *p*erception."

Chunking

A second way to help others remember information in your speech is **chunking.** Chunking refers to the recognition or creation of patterns among sets of perceptions. Chunking groups together individual bits of information to facilitate comprehension and memory. For example, remember when you learned to write. At first, you had to focus your attention on each separate line that composed each letter. Later, you could write each letter without concentrating on the individual lines; that is, you chunked the lines into larger units called letters. Similarly, the letters became chunked together as you learned to spell words. Words became chunked into sentences, sentences into paragraphs, and paragraphs into term papers and reports.

Research indicates a person can process approximately seven chunks of information at any one time.[6] Once a set of information exceeds seven or so individual pieces, the person creates a larger category or chunk by which to refer to several pieces of information simultaneously. Chunking capitalizes on the organization function of perception (see chapter 2) by showing similarities among the information. We remember chunks of information more easily if the information in each chunk is related. Speakers who recognize this as they organize their speeches can help the audience chunk information appropriately.

For instance, you know that others cannot remember long lists of procedures or a large number of unrelated facts. You have to organize information into chunks the audience can easily grasp and identify. Therefore, if you are giving a speech on the causes of war in the Persian Gulf, you may divide your speech into the following major ideas or chunks:

1. Enforcing the United Nations' resolutions against Iraq.
2. Protecting the oil supply for dependent industrial nations.
3. Maintaining a balance of power in the Middle East.

Another example might be chunking information regarding a visit to New York City into the following categories:

1. museums
2. theaters
3. restaurants
4. athletic events
5. shopping areas
6. historic sites

Even this list may be too long to easily remember. You could reduce the list to smaller chunks:

1. Culture
   a. museums
   b. historic sites
2. Entertainment
   a. theaters
   b. athletic events
3. Relaxation
   a. shopping
   b. restaurants

As you may realize from looking at the last example, chunking is the process by which you organize ideas into major ideas and supporting ideas. A speech outline helps you visualize the way information is chunked. The major ideas indicate the relationship among the supporting information, that is, major ideas explain how supporting ideas are chunked. (Appendix A explains the process for creating an outline of your ideas.) The chunking process helps us perceive and store information.

As a speaker, you have to help others process information by organizing it into manageable chunks. Make it easy for everyone to put the information together appropriately. If you do this, you increase the odds of competent communication.

Use Multisensory Inputs

Creating memories occurs through our perceptions and our need to use the information later. An audience interprets your message as it is decoded through their senses (the use of multisensory validation is discussed in chapter 3). People remember information better when they perceive it through more than one sense. Research indicates that after three days, individuals remember about 10 percent of what they hear and 20 percent of what they see, but 65 percent of what they both see and hear.[7] Because you must be concerned with the impact of **multisensory input** on the retention of your information, work to encode the message so that others both see and hear it.

One method for increasing the sensory input in a speech is to use visual aids to support the verbal message.[8] As you recall, visual aids are effective tools for presenting statistics, restating the main points or key phrases of the speech, and/or showing the exact steps in a process. Examine the information in your speech to determine which information requires visual aids for reinforcement.

You can also supplement your verbal message with appropriate nonverbal messages.[9] Nonverbal communication, as we discuss in chapter 7, can illustrate, emphasize, or substitute for your verbal statements. Studies indicate that more than half of the attitudinal and emotional content in messages is communicated nonverbally. Nonverbal messages provide additional clues to the meaning of your information. Listeners are better able to understand your information after both

seeing it and hearing you than by hearing the information alone. Nonverbal messages provide additional reinforcement to help the audience remember information.

Gestures, movements, facial expressions, voice, and eye contact enhance the clarity and impact of the verbal message. (Chapter 16 discusses strategies for nonverbal delivery.) Using hands to indicate shapes and sizes, using facial expressions to show pleasure or surprise, using the voice to emphasize important ideas, and using eye contact to increase involvement in the communication affects the understanding and retention of your information. For example, a student giving a speech about the appropriate tennis racket grips when hitting forehand and backhand strokes could illustrate the movements through gestures more clearly and simply than describing the motions or showing pictures of the grips.

"Before You Go On"

You should be able to answer the following question:

What are the advantages to using multisensory media in a speech?

Remembering information is necessary for people to function in our culture. You can construct speeches to help others create strong mental associations between your information and their memories by highlighting important ideas through verbal statements and nonverbal delivery, creating mnemonic devices, and using multisensory inputs through visual aids and nonverbal descriptions. By chunking information; encouraging involvement by everyone through questions, applications, and practicing; and creating immediacy you increase your listener's understanding and ability to remember.

Appendix B includes a speech that illustrates many of the strategies for giving information. As you read "The Exploration of Space" by Richard H. Truly notice the strategies he used to help his audience understand and remember his ideas.

Responses to *"Before You Go On"* Questions: A Chapter Summary

---

1. What are the two primary purposes of sharing information during a speech?

First, the speaker wants to make sure listeners understand the message as it is intended. Second, the speaker wants to make sure that listeners are able to remember information for later use. These related purposes are equally important for communication competence.

2. What are three concerns when creating strategies for increasing understanding?

First, you want to make sure that the audience is paying attention and listening carefully to your speech. Second, you want the audience to co-create shared meanings for the information in your speech. Third, you want listeners to believe you and the information in your speech.

3. What four strategies can you use to help develop shared meanings with your listeners?

First, define words and ideas. One way to ensure your audience understands your words is to define them by citing authorities and dictionaries, through examples, and by analogies. Second, compare and contrast information in your speech. Relate unfamiliar information with information the audience already knows.

Third, use examples to help others co-create shared meaning. Hypothetical examples are relevant, believable, and used to support ideas. Real examples actually occurred and are even better if they actually occurred to you.

Finally, using statistics can help co-create shared meaning. Use statistics carefully, accurately, and honestly; make them meaningful to your listeners.

4. What is accomplished by repeating ideas during a speech?

First, when you repeat information, you are helping to make sure that others perceived it. Second, repeating information reinforces the association with established memories and helps the audience remember it.

5.   How do rhetorical and responsive questions help listeners remember information?

A speaker can ask a rhetorical question to which people mentally respond. When a speaker asks a responsive question, the audience is expected to give a verbal or visual response. Questions increase listeners' involvement with the message and require them to actively relate information to their own experiences.

6.   What are the advantages to using multisensory media in a speech?

The major advantage of using multisensory media is that people tend to remember information better when they have used more than one sense to perceive it. Research suggests that people remember 10 percent of what they hear and 20 percent of what they see; but they remember 65 percent of what they both see and hear.

S T U D E N T   E X E R C I S E S

---

1.   Awareness of information strategies.

Watch your instructors for a week and identify the specific information sharing strategies they use. Keep a log listing the types and frequency of each strategy used. Did some teachers use a lot of repetition? Were others able to involve the audience more actively? Did any of them employ mnemonic devices?

After observing your teachers, decide which teacher was most effective in getting you to listen to and remember the week's material. Did some information sharing strategies seem to work better than others? Why? Which ones were most effective? What insights into your own information sharing strategies did you gain by watching others?

2.   Defining words and phrases.

Define each of the following terms in the left column in five ways by using all of the strategies for definitions on the right.

Word or phrase	*Strategies for definitions*
Friendship	Quoting authoritative sources
Image	Hypothetical examples
Good work	Real examples
Politician	Dictionary
Obfuscation	Analogies

3.   Multisensory input analysis.

Begin by picking up one of the weekly news magazines. Cut out advertisements for a specific car or a particular store. Tape each ad to a separate piece of paper. Now read each one, wait five minutes, and then on the back of the paper write down the information you remember from reading the ad.

Next, listen to radio advertisements for the same car or store. Write down on a sheet of paper the information you remember from listening to the ad.

Finally, watch advertisements on television for the same car or store. Write down on a sheet of paper the information you remember from watching and reading the information on the screen. Again, be sure to identify the car company or store.

Spend a few minutes comparing your lists. Which lists contain the most information? Why does that particular list contain more information than the other lists? If the lists from the television ad contain more information than the others, why is that true? If they contain less, in light of what was discussed in the chapter, why do they?

GLOSSARY

chunking The recognition **or** creation of patterns among differing sets of perceptions; helps listeners to group individual stimuli together to facilitate understanding and memory.

comparison Helping listeners understand your message by relating new information to information the listeners already know by identifying similarities.

contrast Helping listeners understand your message by relating new information with information the listeners already know by pointing out differences.

extraneous messages Messages irrelevant to the purpose and information being communicated to listeners; examples include excessive shifting of weight, overly repetitive gestures or movements, poor eye contact, mispronouncing words, and excessive vocalized pauses.

highlighting Places additional emphasis on an upcoming idea or directs listeners' attention to a specific statement.

immediacy of information A speaker creating an urgent or immediate need for information in the listener; shows listeners that they will need this information soon and should pay attention to it.

mnemonic devices Words, phrases, abbreviations, initials, or acronyms that help people recall information.

multi-sensory inputs Using strategies that require the audience to use more than one of their senses; the more senses they use to perceive information, the better people remember information.

responsive question A question asked by a speaker expecting a verbal or visual response from listeners.

rhetorical question A question asked by a speaker to which listeners mentally respond.

NOTES

1. R. A. Cocetti, "Understanding the Oral Mind: Implications for the Basic Course." Paper presented during the Speech Communication Association meeting, Chicago, Illinois, 1990.

2. R. Whitman and J. Timmis, "The Influence of Verbal Organization Structure and Verbal Organizing Skills on Select Measures of Learning," *Human Communication Research* 1, (1975), 293–301.

3. J. N. Cappella, "The Method of Proof by Example in Interaction Analysis," *Communication Monographs* 57, (1990), 236–42.

4. *Consumer Reports Car Buyers' Guide, 1991,* 12, no. 1, 58.

5. G. Mitchell, *The Trainer's Handbook* (New York: American Management Association, 1987), 23. Mitchell states that people learn better if they can practice what is being taught.

6. G. A. Miller, *The Psychology of Communication* (New York: Basic Books, 1967), 14–43.

7. E. P. Zayas-Bayas, "Instructional Media in the Total Learning Picture," *International Journal of Instructional Media* 5, (1977–1978), 145–50.

8. E. G. Bormann and W. S. Howell, *Presentational Speaking for Business and the Professions* (New York: Harper & Row, 1971), 244–56. Bormann and Howell discuss the Cone of Experiential Experiences in this section of their book and relate it to helping others remember information.

9. A. Mehrabian and S. R. Kerris, "Influence of Attitude from Nonverbal Communication Using Two Channels," *Journal of Consulting Psychology* 31, (1967), 248–52.

Strategies for Persuading Others

W e are constantly assaulted by messages intended to persuade: Advertisers try to persuade television viewers to buy their products. Students try to influence teachers to give them better grades; teachers try to influence students to study hard; and children try to persuade their parents to let them stay up late. Understanding persuasive strategies is critical because of the numerous times you are either the target of a persuasive appeal or try to persuade someone else.

Persuasion is a process of communication that influences attitudes and/or behavior. The assumption is that your attitudes and behavior are related, so a change in one results in a change in the other. The traditional perspective holds that persuasion is related to the modification of attitudes which should, ultimately, lead to a modification of behavior. However, the process could operate in the opposite direction: a change in behavior could lead to a modification in attitudes.[1]

The purpose of a persuasive message is to convince listeners to voluntarily change behaviors or attitudes. If you believe you have no choice but to comply with a persuasive appeal, you may perform the required behavior but not change your attitude. At the earliest opportunity, you may revert back to behaviors more consistent with your established attitudes. If you are convinced that the requested changes are desirable, however, you will believe that you are making the change because you want to do so. Voluntary compliance usually results in more enduring adherence to the proposed change.

Strategies for Identifying Persuasive Goals

To be a successful speaker, you must design persuasive strategies for multiple communication contexts. By understanding the goals of persuasion and the processes by which people change their attitudes or behaviors, you can plan persuasive appeals.

Types of Persuasive Goals

The ultimate goal of persuasion is to effect change in others. In attempting to achieve long-term goals, you have to use persuasive messages often during a persuasive campaign. A campaign involves accomplishing a series of short-term or interim goals leading to the achievement of a larger goal. While an immediate, short-term goal may be to change attitudes *or* behaviors, most persuaders have the long-term goal of changing listeners' attitudes *and* behaviors.

For example, advertisers design television commercials primarily to influence consumers to buy a particular product. Would McDonald's be completely satisfied with simply making you think positively about hamburgers, french fries, or their restaurants? No, the creation of positive attitudes toward McDonald's is a critical step in the persuasive process, but ultimately McDonald's wants you to buy its products.

Conversely, a short-term purpose might be to change your behavior with a long-term goal of changing your attitudes. McDonald's would probably not be satisfied merely with convincing you to buy a hamburger today, if they could not also convince you that McDonald's was a good place to eat in the future.

In the following sections, persuasive goals fall into four categories: continuance, discontinuance, deterrence, and adoption.[2]

Continuance

You may want others to increase the frequency of behaviors they currently perform or to rededicate their efforts toward an already agreed-on goal. The persuasive goal of **continuance** is concerned with reinforcing existing attitudes and behaviors. A persuasive speech at a local political rally for party workers, for example, tries to reinforce current behaviors and attitudes. The candidate is satisfied that the supporters are employing appropriate campaigning techniques, are displaying suitable attitudes toward potential voters, and have the correct perception of their job duties. The politician's purpose, therefore, is to reinforce current behaviors and encourage the campaigners to build additional enthusiasm and strengthen their belief in the campaign.

Discontinuance

When you want listeners to stop doing something, your persuasive goal is **discontinuance.** For example, a student union cafeteria manager had difficulty enforcing an employee no smoking rule while the cafeteria was open for business. The manager finally called all of the student employees together. The manager discussed health and safety issues: smoking near open natural gas burners, inhaling second-hand smoke, and preparing food around smoke and ashes. The goal of this speech was to discontinue employees' smoking behavior.

Deterrence

The persuasive goal of deterrence is accomplished if you convince others not to begin a new behavior or to embrace an attitude that they currently do not hold. For example, two police officers visit a fourth-grade class to talk about drugs. Their intent is to educate students about the dangers of drugs before they find out for themselves through direct experience. The officers' persuasive goal, therefore, is **deterrence,** because they are trying to prevent children from using drugs before they start.

Adoption

The type of behavioral or attitudinal change usually associated with persuasive speeches is adoption of behaviors that people are not currently doing (though they may have done them in the past). Attempting to persuade management to adopt a new payroll system, convincing your friends to join a softball team, and persuading someone to begin an exercise program are examples of adoption. **Adoption** goals focus on the acquisition of new behaviors or the formation of new attitudes.

The persuasion strategies for each purpose are different. The first step in designing a persuasive speech is to decide which persuasive goal or goals to pursue. Base this decision on your initial analysis of the situation and your audience. Such an analysis can prevent you from trying to persuade an audience to adopt a behavior that they already do or to discontinue a practice that they have never done.

"Before You Go On"

You should be able to answer the following question:

What are the different persuasive goals you can have when preparing a public speech?

Strategies for Using Proofs

Assertions are statements about a specific topic that may or may not be valid. When you state that older people make the best employees, you are making an assertion. People could subsequently ask you to defend or prove that statement. In a persuasive speech, the assertion you make becomes the core proposition that guides the development of your message. To develop the proposition, you must provide additional supporting propositions asserting why you think the core proposition is true. For example, in the previous assertion, you could develop supporting propositions such as:

1. Older employees are more dependable in showing up for work.
2. Older employees are more concerned about the quality of their work.
3. Older employees are more likely to figure out problems on their own.

A universal axiom in persuasive speaking is that the speaker has to convince others to change their attitudes and behaviors by proving the propositions are true. Three forms of proof support a proposition: logical proofs, emotional proofs, and personal proofs.[3] You may use any combination of these proofs to convince the audience that the proposition is true.

People are convinced for different reasons. Some people might be convinced that the proposition about older employees is true if you provide them with logical facts. As an example, the absence rate among workers over 60 years old is 22 percent lower than for all other age groups. Others might be convinced if they trust the speaker as an expert. Such a speaker may say, "Trust me. I have hired eighty older workers in the past two years and consider them to be more conscientious, to have more common sense, and to work harder than younger people." Other listeners might be convinced through appeals to their emotions. A speaker could remind them, "You are going to be old someday, too. Do you want to be cast off as an unproductive member of our society? Don't think of older people as elderly, think of them as 'chronologically gifted.' "

You can develop persuasive messages once you understand the forms of proof and their applications in persuasive communication situations.

"Before You Go On"

You should be able to answer the following question:

What three types of proofs can you use to support your persuasive proposition?

Using Logical Proofs

One way to construct a persuasive speech is to support assertions with believable information and arguments. **Logical proofs** appeal to the rational minds of the listeners.[4] This proof assumes others accept the validity of an assertion if they are given good reasons backed by verifiable facts. Information creates, modifies, or reinforces people's attitudes and images of reality.[5] Because attitude change is one of the goals for persuasive speaking, using information to support persuasive propositions and assertions facilitates their acceptance.

Facts in and of themselves do not persuade people to change their attitudes or behaviors. Logical proofs rely on facts and information to structure *arguments*. To formulate an argument, show the relationships between information and the assertion.[6] Construct arguments in the following manner:

1. State the assertion.
2. Provide information related to the assertion.
3. Draw a conclusion about the validity of the assertion (by relating the information to the assertion).

Although these three elements of an argument may be presented in any order, all three must be present in some form to construct a valid argument.

For example, Jane, a student employee working for the university grounds department, wants to convince her supervisor to let her go work on the landscape redesigning project developed by the university facilities department. Jane could have simply stated that she was well-qualified for the task, in which case the supervisor might or might not have believed her. Rather than risk this possible outcome, Jane presented logical proof showing her unique qualifications. She presented supporting information concerning her educational background, and her major in landscape architecture. She mentioned her past experience with similar projects with private landscaping companies, and her abilities to calculate material and plant needs as well as cost. She structured her argument according to the three steps just listed:

Assertion:	I am well qualified for the job.
Information:	a. The person working on this project needs to be knowledgeable, must know surveying methods, plant care, and must have past experience.
	b. I have all of these qualifications: courses in college, experience on three similar projects, and practice in plant installation and maintenance.
Conclusion:	Because I meet all of the requirements, I am well-qualified for the job.

Notice that the conclusion is based on the relationship among the facts presented and the assertion. Be sure to draw specific conclusions from the information you present. Conclusions drawn from information are based on types of reasoning.

Reasoning from Specific Instances

When you argue that your assertion is valid based on examples that illustrate the assertion, you are reasoning from specific instances, often called **inductive reasoning.**[7] People draw conclusions about general assertions from the existence of specific cases. The following argument illustrates this type of reasoning:

Assertion:	Older workers are better than younger workers.
Information:	a. Joe and Alice are the best workers in the company and they are both over fifty-eight years old.
	b. Fourteen of the people I hired who were over fifty-five were outstanding workers.
	c. The older workers in the clerical services department make fewer errors than the younger workers.
Conclusion:	Because lots of examples show older workers are better than younger workers, the assertion is true.

The conclusion is based on reasoning from example; that is, because the examples are true, the general assertion covering all older workers is true. If it is true for some cases, it is true about most cases.

Be cautious about drawing false conclusions based on too few instances or examples that are not representative. Arguments based on a few examples are not persuasive because listeners may perceive the examples to be an exception rather than the rule.

Reasoning from General Rules, Axioms, or Truisms

When you argue that a specific case is true because a general rule is true, you employ **deductive reasoning.**[8] This reasoning is the opposite of reasoning from specific instances. Instead of drawing general conclusions from specific examples, you draw conclusions about specific examples from a general rule. The following argument illustrates reasoning from general rules:

Assertion:	As a general rule, student athletes who are on full athletic scholarships need close supervision.
Information:	Peter is on a full athletic scholarship. Georgia is also on a full athletic scholarship.
Conclusion:	Peter and Georgia need close supervision because they are on full athletic scholarships at the university.

The validity of the conclusion is based on the assumption that a general rule applies to specific cases. Since Peter and Georgia fit into the classification of athletes on full athletic scholarships specified by the general rule, the rule should apply to them.

Speakers must be sure that others accept the validity of the general rule and that they perceive the specific cases to be governed by that rule. When the general rule is false or if the rule does not apply to the specific cases, the reasoning is unsound. In the previous example, listeners may not believe that athletes with full academic scholarships need close supervision or they may feel that only male or only female athletes with full scholarships need close supervision. In any of these instances, listeners would consider your reasoning to be false.

Reasoning from Analogy

People reason from analogy by drawing comparisons between two or more similar ideas or cases. They base the conclusion on the assumption that what is true in one case is true of the other case, since they are similar. For example, consider the previous argument by Jane who wanted to work on the landscaping project. One of the reasons for her belief that she could do the job was her past experiences with similar projects. Her arguments might have been structured as:

Assertion:	The present job is similar to past jobs.
Information:	The jobs require the same skills and knowledge. I was commended for my work on past jobs.

| *Conclusion*: | Because I could do the other job and because that job is similar to the new one, I know I can do the new job. |

In this argument, the validity of the conclusion depends on the degree of similarity between the two jobs. If the supervisor thinks the new job requires skills or knowledge that Jane did not acquire in her previous jobs, the argument is not convincing. Be careful to identify exactly how the comparative cases are alike. When people are not convinced of the similarity, your reasoning cannot persuade them.

Reasoning from Cause to Effect

Cause-to-effect reasoning suggests that an event or condition occurs because of the presence of a previous event or condition. The statements, "Lightning causes thunder," and "Missing my bus caused me to be late," are simple examples of cause-to-effect reasoning. In each case, the cause is a previously occurring event or condition resulting in a subsequent event or condition. The following message illustrates cause-to-effect reasoning:

Assertion:	Paying Henry more money will motivate Henry to study harder.
Information:	People will work if they need money. Henry needs money to go on dates, play golf, put gas in his car, pay car insurance, and buy new clothes. Henry has studied harder in the past when given more money.
Conclusion:	Giving Henry more money will cause him to study harder.

Cause-to-effect reasoning is valid to the degree that the result can be directly related to a specific event or antecedent condition. The validity of the reasoning is also increased if the effects can only be the result of the specified causes; that is, there is only one possible set of causes for a specific event. Listeners who perceive that a different set of events may account for the result will not be convinced that your argument is valid. In Henry's case, people may assume that he will study harder for a variety of reasons: future employment, self-satisfaction, pride, and/or personal growth. If all of these causes can produce the same effect, then money alone might not be enough to produce the desired outcome of Henry studying harder.

"Before You Go On"

You should be able to answer the following question:

What forms of reasoning are available to you in creating a persuasive argument?

Choosing the correct form of the argument depends on the audience's knowledge about the topic and the nature of the relationship between the assertions made in the speech and the information included to support them. By working diligently, you can construct valid arguments, that is, make clear assertions, provide sufficient information, and draw specific conclusions.

Using Emotional Proofs

By appealing to their emotions, people can also be persuaded that your assertions are acceptable. By using logical proofs, you can establish belief in the assertion through reasoned argument. With emotional proofs, you persuade others to accept the assertion through appeals to feelings and emotions. **Emotional proofs** depend on your abilities to vividly describe emotional events and to involve others in emotional situations.

Emotions are feelings and sentiments such as fear, joy, anxiety, pride, and love. For instance, listeners may react with strong emotions to a speech on drunk driving if their relatives or close friends were killed or injured by drunk drivers. The emotion of fear may result in adoption of new beliefs or behaviors. Advertisers attempt to arouse our emotions of fun and adventure to persuade us to buy their products (manufacturers of diet drinks and sports cars, health insurance, life insurance, cereals, and cosmetics). They appeal to pride in our country or community to convince us to join an organization (the National Rifle Association, the National Organization of Women, or the American Civil Liberties Union). Or, they request that we contribute money to charity by appealing to sympathy, love, and our need to help others (The American Cancer Society, the American Heart Association, Planned Parenthood, or the local United Way). The armed forces recruit volunteers through appeals to adventure and patriotism, and encouragement to "be all that you can be."

When people respond emotionally to messages, they often disregard the facts surrounding the topic, situation, and/or speaker. Speakers may use emotional appeals to arouse interest in and acceptance of assertions more effectively than by using logical appeals.

SECURITY BLANKET

You invest to grow. To help provide a better tomorrow for you and your family.

To select an investment is an act of trust.

For years, families all over America have felt secure in placing that trust in the Kemper name.

Ask your financial representative about the investment products of Kemper Financial Services.

• Kemper Money Market Fund
• Kemper Mutual Funds
• Kemper Tax-Advantaged Insurance

For more complete information about these investment products including charges and expenses obtain a prospectus by calling 1-800-621-1048. Read them carefully before you invest or send money. Insurance products issued by Kemper Investors Life Insurance Company.

Kemper Financial

A concern for your future.

For example, the faculty at a major university were threatening to strike because of low salary increases and budget cutbacks. Economic facts and logical appeals did not seem to change the faculty's opinion that the university was being unfair. A university administrator gave a speech attempting to persuade the faculty union not to strike by appealing to their loyalty to the university and its students. She described the university as a big family, stressed the warmth and regard the administration had for its faculty. She emphasized the tradition of faculty pride in and loyalty to the university. By citing examples of employees'

GUESS

GUESS   Westside Pavilion   (213) 470-9910
GUESS   South Coast Plaza   (714) 540 -6702

dedication to the university and the university's assistance to employees with personal and financial problems, she made the emotional appeals vivid. Her appeals to emotions of pride and loyalty were effective, whereas logical proof at the bargaining table had failed to persuade the faculty not to strike.

When arousing emotions, be sure to provide an outlet for people's feelings. Emotions provide a reason to change; when others are emotionally aroused, they need a target for their behavior. Research on fear appeals, for example, indicate that fear is usually effective in persuading people only when they were told specific ways to reduce the fear or to avoid the danger.[9] For example, advocates of

U.S. and allied military intervention in the Persian Gulf argued that Saddam Hussein must be stopped before he became an even bigger threat in the future. Iraq's president was portrayed as someone willing to kill his own people with chemical bombs. Noted for his ruthlessness in killing family members, he was presented as a bully who would conquer and kill defenseless people. He was referred to as the new Hitler who would not stop until he ruled the Middle East. Through appeals to our fears of a great danger to the world's future, many people were convinced that the only solution was to take military action to force Iraqi troops out of Kuwait and to defeat Saddam Hussein.

Emotional appeals may fail to be effective if others perceive that you are trying to manipulate them. When emotional appeals are too obvious, overstated, or overly dramatic, people perceive them as insincere attempts to manipulate. For instance, many people rejected involvement in the Iraq situation because they believed the references to Hitler and the descriptions of ruthless killing were exaggerated. People who believe their emotions are being exploited, discount the speaker's message.

Using Personal Proofs

Personal proofs are also referred to as *credibility*. You may convince others to accept the validity of your assertions because of who you are rather than due to logical or emotional appeals. Credibility is the respect and regard others have for you.[10] Credibility is given to you by others; it is not a characteristic you are born with or possess. Several important factors influence listeners' perceptions of your credibility. Commonly accepted dimensions of credibility are expertise, trustworthiness, and dynamism.

Expertise

People considered experts on specific topics are believed whether or not they provide logical reasons or emotional appeals. People are perceived as experts because of their roles or status within the community, their academic or professional credentials, or their experience. People believe that physicians are correct in their diagnoses of illnesses because they are doctors. A new student may accept assertions concerning the proper procedures for using the university library and physical fitness facilities because the upperclass student presenting the information has been attending the university and using these facilities for some time.

Sometimes credibility based on our perceptions of another person's expertise can be misplaced. We must be careful not to generalize expertise on one topic to other topics outside the person's actual area of expertise. This *halo effect* occurs when people perceive the speaker as an expert on all topics because this person is an expert on one topic. For example, an individual may have twenty years' experience as a test pilot and astronaut. As a consequence, others could believe the person to be an expert on over-the-counter drugs, automobile parts, computers, or international affairs as well. This may not be true.

Trustworthiness

People believe the assertions of people they trust. Trust is developed through our experiences with others, through information we get from other sources, and from impressions we have about other persons based on our impressions of their appearance and mannerisms. Trustworthiness includes perceptions of a speaker's honesty, fairness, morality, and good will.

If others decide that you are trying to help them and have their interests in mind during the speech, they are more likely to trust you and believe you. When you distrust a speaker because of appearance, a past betrayal, or a doubtful character, you disregard the speaker's assertions.

Dynamism

People believe assertions made with enthusiasm and confidence. Be emphatic in stating your assertion; often your confidence makes a statement sound valid and believable. People believe speakers who are active, passionate, and lively more than those who are soft-spoken, dull, and understated. They base their judgments of dynamism on the speaker's vocal variety, volume, facial expression, eye contact, gestures, and movements. Listeners perceive dynamic speakers as credible partially because of their enthusiastic and forceful styles of delivery.

For instance, at a neighborhood meeting about storm damage resulting from flooded streets and backed up sanitary sewers, a rather quiet, reserved neighbor offered a suggestion to solve the water drainage problems that caused flooding in many houses. Hesitantly, and without noticeable conviction, he suggested building a retaining pool, cleaning the storm sewers, and widening the local run-off creek. The other neighbors at the meeting immediately objected to these suggestions. After a brief discussion, another neighbor made essentially the same suggestions with confidence and enthusiasm. Using vivid language, rising from her chair and walking to the front of the room, smiling, and gesturing emphatically, she repeated the initial suggestions and called for a vote. Surprisingly, without further discussion and with essentially no new information, the neighbors voted to adopt the solutions she presented. The conviction in her voice helped persuade others to adopt the original suggestions. The point is that a dynamic speaking style influences believability and acceptance of a proposition.

A speaker may be perceived as credible on all three dimensions or only one or two. A trustworthy expert may be believed despite a less than dynamic delivery. Someone who is dynamic may be believed even though not an expert. Conversely, a person who is untrustworthy may not be believed even though he or she is dynamic and knowledgeable. When you speak, capitalize on others' perceptions of your expertise, trustworthiness, and dynamism. Whenever possible, tell your audience why you are an expert based on your personal experience with a topic, your specialized training, your work experience, your research efforts. Tell them you can be trusted, you are trying to help them, and you have their interests in mind. And, show them you are confident and enthusiastic about your assertions through vivid language and emphatic delivery.

"Before You Go On"

You should be able to answer the following question:

What are the three commonly held dimensions of credibility?

Emotional, logical, and personal proofs help others believe and accept assertions. Competent persuasive situations require that speakers use each of the three forms of proof appropriately to persuade others to understand and accept their ideas.

Organizing the Persuasive Speech

The initial step in developing a persuasive speech is to determine exactly which change you want others to make (adoption, deterrence, discontinuance, continuance). Once you have selected the change, decide which forms of proof influence the particular audience's attitudes and behaviors. Finally, determine the best strategy to organize your persuasive appeals to create interest and involvement in your message.

Two useful strategies for persuasive speaking are strategies based on others' needs and strategies based on others' attitudes.

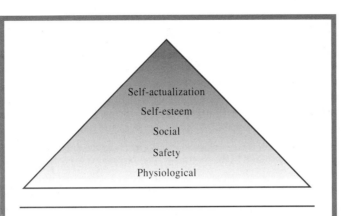

FIGURE 18.1
Maslow's hierarchy of needs.

Self-actualization: need to reach your full potential; to grow and develop.

Self-esteem: need to feel good about the self; to receive positive feedback.

Social: need to belong; to form social relationships; to like and be liked by others.

Safety: need to feel secure and protected.

Physiological: need to survive and maintain health.

The most important need at any specific time is the lowest need that is unfulfilled.

Persuasive Strategies Based on Others' Needs

One approach to understanding how to change others' attitudes and behaviors is *need reduction theory.* As shown in figure 18.1, it suggests people behave in particular ways to satisfy unfulfilled needs.[11] Persuasive strategies based on this theory create, identify, or emphasize the needs of others and demonstrate how those needs can be satisfied.

The first step in developing persuasive strategies based on need reduction theory is to determine which needs are most relevant to the topic and other people. Analysis of others' involvement and characteristics can provide clues as to which needs are most salient. Fast-food chains, for example, create different advertisements to appeal to a wide variety of their clients' needs. Ads emphasizing quality food and low prices appeal to our basic needs for food and saving money. Ads emphasizing cleanliness and the image of the restaurant being a home-away-from-home focus on our needs for safety and security. Other ads emphasize our social needs of being with friends and family. Still other ads illustrate ways in which the chain boosts community spirit and supports charities, appealing to the pride and self-esteem through helping others. Advertisers design each ad to appeal to the needs of a specific group. Persuasive speakers also spend time ascertaining specific needs that can persuade others to adopt desired changes in attitudes or behavior.

One specific organizational pattern helpful in pointing out needs and ways to satisfy them is Monroe's Motivated Sequence.[12] This sequence suggests a general pattern of problem solving useful in gaining acceptance for a specific proposal (see the discussion in chapter 5).

Monroe's Motivated Sequence

Step 1: *Getting Attention*

Arousing listener interest in the topic
Focusing the listeners' attention on the message

Step 2: *Showing the Need: Describing the Problem*

Explaining what is wrong with current situation	(statement)
Clarifying the problems with examples	(illustration)
Showing the extent and the seriousness of need	(ramification)
Relating the problem directly to the listener	(pointing)

Step 3: *Satisfying the Need: Presenting the Solution*

Stating the proposed changes from the present	(statement)
Explaining the mechanics of the solution	(explanation)
Showing how the solution solves the problem	(demonstration)
Showing that the proposal is workable	(practicality)
Answering objections to the proposal	(rebuttal)

Step 4: *Visualizing the Results*

Describe future benefits if the plan is adopted	(positive projection)
Describe future consequences if the plan is not adopted	(negative projection)
Describe both positive and negative projections	(contrast)

Step 5: *Requesting Action or Approval*

Describing specific actions for listeners to take
Asking for commitment from the listeners

Attention Step

The first step in every speech is to gain the attention of the audience. An audience that isn't listening cannot recall information, understand ideas, or be persuaded by your assertions and supporting materials.

Need Step

In a persuasive speech, identify a specific need and bring it to the audience's attention. Once the audience has focused on the need for action or change, you can explain its significance and relevance to them. State the need clearly and explain it so that all members of the audience see its relevance to them (immediacy). Show the significance or magnitude of the need or problem by providing proof that the problem is not limited to a few examples but is widespread. Once you have presented the need, shown that it exists by using examples, demonstrated the magnitude of the need, and made it relevant to each person, the audience should be ready to listen to your plan for satisfying the need.

Satisfaction Step

State your plan for satisfying the need specifically and in sufficient detail to persuade others that it can satisfy the need. Before they can approve a plan, the audience must understand how it works and realize its relationship to the need.

A helpful strategy for gaining acceptance of a plan is to anticipate the audience's objections and answer them during your speech. In many cases, objections concern the workability of the plan such as financial constraints, time demands, or excessive demands on the individuals involved. To counter these objections, provide specific answers and information to show the cost and time are justified and that the people executing the plan would not be unnecessarily burdened.

Visualization Step

People can be convinced to change behaviors if they are told the benefits of adopting the plan or the disadvantages of not adopting the plan. An excellent strategy for describing the effects is to have others imagine what the future would be like after adopting the plan. The visualization can focus on the benefits of satisfying the need, or the dissatisfaction and problems if the plan is not adopted.

Action Step

The final step in developing a persuasive speech using the needs strategy is to make a specific call for action. The conclusion to a persuasive speech based on needs reduction should be similar to conclusions for other speeches. It should summarize the major reasons for change, restate the plan, reemphasize the advantages of adopting the proposal, and end with a strong and memorable closing statement. Prior to the closing statement, remind everyone specifically what action they are to perform. Identify the behavior they should adopt to satisfy their needs, and try to provide an immediate opportunity for them to commit themselves to a course of action. The more specific and immediate the action step is, the better the chances of your plan gaining acceptance.

To summarize the application of need reduction theory to a persuasive message, let's examine a sales trainer's persuasive speech to new salespeople. The product is high-quality cookware sold door-to-door during the summer and just before Christmas. The sales trainer called the sales force to a meeting with the goal of persuading them to increase their sales by doubling the number of calls they made each week and by explaining the three *C*'s of closing (see the example of using repetition and mnemonics in chapter 17).

The sales trainer began by asking the salespeople to state how many calls they made and how many sales they closed. After each response, the trainer looked sad and offered everyone condolences. The audience knew immediately that the problem was the number of calls they were making and that it was their problem. The trainer had *gained their attention* quickly and dramatically.

Then the trainer proceeded to *create the need* and make it significant. Graphs indicated the number of sales calls made in this area compared with the average of similar groups in other cities. The trainer cited statistics indicating that overall sales in the area were dropping. Each statistic showing a decrease in sales was related to the money the company and the sales force were losing.

Once the need was established, the trainer moved to the *satisfaction step* which proposed a plan to satisfy the need by increasing sales. The trainer discussed the three *C*'s of closing, went through a demonstration of the method with a volunteer, and gave each person a copy of the procedures to take home and review. He showed the plan was workable through the live demonstration.

The *visualization step* was perhaps the most dramatic and most convincing strategy used by the trainer. The trainer asked the group to visualize how much additional money they could make in commissions if they used the three *C*'s of closing and increased sales by just one customer each week. Since the commission in a single set of cookware was $50, the trainer handed a $50 bill to a salesperson in the front row. The trainer asked the salesperson to tell everyone what she could do with the extra $50. On hearing the answer, the trainer smiled and asked if the person would like to have an extra $100, or perhaps $500 each month. Of course, she answered yes! The trainer observed that if each of the sales staff could sell just ten more sets of cookware each month, only a couple per week, in a year's time they would have not $50, or $500, but $6,000. At that point, the trainer opened a briefcase, took out 600 $10 bills and threw them into the group.

All that remained for the trainer was the *action step*. He asked the salespeople to raise their hands if they believed the plan would help them increase sales. Next, they had a chance to practice the closing technique with the other salespeople. Finally, he asked the group to make sales calls immediately and return at five o'clock with orders in their hands. Each member of the sales staff left the room committed to the goal of using the new technique.

A persuasive speech following need reduction theory capitalizes on everyone's desire to satisfy unfulfilled needs. Speakers use strategies to arouse specific needs in listeners and provide specific means by which to meet those needs. The assertion of needs, the workability of the plan, and the effects of the plan require proof using logical, emotional, and/or personal appeals. Application of the communication skills of analysis, organization of ideas, phrasing of statements, and nonverbal communication are all essential elements of persuasive speeches.

Persuasive Strategies Based on Attitudes

Attitudes vary in specificity, stability, and strength. Some attitudes are general, vague opinions such as, education is important, or I'm politically conservative. Others are very specific such as, minorities must have the opportunity to attend the colleges of their choice, or women should not be allowed to engage in combat. Some attitudes are very strong and stable such as, "I will always be a Republican," or "There's no way you can change my mind that abortion is wrong." Others are weakly held such as, "I'm sort of a Republican, but I'm not sure how I'll vote in the election," or "I think a living will is a good idea, but I don't know how I would feel if I were in a coma."

People tolerate a range of attitudes that are closely related. We may be willing to accept the validity of a variety of positions that are similar. We reject positions that are too different from our attitudes. Strategies based on changing attitudes increase or decrease the range of our acceptance and rejection. The more specific our attitudes, the fewer attitudes that are perceived as similar, and hence the fewer the attitude positions we accept. The stronger and more stable the individual's attitude, the less likely it is to change. Analyze the strength and stability of listeners' attitudes toward your assertions so you can choose appropriate strategies for constructing your persuasive message.[13]

Strive for Incremental Changes in Attitudes

Do not expect immediate acceptance of a behavior initially rejected by your audience. Instead, design your speech to gradually shift attitudes toward the desired goal through a series of smaller, incremental changes. Through a series of assertions during a speech or sequence of speeches, you may move others gradually to your desired attitude position.

People involved in advertising campaigns, political campaigns, sales presentations, and business policy changes adopt this strategy when trying to persuade people to change well-defined, stable attitudes.[14] In politics, for example, people usually resist changing significantly from their established political views. "But I've always voted for Democrats," or "But I've been a Republican all my life," or "I would never join a political party," are common responses to persuasive speeches aimed at changing voting patterns. However, political stances can be changed through incremental decisions, that is, decisions making small changes in political orientation. Over time, a series of incremental changes, each close to the current procedure or policy, can result in a shift in the original preferences.

You can sometimes be more effective by striving for smaller changes in attitude positions than by attempting to make radical changes that others will reject immediately. An example of this is trying to change attitudes toward abortion or capital punishment. When listeners' attitudes are strongly for or against these issues, the likelihood of quickly changing their attitudes is not very promising.

Refute Arguments against the Desired Attitude Position

You may find that others have strong reasons for rejecting your attitude position. Simply showing positive reasons why your position is valid is not sufficient. You have to develop strategies demonstrating why their arguments against your position are not valid. Refuting their reasons is an effective strategy to decrease their rejection.[15] Read the following statement illustrating how you might refute listeners' attitudes regarding motorcycle helmet laws:

> If you believe that mandatory motorcycle helmet laws are unconstitutional, all my arguments about safety will be unconvincing. You might even agree with me about safety but reject my position because of your strong attitude toward the right to choose. First, I will explain the Supreme Court's reasons for concluding that helmet laws are, indeed, constitutional. Your right to choose is not being violated by any law that seeks to protect you from harm.

One method for convincing others that their reasons for holding attitudes are invalid is to refute the evidence supporting their attitudes. If you can show others that the facts and information on which their attitudes are based are incorrect, biased, or outdated, they are more likely to shift their attitudes. Consider the following message advocating that a neighborhood be incorporated into the city:

> I know that many of you think incorporating our neighborhood into the city is wrong. You have heard that the city's financial health is questionable and that the state is conducting an audit to attest to its poor financial condition. If this were true, I would agree that we should not be incorporated. However, these assumptions are no longer true. I have received the report from the state auditor attesting to the financial stability of the city. The city's latest financial statement indicates a healthy increase in cash reserves and a solid financial future. Educational and civic leaders around the state have affirmed that our neighborhood being incorporated into the city will be in our best interest and in the best interest of our children for decades to come.

Notice how the speaker defined the opposing arguments and then refuted the evidence and facts supporting them. Once the reasons for holding a negative attitude toward incorporation were questioned, the audience might be more likely to listen to the reasons for change.

When you advance arguments against currently held positions, do it early in your persuasive speech. If you only present one side of the issue or if you wait until late in your speech to refute counterarguments, others are less likely to listen to your arguments with open minds. As long as they have unrefuted reasons for rejecting your position, others listen to your message with a great deal of skepticism. By demonstrating that their rejection is inappropriate, you have a better chance of changing their attitudes to the position you advocate.

Show that the Desired Attitude Position Meets Accepted Criteria

Another strategy for counteracting rejection is to demonstrate that your position meets their own criteria for acceptance. In using this strategy, develop criteria on which others would judge the acceptability of your attitude position. If possible, use criteria others already believe are valid and currently use to decide the acceptability of their attitudes. Once others accept the criteria as a valid method for judgment, you must show that the attitude you want them to accept meets that criteria. The following example illustrates the use of this strategy:

> I think we can all agree that there are two basic criteria which any proposal for a salary increase for our part-time sales staff must meet. First, it must be fair to the part-time employees. Second, it must be flexible enough to meet ever-changing economic conditions. If a proposal fails to meet either of these criteria, it must be rejected; if it meets both of these criteria, it should be accepted. If you carefully examine the proposal currently being considered, you will notice that it has an across-the-board increase for all the part-time workers. At the same time, it includes a merit increase structure to reward exceptional part-time workers. What could be more fair? It also contains provisions for adjustments in the base pay scale to meet increases in inflation and to benefit from increased profits. This proposal is fair to all part-time workers and is flexible enough to adapt to changing economic conditions. I propose it should be adopted.

In this example, the speaker established criteria with which the audience could agree. The proposal was then shown to meet each of the criteria.

Take care to establish valid criteria that others accept and to use all of the criteria they will use to decide the acceptability of your proposal. If you do not discuss a particular criterion that others consider important, they are likely to reject your proposal. In the previous example, people could reject the proposal if they believe the salary increase must also meet the criterion that the pay scale be the highest in the community. Showing that a desired change meets the accepted criteria is an effective strategy for persuading others.

Inoculate the Listeners Against Future Counterarguments

Especially important in meeting continuance and deterrence persuasive goals is reinforcing existing attitudes. In seeking adoption and discontinuance, you want to persuade people to adopt a new attitude position and to ensure that they maintain that position in the future. Much as a doctor inoculates a patient against exposure to disease, speakers can inoculate others against possible arguments challenging their new attitude positions.

One way to maintain and reinforce existing attitudes is to present both sides of an issue, or a two-sided argument.[16] Even though results of research are somewhat inconsistent, two-sided arguments are usually more persuasive and can strengthen the listeners' resistance to counterarguments.

By showing others arguments against their established positions and providing counterarguments, you provide reasons they can use to discount future arguments attacking their attitudes. Sometimes referred to as *inoculation theory,* this exposure to unfavorable arguments warns others to be prepared for disagreement. By helping them understand the counterarguments and helping others practice refuting them, you decrease the likelihood that unfavorable arguments can change their attitudes.[17] This idea is called emotional inoculation. For example, a patient decided to have an operation. The doctor tried to prepare the patient for the negative side effects so she could deal with them. The patient anticipated the side effects and constantly repeated arguments to persuade herself that she made the right decision even though she experienced some pain. She maintained a positive attitude toward the operation because the doctor had prepared her for negative consequences and she was able to counter their impact on her attitudes toward the operation.[18]

A second way to reinforce a commitment to and the stability of attitudes is to use *follow-up messages.* This is different than merely repeating what you have already said. It is following up the initial message with additional messages reinforcing the reasons for holding attitudes. Remind others that their attitudes are appropriate and reinforce their reasons for holding those attitudes. This makes the attitudes more stable for each person. If they receive little or no reinforcement, listeners are more likely to later change their attitude positions. People who are persuaded to quit smoking often need repeated reminders and motivational messages to reinforce the appropriateness of their new attitudes.

"Before You Go On"

You should be able to answer the following question:

What strategies are available when attempting to change others' attitudes?

Design your persuasive messages through careful analysis of your audience and by choosing those persuasive strategies that best meet your audience's characteristics. No single persuasive strategy is guaranteed to work for all people in all situations. Persuasion is not an action you perform or something that you do to people. The transaction approach to communication requires that the audience and speaker cooperate to determine the effects of persuasive messages. The persuasive strategies we have discussed help people cooperate to create competent persuasive communication.

1.   What are the different persuasive goals you can have when preparing a public speech?

The four persuasive goals for a public speaker are continuance, discontinuance, deterrence, and adoption.

In the persuasive goal of continuance, you seek to increase the frequency of behaviors or to rededicate your listeners' efforts toward an already agreed-on goal. Discontinuance is just the opposite. You try to get your listeners to stop doing something or stop believing something.

With a goal of deterrence, you seek to have the audience refrain from beginning something they are not currently doing or to accept a belief or perception they currently do not hold. Adoption is similar to deterrence. However, in this case you try to get your listeners to do something or adopt a new belief or perception.

2.   What three types of proofs can you use to support your persuasive proposition?

The three forms of proofs are logical proofs, emotional proofs, and personal proofs (credibility). Logical proofs suggest that the speaker use reasoning or logic to support propositions. Evidence, testimony, statistics, and other forms of data are used when reasoning with listeners. Emotional proofs are appeals to listeners' emotions. Fear, anger, love, and disgust are emotional proofs commonly used in persuasive speeches. Personal proofs relate to the amount of trust listeners put in you and your ideas. You can enhance your credibility in your speech by using believable sources and oral footnotes in your persuasive speech.

3.   What forms of reasoning are available to you in creating a persuasive argument?

You can reason from a specific instance (inductive reasoning). In this case, you are drawing conclusions from specific instances or events. You can reason from general rules, axioms or truisms (deductive reasoning). In this case, you are drawing conclusions to specific instances from general rules or facts. A speaker can also argue from analogy in a persuasive speech. When using this type of reasoning, you are drawing similarities between two or more similar ideas. Finally, you can argue from cause to effect in persuasive speeches. You are trying to draw relationships between current and past events or current and future events.

4.   What are the commonly held dimensions of credibility?

The three dimensions of credibility are expertise, trustworthiness, and dynamism. Expertise is related to your past experience with a topic, your knowledge of the topic, and the listeners' awareness of these things. Trustworthiness refers to the amount of belief listeners place in your propositions and ideas. Dynamism refers to the enthusiasm and confidence that a speaker demonstrates during the delivery of the speech.

Strategies for Persuading Others

5.   What are the five steps of the Motivated Sequence?

The five steps of the Motivated Sequence are attention, need, satisfaction, visualization, and action. In the attention step you work to gain the interest of the audience. The need step dictates that you create a need or problem for the audience. In the satisfaction step, you present your solution to the problem just created in the need step. The visualization step allows you to demonstrate how well your solution solves the problem or satisfies the need. Finally, in the action step you try to gain immediate commitment or action.

6.   What strategies are available when attempting to change others' attitudes?

When trying to change others' attitudes, you have several strategies available. First, you can strive for incremental changes in attitudes. This enables you to change others' attitudes in small parts, eventually attaining your total persuasive purpose. A second strategy is to refute arguments against your desired attitude position. For every change you seek, there are arguments against your change. You have to anticipate these arguments and develop messages to refute them.

A third strategy is to show that your desired attitude position meets generally accepted criteria. If you can demonstrate that your proposed change in attitude meets listeners' criteria for acceptance, it is easier to achieve your persuasive purpose. Finally, you should inoculate your audience against future counterarguments. Provide them with the information necessary to counter arguments against the attitude change you advocated.

S T U D E N T   E X E R C I S E S

1.   Developing strategies based on need reduction theory.

Choose one of the following propositions. Construct an outline of a speech you might give in class that follows the steps of the Motivated Sequence. Specifically label each step in the outline. (If you find yourself on the opposite side of any of these issues, develop a speech reflecting your own point of view.)

   a. The United States Supreme Court should hear more cases.
   b. The United States allows too many immigrants into the country each year.
   c. The university should adopt a no smoking policy on the entire campus.
   d. The National Rifle Association should spend more money in fighting gun registration laws.
   e. Consumers have the right to know what ingredients are included in all products they might purchase.

2.   Constructing logical proofs.

By showing the relationship between an assertion and supporting information, we formulate logical arguments. Try to construct a logical argument for each of the following assertions. Use each form of reasoning for each assertion. The forms of reasoning are reasoning from instances, reasoning from rules, reasoning from analogy, and reasoning from cause to effect.

1. I deserve a raise at my current place of work.
2. The university should guarantee a convenient place to park for all students.
3. It is not reasonable for students to have to wait in lines to register, change registration, or pay any bills at the university.
4. Every student who graduates from high school or passes the high school equivalency test should be guaranteed a college education.

What type of information and supporting material was necessary to develop each type of reasoning? Share your arguments with others. Were they persuaded?

3.   Constructing emotional proofs.
Using the assertions in exercise 2, construct an argument for each using emotional proofs. Identify a specific emotion that would be persuasive for each assertion. Write a short statement or message illustrating an appeal to that emotion.

4.   Constructing personal proofs.
Using the assertions in exercise 2, construct an argument for each using personal proofs (credibility). Write a short statement illustrating that you are trustworthy, have expertise, and are dynamic.

5.   Applying the concepts of need reduction theory.
Commercials often appeal to consumers' needs to sell a product or service. Watch one hour of television, listen to the radio for one hour, or look through a popular magazine. Make a list of all the commercials you see, hear, or read. For each commercial or ad, identify the specific needs to which the ad or commercial appeals. Which needs were appealed to most frequently? Were there any trends in the type of needs and type of product sold?

Do you notice any trends that might be helpful to you in developing needs in your persuasive speeches? Make a list on a note card of the needs most frequently used. Keep it for future reference when you prepare your persuasive speech for class.

GLOSSARY

adoption A persuasive goal when you try to convince your audience to start a new behavior or adhere to a new attitude or belief.

assertions Statements a speaker makes on a certain topic that may or may not be true; the speaker attempts to persuade the audience that the assertion is true or valid.

continuance A persuasive goal where the speaker wants to reinforce others' attitudes or beliefs, or urges them to continue to do what they are doing.

deductive reasoning When you argue that a specific case or instance is true or accurate because it fits into a general truism, rule, or axiom.

deterrence A persuasive goal when you try to prevent others from beginning a new behavior or adopting a new attitude or belief.

discontinuance A persuasive goal where you try to get your audience to stop doing something they are doing or believing something they believe.

emotional proofs Supporting an assertion by using proofs that appeal to others' emotions or passions; used frequently in contemporary media advertisements.

inductive reasoning Making a generalization to a broad class of events or instances based on a specific instance or event.

logical proofs The use of reason and evidence to support assertions in a persuasive speech; using a rational approach to persuade others that an assertion is true or valid.

personal proofs Also known as credibility; using the characteristics of trustworthiness, expertise, and dynamism to help people believe what you are telling them.

persuasion A process of communication influencing attitudes and behaviors.

N O T E S

1. For historical explanations of the relationship between persuasion and communication, see C. Hovland, I. Janis, and H. Kelly, *Communication and Persuasion* (New Haven, Conn.: Yale University Press, 1953); or M. Sherif, C. Sherif, and R. Nebergall, *Attitude and Attitude Change* (Philadelphia: Saunders, 1965).

2. F. C. Fotheringham, *Perspectives on Persuasion* (Boston: Allyn and Bacon, 1966).

3. L. Cooper, *The Rhetoric of Aristotle* (New York: Appleton-Century-Crofts, 1932). This translation of Aristotle's writings offers the reader a clear explanation of the three forms of proof: ethos, logos, and pathos.

4. For explanations of how to develop rational arguments, see C. Perelman and L. Olbrechts-Tyteca, *The New Rhetoric: A Treatise on Argumentation* (London: University of Notre Dame Press, 1969); or M. J. Smith, *Persuasion and Human Action* (Belmont, Calif.: Wadsworth Publishing Company, 1982).

5. K. Boulding, *The Image: Knowledge and Life in Society* (Ann Arbor: University of Michigan Press, 1977).

6. S. Toulmin, *The Uses of Argument* (London: Cambridge University Press, 1958).

7. J. Z. DeWitt, "The Rhetoric of Induction at the French Academy," *Quarterly Journal of Speech* 69, (1983), 412–22.

8. V. E. Cohen and N. Mihevc, "The Evaluation of Deductive Argument: A Process Analysis," *Communication Monographs* 39, (1972), 124–31.

9. K. L. Higbee, "Fifteen Years of Fear Arousal: Research on Threat Appeals," *Psychological Bulletin* 72, (1969), 426–44.

10. C. C. Staley and J. L. Cohen, "Communicator Style and Social Style: Similarities and Differences between the Sexes," *Communication Quarterly* 36, (1988), 192–202.

11. A. H. Maslow, *Motivation and Personality,* 2nd ed. (New York: Harper & Row, 1970).

12. D. Ehninger, B. E. Gronbeck, and A. H. Monroe, *Principles of Speech Communication,* 9th Brief Ed. (Glenview, Ill.: Scott, Foresman, 1984).

13. W. F. Eadie and J. W. Paulson, "Communicator Attitudes, Communicator Style, and Communication Competence," *Western Journal of Speech Communication* 48, (1984), 390–407.

14. G. J. Shepherd, "Linking Attitudes and Behavioral Criteria," *Human Communication Research* 12, (1985), 275–84.

15. J. C. Reinard, "The Role of Toulmin's Categories of Message Development in Persuasive Communication: Two Experimental Studies on Attitude Change," *The Journal of the American Forensics Association* 20, (1984), 206–23.

16. M. Karlins and H. I. Abelson, *Persuasion: How Opinions and Attitudes Are Changed,* 2nd ed. (New York: Springer Publishing, 1970).

17. M. Pfau, H. C. Kenski, M. Nitz, and J. Sorenson, "Efficacy of Inoculation Strategies in Promoting Resistance to Political Attack Messages: Application to Direct Mail," *Communication Monographs* 57, (1990), 25–43.

18. I. Janis and L. Mann, *Decision Making: A Psychological Analysis of Conflict, Choice, and Commitment* (New York: Free Press, 1977), 157–59.

Guidelines for Outlining

Fundamentals of Outlining

Outlining is the process by which you construct a visual blueprint of your message. Outlines can take several forms: a full-sentence outline, full-phrase outline, and key-word outline. All outlines, however, follow three general principles which enable you to show the order and relationship of your ideas.

Principle 1:

Outlines Show Subordination of Ideas

When you are planning a message, you have some ideas that are more important than others. You want these ideas to stand out in the message so that listeners are sure to understand and remember them. These ideas are called *main ideas* or *main propositions*. Each main idea may also need explanation and support to show that it is true or to help develop it. Ideas that develop the main points are called *subordinate ideas,* or *supporting propositions*.

The outline shows which ideas are main ideas and which ideas are subordinate ideas through the use of symbols and indentation. Main ideas are designated by Roman numerals (I, II, III, IV) and subordinate ideas by capital letters (A, B, C), lowercase letters (*a, b, c*), and Arabic numerals (1, 2, 3). Examine the sample outline and notice how each main idea is designated with a Roman numeral and each succeeding subordinate idea is labeled with letters or numbers. Normally, each successive subordination of ideas uses a different style of nomenclature, alternating between letters and numbers. This is illustrated in the accompanying box entitled Outline Showing Principle of Subordination.

    I.   Your company benefits package includes comprehensive insurance coverage.

        A.   Health care is provided in the hospitalization plan.

            1.   The company pays the total premium for your hospitalization insurance.

                a.   This practice saves you $200 to $300 per year.

                b.   We pay premiums for yourself and your family.

            2.   The company also provides coverage for catastrophic illnesses.

                a.   This type of coverage is seldom part of benefits packages.

                b.   We pay 80 percent of costs for any catastrophic illness.

        B.   Life insurance is also included in your benefit package.

            1.   You can choose whichever type of life insurance you desire.

                a.   Whole life insurance is available.

                b.   Decreasing term insurance is also available.

            2.   The company pays for all premiums for you and your family.

                a.   It will pay the premiums until you retire.

                b.   It will pay premiums for your family if you die before retirement.

    II.   Your benefits package includes a generous retirement/pension program. (This main idea would be developed in a similar format.)

Principle 2:

Outlines Show Coordination of Ideas

An outline shows which of your ideas are equally important. All of the main ideas (all ideas labeled I, II, III) should be equally important. All of the first level of subordinate points (all the ideas labeled A, B, C) should be equally important. Coordination of ideas allows you to show how the ideas relate to each other.

    To coordinate your ideas, inspect each of the main points you have labeled with Roman numerals to see if they are similar in importance and development. If you find a main point that seems much less important than the others or that has very little development with subordinate points, you may decide the idea is not really a main idea. Likewise, inspect each of the subordinate points to see if they are equal in importance.

    For example, the first outline in the accompanying box entitled Outline Illustrating the Principle of Coordination shows main points that are not equally important. How would you change this outline to meet the principle of coordination? Could you rewrite the outline to show three equally important ideas? Our version of a better outline follows the first outline.

(INCORRECT)

I. One cause of poor production this quarter has been machinery breakdowns.
    A. The labeling machine was broken for two weeks.
    B. The packaging machine was down periodically for a total of 100 hours.
    C. Last week one of the delivery trucks had a dead battery.
    D. Two weeks ago a delivery truck broke a water hose.
II. A second cause of poor production this quarter has been employee absences.
    A. Fourteen workers called in sick with the flu last week alone.
    B. Employees have been consistently late because of inclement weather.
    C. My secretary had to go to the hospital to see her mother.
    D. The shipping clerk was gone three days for a father-son camping trip.
III. A third cause of poor production this quarter has been employees' taking long lunch breaks.

(CORRECT)

I. One cause of poor production this quarter has been machinery breakdowns.
    A. The labeling machine was broken for two weeks.
    B. The packaging machine was down periodically for a total of 100 hours.
    C. Poor maintenance of our delivery trucks caused breakdowns.
        1. Last week one of the delivery trucks had a dead battery.
        2. Two weeks ago a delivery truck broke a water hose.
II. A second cause of poor production this quarter has been employee absences.
    A. Fourteen workers called in sick with the flu last week alone.
    B. Employees have been consistently late because of inclement weather.
    C. Employees have been abusing their personal days and flexible hours.
        1. Some employees have taken off work for invalid reasons.
        2. Some employees have been taking overly long lunches.

Principle 3:

Ideas Should Be Expressed in Parallel Form

To use the outline effectively, you must be able to visually inspect the order and development of your ideas. One way to facilitate this process is to express ideas in the same form and structure. First, use the same type of statements throughout the outline. If you express your ideas as complete sentences (a procedure we recommend), then use complete sentences throughout the outline. If you use full phrases for your ideas, use phrases throughout. Similarly, key-word outlines should be expressed as single words or short phrases throughout.

A second application of the principle of parallel structure is to have at least two separate ideas for each level of subordination. If you have a point labeled I you need at least one idea labeled II. If you have one idea labeled A, you also need at least one point labeled B; if you have a 1 you need at least a 2, and so on. If you have less than two points for a specific level of subordination it probably means that you either (1) need to find more support or develop the idea further, or (2) need to rethink the structure or phrasing of your ideas. In the first case, more research may be needed. In the second case, the subordinate idea and its immediately preceding superordinate idea may be combined into one idea. The box entitled Outlines Illustrating the Principle of Parallelism illustrates an outline which violates the principle of parallelism and how it might be restructured to correct the violation.

Outlines Illustrating the Principle of Parallelism

(INCORRECT)

I. Cooking hamburgers in a fast-food restaurant is easy as ABC.
   A. Arrange the patties.
      1. Straight rows
   B. Wait till the juices bubble to the top of the patty.
      1. The juices tell you the patty has cooked all the way through.
   C. Flip them.
      1. Only once
      2. Sear the other side briefly so you don't overcook them as they will continue to cook after they have been taken off the grill.

(CORRECT)

I. Cooking hamburgers in a fast-food restaurant is easy as ABC.
   A. Arrange the patties on the grill.
      1. Put all of the patties in straight rows from the bottom of the grill to the top.
      2. Keep the patties an equal distance apart.
   B. Broil the patties until they are ready to turn.
      1. You'll know they're ready when the edges turn brown.
      2. Another sign they are ready is that the juices bubble to the top.
   C. Flip the patties as soon as both of the signs occur.
      1. Flip each patty only once.
      2. Sear the other side briefly.
         a. They'll continue to cook after they leave the grill.
         b. Overcooking makes the meat dry and tough.
II. A well-cooked hamburger looks good as well as tastes good. (and so on to develop point II)

Once you have mastered the mechanics of outlining suggested by the three principles, you can begin to use outlines to plan and develop your messages. The box entitled Suggested Outline Form provides a general outline format that you can use for most messages. Notice that the parts of the message (introduction, body, and conclusion) are included to help you clearly identify the development of your message. Also notice that these labels for the three parts of the message are not given symbols, they are not ideas. They simply serve as an easy reference to let you check to be sure you have included all necessary ideas and materials in the development of your message. It is often helpful to label the specific purpose of each part of your message in the margin.

Suggested Outline Form

INTRODUCTION

I. Attention-getting statement
   A. Supporting material (if necessary)
   B. Supporting material (if necessary)
II. Statement that establishes your credibility
   A. Supporting material or explanation of expertise
   B. Supporting material or explanation of trust and goodwill
III. Statement relating topic to the listener
   A. Supporting material establishing immediacy of topic
   B. Supporting material establishing relevancy of the topic
IV. Preview of the main ideas—statement of core proposition
   A. First main idea or area to be discussed
   B. Second main idea or area to be discussed
   C. Additional areas to be discussed (label each with a separate number)

BODY

I. First main idea
   A. Subordinate idea which develops or explains main idea I
      1. Statement of support for subordinate idea A
         a. Research material which supports 1
         b. Research material which supports 1
      2. Statement of further support for subordinate idea A
         a. Research material which supports 2
         b. Research material which supports 2
   B. Second subordinate idea which develops or explains main idea I.
      1. Statement of support for subordinate idea B
         a. Research support for B1
         b. Research support for B1
      2. Statement of support for subordinate idea B
   C. Additional supporting statements can be used following the same format as for A and B

II. Second main idea
    A. Subordinate idea which develops or explains main idea II (develop in same format as above)
    B. Statement of further support or explanation for main idea II (develop in same format as above)
III. Third main idea (develop in same format as other main ideas)

CONCLUSION

I. Statement of transition between body and summary
    A. Summary of main ideas
        1. First main idea
        2. Second main idea
        3. Third main idea (additional main ideas should be listed in the same way)
    B. Major conclusion from main ideas
II. Statement relating topic and ideas to listener
    A. Statement of immediacy (develop subpoints if necessary)
    B. Statement of relevance (develop subpoints if necessary)
III. Closing statement

B APPENDIX

Sample Speeches

Sample Informative Speech

The Exploration of Space
THE PAST AND FUTURE IMPACT ON HUMAN SOCIETY

By RICHARD H. TRULY, Administrator, National Aeronautics and Space Administration

Delivered as an Alfred M. Landon Lecture, Kansas State University, Manhattan, Kansas, December 12, 1990

THANK YOU, Dr. Wefald. NASA people don't get the opportunity to visit the heartland of America very often because virtually all our research and operations centers are along the Atlantic, Gulf, and Pacific coasts. So I am especially honored to be here this morning and become a part of this renowned Alf Landon Lecture series. — *Personal greeting*

Foreign visitors often remark that they did not understand America until they saw the magnitude of the nation's heartland—the great plains, the rich farmland, the towering cities rising along broad rivers. Then the reason for the optimism associated with the American character becomes clear.

Optimism is not the only thing rooted here. You find wisdom too—especially in Kansas. I can personally vouch for this. — *Adapting to audience to establish trustworthiness*

Standing here as the administrator of NASA, and having suffered through a summer of shuttle fuel leaks, the inheritance of a myopic space telescope, a budget battle that left us $6 billion short in the space station account over the next five years, I can — *Establishing credibility through references to credentials*

assure you that your forefathers were realists when they decided that the state motto should be: "To the stars through difficulties." — *Relating topic to audience*

I knew at least one Kansan who lived by the motto. He was my old space shuttle flying buddy, Joe Henry Engle from Chapman, Kansas. Joe Henry and I flew both the space shuttle *Enterprise* and the *Columbia* together . . . and he never failed to let me know that he was as good as he was because he hailed from "Chapman, by God, Kansas, buckle of the wheat belt." — *Personal example to relate topic to audience*

NASA has other links with this great state. Some are especially strong, like the memory of Dwight Eisenhower, whom you commemorate so eloquently with the museum in Abilene. It was his role to be president when the Soviet Union launched Sputnik and presented the first serious challenge to America's technological preeminence. — *Example to relate topic to audience*

Reprinted with the permission of *Vital Speeches of the Day* and Richard H. Truly.

459

Ike was urged to respond with an intense program lodged in the agency already in the forefront of the dangerous U.S.-Soviet competition—the Department of Defense.

But Ike feared creation of a massive, single-minded, centrally directed American technical bureaucracy—so, instead, he created a highly visible civilian space agency, my space agency, your space agency, NASA. In his vision, it would reflect traditional American values of individual creativity, diversity, elevation of the human spirit, and, especially, openness.

NASA's other important link to Kansas is between our decades-long aeronautics research program and your aircraft manufacturing industry with famous names like Boeing, Cessna, Beech and Lear.

Example to relate topic to audience

Because of the fascination with space exploration, a lot of people forget that the first *A* in NASA stands for aeronautics, and a 75-year old flight research program that has been unsurpassed in the world.

If you visit the aircraft manufacturers in Wichita today you will find their products loaded with technology developed by NASA. Technology that makes aircraft stronger, safer, faster, and more economical.

Core proposition: The development of aviation is astonishing

When you think about it—it's astounding to consider what has happened since the Wright brothers first flew on December 17, 1903.

Use of descriptive language to create vividness

In 87 years—a mere instant in the long history of intelligent beings—we have progressed from the sands of Kitty Hawk to the dusty mountains and deserts of the moon; from Robert Goddard's four-second rocket flight to the passage of the pioneers and the voyagers beyond the planets of our solar system into the void of deep space.

How, against such an extended human history, could these great events happen so quickly?

Rhetorical questions to create audience involvement

And why here, in America? Why did the human race fly first here? Why were Americans the first—and so far only—humans to walk on another body in space? Why is it, today around the globe, that technological achievement is measured against American standards?

I think two factors have distinguished America from the other nations of the world.

Subproposition: reasons for historical events

First, America was—and is—the land of opportunity. From the beginning, it opened its gates to all people regardless of race, religion and origin. Today the door remains open, and they still come, bringing their skills, their hopes, their willingness and their determination.

Effect to cause organizational pattern

The other is America's emphasis on freedom—freedom of religion, freedom of speech, freedom of the press, freedom of movement, freedom to choose the government, freedom to make economic decisions, freedom to set your own goals and pursue your own life. Freedom to reach for the stars!

This has been a climate in which new ideas and new capabilities could flourish. And flourish they have. And they have flourished most in this wonderful field of activity—flight—that has filled the lives and aspirations of all of us.

Preview: historical development, current events, and future aspirations

Today I want to talk most about the beginning of the exploration of space; about the moment in history you and I share; a period now only 33 years old. It commenced on October 4, 1957, when the Soviet Union showed us all that mankind could break the chains of gravity and place a man-made object in orbit around the earth.

This event has had a profound effect on humanity. It has led to:

A revolution in global communication made possible by satellites.

Examples of effects of aviation to create interest and relate topic to audience

A revolution in all aspects of electronics, including information processing, made possible by the miniaturization driven by space programs.

A revolution in military intelligence gathering that has helped keep the peace for a generation.

A revolution in new products and processes—in fact, more than 30,000 of them—to simplify life, do away with onerous tasks, save time and improve the quality of living.

A revolution in our knowledge of our home planet and our sense of responsibility to preserve those conditions that allow life to flourish.

Perhaps the greatest argument ever in behalf of the environment, and against pollution and nuclear war, was the first spacecraft photograph of earth in its entirety—a beautiful, inviting but fragile blue ball suspended very much alone in the harsh black void of space.

And then . . . the revolution in our knowledge of our solar system and the universe beyond, raising profound questions about mankind's role that, today, have yet to be settled.

Our ancestors looked into the night sky and saw a majestic canopy of changeless stars. Then came the telescope, and the night sky suddenly was transformed. As time moved toward our generation, instruments of great power began to unveil the immensity and complexity of the universe, but always constrained to that small window surrounding the visible wavelengths that could find its way through the earth's atmosphere.

But, finally, in our own lifetime and our own generation, space flight has enabled astronomers to place their instruments above the obscuring atmosphere and see all the messages—all the radiation from all the sources at all the wavelengths—the universe was sending us.

This explosion of technical capability changed our view of the universe radically. Today we know it is enormously large and violently dynamic. It is populated by vast structures, like galactic strings and walls. It contains mysterious objects of unimaginable energy, like quasars and black holes.

In our own neighborhood, the solar system, we have visited every planet but Pluto—some several times—and discovered extraordinary things. We have found atmospheres reminiscent of the early earth, evidence of water, active volcanoes, and even the possibility of ancient oceans. We have encountered enormously deep canyons, mountains that dwarf our own, and unimaginably turbulent skies with storms that last for centuries, like Jupiter's great red spot.

We have found oxygen locked in the rocks of earth's moon, which someday might be used as propellant. We have found helium 3 in the same rocks which some people believe in some future decade could help produce energy on earth through clean fusion.

We succeeded in placing a lander on Mars to analyze the soil. Our orbiters there found evidence of ample frozen subsurface water on the planet. And we have found more—so much more—in our initial journey through our solar system.

But we have not found what we really hoped to find—evidence of life. Thirty years of robotic and human exploration and observation have failed to disclose life anywhere except here on earth. The message we have gathered from this failure is this: keep looking; and look harder.

Let me tell you where we stand today.

On January 28, 1986, America's space program was rocketing along. We had been flying the world's only returnable space vehicle—the space shuttle—for almost five years. The ability to routinely send large crews into orbit gave a great boost to the life sciences. We had embarked on the new science of microgravity materials processing. We were well along on the design of America's first permanent home in orbit, space station *Freedom*. Our robotic explorers were ranging the solar system. A commercial sector was coming into being. And we had even begun working on the technologies needed for people to return to the moon and explore Mars.

Then, on that day, we had a terrible accident. And not just *Challenger*; in the few months, that tragedy, two Titan 34'D's, a Delta, an Atlas, a French Ariane, and a Soviet

Chronological organizational pattern to develop history of aviation

Use of examples to illustrate subpropositions

Transition to second main proposition

Second main proposition: current events in aviation

Examples of current projects

Climactic topical organization of subpropositions

Proton were lost. Here at home, this combination forced us to stop and focus all our attention on what we had done wrong and correct the problems. In the case of the shuttle, it took two and one-half years, but we did it and resumed human space flight on September 28, 1988.

That flight has opened the door to an intense, unprecedented period of activity in all areas of space science and exploration.

Reference to introduction to reestablish credibility. Use of analogy to create vividness

Magellan is already mapping Venus. *Galileo* is on its long journey to Jupiter, and *Ulysses* is moving out of the solar system's ecliptic plane to examine the poles of the sun. *Cassini* will orbit Saturn and send a probe to Titan in 1996. Just as Joe Henry and I flew close formation together, the comet rendezvous asteroid flyby mission will fly formation with a comet beginning in the year 2000. Orbiters also will be sent to the moon and Mars to pave the way for human exploration.

We are learning much about climates, atmospheres, topology, geology, and chemistry, especially the kind that might produce life.

Specific example

In astrophysics, we will orbit four great observatories to look at the universe across the electromagnetic spectrum—from infrared and gamma rays—with unprecedented resolution and clarity. The first, despite what you hear, the Hubble Space Telescope, is already returning superb science. The gamma ray observatory will fly in April, and the advanced x-ray facility and the space infrared telescope facility will follow.

Earlier this year, the cosmic background explorer confirmed predictions based on the big bang theory of creation, and produced the first clear picture of our galaxy's center. And after conquering early mechanical problems you just read about, the Astro-1 astronauts and scientists were elated with the data they got, some of which is unique in the history of astronomy, and I was elated the night before last at their safe return. Thirteen

Statistics: magnitude and average

successful shuttle flights in just 26 months. On the average, a flight every other month!

Our goals in astrophysics are ambitious—to uncover the nature of quasars and black holes, to discover places where life might exist, to learn the age and size of the universe, and to predict its ultimate fate.

Subproposition of value: importance of space exploration

To do all I have just described requires us to look out from earth, but it is just as important to look back.

In the 1990s, virtually every country in the world will participate in an effort to understand how earth's global systems work interactively. The purpose is to give this and future generations the data required to make accurate and timely decisions to prevent further deterioration of the environment.

Example to illustrate subproposition

This effort is our mission to planet earth. A key American contribution will be the earth observing system, a comprehensive series of polar orbiting spacecraft able to view the earth with a variety of instruments simultaneously. Other spacefaring nations will launch satellites, too.

Another area of intense interest is microgravity science.

Relating topic to audience

Right now, 16 NASA centers for the commercial development of space are developing ideas to test in microgravity. Fifty-two universities—including Kansas State—are associated with these centers, plus 175 corporations, including many of America's largest.

Key to major progress in this area will be the international space station *Freedom.* It will provide large, well-equipped laboratories without the requirement of returning to earth every few days. The United States, Canada, the European Space Agency, and Japan will build the station and furnish the laboratories.

But the chief reason we need *Freedom* is to learn how the human body and psyche react to long-duration exposure to microgravity. This is key for that future day when the first human lifts off the launch pad for that inevitable journey to Mars.

As you perhaps have detected, a great deal of our 1990s activities will help set the stage for human expansion beyond earth orbit. President Bush announced that as a national goal in a talk July 20, 1989—the 20th anniversary of man's first landing on the moon.

Testimony: paraphrase of Bush's speech

In that speech, the president called for the completion of space station *Freedom,* then a return to the moon, this time to stay, then exploration of Mars.

Human exploration, preceded by robots, will expand the frontiers of scientific knowledge by employing our most powerful computer—the human mind. Only the human mind can make giant leaps of inference. Maybe computers will do that someday.

Third main proposition of value: future aspirations are important and the correct things to do

What I have outlined for you this morning obviously is a most ambitious program. Is it the correct space program for America?

Last August we decided to step back and ask that question again. With support from the top from the president and the vice president, who is chairman of the National Space Council, I appointed a committee of distinguished, experienced citizens to review the nation's space program and NASA and make recommendations. The group has completed its work, and last Monday its chairman, Mr. Norman Augustine, of Martin-Marietta, explained its findings to the press.

Establishing credibility of source of subsequent quotation

I am happy to report the committee concluded that—and I quote—

"America does want an energetic, affordable, and successful space program."

I am also happy to report that the program this independent group recommended coincides very closely with the programs and policies NASA has been pursuing. The committee stated that the United States should maintain a civil space program balanced among five elements:

—Space science.

—Mission to planet earth.

—Mission from planet earth—first to the space station, then to the moon and then to Mars with human beings.

—A greatly expanded technology development program.

—And creation of a more robust space transportation system.

Use of direct quotation to support proposition

While NASA took some lumps in the last two days from a media which seems to have turned NASA-bashing into a journalistic art, the committee said of us, and I quote again:

"The committee believes that NASA, and only NASA, realistically possesses the essential critical mass of knowledge and expertise upon which the nation's civil space program can be sustained—and that the task at hand is, therefore, for NASA to focus on making the self-improvements that gird this responsibility."

Direct quotation to support proposition

NASA will study this report in great detail and will live up to its responsibilities. We hope that other organizations with responsibility for the nation's space program will, too.

Earlier in this talk, I noted how the technology invented to get us into space and out to the planets had been transformed by private enterprise into products and processes—and even whole industries—that changed the way we live.

Relating topic to audience to create involvement

To live permanently in space and on bodies other than earth will require a vast amount of additional new technology. If the past is prologue, that means another wave of new products and processes that will have an impact on us just as great as the impact of microelectronics, computers, communications satellites, and all the rest.

Examples develop subproposition about future directions and events in space exploration

Some of the new technologies we are or will be working on to return to the moon and go on to Mars are artificial intelligence, virtual reality, advanced robotics, telepresence and teleoperation, ultra high-strength and high-temperature resistant materials, supercomputers, wireless power transmission, and many others.

And I expect that we will experience over the next quarter century of space exploration a major breakthrough. Certainly, Benjamin Franklin did not envision New York City lit up at night or our digitized society when he flew a kite in a thunderstorm. And it is doubtful that those who first dissected the atom realized they had found a new, practical energy source.

Climactic topical organizational pattern

Expanding our presence into space sets the stage for discovery; perhaps in medicine or materials or energy or transportation.

Now we are lofting telescopes and other instruments of enormous power. They will radically change our view of time and space again.

The continuing exploration of space will involve greater international cooperation. Rising costs and political imperatives are bound to drive today's spacefaring nations to cooperate. But the real driver, I think, is increasing belief that not individual nations, but the human race, should undertake the expansion of the planet.

Rhetorical question to involve audience

Finally, there is the question of life elsewhere.

Is there any? In a sense, everything NASA does seeks to answer that one question. We know one place in the universe where life exists. We have identified its vital components. We know the factors that allow it to flourish.

As we search the solar system with our robots, and scan the sky beyond with our telescopes, we look for similar components and factors.

What if, after having acquired the ability to search, and having searched for decades or centuries, we find nothing? Then, we will have gained a sobering bit of knowledge. We may come to see ourselves as the sole keepers of the flame with a terrible responsibility to never let it go out.

Rhetorical question to involve audience

But suppose, some night, a NASA receiver hears the dim remnants of a far away signal that is unmistakably not random . . . and therefore of intelligent origin?

How would the human race react? Certainly, fear by some, and certainly elation by others. Undoubtedly, a heightened sense of our humanity. Perhaps a new view of certain conflicts which suddenly would seem so trivial.

Conclusion: restatement of core proposition

But one thing for sure, it would change our world, and the human race would be off on another great adventure—a learning adventure.

Review of third main proposition

We would become eavesdroppers on an unprecedented scale, listening intently, and trying to decode the conversations of another civilization. We would want to know what they are like physically and intellectually, where they get their energy, how they combat disease, how and where they travel, what natural resources they have and how they use them, what traditions they hold dear and gods they hold sacred.

Review of first main proposition

This certainly would happen because, if nothing else, mankind is curious. It has been all its existence. More than anything else, curiosity impelled folks over the next hill, across the next river, across the oceans, then the continents, then into the atmosphere and, now, into space. Soon it will drive us to the next planet and then its moons, and then on to the next and the next and the next.

Closing: reference to introduction and speaker's relation to Kansas audience

Your invitation to me to deliver the Alfred M. Landon Lecture today has been a wonderful honor I will not forget. This opportunity for me to return to the center of this land I love has been a personal pleasure of immense proportions.

Thank you.

Sample Persuasive Speech

How Women and
Minorities Are
Reshaping Corporate
America

MANAGING DIVERSITY

By LINDA WINIKOW, Vice President, Corporate Policy and External
Affairs, Orange and Rockland Utilities, Inc.
Delivered to the Women's Bureau Conference,
Washington, D.C., October 23, 1990

T HANK you very much. I appreciate the opportunity to speak to you on a subject that's been important to me for many years. I must confess, though, that in some ways it's a very difficult speech to make, because so many things come to mind and so much personal emotion is vested in the subject.

Attention step: startling statement to gain interest

There's no question in my mind—none whatsoever—that we have an opportunity today to tap a huge reservoir—the pool of cultural diversity. Our challenge is not only to *accommodate* diversity, but to actually *use* it to bring new and richer perspectives to our jobs, to our customers, and to our whole social climate.

Use of repetition for emphasis

Core proposition

But we have a long, long way to go. For generations, our view of women and minorities in the workplace was an impoverished one, and that narrow focus resulted in incalculable harm.

Development of need step— historical problems

Think about the intellect, the cultures, the ideas, and the creativity that was wasted by ignorance and by prejudice.

The fundamental question we have to ask ourselves, of course, is "How much has changed in the last eighty or ninety years?" The answer is mixed.

Rhetorical question to create audience involvement

On the one hand, civil rights legislation and labor laws have done an enormous amount to wipe out the legal impediments to inequality. And the Department of Labor has played a key role in our progress.

But while the *laws* to combat discrimination have changed, all-too-many of the *attitudes* that prevented the flowering of diversity still exist.

Metaphors and contrast to emphasize problem

But the issues aren't clear-cut—there are no simple "rights" and "wrongs."

Let me give you an example. Just two weeks ago, the Supreme Court heard a case where in 1982 Johnson Controls said that women of childbearing age couldn't work in certain jobs because their exposure to lead would exceed the limits believed to cause fetal defects.

The company said that it had a duty to protect its employees from health and safety hazards. On the surface, this sounds like responsible corporate policy.

Real example to illustrate need; inductive reasoning from specific example to general rule

Many women employees, along with labor unions, on the other hand, claimed that this action was discriminatory, resulting in their losing their jobs or the opportunity to advance. So they sued, claiming that *all* employees should be adequately—and equally— protected from lead exposure.

Drawing conclusion from example relates example to proposition	Whatever the merits of either side, this is a classic case of the difficulty of managing diversity—where issues of fairness, equity, competing rights, multiple standards, ethics and law meld together in confusion. Where the difference between right and wrong is not as absolute as we would hope for in an ideal world.
Further development of need: current problems	In corporate America, this is an era of remarkable change. It's no longer the homogeneous white, male-oriented work force it once was. Today, our business world is being enriched by an infusion of different cultural perspectives. Today's co-workers bring new ideas—whether from Japan or from the inner city.
Cause-effect reasoning	A culturally diverse work force will mean *less* bias, not more. As minorities make up more and more of the work force, people will become less and less tolerant of bigotry and discrimination. And the smart employers will seek out diversity; they will recognize that *everyone* can add value to the companies' ability to do its job—and to do it well.
Argument from analogy: corporations are like the United States	Just as the United States was made great—not by making everyone the same but rather by respecting their differences—so, too, can corporations achieve new levels of greatness. Cultural, religious, and ethnic diversity in both the corporate boardroom and in the corporate trenches make that company better understood and more in tune with its customers.
Transition to satisfaction step	Today, workers deserve to be recognized for what they *are,* as well as what they *produce.* If management learns to understand the *whole* person, the corporate culture will be enriched beyond imagination.
	This is no easy task.
	But regardless of how difficult the issues are, we as corporate executives have an obligation to recognize that these aren't simply side issues to running a business. It's really the opposite: These are the *fundamental* management issues.
Satisfaction step	I believe that a corporate manager's first job is to manage—to bring people to their full potential—to encourage employees to grow, to take risks, to be comfortable with who they are and to be able to learn from their own mistakes and from other people's achievements.
	But let me be more specific:
Development of satisfaction step	I believe that it's the obligation of corporate managers to *learn* about the people who work for them. To *understand* the Orthodox Jewish holidays; to *appreciate* the Chinese New Year; to *reflect* on the Hispanic heritage. Each of these—and every other culture—brings something enormously valuable to the workplace, and we'll never tap it if we don't understand it.
Rhetorical questions to create audience involvement	Further, I believe that corporate managers must *respect* those cultural differences. If we don't respect them, who will? If we don't value differences, can we expect harmony among others?
	Finally, I believe that corporate managers must *communicate* with those above—and below—them. All the understanding in the world is for nothing if we don't *act* on our convictions.
Personal example to increase credibility	Six years ago, I joined Orange and Rockland Utilities as the first woman vice president in the company's history. I'll be candid with you—not everyone gathered at the front door to greet me!
Personal proof	
Statistical data to create logical proof	Simply put, for 100 years the utility industry was white male-dominated. And it still is. Today, only 17 percent of this nation's total work force are women. And only 9 percent of all managers are women.
	Minorities fare even worse. Only 10 percent of the utility work force nationwide is black, and 5 percent Hispanic. Among managers, blacks make up only 4 percent, and Hispanics 2 percent. Asians and other minorities are represented by even smaller numbers.

466   Appendix B

But progress is being made, and at all levels. Since 1985, minority employment in the utility industry has increased 3 percent—progress, yes; but altogether too slow.

On the corporate ladder, we've also seen some changes. A woman—Joan Bok, is chairman of the New England Electric System, and there are now literally dozens of women vice presidents across the country.

This progress is fine—we all applaud it. But we shouldn't lose sight of the fact that:

—There are less than half a dozen female chief executives in the Fortune 500;
—Only 5 percent of all corporate board members are women.

Not a wonderful record, particularly in view of the fact that according to a study conducted in 1988 by The Conference Board, women make up nearly half the U.S. work force, and two-thirds of the new entrants to the work force are women.

So why the poor showing at the top? The Conference Board lists four reasons—or excuses—that are most often cited:

—First, *discrimination*. That is to say, promotions and pay are affected by biases and stereotypes.

—Second, *genetics and gender*—The argument that women are simply born with inherent limitations, or that the prospect or actuality of motherhood makes them unsuitable for the workplace. You can imagine how I feel about *that* one!

—Third, *contradictory expectations*—Women are expected to be tough, but can't be macho; or they're expected to take responsibility, but also to follow advice.

—Fourth, *corporate culture*—meaning that no matter how well a woman performs, corporate policy and social climate are stacked against her.

So getting to the top has lots of obstacles. That's the theme of an important book that I recommend to everyone: It's called *Breaking the Glass Ceiling*. The ceiling is a transparent barrier that keeps women from rising above a certain level in corporations.

The ceiling occurs at different levels at different companies, but the main point is that the glass ceiling applies to women, as the book says, simply *because* they are women!

Let me go back to my own experience.

When I first became involved in politics, back in the early 1970s, men found it difficult to swallow that I could be a member of the Zoning Board of Appeals and be pregnant simultaneously!

And when I was a New York State Senator, I was stopped by the State Police on the New York State Thruway because they thought my car—with its Senate license plate—must be stolen, since a woman was in it!

That's not a glass ceiling, that's a glass wall! Given this kind of experience, it's no wonder that now—in the corporate climate—I have more women managers than any other vice president does. Is that by accident? Of course not. But let there be no mistake about it: There's no free ride. Any woman I hire has to be the best, just like *anybody* I hire has to be the best.

In some respects, women have to be even *better* than the best. I'm reminded of the story told by the Chief Executive Officer of ConEd, New York's largest utility.

He says that every woman he's ever interviewed is head and shoulders above their male counterparts. Why? Because for these women just to get to that point in the interview process means that they're extraordinary!

So I think we can agree that a woman can do any job she sets out to do, given the requisite skills and training. The glass ceiling exists, but senior management's job—and especially women senior management's job—is to do everything possible to provide that training and the climate for success.

Marginal annotations:

Development of trends from statistical data

Proposition of value

Inductive reasoning

Cause-effect reasoning

Conclusion from cause-effect argument

Personal proof

Metaphor to create vividness

Personal proof

Paraphrase testimony with oral footnote

Transition to visualization step

Visualization step of problems and advantages of solution	But there are lessons both for the managers *and* the managed. First, most traditional managers are afraid of change. Recognize that fear as something natural, and work with them to overcome it. Be sensitive to the white male manager who may be having trouble coping, just like you're sensitive to the woman or minority employee coming up the ladder.
Metaphor to create vividness	As we progress as a society, that ladder becomes increasingly crowded. But it certainly comes as no surprise to learn that women are still being excluded from the top, any more than it's a surprise to learn that women and minorities hold a disproportionate share of the menial or lesser-paying jobs.
Metaphor to create vividness	But the real measure of progress is not taken only by counting those at the top and those at the bottom; another real measure is the increasing numbers of women and minorities in *middle*-management positions. These are the people with the greatest opportunity. And, unhappily, they are also the ones who most acutely feel the disadvantage of their gender or heritage or color in today's work force.
	Too often, nontraditional middle managers get squeezed by the doubtful expectations of their superiors on the one hand and by the cynical views of those reporting to them on the other.
	Too often, minorities are stereotyped as less assertive or more emotional, less mathematical or more artistic, less persuasive or more sensitive, less open or more introspective, or any one of a hundred generalities without foundation.
Transition to action step	My job as a woman executive—and the job of *every* executive, regardless of sex—is to dispel the myths and get on with the business of managing.
	That's not easy. Women executives—and minority executives—have to be very secure, because managing diversity really means managing the unknown.
Action step: tells audience what they must do to correct problems	And to do that, you have to be willing to take risks. You can't be afraid of having people grow in their jobs. You can't feel threatened. You have to recognize that *our* job is *not* to make a widget. *Our* job is to make a *difference*. And in American industry, there's still plenty to be done.
	—We must guarantee equal opportunity in our hiring, and this must go *beyond* affirmative action; it must truly recognize the *value* of ethnic, racial and sexual diversity;
Immediacy to create involvement	—We must understand the cultural diversity of the work force;
	—We must ensure that there's equal pay for equal work.
	These aren't just *business* issues. These are *societal* issues, and how we deal with them will affect every person in this nation.
Personal proof	Today, I'm talking as a businessperson. But this wasn't always the case. For 10 years, as a New York State Senator, the struggle for women and minority rights was always at the top of my agenda.
	What I did in the Senate was respond to constituents' needs by changing laws, creating programs, and shaping attitudes. Legislation which protected working women and minorities were among my proudest achievements.
	But I wish that had been enough. Instead, we find that there are still problems, so we need more people—in the community and in business—taking up the challenge.
	As a senator—and particularly as a *woman* senator—I was privileged to be in a leadership role in finding solutions to those problems.
	Now, I'm with Orange and Rockland, and I recognize that it's not just government that has a role in righting the wrongs. At O&R, we take our responsibilities seriously, and I'll just mention one program that I'm particularly pleased with.

Shortly after I joined the Company, we established a Women's Council, made up exclusively of women employees. The council was formed in recognition of the fact that women often have special pressures on them—sometimes it's balancing careers and home life, sometimes it's real or imagined prejudices, sometimes it's just being an island in a sea of men.

The council is dedicated to supporting programs and running events of special interest to women employees, and since its inception about five years ago, it's been a great success. Among the really successful programs the Women's Council has sponsored are

—One on *Eldercare*—a subject that is becoming tremendously important as people are living longer and as the nuclear family of a few generations ago is disappearing;

—A program on *Financial Management*—something of special importance to every working woman;

—Another program devoted to *Time Management*—how to balance all the competing demands both at home and in the workplace.

Well over 200 women—nearly *two-thirds* of our entire women work force!—have attended one or more of these sessions! That speaks volumes not only for what *can* be done but also for the critical need to get out there and *do* it.

Have we solved the problems of every woman employee? Not by a long shot. But there's not a woman at Orange and Rockland who doesn't at least have a sense of the company's intentions. And while I've touched on the company's intentions, let me make one other observation.

The good things the Women's Council has been doing wouldn't be possible without the active encouragement and support of Jim Smith, our chairman and chief executive officer. It's just not enough for Linda Winikow to believe in these things; our chairman has to be behind it to make it stick, and he is—100 percent.

Now, as much as I enjoy singing Orange and Rockland's praise, let me close my talk not with what *we're* doing, but rather what remains unfinished.

I began my talk by saying that cultural diversity—as complex as it is and as threatening as some find it—is the thing that can make American business even greater. Our challenge is to manage diversity—to put that great force to work for us.

That's no small challenge, but I'm convinced that it's one that we can achieve. I think that this conference has shown what people can do, working together, to break the glass ceiling.

Thank you.

Margin annotations:
- Personal example to illustrate action step
- Inductive reasoning
- Metaphor to create vividness
- Examples of program successes to show workability of solution
- Reference to authority to bolster personal proof
- Transition to conclusion
- Summary of core proposition
- Relates topic to audience
- Closing with impact

C R E D I T S

Illustrations

Chapter 3

pp. 61–62
Gibb's Defensive Climates
Gibb, Jack (1961). Defensive Communication. *Journal of Communication 11*, 141–148. New York, NY: Oxford University Press.

pp. 65–66
Gibb's Supportive Climates
Gibb, Jack (1961). Defensive Communication. *Journal of Communication 11*, 141–148. New York, NY: Oxford University Press.

Chapter 5

p. 109
Monroe's Motivated Sequence
Monroe, Alan (1935). *Principles and Types of Speech*. Glenview, IL: Scott, Foresman & Co.

Chapter 6

Opening Quotation
"Kinder, Gentler Monikers Sought for Hated R-word." *Dayton Daily News*, Nov. 30, 1990, p. 8-B, Dayton, OH.

Chapter 9

Figure 9.2
Knapp's Stages
Originally developed by Mark Knapp. This version of Knapp's Model is taken from Fisher, B. Aubrey (1987). *Interpersonal Communication: Pragmatics of Human Relationships*. By permission of McGraw-Hill, Inc.

Chapter 10

Figure 10.1
Thomas Model of the Conflict Episode
Thomas, K. (1976). Conflict and conflict management. In M. Dunnette (Ed.), *The Handbook of Organizational and Industrial Psychology*. Chicago: Rand-McNally.

Chapter 11

p. 272
Strategies for a Supportive Climate
Gibb, J. (1961). Defensive Communication. *Journal of Communication 11*, 141–148. New York: Oxford University Press.

Chapter 13

pp. 305–306
The Janis & Mann Model (Explanation)
From DECISION MAKING: A Psychological Analysis of Conflict, Choice, and Commitment by Irving L. Janis and Leon Mann. Copyright © 1977 by The Free Press, a Division of Macmillan, Inc. Used by permission of the publisher.

p. 309
Goldberg & Larson's Ideal Solution Model
Alvin A. Goldberg/Carl E. Larson, GROUP COMMUNICATION, © 1975, p. 149. Adapted by permission of Prentice Hall, Englewood Cliffs, New Jersey.

pp. 315–316
Janis & Mann's Five-Step Model of Decision Making
Janis, I. L., & Mann, L. (1977). *Decision Making: A Psychological Analysis of Conflict, Choice, and Commitment*. New York: The Free Press.

Figure 13.1
A Basic Model of Decision Making
MacCrimmon, K. R., & Taylor, R. (1976). In Dunnette, M. (Ed.), *Handbook of Industrial and Organizational Psychology*. Chicago: Rand-McNally.

Chapter 14

p. 326
Webster's Dictionary Definition of "Culture"
By permission. From Webster's Ninth New Collegiate Dictionary © 1991 by Merriam-Webster, Inc., publisher of the Merriam-Webster © Dictionaries.

p. 337
Practical Advice
Broome, B. J. (1991). Building Shared Meaning: Implications of a Relational Approach to Empathy for Teaching Intercultural Communication. *Communication Education 40*, 235–249. Annandale, VA: Speech Communication Association.

Chapter 18

Figure 18.1
Maslow's Hierarchy of Needs
"Hierarchy of Needs" from MOTIVATION AND PERSONALITY by Abraham H. Maslow. Copyright 1954 by Harper & Row, Publishers, Inc. Copyright © 1970 by Abraham H. Maslow. Reprinted by permission of HarperCollins Publishers.

Figure 18.2 and pp. 440–443
Monroe's Motivated Sequence (Fig. and explanation.)
From PRINCIPLES AND TYPES OF SPEECH COMMUNICATION by Douglas Ehning, Bruce E. Gronbeck, Ray E. McKerrow, and Alan H. Monroe. Copyright © 1990 by Bruce E. Gronbeck and Ray E. McKerrow. Reprinted by permission of HarperCollins Publishers.

Appendix B

pp. 459–464
Richard H. Truly. "The Exploration of Space." (1991) *Vital Speeches of the Day.* Vol. LVII, No. 9, Feb. 15, 1991, pp. 280–283. (Mt. Pleasant, SC: City News Publishing Co.)

pp. 465–469
Linda Winikow, Vice President, Orange & Rockland Utilities, Inc. (NY), "How Women and Minorities are Reshaping Corporate America." (1991) *Vital Speeches of the Day.* Vol. LVII, No. 8, Feb. 1, pp. 242–244.

GBR Graphics

1.1, 1.2, 1.3, 2.1, 2.2, 6.1, 6.2, 9.1, 9.2, 10.1, 13.1, 15.1 A & B, 15.2 A–E, 15.3 A & B, 17.1, 18.1

Photographs
Part Openers

Parts 1, 2, 3: © Jean Claude Lejeune; 4: © George Bellrose/Stock Boston

Chapter 1

Pages 5, 7: © Jean Claude Lejeune; p. 11: © James L. Shaffer; p. 15: © Jean Claude Lejeune

Chapter 2

Page 25: From FIND WALDO NOW by Martin Hanford. Copyright © 1988 by Martin Hanford. By permission of Little, Brown and Company; p. 30: © Kathy Aduddell Yoder; p. 36 top: © R. K. Workman; bottom left: © Michael Siluk; bottom right: © Jean Claude Lejeune; p. 45: James L. Shaffer.

Chapter 3

Page 58: © Robert Eckert/EKM Nepenthe; p. 60: © Michael Siluk; p. 63: © Elizabeth Hamlin/Stock Boston

Chapter 4

Page 77: © Eric Neurath/Stock Boston; p. 80: © Dion Ogust/The Image Works; p. 86: © James L. Shaffer; p. 89: © Michael Weisbrot/Stock Boston; p. 91: © Michael Siluk

Chapter 5

Page 103: © Marilyn Nolt; pp. 105, 107: © Michael Siluk; p. 111: © Jean Claude Lejeune

Chapter 6

Page 130: © Kathy Aduddell Yoder; p. 134: © Michael Siluk; p. 138: © Marilyn Nolt

Chapter 7

Page 152: © James L. Shaffer; p. 155, 158: © Jean Claude Lejeune; p. 162: © Peter Vandermark/Stock Boston; p. 169: © Paul Fortin/Stock Boston

Chapter 8

Page 177: © Marilyn Nolt; p. 181: © Kathy Aduddell Yoder; p. 186 © James L. Shaffer; p. 188: © Richard Anderson

Chapter 9

Pages 201, 203: © Michael Siluk; p. 205, 210: © Jean Claude Lejeune; p. 219: © James L. Shaffer

Chapter 10

Page 232: © Alan Carey/The Image Works; p. 235: © James L. Shaffer; p. 236: © Peter Menzel/Stock Boston; p. 238: © Paul Fortin/Stock Boston

Chapter 11

Page 259 top left & right: © Jean Claude Lejeune; pp. 259 bottom, 262, 271: © Michael Siluk

Chapter 12

Page 279: © Michael Siluk; p. 280: © J. Berndt/Stock Boston; p. 290: © Michael Siluk; p. 293: © Jean Claude Lejeune

Chapter 13

Pages 303, 316: © Michael Siluk

Chapter 14

Pages 325, 327: © Marilyn Nolt; p. 330: © Monique Salaber/The Image Works; p. 335: © Jean Claude Lejeune

Chapter 15

Page 350: © Dan Chidester/The Image Works; p. 354: © Dion Ogust/The Image Works

Chapter 16

Pages 381, 384, 386: © Michael Siluk; p. 391: © Wells/The Image Works

Chapter 17

Page 416: © Michael Siluk; p. 420: © Beringer-Dratch/The Image Works

Chapter 18

Page 434 top: Reprinted with permission of Kemper Financial Services, Inc.; bottom: © Eric Aeder; p. 435: Courtesy of Guess?®; p. 437: © Bob Daemmrich/Stock Boston

INDEX

barriers to, 176–180
closure, 178–179
distractions, 177–178
mind speed, 176–177, 182
perceptual bias, 178
self-focus, 179–180
conflict intensity and, 241–242
conflict strategies, and, 243–244
importance of, 4–5, 176
misinvolvement and, 178, 387–388
relationship development and, 314–315
skills, cognitive, 182–183
skills, expressive, 184–186
types of, 180–181

M

Maslow's Hierarchy of Needs, 439
Messages
content and relationship, 16
verbal responsibility, 43–44, 93–94
Metacommunication, 248
Miscommunication, 13
Mnemonic devices, 417
Monroe's Motivated Sequence, 109, 440–441

N

Need reduction theory, 439–441
Noise, 9
Nonverbal communication, 150–169, 385–387. *See also* Delivery
attraction and, 206
continuous, 151
creating interest, 385
creating involvement, 386, 416
credibility, 385–386
defined, 11, 150
delivery and, 384
difficult messages, 151
evaluation of others, 151
learned, 152–153
listening and, 387

percent of meaning, 150–151
supporting verbal message, 387
Nonverbal communication, functions of, 165–169
communicates emotions, 166
contradicts verbal communication, 167–168
defines relationships, 166
regulates communication, 168–169
reinforces verbal communication, 166–167, 387
substitutes for verbal communication, 167
Nonverbal communication, types of, 153–165. *See also Specific types of nonverbal communication*
appearance, 165
eye contact, 153–155
kinesics, 155–158
proxemics, 161–164
time, 164–165
touch, 164
voice, 158–161
Norms, 281

O

Open mind, 336
Organization, 101–117
competence and, 104–105
interviewing, and, 267–269
persuasion strategies, and, 438–446
public speaking, and, 358–361
purpose of, 102–104
Organization, patterns of
choosing, 358–361
types of
cause-effect, 108–109, 358
problem-solution, 109, 358
sequential (chronological), 105–106, 358
spatial, 106–107, 358
topical, 107–108, 358
Outlining, 453–458

P

Paralinguistics. *See* Voice
Paraphrasing. *See* Expressive listening, skills of restatement
Perception
bias, 30–31
defined, 24
listening, and, 178–180, 182
organization, and, 105
Perception, functions of
interpreting function, 30–32
organizing function, 27–29
selecting function, 25–27
Perception, validation strategies
consensual, 33–34
multisensory, 32–33
predictive, 33
repetitive, 33
Persuasion
defined, 426
goals, 426–428
Persuasion, organization of messages and, 438–446
based on attitudes, 443–446
based on others' needs, 438–443
Persuasion, proofs and
emotional proofs, 433–436
logical proofs, 429–433
personal proofs, 436–438
Physical environment
analyzing, 90–94
distractions, 177–178, 182, 386
elements of, 42–44
managing, 390
proxemics, and, 161–163
Planning speeches, 345–370
determine a purpose, 351
develop a proposition, 350
select a topic, 347–350
state a proposition, 351
strategies for, 347
Power
conflict and, 230–231, 240–241
defined, 209
dependency, 211